Pictorial History of

Philosophy

Pictorial History of Philosophy

by Dagobert D. Runes

BRAMHALL HOUSE · NEW YORK

This edition published by Bramhall House,
a division of Clarkson N. Potter, Inc., by arrangement
with Philosophical Library, Inc.

(H)

Printed in the United States of America

Contents

Philosophy, Man and Morals

A WORD TO THE READER

Like all introductions, this one is written at the end of making the book, and not at the beginning. Looking back after a necessarily hasty journey through the main roads and byways of philosophy, one wishes to resolve the multiple impressions and experiences into some definite form of judgment.

What is this metaphysical world, inhabited by so complicated and divergent a population, all about?

There are kings and beggars, sinners, saints, and monks, teachers, shoemakers, and esthetes, physicians, and vagrants all imbued with a yearning for the unknowable. Of course, we can judge philosophy only by those who spoke of it or wrote of it. It may be that the most profound philosophers of all have never uttered a blessed word about what moved them most deeply.

For those who look to philosophy for a solution of problems in scientific methodology, I can find none that was ever applied by any scientist of note. The scientists seem to have gone their own way, wherever the politicians and the churchmen permitted it.

The history of scientific and technical discoveries fails to provide a single clue proving the influence of philosophical methodology in the making of their numerous findings. Much of scientific accomplishments—for instance, in the fields of electricity, medicine, and chemistry—is due to experimentalists who never opened a philosophic treatise in their lives. Some of the modern physicists, already resting on laurels plucked in their specific realm, have dabbled a bit in metaphysical cogitations, but more as a matter of frills than fundamentals.

If one expects to find in philosophy the key to theological verities, I can only offer this discouraging statement: throughout the history of the Western and Eastern world, philosophy has often served as the handmaiden of theology, but never was the relationship reversed. Maimonides and Aquinas used Aristotelianism to bolster their dogmas, even as Philo Judaeus and Albertus Magnus used Plato. The same, of course, holds good for the Arabic philosophers serving Mohammedanism and the writers of Upanishads serving Hinduism. Always the Vedantas followed the Vedas with their intricate ritual—never the other way round.

If one seeks in philosophy a solution for social and political problems, there too, I would say, a mere glimpse of the intellectual facts of the past points clearly to philosophy having been used as the "great rationale" by reformers as well as reactionaries, by usurpers as well as traditionalists, by kings and conquerors, to make vile and

---

The Golden Rule

Confucianism

What you don't want done to yourself, don't do to others. —SIXTH CENTURY B.C.

Buddhism

Hurt not others with that which pains thyself. —FIFTH CENTURY B.C.

Jainism

In happiness and suffering, in joy and grief, we should regard all creatures as we regard our own self, and should therefore refrain from inflicting upon others such injury as would appear undesirable to us if inflicted upon ourselves. —FIFTH CENTURY B.C.

Zoroastrianism

Do not do unto others all that which is not well for oneself. —FIFTH CENTURY B.C.

Classical Paganism

May I do to others as I would that they should do unto me. *Plato*—FOURTH CENTURY B.C.

Hinduism

Do naught to others which if done to thee would cause thee pain. *Mahabharata*—THIRD CENTURY B.C.

Judaism

What is hateful to yourself, don't do to your fellow man. *Rabbi Hillel*—FIRST CENTURY B.C.

Christianity

Whatsoever ye would that men should do to you, do ye even so to them. *Jesus of Nazareth*—FIRST CENTURY A.D.

Sikhism

Treat others as thou wouldst be treated thyself. —SIXTEENTH CENTURY A.D.

Perhaps the oldest ethical proposition of distinctly universal character

---

devious acts appear to be God-ordained or a plan of public welfare.

For Philip and Alexander, as a preamble to their bloody conquests, Aristotle wrote a touching thesis on the Divine division of men into free persons and slaves. From Plato to Hegel, from Hobbes to Stalin's Alexandrov, there stand the giant metaphysical bulwarks, defending the political atrocities of their scepter-wielding benefactors!

Sumerian Worshiper, Iraq, c. 2600 B.C.,
Alabaster with Shell Inlay
(Metropolitan Museum of Art)

Hammurabi's Code, Basalt Stele, from Babylon
(The Louvre)

Plato and Aristotle deemed common slavery a measure of Divine Providence; to them, the little man was meant only to serve in the shadow of the aristocratic rich, cultured, and bellicose. These two cardinal enemies of social equality dominated the realm of metaphysics for two thousand years. It is only with the discarding of their systems that social equality could begin, although nostalgic remembrances of the post-Socratic dream-world still linger on.

One of the Hebrew sages relates the story of a vicious king who was admonished by one of his advisors to be more merciful with his victims because history might blacken his image. The king replied: "My scribes will write my history; I will not permit history to write itself" —and how right this shameful king was! How often have philosophers scribbled justification of the misdeeds of tyrants, of deceptions of the people and of churchish super-

Temple of the Incas, Peru

Traditional Likeness of Zarathustra

Assyrian Tablet of Law, Fourteenth Century, Clay
(Museum of the Near East, Berlin)

Traditional Mausoleum of Zarathustra, near Persepolis
(Fifth Century B.C.)

stitions, not only during the sack of Asia by Alexander, but during the sack of Europe by Hitler, when the founder of contemporary Existentialism, Heidegger, wrote profound pieces glorifying National Socialism. It is more than coincidence that the other great Existentialist, Sartre, a student and epigone of Heidegger, became a vociferous protagonist of Stalinism, strewing fine metaphysical petals on the muddy roads that lead from the Kremlin to the Siberian concentration camps. (Shall I omit the obvious? The blissful union reached by the two statesmen-philosophers of our time, Nehru of India and Mao of China, who, in metaphysical oblivion to the multi-million massacres of innocent people from Peking to Warsaw, share sweet love of Hindu and Confucian philosophical dissertations—with a touching reverence for the Ukases of the Kremlin.)

Then what is philosophy? All the scientific, political, sociological, and theological camouflage put aside, what is the true scope of philosophy? In whom do we find the true character of philosophy personified? To my mind, the three who have come nearest the philosophers' stone of wisdom were Solomon the King; Socrates, the vagrant; and Spinoza, the renegade.

These three, each in his own manner, have trod the road to Inner Freedom, deviating at no time for any church or churlish purpose, serving no one but the voice of their own conscience, the demon within their soul.

It is this still voice of man's conscience that accounts for the only goodness that is left in this world and it is the only substance that makes life more than a mere daily hacking out of existence among savage nations and selfish peoples.

It is this Inner Conscience that sees man as a mere form in an infinite ocean of Being. And from this intelligence—in the words of the kindly Sage—man as a mere breath of the wind, flowers the love of man to man which is no more than the understanding of man in his relationship to the creative universe. Such cognition and such affection are self-same.

Philosophy is no more than man's orientation in the cosmos, and from this orientation stem the kindness, tolerance, and generosity which are the basis of all true teaching. Beyond these simple tasks of ethics there is nothing that falls in the realm of philosophy.

Philosophy is ethics, or it is nothing at all.

Limitations of space preclude inclusion of some philosophers whom the editor considered of lesser importance than those dealt with in the present work.

The editor assumes full responsibility for his judgments, with the admission that others in his place might have displayed different preferences. Historians and teachers have attributed great significance to thinkers whom, at least as far as this anthology is concerned, the editor has relegated to oblivion. Perspectives differ, and so do the colors of evaluation.

The editor has gone to considerable effort to obtain original likenesses of the philosophers. But in many cases it was necessary to be satisfied with traditional and even fanciful representations. The Hebrews and Moslems especially were opposed to personal picturization, and in Chinese portraiture it is almost impossible to differentiate between the real and the imaginary.

The editor sends the book out with the hope that this personal touch of seeing the faces and some of the milieus of the philosophers, will stimulate study of their writings.

He wishes to express his thanks to the many institutions, particularly the European and Asian libraries, museums, and universities which have cooperated in supplying reproductions and photographs of items in their possession.

As this is a pioneer publication, the editor will welcome suggestions from serious readers and students for future editions.

Weighing the Soul in the Judgment Hall of Osiris, from the Egyptian
Book of the Dead
(*British Museum*)

Judaism

JUDAISM

If philosophy is the search for a general ethical regulative, then it is only logical to assume that we will find the origins of early philosophy in the flow of ancient religious thought. Indeed, for a period of three thousand years and more, philosophy not only ran parallel to religion, but was so intermeshed with theology that we can safely say that up to the seventeenth century of our era there was no philosophy without theology; even in the last three hundred years philosophy has never ceased drawing from the rich treasures of religious thought.

Philosophy, the love of wisdom or the search for ethical principles, thus has persisted close to religious meditation since time immemorial. On the other hand, history shows one can stand at the pinnacle of scientific knowledge and have as much feeling for ethics as the primitive savage cutting up his enemy's leg for lunch.

It has been a tradition, however, in the Western world to credit the beginnings of philosophy to Thales of Miletus and his fellow holozoists, who attempted in a naïve and often clumsy manner to explain the composition of matter. These primitive essays in physics and chemistry should not rightly be called philosophy. They are to be classified as scientific, and they have their place in the history of science. From antiquity to our time, science has traveled a path independent of philosophy. The great scientists from Euclidean days to the atomic physicists were, by and large, not philosophers, although a few of them dabbled in it as laymen would. And, similarly, the great philosophers, from Socrates to Bergson, were not scientists, although they too wrote an occasional paper in some field of science, as might any educated layman.

Philosophy is the study of ethical principles, and as such it has found and will find devotees among all groups of civilized men, among all nations and castes and professions. This volume has as its scope the illustration of the catholic character of philosophy, not only geographically, but also socially. While in our days philosophy has been confined to the classroom and may be in danger (as some feel) of being reduced to a self-perpetuating clique of college teachers and students, in the past philosophy lived within the whole body of society.

To place the beginnings of a particular movement or science at a given date is extremely difficult because we are inclined to confuse the historical data that happens to be available to us with the whole of history. That is, if the earliest piece of writing we have found is seven thousand years old, we are inclined to say the alphabet began seven thousand years ago.

In addition to this difficulty, there is that of traditional concepts and prejudices. We are accustomed to pinpointing cultural movements somewhere in the Western world, although all facts cry out against such bias.

Although we have not a page of philosophical writings worth print and paper from the European scene prior to the Sixth Century B.C., we persist in placing the beginnings of philosophy in Greece; yet there is a large body of philosophical literature available in Asia that pre-dates the Socratic era by many hundreds of years.

There was a whole world of philosophy in India, China, and Israel when Europe was still in its savage state.

It was Ur whence Abraham started his trek to Canaan

We shall therefore begin this book with the philosophy of one of the three, Israel, because the ethics of Israel are familiar to us and because they have been retained more clearly in their historic sequence. The books of King Solomon of the year one thousand are one of the best examples of concentrated study of ethical principles.

How much of Solomon's thought is retained in its original formulation is impossible to determine, nor is this the place to go into Biblical exegesis.

We have before us the books of this great man, whose reputation was worldwide in his lifetime. We find traces of it in the fairy-tales of India and Persia and the whole Middle East; and this man's philosophy has not ceased to offer guidance to people of our generation from one corner of the world to the other.

1

King Solomon makes no effort to present his thoughts as original contributions to the science of human behavior and conduct. Rather does he emphasize the wisdom of the Fathers, the teachings of Judaism,

Traditionally, the mainstream of Judaism is traced back to Moses, Prince of Egypt, but undoubtedly there was a Torah, or guide, before Moses. Perhaps some day we will find more definite evidence of the Judaic teachings of Abraham and the men who held the people of Israel together from the days of Ur through the days of Jericho.

Many changes have occurred in the philosophical writings of the people of Israel from the Abrahamic desert nights to the modern dissertations of contemporary Jewish philosophers. But in all these writings, the spirit of man's moral responsibility toward his fellowman has lived on, as expressed in the three major works—the Torah, the Talmud, and the Cabbalah. In fact, the last of the three, which means *tradition*, is still an unfinished book.

Since the sixth century before our era and the destruction of Jerusalem at the hands of the Babylonians, Israel has never been entirely free from conquerors and intrusive strangers, and its people have been subjected to the most cruel pressure to drop their affiliation with Judaic teachings. They have unflinchingly withstood inhuman sufferings at the hands of their Christian neighbors, but they would not deviate from their fundamental principle that the Lord is one and that man's major duty is observance of His precepts and His alone.

It is natural that such faith, as well as the accompanying persecution, should be reflected in the philosophy of the Jewish people.

Burial Place of Abraham in Hebron

FROM THE DEAD SEA SCROLLS

Facsimile of part of "The War of The Sons of Light and The Sons of Darkness"
(Courtesy Rina Gallery, Jerusalem)

The TORAH

Torah means, in the literal Hebrew, *instruction,* or *guidance,* and is used in this sense by the ancient prophets and sages.

Prior to the first destruction of the great Temple in Jerusalem, by "Torah" the Hebrews meant the Books attributed to Moses. Shortly after the time of the second Temple, the final settlement of the Canon was made at Jamnia about 100 A.D. leading to the Bible's present form as codified by the seventh century rabbis known as Masoretes. Therefore, the Hebrew Bible *in toto,* as well as all Talmudic and later literature was often referred to as Torah.

The Hebrew Bible as it appears in our texts today is an anthology of thirty-nine books, reckoned as twenty-two, written for the most part in Hebrew, a little of it in Aramaic. (The uncanonized apocryphal sections are in Greek as well as Hebrew.) There is hardly any doubt that these books were written over a time stretching more than a thousand years. A much larger segment than commonly supposed is written in poetic and aphoristic form. In this sense the Torah is to be considered one of the world's greatest collections of pure literature.

Basically it contains five types of material:

(1) the legendary tales, frequently influencing faraway Asian story writers, as in India and Persia;

(2) the historical books (of remarkable accuracy, as shown by recent archaeological findings);

(3) the ritualistic codes with their 613 commandments and prohibitions as to diet, habitat, marriage, prayer service, sacrifices, and legal procedure;

(4) the prophetic sermons on current political and social issues;

(5) the philosophical and poetical works.

Pray tell me if there is anywhere, or was at any time, another volume of writings such as this, whose impact set aflame the lands between the Nile and the Euphrates more than three thousand years ago—a flame that has never ceased to burn all these millennia and has leapt from continent to continent, from tongue to tongue, from heart to heart.

Show me a village of people and I will find somewhere among them a trace of the Mosaic flame, be it in a book, a house of worship, a painting, a sculptured figurine, a phrase of music, or the memory of a sage proverb from Solomon, the king of kings. And even in places where the Torah has been defiled and its people erased, you will find the ashes of Israel still glimmering to remind the forgetful.

The Torah cannot be forgotten nor can it be thrown aside. If one had such intent, he would have to rip out a thousand books from a thousand shelves, a thousand statues and portraits from a thousand walls, and a thousand temples and churches from land to land. For millennia the people of the East and the West have grown and flourished in the breath of the Torah. The songs of its inspired sages reverberated in the poets, the dramatists, the painters, the sculptors, the fabulists, the preachers, the statesmen, the legislators, the philosophers, and the people at large, forever seeking justice.

If there ever was a book that has moved the world, this is it. It was of this Torah that Jesus said, "I come to fulfill

Earliest Preserved Greek Manuscripts of the Bible. ABOVE: *Fragments of Deuteronomy, Second Century B.C.* BELOW: *St. John's Gospel, Ch. xviii, Second Century A.D.*

it, not to destroy it." And it was because of the Torah that Mohammed called the Hebrews the People of the Book.

So much has been written on the subject of the authorship of the various Biblical books that I certainly do not wish to add to the already existing commentaries. There is no doubt that the majesty of Moses appears in many a page attributed to him, as does the wisdom of King Solomon in the writings named after him, and the incomparable poetry of his father in the Psalms.

Little difference would it make today if these three greatest of the children of Jacob were princes in the palace, as in truth they were, or shepherds on a hill.

Moses, the Lawgiver

MOSES, The Prince

Of the teachings of this greatest of the Hebrew sages, far too little has come down to us. Through the theological and legendary setting of the five-chaptered book attributed to him shines the indomitable light of a great Teacher, imbued with the spirit and vision of a God-devoted life for his people under a social order founded on justice, neighbor-love, and self-discipline.

All available historical writings serve to emphasize the unique and precious personality of the profound lawmaker who carved in imperishable stone the very breath and beauty of the Lord's commandments. We do not know which of the legendary, historical, or ritualistic segments of the Mosaic books were written by this strange and princely shepherd, but dull must be the reader of the Bible who fails to detect the thunderous step of this benign and melancholy giant, wandering through the desert.

This is the immortal tribute the Torah pays to its relentless leader: "So Moses, the servant of the Lord, died there in the land of Moab . . . and he was buried in the valley of Moab . . . and no man knoweth of his grave unto this day . . . And there hath not risen a prophet since in Israel like unto Moses whom the Lord knew soul to soul."

Semitic Captive in Egypt. Stone Relief from Luxor (Thirteenth Century)

4

DAVID, The King

Like Moses, he was a shepherd before he became a leader of his people. This second of the Hebrew kings, conqueror of Jerusalem and unifier of the Hebrew nation, was by far the most colorful of Biblical authors.

Called to the court of King Saul as a young man because of his musical talents, he was a bear and lion killer as a boy, a mercenary soldier, a captain of outlaws, a shining hero who bested Goliath, a magnanimous adversary who more than once spared the life of his enemy king while the monarch was at his mercy, a saintly servant of the Lord, and a very great sinner indeed.

David was the most human among kings and, with all his blunders and failings, a kingly human.

King David
(Painting by Rembrandt)

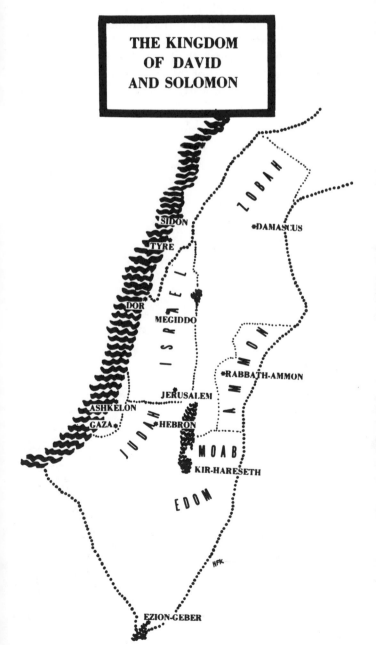

THE KINGDOM
OF DAVID
AND SOLOMON

David forgives Absalom: ". . . he came to the king, and he bowed himself on his face to the ground before the king, and the king kissed Absalom."

5

SOLOMON, Son of David

By far the most eminent personality of the era of the tenth century B.C., Solomon put his stamp on the world of his time as well as all times to follow. He developed Israel into a highly organized empire, reformed its government, sponsored voyages of discovery to West Africa and probably India, and encouraged an architecture the traces of which even a cruel three millennia did not eradicate. He was, as his name bespeaks, a lover of peace, and while wealth was his share, he was unfailingly true to his prayerful wish to become endowed with the blessings of true judgment first and last.

This gifted king of kings gave himself to the study of living nature, and so widely known was his scholarship that for a hundred generations people of all three continents thought him a ruler not only of men, but also of the spirits of the air and the waters. They even attributed magical powers to the plant that bears his name, and many a mystic order claims him as its founder.

Solomon made Jerusalem, the city of his birth, a religious and literary center, the fame of which spread to the East and West. This first of the great polyhistors, who was as much at home in the warrior's chariot as at the writing

"King Solomon," by E. M. Lilien

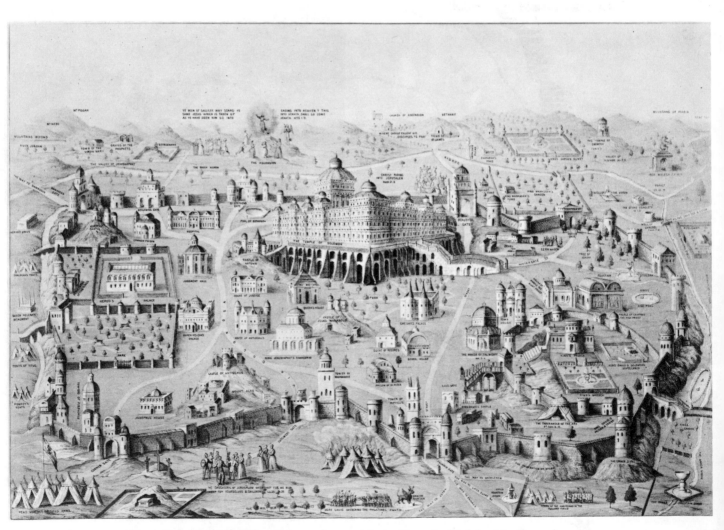

The Ancient City of Jerusalem, with the Temple (Original in Rome)

6

table, became the symbol of story and thought from Iceland to India. Wherever and whenever people spoke or wrote of a wise monarch it was him they envisioned.

The Biblical books are a great (but not the only) document to this astounding man; no wonder that even a thousand years after his death scholars and poets named their writings after this king. Be it so that not every chapter and verse of Solomonic literature is of his pen, they all are of his heart and soul.

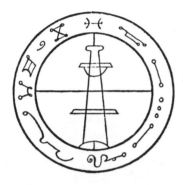

Secret Seal of Solomon, from the Lemegeton

The ruins of Babylon, to which masses of Judeans were deported in 597 B.C. by their conquerors. Cyrus, the Persian emperor who took Babylon, granted the Hebrews return to their lands in 538 B.C. under the leadership of Ezra.

Isaiah, the Eighth-Century Mystic and Moralist
(Engraving by Doré)

Ezra reveals the text of the Law after the return of the Judeans from Babylon
(Engraving by Doré)

*The Destruction of Jerusalem and Its Great Spiritual Riches
by the Romans under Titus (70 A.D.)*

Titus

*Bar-Kochba
Coin of Liberation
with
Temple Façade*
(Jewish Museum)

The Seven-Armed Candelabrum from the Temple of Jerusalem

Wailing Wall at the Foot of the Temple of Jerusalem

Spoils of the Temple, on the Arch of Titus, Rome

This painting by Lilien illustrates the perennial hopes of the Children of Israel of return to their homeland

Commentators, Talmudists and Cabbalists

SIRACH, JESUS

SIRACH, JESUS, son of (About 200 B.C.). Ever since the book written by Jesus, son of Sirach, has become known it has edified readers of all succeeding generations up to the present day. It has confirmed pious people in their faith. It has impressed sceptical-minded readers by its vigorous conviction. It has inspired poets, philosophers, statesmen and plain people. Above all, it has been valued as a rich fountain of proverbial wisdom and the personal confession of a man of large experience. Although it has not been accepted into the Protestant canon and was placed among the books of Apocrypha, it has generally been as highly appreciated as the books of the Bible itself.

The author was a contemporary of the high priest Simon II who died in 199 B.C., and he certainly was no longer alive when the Jewish people were afflicted by the persecutions which preceded the rise of the Maccabees. In his youth, Jesus ben Sirach had studied the Bible and books of popular wisdom. Then a calumniator endangered his life and forced him to flee from his native town, but after a while he was vindicated and lived for the rest of his life in Jerusalem. During his exile, he meditated on his misfortune, and observed the vicissitudes of life which others had to endure. These experiences, and not so much his previous readings, are the substance of his book. He was neither a priest nor a *Sofer* (skilled interpreter of the law), but a layman who used to deliver popular speeches. His book was translated into Greek by his grandson under the title *Wisdom of Jesus the Son of Sirach*. Its Latin title is *Ecclesiasticus*. It also was translated into many other languages. The Hebrew original was lost. In 1896, some parts of it were found in a cellar of the Ezra Synagogue in Cairo. Later these were augmented so that now about three fifths of the original are extant.

Philo, the Earliest Portrait Type
(From a IX century Ms. in the Bibliothèque Nationale)

PHILO JUDAEUS

PHILO JUDAEUS (About 25 B.C.—Before 50 A.D.). The importance of Philo to the history of philosophy is incomparably greater than the power of his personality or the relevance of his personal thinking. For about seventeen centuries his example was, consciously and unconsciously, followed by all European thinkers, notwithstanding their differences, no matter whether they were nominalists or realists, idealists or naturalists, orthodox or heretics, and today Catholic Neo-Scholasticism is still following him, not to mention his influence on Islamic and Jewish philosophy.

Philo was the first thinker to introduce into epistemology, metaphysics, physics and ethics the problem of reconciling speculative thought with the data of Biblical revelation; or, rather, he established these data, especially their characteristics of God, Man and Nature as the perfect truth with which the philosopher had to harmonize the results of his thinking. In this way, Philo created a spiritual situation, completely unknown in pagan Greek

Philo Judaeus

The first printed text of Philo (Reduced)

philosophy, which had not to regard Sacred Scripture as the standard and source of truth. The impact of the belief in the pagan gods on philosophical thoughts had only occasionally caused conflicts and had become negligible. As a positive support of thinking, as a source of knowledge, the belief in the pagan gods was of no account even when some philosophers used the gods as symbols of forces which were comprehended by speculative methods. Philo initiated a new era in the history of philosophy, the earliest documents of which can be noted in the Gospel of St. John. Its great development begins with the Fathers of the Church, comprises the whole Middle Ages and part of modern times, Descartes included. It was Spinoza, a Jew like Philo, who removed Biblical revelation from the realm of philosophy.

But, unlike Spinoza, Philo, a contemporary of Jesus Christ and St. Paul, remained a faithful, professing Jew. He devoted the main part of his life to the interpretation of the Pentateuch and to the defense of the Jewish faith against attacks on the part of gentile critics by explaining the essence of Judaism from the historical, philosophical, ethical and juridical points of view. When he was elected leader of a Jewish embassy to Rome in 40 A.D., he tried also to defend his co-religionists against the arbitrary power of Emperor Caligula.

Although Philo borrowed much from Greek philosophers, his system deviates widely from purely Greek lines. It is the doctrine of monotheistic mysticism, teaching that human mind is capable, by intuition, not by reasoning, to apprehend God's existence but not His nature. In this way, Philo was the first to outline a psychology of faith.

The TALMUD

The *Talmud,* which may be rendered from the Hebrew as "Research," is one of the world's ten great works of divinely inspired literature. Like the Koran and other post-Judean books of holy nature, it is impossible to conceive of the *Talmud* without the *Torah,* the ancient Books of Moses. In fact, the *Talmud* is the *Torah* perpetuated.

As long as the great Solomonic Temple towered over the lands along the Jordan, the rituals, ceremonies and observances, sacrifices, commands and prohibitions made the *Torah* a living spirit in Israel. It was both 'state law and religious fountainhead, the guide to daily conduct and the basis of family and social structure for all the adherents of the Covenant.

But with the sudden advent of the overbearing and hostile Caesarian Empire, the sacred walls of the Temple crumbled under the Roman ram and the people of Palestine were scattered to the four corners of the world, to become the most remarkable wandering people of all time. Thrust into strange lands with alien customs to which they were forced to adjust their own deeply felt faith, the dispersed Hebrews were often and in many places bewildered as to how to abide by the laws of the *Torah,* the Covenant they had made with their Lord.

A thousand practical problems arose before the Jews of

Gamaliel, descendant of Hillel, religious philosopher of the first century, with his pupils

Ancient academies. Outdoor teaching as practiced in Palestine and Babylonia during the Talmudic period. Neither teacher nor pupils carried notebooks, as all lessons were committed to memory. The lesson was a discourse, after which the pupils asked questions or engaged in discussions

the First Century of the Common Era: problems concerning marriage and divorce and other aspects of family life; concerning personal hygiene and ritual purity; concerning civil and ceremonial law, dietary obligations and sacrificial cults; concerning the observance of holidays and festivals, the keeping of the Sabbath, the treatment of illness, the care of the poor, and so on.

For a hundred years and more, distinguished scholars labored to formulate a new set of laws which would reinterpret the ancient Mosaic concepts to the sons of Israel living in a pagan world.

Finally, in third-century Palestine, under the editorship of Rabbi Judah, called "The Prince," all the new writings of Biblical interpretation were correlated into a volume of six books known as the *Mishnah,* or "Repetition." This became the core of the Talmud.

During the next three hundred years the *Mishnah* was supplemented by many recorded discussions or commentaries, contributed by Babylonian as well as Palestinian rabbis. Some of these were legalistic, some philosophic, some folklorist, some allegorical. These later writings,

Meir b. Baruch of Rothenburg
(b. Worms, 1215; d. Alsace, 1293)

A typical disputation between monks and rabbis
(*woodcut*)

known as the *Gemara,* or "Learning," were intended to expound the *Mishnah* and to facilitate the understanding of its difficult passages.

Thus for almost five hundred years the great *hakhamim,* or sages, of Babylon, Jerusalem and other academic centers worked in setting down first the *Mishnah* and then the *Gemara,* which together constitute the *Talmud.*

By the fifth century the compilation of the *Talmud* had come to an end, but the commentaries and addenda have never ceased, even up to our own days. In the Middle Ages, the philosopher Maimonides, the commentator Rashi, and the codifier Caro were among those who brought about a renaissance of Talmudic study in Western Europe. Many sayings and parables from such Talmudic scribes as Hillel and others became proverbial in the non-Jewish world also.

The books of the *Talmud* are uneven. They range from severe theological legalism to unsurpassed beauty of legendary literature. To borrow a phrase from one of our masters, "Who would forego a walk through the forest because some of the trees are dry and barren?"

13

CABBALAH

CABBALAH is that great body of Hebrew literature that sprang up and grew parallel to the traditional writings of rabbinical literature, for a period of over a thousand years. Its origins are clouded in uncertainty, its authors doubtful or anonymous, and its forms of expression varied as they are unusual.

Cabbalah signifies "receiving." However, only few were given the inner light by which they could behold the visions of eternity. The secret doctrines concerning God are revealed to the spiritually prepared only.

In a sense, the Cabbalah was a silent protest movement of the mystic element against formalism; a role which it played not only in Judaism but also in Christian Protestantism (Reuchlin a.o.).

The great theme of the Cabbalah is God before creation, and the soul of man after it.

God is *ain soph,* the endless, ever creating; or, in the words of the great philosopher of Mysticism, Baruch Spinoza, *"Natura naturans"* (infinite creative substance).

Allegory of the Cabbalah

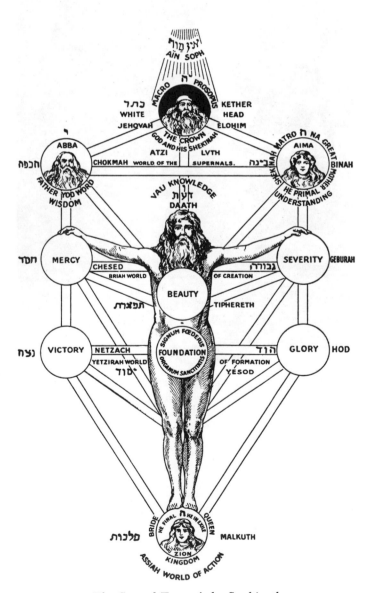

The Sacred Tree of the Sephiroth

God manifests Himself in ten emanations, or *Sephiroth.* His divine attributes are: Wisdom, Reason, Knowledge, Greatness, Strength, Beauty, Eternity, Majesty, Principle, and Sovereignty (*Chokmah, Binah, Daath, Gedulah, Geburah, Tiphereth, Netzach, Hod, Yesod, Malkuth*).

Man is part of this created world, but man is also given to glory in the emanations of the heavens. Man can lift the curtain of the great Unknown and raise himself into the abode of the blessed spirit by dedicating his life to *Chabad* (Wisdom, Reason, Knowledge), the first three of the Divine Emanations.

This sublime love of the Divine transcends physical being and transforms mere man into the *Zaddik,* the Righteous One, who, seeing the inner stream of creation, lives in the bliss of fundamental faith and equanimity. His body is earthly but his soul is of the heavens. He is united with God in a mystical union which can be comprehended by the initiated only (*Yihud*).

Again we are reminded of Spinoza and his theorem, "The love of man to God and the love of man to man are one and the same."

The Cabbalah, although offering no moral regulative or system of precepts, is inherently a philosophy of ethics. Its writings may point to examination of the symbolic meaning of the Hebrew alphabet; they may encourage a semanticism based on initials and numbers; they may become involved with incarnation and magic, with amulets and spiritism, demonology, exorcism, or Messianism; the essence of the Cabbalah has ever been man's mystical union with God in thoughts of wisdom and deeds of kindness.

*Amulet used to protect women in childbirth
from evil spirits*

(From collection of the Jewish Historical Society of Strasbourg)

The literature of the Cabbalah has its beginning in Palestine and Babylon in the post-Talmudic era. Of the systematic books of the early epoch are *Shiur Komah,* dealing with the measures of God, and *Sepher Yetzirah,* Book of Creation.

In the early middle ages the center of Cabbalist study moved from the Middle East to the Mediterranean countries and Germany. The major works of that era are *Masechet Azilut,* a treatise on emanations; *Sepher ha-Bahir,* the Book of Enlightenment; *Sepher ha-Temunah,* the Book of the Image; and last and foremost, the *Zohar,* or Splendor.

The *Zohar* is generally and rightly regarded as the main work of the Cabbalah. It was written in Aramaic in the manner of a commentary to the Torah. It was composed and published toward the end of the thirteenth century by Moses ben Shemtov de Leon, of Castile (d. 1305). It is the only piece of post-Talmudic literature that was to be used by many as a text, almost equal to the Torah and Talmud. The *Zohar* was and still is the classical expression of Jewish mysticism. Like the Midrash, it is written in a homiletical manner, following the Platonic style of attributing dominance in the dialogues to the Socratic Rabbi Simeon Ben Yochai.

In the sixteenth century the center of Cabbalah veered back to Palestine, especially the city of Safed. Its great representatives were Moses Cordovero, the profound theoretician of Cabbalism; Isaac Luria, the Saint; and his disciple Hayim Vital, who put his master's teachings on paper.

The Safed school of Cabbalah became a source of great inspiration to the fervent religious movements of Eastern Europe of the later centuries, culminating in the tremendously powerful revival movement of Jewish mysticism in the eighteenth and nineteenth centuries, known as Chassidism.

Founded by Rabbi Israel ben Eliezer (1700-1760), called Baal Shem-Tov, Master of the Good Name, Chassidism (Pietism) is based on the application of Cabbalistic principles of union with God. Its emphasis is on the guidance of the Zaddikim, the righteous, and constant direct communion with the Heavens.

The Cabbalah in all its ways and byways is based on the theology of *Schechinah,* God's indwelling in man.

Man can reach the Divine in his own heart, in his own faith.

Man can reach the Divine in meditation of the oneness and infiniteness of the Lord.

Man can reach the Divine in deeds of kindness, as love to man is but love to God in another form. Man's destiny is the practice of *Tikkun,* to restore harmony to the world by spreading God's scattered light into every corner.

The Cabbalah is called the third of the great literatures in the Hebrew faith, next to the Bible and Talmud. Indeed, they are all three but one. And if some may point out that not always did holy wisdom guide the scriptural text, it is not difficult to pull back the frilly curtain of the incidental and gaze upon the celestial splendor of what is forever the Faith of Israel.

The Golem. The Golem was a clay servant into which life had been breathed by the Rabbi of Prague, Judah Loew ben Bezaleel (1520-1609), an ethical and homiletic writer who became the central figure in the Golem legend

15

Monument to Rabbi Judah Loew; Hero of the
Golem Stories

Sabbatai Zevi (1626-1676)

Rabbi Loew's Grave
(E. M. Lilien)

*Letter of the community of Tiberias to the community of
Modena regarding Sabbatai Zevi*

16

Jacob Franck (1726-1791), false Messiah following Sabbatai Zevi, who later became a Catholic

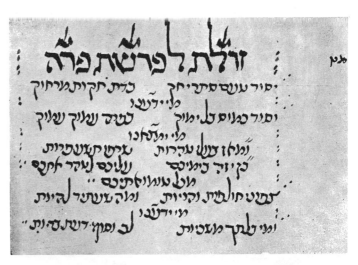

Piyyutim in Spanish Rabbinical Writing
(Manuscript in El Escurial Museum)

Memorandum by the Exilarch David ben Zaccai on the Calendar Controversy, 921-22, composed by Saadia

SAADIA

SAADIA (892-942). Until Saadia began to formulate his ideas, the spiritual atmosphere of his times had been, as one of his contemporaries complained, as follows:

Muslims, Jews, Christians and Magicians, they all are walking in error and darkness. There are two kinds of people left in the world: the one group is intelligent but lacking in faith, the other has faith but is lacking intelligence.

And so it became Saadia's purpose to teach not only his Jewish co-religionists but also Islamic and Christian thinkers that faith is not opposed to reason but only to pseudo-reason.

Born in Egypt, and educated as well in all branches of Arabian culture as in Biblical and Talmudic scholarship, Saadia went to Palestine, and then to Babylonia. There he accomplished his great work which became the foundation of Jewish philosophy and science. Acquainted with Greek philosophy, the various formulations of the Christian dogma, the doctrines of the Manicheans, of Zoroaster and even with the philosophy of India, Saadia developed the idea that Judaism is compatible with all truth, whatever its source. In his explanation of the nature of religion, the character of man and the way of conceiving God, Saadia criticized Plato's cosmology and refuted gnostic doctrines. He tried to reconcile the idea of freedom of man with that of the all-embracing foreknowledge of God.

Saadia was also a learned mathematician and a trained philologist, and he composed the first Hebrew dictionary as well as the first Jewish prayer-book.

17

Rashi (Solomon ben Isaac, 1040-1105) of Troyes. Eminent Talmudist commentator; his notes on Bible and Talmud virtually became a part of the text.

Chapel of Rashi, Most Prominent Medieval Talmudist

AL-MUKAMMAS, DAVID IBN MERWAN

AL-MUKAMMAS, DAVID IBN MERWAN (died c. 937). Born in Babylonia, author of the earliest known Jewish philosophical work of the Middle Ages—a commentary to the Sefer Yetzirah (the Book of Formation) —chiefly responsible for the development of the Cabbalah, Al-Mukammas' manuscripts lay forgotten for centuries. The aforementioned was discovered in 1898 in the Tsarist Library; fragments of another work on the unity of God were found in the basement of a Cairo synagogue. Al-Mukammas established three ascending categories of science: practical philosophy, theoretical philosophy, and knowledge of the Torah.

IBN GABIROL, SOLOMON

IBN GABIROL, SOLOMON (About 1021—about 1058). From the middle of the twelfth to the end of the fourteenth century, Dominicans and Franciscans struggled with great bitterness over the ideas expressed in the book *Fons Vitae,* which the monk Dominicus Gundisalvi, assisted by the baptized Jew John Hispalensis, had translated from the Arabic. Its author was called Avicebron. The Franciscans, among them famous philosophers like Alexander of Hales and Duns Scotus, accepted its ideas and used it as a source for their own work, while the majority of the Dominicans, including Thomas Aquinas, opposed them. The importance of *Fons Vitae* as a source of medieval Neo-Platonism can hardly be exaggerated. It was not until 1840 that the great orientalist Salomon Munk discovered the real author of the book—namely, Solomon Ibn Gabirol, who, up to then, was known only as one of the greatest Spanish-Jewish poets. The Hebrew title of Ibn Gabirol's book is *Mekor Hayim (Fountain of Life).* It deals with the total subject matter from the point of view of the antagonism of form and matter, and establishes a hierarchy of all things, a graduation which, on each higher level, shows a more perfect relation between form and matter. Gabirol, who continued to express his Jewish convictions in his poetry, dealt with the philosophical problems of his metaphysical work without any relation to Judaism. (W) *On the Improvement of Moral Qualities.*

A Street in Old Toledo, a Center of Sephardic Culture

Manuscript Page from Abraham Ibn Ezra's Grammatical Excursus—Introduction to Commentary on the Book of Exodus

Abraham Ibn Ezra (Spanish-Hebrew, 1092-1167), wandering hymnist and philosopher. Traveled through many non-Moslem lands, becoming first Hebrew Spaniard to write entirely in Hebrew. Wrote many liturgical poems, philosophic works, and an Arabic study of Spanish-Hebrew poetry

HIYYA, ABRAHAM BAR

HIYYA, ABRAHAM BAR (About 1065-1136). While Christianity and Islam met each other on the battlefield, Abraham bar Hiyya, called by his fellow Jews "the prince," and by non-Jews "Savasorda" (Latinization of his Arabic title Sahib al Shurta, governor of a city), took a leading part in promoting spiritual interchange between the representatives of the Christian and Arabic civilizations, without neglecting his principal task, namely the vindication of the Jewish faith and its harmonization with science and philosophy.

His treatise on areas and measurements which introduced new scientific terms and new methods for the measurement of surfaces, was translated into Latin under the title *Liber Embadorum,* and, for centuries, it remained a standard work. His contributions to mathematics, astronomy, music and optics were highly appreciated by Jewish, Christian and Moslem scholars. In his *Hegyon Hanefesh* (Reflection on the Soul), Abraham bar Hiyya, while exposing his ideas on creation and the destiny and conduct of Man, showed a strong inclination to an ascetic conception of life.

BAHYA IBN PAKUDA

BAHYA IBN PAKUDA (c. 1050). Little is known of the personal life of Bahya, except that he was a *dayyan* (judge at the rabbinical court) in Saragossa toward the end of the eleventh century. His book, *Hobot ha-Lebatot* (The Duties of the Heart), expressed his personal feelings more elaborately than was usual for the Middle Ages. It depicted the noble, humble soul and pure, imperturbable mind of a man ever-grateful to God, motivated by his love of God. Bahya regarded the soul elevated toward God and liberated from the shackles of earthly existence as evidence of purification, communion with God as the ultimate goal. However, his teachings neither imply nor result in neo-Platonic ecstasy. He remained faithful to the Bible and the Talmud. Unlike many other schools of mysticism, he differentiated between man and God. Although a religious moralist, he resolutely subordinated moral righteousness and lawful action to the pious contemplation of God, for the latter served as the most effective control of egoistic instincts and passions.

19

JUDAH HALEVI

JUDAH HALEVI (About 1080-1140). As a "flaming pillar of song," Judah Halevi, the greatest Jewish poet of the Middle Ages, was exalted by Heinrich Heine, who, himself an undeniable expert, sensed through the medium of a translation Halevi's mastership of versification and his fervent soul. Halevi sang of love and friendship, of virtue and beauty, and most passionately of the fate of the Jewish people, of Zion and God. Several of his sacred poems form part of Jewish prayer-books in every country where Jewish congregations exist.

But Halevi was also an important philosopher of religion. His *Kitab Al Khazari,* written in Arabic and translated into Hebrew under the title *Sefer Ha-Kuzari* (Book of the Khazar), referring to the conversion to Judaism of the Khazar King Bulan II (about 740), is a defense of the Jewish faith against Christian and Islamic attacks and at the same time, a profound meditation on Jewish history and an acute demarcation between philosophy and religion. The close connection between the revealed religion and the history of the Jewish people is characteristic of Halevi's position. He maintained that Judaism does not center in the person of its founder as the religions of Christ and Mohammed do but in the people to whom the Torah has been given, and he goes so far as to declare: "If there were no Jews there would be no Torah." But he by no means idolizes his people in the way modern nationalists do. Jewish history is the work of Divine Providence which he regarded as the continuation of the Divine creative activity. Halevi was opposed to Aristotelianism which he reproached for subjecting the Deity to necessity and for being incompatible with the idea of a personal God. Platonic tradition seemed more fitting to him, for he was inclined to regard God as the principle of form that moulds the eternal material principle. Fundamentally, however, Halevi remained reluctant to use philosophical categories in matters that concern religion, and he often expressed his dislike of philosophy and philosophers, although he proved to be one of them.

Another View of Toledo

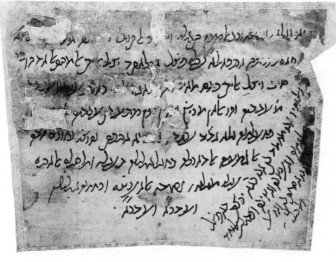

Judah Halevi's Holograph

A letter in Hebrew from a Khazar Jew, dated 950 A.D., five years prior to the letter received by Hasdai ibn Shaprut, the Jewish Vizier of the Caliph in Spain, from King Joseph of Khazaria. In this letter are recounted the incidents that led to the conversion of the Khazars to Judaism and events that took place in Khazaria during the 10th century

MAIMONIDES (Moses Ben Maimon)

MAIMONIDES (MOSES BEN MAIMON) (1135-1204).
Among the rabbis of the later Middle Ages and centuries
thereafter, an adage was current, saying, "From Moses to
Moses there is none like unto Moses." It means simply
that Maimonides is to be regarded as the greatest figure in
Jewish history since the man who delivered the Ten Commandments to the Jewish people. In fact, the spiritual
development of Judaism up to the present age is incomprehensible without taking account of Maimonides' activities as a codifier, judge and commentator of the Bible and
the Talmud. His *Mishnah Torah* (Copy of the Law) was
the first systematic exposition of Jewish religion. His "articles of faith" are either quoted or poetically paraphrased
in modern Jewish prayer books.

The philosophical thoughts of Maimonides strongly influenced not only Jewish but also Islamic and Christian
philosophers. The intention of his main work *Moreh
Nebuchim* (Guide of the Perplexed, in Arabic *Dalalat al
Hairin*) was to prove that the teachings of Judaism are in
harmony with the results of philosophical thinking, and
that beyond that, they offer insight which reason alone
cannot obtain. For this purpose, Maimonides prevalently
used the works of Aristotle, and, to a lesser extent, those
of Plato. Christian philosophers were eager to apply Maimonides' doctrine to the defense of their own religion or to
the explanation of general principles. Thus did William of
Auvergne, Alexander of Hales, Albertus Magnus, Meister
Eckhart, Thomas Aquinas and, through him, all medieval
and modern Thomists. The great jurist, Hugo Grotius, was
inspired by Maimonides' views on the history of religion.

Born in Cordova, Spain, Maimonides was forced to
emigrate, at first to Morocco, then to Egypt where he
earned his living by practicing medicine. In his medical
treatises he anticipated modern discoveries concerning the
affliction of the body by psychic factors, allergies, epilepsy,
the nervous system and individual constitution. Almost all
of his books were written in Arabic and shortly thereafter
translated into Hebrew and Latin.

Signature of Moses Maimonides
(*From a Twelfth Century Manuscript in the Bodleian Library at Oxford*)

Autograph from Maimonides, "Perush Hamishnajoth"
(*by courtesy of the "Israelitisches Familienblatt," Berlin*)

Maimonides fled Morocco in 1165 to escape religious persecution. He wrote dietetic rule book for Saladin

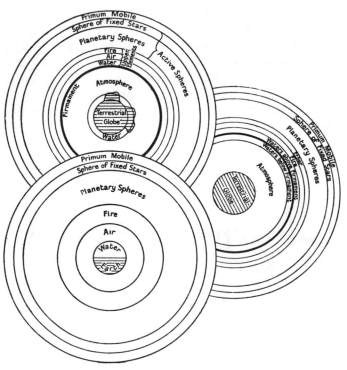

Three typical medieval diagrams of the structure of the universe. The uppermost accords with the scheme of Maimonides, the lowermost with that of Dante. A separate planetary sphere was believed to exist for each planet including the sun and moon

שג גאולת עולם תהיה ללויים   ישראל שירש את אבי
אמו לוי   הרי זה נגול מלוי אעף שאינו לוי הואיל והערי
או השרות של לויים נגול לעולם   שרק זה תלוי במקומות
או ולא בבעלים ולי שירש את אבי אמו ישראל נגול כישראל
ולא כלויים שלא נאמר גאולת עולם תהיה ללויים אלא בערי
הלויים   כל שבט לוי מוזהרין שלא ינחלו בארץ
כנען וכן הן מוזהרין שלא יטלו חלק בבוה בשעה שכובשין
את הערים שנאמר לא יהיה לכהני הלוי כל שבט לוי חלק
ונחלה עם ישראל חלק בבוה ונחלה בארץ   וכן הוא אומר
בארץ לא תנחל וחלק לא יהיה לך בתוכם בבוה וכן לוי
או כהן שנטל חלק בבוה לוקה   ואם נטל נחלה בארץ
מעבירי אותה ממנה יראה לי שאין הדברי אומרין
אא בארץ שנכרתה עליה ברית לאברהם ליצחק
ולעקב וירשוה בניה ונתחלקה להם אבל שאר
כל   הארצות שכובש מלך ממלכי ישראל
הרי הכהני והלויי באותן הארצ ובביתן
ככל ישראל   ולמה לא זכה לוי   בנחלת
ארץ ישראל ובבזתה עם אחיו ספני
שהובדל לעבוד את   ה ולשרתו
ולהורו דרכיו הישרי ומשפטיו
הצדיקים לרבים שנא יורו
משפטי ליעקב ותורתך
לישרא לפי הובדלו
מדרכי העול לא
עורכין
מלחמה כשאר
ישראל ולא נוחלין
ולא זוכין   לעצמן
בכח גופן   אא הם חיל
ה שנאמ ברך ה חילו והוא
ברוך הוא זוכה להם   שנ אני
חלקך ונחלתך   ולא שבט לוי
בלבר אא כל איש ואיש מכל באי
העולם אשר נדבה רוחו אותו והבינו
מרעו להבדל לעמור לפני ה לשרתו
ולעברו לרעה את ה והלך ישר כמו טעשהו
האהים ופרק מעל צוארו עול החשבונות הרבי
אשר בקשו בני האדם   הרי זה נתקרש קורש
קרשים ויהיה ה הלקו   ונחלתו לעולם ולעולמי
עולמים   ויזכה לו בעולם רבר המספיק לו כמו שזכה
לכהנים וללויים   הרי דוד עליו השלום אומ ה מנת חלקי
וכוסי אתה תמיך גורלי

A page from Maimonides' "Mishnah Torah," printed before 1480 by Solomon ben Judah and Obadiah ben Moses in Italy

The Grave of Maimonides at Tiberias

Illustration from the Manuscript of Maimonides'
Mishnah Torah *(1295)*

Moses ben Nachman (Gerona, 1194—Acre, 1270). Spanish Talmudist and Cabbalist who died in Palestine; also rabbi and physician. Public defender of Judaism against a renegade Jewish Dominican. Known as Nachmanides

Statue of Maimonides by Doris Appel

JUDAH BEN SAMUEL OF REGENSBURG, HEHASID

JUDAH BEN SAMUEL OF REGENSBURG, HEHASID (12th and 13th centuries). The Hebrew word *Hehasid* means "the Saint." Judah's co-religionists revered him because he was an extremely pious man, absorbed in mystical contemplation, a great teacher, scholar and a careful leader of the Jewish community of Regensburg where he settled in 1195. He was the initiator of Jewish mysticism in Germany, a way of thinking and feeling that is different from cabbalistic mysticism because it insists more on prayer and moral conduct. Judah denied all possibility of human understanding of God. Man must fulfill his religious duties, as they are prescribed in the Bible, without reasonable knowledge of the Almighty, but, by purification, obedience to ceremonial life and asceticism, he may obtain union with God that is beyond reasoning. In this way, Judah tried to reconcile the demands of orthodox Judaism with enjoyment of mystical ecstasy.

Judah's biography is adorned with many legends which testify to the admiration of his contemporaries and succeeding generations. He wrote *Sefer Hasidim* (Book of the Pious), and *Sefer Hakavod* (Book of Glory). The second book has been lost. It is known only by quotations other authors have made from it.

Samuel Abulafia's synagogue at Toledo. Abulafia (1240-1291) was a profound Cabbalist who attempted to convert the Pope to Judaism

Asher ben Jechiel (Germany, 1250–Spain, 1327). Greatest authority on Jewish law of his time; wrote responsa, commentaries, and a collection of halakhot up to his time called Piske Ha-Rosh *(he was called Rosh for Rabbi Asher) or* Ha-Asheri

BERACHYAH

BERACHYAH (c. 12th or 13th century). The literary fame of Berachyah is chiefly founded upon his *Mishle Shualim* (Fox Fables). Some of these were of his own invention; others were derived from the fables of Aesop, the Talmud, and the Hindus, but even in the adaptation of plots to his own Hebrew style, he displayed poetic originality and narrative talents. The best-known of his philosophical works, encyclopedic in quality, is *Sefer Hahibbur* (The Book of Compilation). Here, he developed the ideas of Saadia, Bahya Ibn Pakuda, and Solomon Ibn Gabirol. He was versed in the eastern and western branches of Jewish philosophy, and was well acquainted with medieval French and English literature.

The personal life of Berachyah is solely conjecture. He was called Berachyah Ben Natronai Hanakdan. His father's name indicates descent from the Jewish scholars of Babylonia, which may help to explain Berachyah's knowledge of Hindu stories. His surname means "punctuator," probably an allusion to his profession of scribe or grammarian. There is no agreement as to the time, place, or country in which he lived. Some of his biographers assume that he wrote during the twelfth century; others during the thirteenth century. Some maintain that he lived in Provence; others in Northern France, and still others in England. It is not improbable that he was an itinerant teacher, scholar, and writer.

GERSONIDES

GERSONIDES (1288-1344). Levi ben Gershom, called Gersonides, was the greatest astronomer of his time. His writings attracted the interest of Kepler and his inventions, the "Jacob's staff" to measure visual angles and the *camera obscura*, became of great use. He also wrote on physics, physiology, mathematics, logic, ethics, psychology, metaphysics, the Bible and Talmud. Whatever he dealt with, he did so in a new manner. In some regards he was a precursor of Galileo, in others even of modern thinkers like Bertrand Russell, for Gersonides' principal problem in general philosophy was the relation between individual experience and the body of scientific knowledge, or the way science can be developed and subsist in the course of history. As a philosopher of religion, Gersonides, in his principal work *Milhamoth Adonai* (The Wars of the Lord), made a vigorous effort to integrate the historical experience of the Jewish people into a conception of the universe that rests upon the secular sciences of astronomy, physics and the other branches with which he was acquainted. He insisted that scientific research must be conducted independently of the Torah, which, he said, does not compel men to believe what is not true. But he was convinced that truth, in accordance with modern science, is contained in the Torah, though not explicitly, and that the history of the Jewish people reflects and confirms the universal truth, in whose discovery time plays an important part.

A large part of Gersonides' writings is either lost or still unpublished.

*Two pages from the "Birkath Hamazon" (1514)
by Gersonides*

CRESCAS, HASDAI

CRESCAS, HASDAI (1340-1410). Like almost all Jewish philosophers of the Middle Ages, Crescas developed his philosophy in the face of persecution and imminent personal danger. He was born in Barcelona and was denounced and victimized there, imprisoned and fined, despite the recognition of his innocence. He moved and settled in Saragossa, where he declined appointment as rabbi of the congregation. He then became an authority on Jewish law and ritual tradition, and often intervened diplomatically on behalf of his co-religionists in Aragon and neighboring kingdoms. In a letter from him to the Jews of Avignon, he described the personal pain he and other Jews endured during the persecution of Jews in Spain. It was during this Inquisition period (1391), that he lost his only son.

Crescas did not content himself with bemoaning the fate of the Jews. He endeavored to defend the spirit and doctrines of Judaism against its religious and philosophical opponents. His criticism of Christianity, written in Spanish, is lost, except for those fragments which were translated into Hebrew by Joseph ibn Shemtob in 1451. Crescas' principal work, *Or Adonai* (The Light of God), completed in 1410, the year of his death, was of great consequence. It refuted Neo-Platonism and Aristotle, and implied a sharp criticism of Gersonides and Maimonides because of their efforts to reconcile Judaism with Greek philosophy. Crescas rejected Aristotle's physics, metaphysics, and axiology. He defended the cause of Judaism with a spiritual originality, radicalism, and courage uncommon in the history of the Middle Ages. The importance of his thinking was by no means confined to the history of Jewish philosophy. His rejection of Aristotle, by stating that "there are no other worlds" than the one system in which the earth is situated, inspired such Christian thinkers as Nicholas Cusanus, Giordano Bruno, Marsilio Ficino, and Pico della Mirandola. There is little doubt that Spinoza was indebted to Crescas for his concept of the universe.

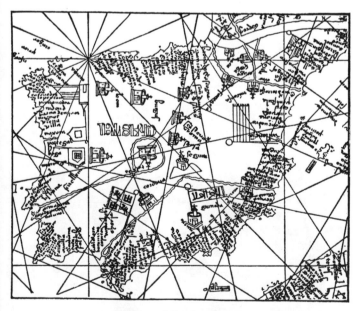

Map of Spain, 1375

ALBO, JOSEPH

ALBO, JOSEPH (c. 1380-1445). Very little is known about the life of Albo, but the few facts that are available present interesting aspects of medieval Jewish life amidst Gentile surroundings. Albo was the representative of the Jewish community of Daroca, where the impact and resultant clash of Jewish, Christian, and Islamic thought gave rise to a number of intellectual disputes. He participated in the great religious controversy at Tortosa (1413-14), where he vigorously defended the Jewish viewpoint of the Talmud.

He attained popularity among medieval Jews because of his book *Sefer-Ha-Ikkarim* (Book of Principles), a defense of Judaism against philosophical criticism and Christianity. Although no new ideas are introduced, the book is important to the general philosophy of religion because it established the criterion whereby the primary fundamental doctrines of Judaism may be distinguished from those of secondary importance. Albo stated that three principles are basic to every revelational religion: a belief in God, the concept of divine revelation, and divine retributive justice.

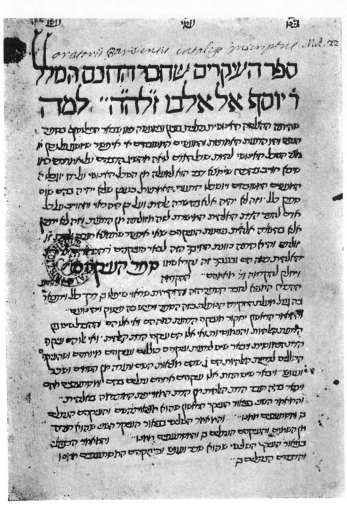

First Page of Manuscript of Joseph Albo's
Sefer-Ha-Ikkarim

Massacre of Jews by the Crusaders

Defecting Marranos or forcibly converted Jews being led to the pyre

ABRAVANEL, JUDAH

ABRAVANEL, JUDAH (c.1460-1530). Abravanel was one of the outstanding figures of the period of transition between the Middle Ages and the Renaissance. He lived not only at the conjunction of two eras, but also in contact with three cultures—Jewish, Spanish, and Italian. He and his father, Don Isaac Abravanel, fled in 1483 from their native Portugal to Spain, and thence to Italy in 1492. Judah practiced medicine, but he was mainly interested in philosophy, mathematics, and astronomy. For a time he lectured at the Universities in Naples and Rome. The intellectuals of both cities requested his friendship; his was a close association with Pico della Mirandola. During his sojourn in Italy, Judah assumed the name of Leone, the translation of Judah, the Lion.

His most famous work, *Dialoghi di Amore* (Dialogues about Love), was published in Italian, and soon after translated into Hebrew, Latin, French, Spanish, and English. A portion of the book was incorporated in a rabbinical commentary on the Song of Songs. The Dialogues are landmarks in the history of aesthetics and of great consequence to the history of metaphysics and ethics. The book promulgates love as a cosmic principle inseparable from being; its spirit, the mirror of reality. The Dialogues stressed the spiritual character of physical beauty and helped develop the field of aesthetic idealism. He maintained that true happiness is the "union of the human intellect with the Divine intelligence," and that it is directly connected to aesthetic enjoyment. There is a pantheistic strain in Abravanel's philosophy, but he always emphasized his orthodox Judaism, and tried to reconcile his pantheistic feelings with the Biblical concept of God.

Isaac Abravanel (1437-1508), statesman and philosopher, was treasurer to the King of Portugal. He attempted in vain at the court of Queen Isabella to stop the expulsion of the Jews from Spain

Nach dem Reisebericht des Seigneur Béthencourt.

Jews Being Expelled from Spain

Columbus Bidding Farewell to the King and Queen of Spain

Joseph Caro (1488-1575)
(A Drawing by Arthur Szyk)

Lived in Turkey and Palestine, where he codified in grand manner the rabbinical Law. His Shulchan Aruch (Covered Table) *was and still is a pillar of Orthodox Jewish observance*

Isaac Aboab (1430-1493), Spanish Rabbi and Author of Biblical Commentaries, as Well as Teacher of Isaac Abravanel

DELMEDIGO, JOSEPH SOLOMON

DELMEDIGO, JOSEPH SOLOMON (1591-1655). A restless spirit made Delmedigo the prototype of the wandering Jew. He peregrinated from Candia, Crete, his native town, to Padua, Italy; thence to Egypt, Turkey, Poland, Hamburg, Amsterdam, Frankfort, Worms, and then finally died in Prague. He earned his living either as physician or teacher but wherever he sojourned, he remembered to study the natural sciences. He was a disciple of Galileo and a keen critic of the medieval philosophy of nature; but he had to be careful, lest the ecclesiastical and secular authorities were offended by his ideas. He was shrewd enough to avoid such disturbances. His only known works are: *Elim* (Palms) dealing with mathematics, the natural sciences, and metaphysics, and some letters and essays.

Joseph Solomon Delmedigo

Eyebeschutz, Jonathan (Cracow, 1690–Altona, 1764). Talmudist, Cabbalist, head of Prague Yeshivah, Rabbi of Altona, Hamburg, and Wandsbeck, writer of legal and homiletic works, called a Sabbatarian by Rabbi Jacob Emden in a famous controversy, Author of Urim Wetumim, Kreti U-Fleti

Elijah ben Solomon (1720-1797). The famed Gaon of Wilna, master of all Jewish knowledge and of mathematics and the sciences; a rational thinker, he vigorously opposed Chassidism

Tombstone of Joseph Solomon Delmedigo at Prague

LUZZATTO, MOSES HAYIM

LUZZATTO, MOSES HAYIM (1707-1747). Some occurrences in Luzzatto's life show a parallel to that of Spinoza. Just as Spinoza earned his living by grinding optical lenses, Luzzatto did the same by lenses. Like Spinoza, he was ex-communicated from his coreligionists. But Luzzatto remained a faithful Jew, ardently devoted to the cause of Judaism. He even felt himself, like the Messiah, bound to rescue the Jewish people from danger and misery, and he believed that the study of the Cabbala would enable him to perform that mission. Notwithstanding pressure on the part of orthodox rabbis, Luzzatto did not turn his thoughts from the mysticism that not only incited his loftiest aspirations but also inspired him to the conception of high ethical principles. Luzzatto was a versatile and gifted writer whose Hebrew style is much admired. He composed a drama, many liturgical poems and philosophical treatises in Hebrew, while his mystical works were written in Aramaic. His best-known book is *Mesillat Yesharim* (Path of the Upright, 1740) which has been compared with Bunyan's *Pilgrim's Progress* though it was not influenced by the latter. In 1746, Luzzatto emigrated to the Holy Land where he died shortly after his arrival.

BAAL SHEM-TOV

BAAL SHEM-TOV (1700-1760). After seven years of solitary meditation, Israel ben Eliezer began to teach, in 1740, a mysticism which later became known as Chassidism. This earned him the title of Baal Shem-Tov (Master of the Good Name), even though in his early years he had been despised by his people as an ignorant and inefficient man.

He taught that the divine spirit is omnipresent in each man and in everything that exists. Therefore, it is possible to serve God in even the most trifling of actions. In contradistinction to other schools of mysticism and to various Jewish mystical doctrines, he declared that the pleasures of the senses are not sinful, because man must serve God with his body as well as with his soul. In his teachings, all things, including the lowest acts, had dignity. Although he did not reject learning, he put prayer above scholarship, insisting that his followers pray "with gladness" and forget, through religious concentration, all the sufferings imposed by life.

The teachings of Baal Shem-Tov gained a large number of adherents among the Jews of Eastern Europe who, at that time, were subject to frequent persecutions and whose economic situation was constantly growing worse. These people were impressed by his kind and humble personality and revered him as a saint. He received gifts of immense value, but ended each day by distributing all his wealth among the poor. He saved many co-religionists from despair, enabled them to endure extreme hardship, and imbued them with the spirit of confident piety.

Baal-Shem's synagogue in Miedziboz, the Ukraine

Old etching of Chassidim dancing; on a Simchat Torah flag

30

That Man Spinoza

(Copper Cut by V. Froer, 1871)

the subtlety of his definitions, Spinoza's mind was unsophisticated, and regardless of the boldness of his thoughts and the sternness of his will to draw his conclusions logically and without any regard to personal inclinations, Spinoza was calm, benevolent, fond of plain people. He earned his living by grinding optical lenses and declined an appointment as professor at the University of Heidelberg because he preferred independence to honors.

Spinoza belonged to a Jewish family which had been exiled from Spain and Portugal, and had finally settled in Holland. Before studying Latin, the natural sciences, and the philosophy of Hobbes and Descartes, he had studied the Hebrew Bible, the Talmud, medieval Jewish literature, and probably Cabbalah. In 1656, he was put under the ban by the Jewish community of Amsterdam because of his opposition to traditional doctrines of Judaism, including those that were also sacred tenets of Christianity. Detached from the Jewish community, Spinoza manifested indifference to Jews and Judaism. With his investigation of the sacred Scriptures he gave an impetus to modern Biblical criticism. But the elements of his Jewish education, especially his acquaintance with medieval Jewish philosophy, remain visible in his conception of the oneness of God and in his personal piety.

Spinoza's chief work is entitled *Ethics*. It could have been named "Metaphysics" with equal justice, for Spinoza was thoroughly convinced that the knowledge of the ultimate reality involves the norm of human action and implies the measure of personal perfection. Philosophical thinking was, to Spinoza, self-education and improvement

SPINOZA, BENEDICTUS DE (BARUCH DE SPINOZA) (1632-1677). For more than a century after Spinoza's works were published, their author was objurgated with embitterment by Catholics, Protestants, Jews and freethinkers alike. Even David Hume, in general a man of kindly disposition, branded him as "infame," and Moses Mendelssohn, the affable advocate of tolerance, was horrified and disbelieving when he heard that his friend Lessing had adopted Spinoza's doctrine. A great change was inaugurated by Herder and Goethe who became Spinozists, and revered Spinoza as a saint. So did Heinrich Heine. Post-Kantian philosophers and Romantic poets in Germany were deeply influenced by Spinoza's conception of nature. In modern times, Spinoza is universally recognized as a philosopher of unsurpassed sublimity and profundity. Even his critics agree that Spinoza had a most lovable personality, one of the purest characters in the history of mankind. Despite his delicate feelings and

The Harbor at Amsterdam, from a Mid-Seventeenth-Century Engraving

of the mind of the thinker. His aim was to obtain, by means of reason and science, the same trust in rules of human behavior that religious traditions claimed to grant their believers. Contrary to Descartes, he denied the possibility of harmonizing reason with Biblical revelation, and, in that way, Spinoza, not Descartes, became the symbol of the end of medieval philosophy. The scientific method offered to Spinoza not only the measure of moral evaluation but a means of gaining eternal bliss. To win supreme happiness or "unceasing joy," Spinoza said, man has to attain knowledge of his union with the whole of nature.

All individual beings, whatever is popularly supposed to be a real thing, are regarded by Spinoza as mere modifications of but one infinite substance which has an infinite number of attributes, of which, however, only two, namely thought and extension, are perceptible by man.

This one substance which is in itself and conceived through itself alone, is the only object of true knowledge, and is identical with God whose will is identical with the laws of nature. He who knows nature knows God. Increasing knowledge of nature means increasing love of God. From this proposition of the oneness and universality of God, Spinoza has deduced *more geometrico,* in a manner following the example of geometrical demonstrations, his definitions of all particular objects in the realms of extension and thought. He finally arrived at his much admired description of the intellectual love of God which is characterized as an absolutely disinterested feeling, the humble cognizance of all-governing necessity and at the same time the complete liberation of the soul from disturbing passions. Neither to laud nor to blame but to understand is the principle of Spinoza's attitude toward life.

In this famous painting by Hirszenberg the young Spinoza is shown appalling his co-religionists by his rigorous criticism of the Bible

Spinoza House in Rhijnsburg

Portrait Painting at Wolfenbüttel
(Copy In The Hague)

Spinoza's Workroom at Rhijnsburg. *The instruments that Spinoza used for his work as a maker of lenses are on the table*

Spinoza House in The Hague

Jan de Wit, with whom Spinoza aligned himself by accepting a secret mission to the French. Spinoza set down his epochal ideas on the right of free speech and free worship in his work entitled The Political Tractate
(Copper Cut by Engelvaert)

cerptam & defcriptam effe neceffario fatendum eft, adeo parum fibi conftare videmus. Cap. enim 47. Genef. narrat quod Jahacob cum primum Pharahonem ducente Jofepho falutavit, annos 130. natus erat, à quibus fi auferantur viginti duo, quos propter Jofephi abfentiam in mærore tranfegit & præterea feptemdecim ætatis Jofephi cum venderetur, & denique feptem, quos propter Rachelem fervivit, reperietur ipfum provectiffimæ ætatis fuiffe, octoginta fcilicet & quatuor annorum cum Leam in uxorem duceret, & contra Dinam vix feptem fuiffe annorum, cum à Sechemo vim paffa eft, Simeon autem & Levi vix duodecim & undecim, cum totam illam civitatem deprædati funt, ejufque omnes cives gladio confecerunt. Nec hic opus habeo omnia Pentateuchi recenfere, fi quis modo ad hoc attenderit, quod in hifce quinque libris omnia præcepta fcilicet & hiftoriæ promifcue fine ordine narrentur, neque ratio temporum habeatur, & quod una eademque hiftoria fæpe, & aliquando diverfimode repetatur, facile dignofcet hæc omnia promifcue collecta, & coacervata fuiffe, ut poftea facilius examinarentur, & in ordinem redigerentur. At non tantum hæc quæ in quinque libris, fed etiam reliqua hiftoria ufque ad vaftationem urbis, quæ in reliquis feptem libris continentur, eodem modo collectæ funt. Quis enim non videt, in cap. 2. Judicum ex verf. 6. novum hiftoricum adferri (qui res à Jofua geftas etiam fcripferat) ejufque verba fimpliciter defcribi. Nam poftquam hiftoricus nofter in ult. cap. Jofuæ narravit, quod ipfe mortem obierit, quodque fepultus fuerit & in primo hujus libri narrare ea promiferit quæ poft ejufdem mortem contigerunt, qua ratione, fi filum fuæ hiftoriæ fequi volebat, potuiffet fuperioribus annectere, quæ hic de ipfo Jofua narrare incipit. Sic etiam capita 17. 18. &c. Samuëlis 1. ex alio hiftorico defumta funt, qui aliam caufam fentiebat fuiffe, cur David aulam Saulis frequentare inceperit, longe diverfam ab illa, quæ in cap. 16. libri ejufdem narratur: non enim fenfit quod David ex confilio fervorum à Saulo vocatus ipfum adiit (ut in cap. 16. narratur) fed quod cafu à patre ad fratres in caftra miffus Saulo ex occafione victoriæ, quam contra Philiftæum Goliat habuit, tum demum innotuit, & in aula detentus fuit. Idem de cap. 26. ejufdem libri fufpi-

P 3

Handwriting of Spinoza. Marginal Notes to his Tractatus Theologico-Politicus *(1670)*

RENATI · DES · CARTES

PRINCIPIORUM

PHILOSOPHIÆ

Pars I, & II,

More Geometrico demonſtratæ

PER

BENEDICTUM de SPINOZA *Amſtelodamenſem.*

Acceſſerunt Ejuſdem

COGITATA METAPHYSICA,

In quibus difficiliores, quæ tam in parte Metaphyſices generali, quàm ſpeciali occurrunt, quæſtiones breviter explicantur.

AMSTELODAMI,

Apud JOHANNEM RIEWERTS, *in vico vulgò dicto, de Dirk van Aſſen-ſteeg, ſub ſigno Martyrologii.* 1663.

Title Page of First Edition (1663)

B. d. S.

OPERA

POSTHUMA,

Quorum ſeries poſt Præfationem exhibetur.

cIɔIɔC LXXVII.

Title Page of First Edition (1677)

Spinoza being instructed by D'Acosta
(S. Hirszenberg, Louvre)

ACOSTA, URIEL

ACOSTA, URIEL (1590-1647). Born in Portugal, the descendant of a Marrano family, religiously observant of Catholicism, the young Acosta prepared himself for the priesthood. But, tortured by doubts about the Christian religion, he decided to flee to Holland. Here he embraced Judaism, not because he was convinced of the truth of his new faith, but he was resolved to deny his former beliefs. He defied Jewish orthodoxy, the very basis of Judaism, because he was incapable of integrating himself into the Jewish community or of understanding its precarious situation and vital needs. His attacks upon the fundamental doctrines of Christianity, which he wrote as a member of the Jewish congregation of Amsterdam, angered the congregation because they felt the Christian authorities who had given the Jews refuge would be offended. Banished, he recanted, revolted anew, was banished anew, and ostracized for seven years. No longer able to endure solitude, he was willing to withstand the most severe penance in order to be allowed to re-enter the Jewish community. But the rigors of the ceremony destroyed his will to survive. Soon thereafter, he committed suicide, unrepenting and irreconcilable. To some extent, he was the victim of his temper, but more so of an era in which it was impossible for an independent thinker to live unharmed outside a religious community.

Many novelists and dramatists, Jew and non-Jew, have idealized his life and thoughts, for the poetic transfiguration of his fate is the tragedy of an uprooted man in revolt against tradition and any community based on tradition— the tragedy of a humiliated man, unable to live in isolation, whose only alternative was death. He entitled his autobiography *Exemplar Humanae Vitae* (Example of a Human Life), but his life was certainly anything but typical.

Bust of Spinoza by Upton Ewing

Massacre of the last Jews of England in 1190. Not until 1656 were Jews readmitted to England, largely upon the appeal of Menasseh ben Israel to Cromwell

MENASSEH BEN ISRAEL

MENASSEH BEN ISRAEL (1604-1657). It was an apocalyptic mystic, expecting the fulfilment of the Messianic promises, who, in 1655, accomplished with extraordinary worldly ability the political and diplomatic task of securing permission for the Jews to settle again in England, from which they had been expelled in 1290. Menasseh ben Israel, who was able to put Oliver Cromwell in a mood favorable to his demands for readmission of the Jews to England, was also highly respected by Queen Christina of Sweden, had studied philosophy with Descartes, and his scholarship was exalted by men like Hugo Grotius and the learned theologian Johannes Buxtorff. Until the end of the 18th century, Menasseh ben Israel was considered a high authority in history, linguistics and theology by great scholars in Holland, England, France and Germany. Even greater was his influence with Christian mystics. He had studied the Cabbalah but was also well acquainted with orthodox rabbinic literature. His own writings, devoted to the vindication of Judaism, to its defense against accusations or to its reconciliation with philosophical and mystical doctrines, show him to be a versatile rather than a profound thinker. Among them, *Hope of Israel* (1650), dedicated to the Parliament of England, and *Vindication of the Jews* (1656) were written for political purposes, while *The Statue of Nebuchadnezzar* (1656), a commentary on Daniel's interpretation of the Babylonian king's dream, outlines a mystical philosophy of history. This book, when first printed, was decorated with four etchings by Rembrandt who, from 1645 on, was his intimate friend.

Menasseh ben Israel (1604-1657), one of Spinoza's teachers, and a philosopher in his own right

The burning of heretics, one of the many horrifying examples of contemporary bigotry which considerably influenced Spinoza's appeal that religion consist of charity rather than abstract doctrine

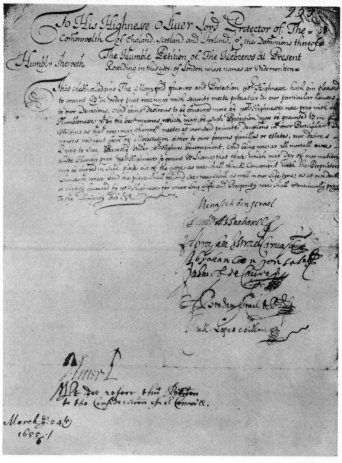

Jewish Petition to Oliver Cromwell, 1656, which led to the legalization of Jewish residence in England

House in the Strand, London, Where Menasseh Issued His Petition to Cromwell

Oliver Cromwell

Heidelberg in the Seventeenth Century. Spinoza declined an appointment as professor at the University of Heidelberg, fearing restriction of his teaching freedom

The Room in Which Spinoza Died

Baruch Spinoza, Statue by Mark Ontokolski

Judaism in the Modern World

MENDELSSOHN, MOSES

MENDELSSOHN, MOSES (1729-1786). In the late seventeenth century, Father Pierre Bonhours, a Jesuit and a refined art critic, published a pamphlet in which he held that a German could never be a poet or an artist, nor could he understand aesthetical problems and phenomena. Of course, the booklet aroused indignation in Germany, and provoked violent counter-attacks. At that time, however, Frenchmen and Germans agreed that a Jew could never become integrated into modern culture, let alone contribute to its development. This opinion remained constant until, by 1755, the surprising news was spread in literary circles that there was in Berlin a Jew called Moses Mendelssohn who could not only speak and write German flawlessly but who could discuss philosophical and literary problems and was even esteemed by Lessing, the most feared German critic of his time, as an authority in aesthetics and psychology. Many otherwise independent thinkers would simply not believe that the news was true. Some of them went to Berlin in order to gaze in astonishment at such a curiosity. Then, for some years, even Mendelssohn's sincere admirers, such as Kant and Lessing, expressed doubts that he could continue to be devoted to German culture and at the same time remain loyal to Judaism. Later they recognized that he could do both.

Mendelssohn enriched descriptive psychology by his treatise on mixed sentiments. His essay on evidence in metaphysical sciences was awarded the prize by the Prussian Academy against his competitor, Immanuel Kant. His *Phaedon* (1767), defending the idea of the immortality of the soul, was a favorite book of German Jews and Christians alike for more than two generations. With his *Jeru-*

(Copper Cut by J. G. Müller)

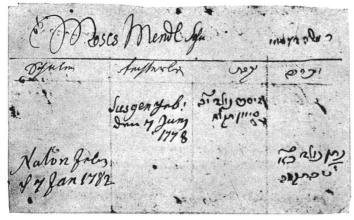

Registration of Two Children of Mendelssohn in the Berlin Family Register

salem (1783), he deeply impressed Kant, who became convinced that Judaism was a true world religion. Mendelssohn also translated the Hebrew Bible into German and demanded civil rights for the Jews as well as the separation of Church and State. With him came the beginning of a new epoch in the history of the Jews, not only those of Germany. Still four decades after his death, hymns to his praise were sung by Christians and Jews united in their adherence to Mendelssohn's ideas. Lessing raised a poetic monument to his friend by using him as model for the hero of his drama *Nathan The Wise*.

*Moses Mendelssohn entertaining Lavater and
Lessing at his home*

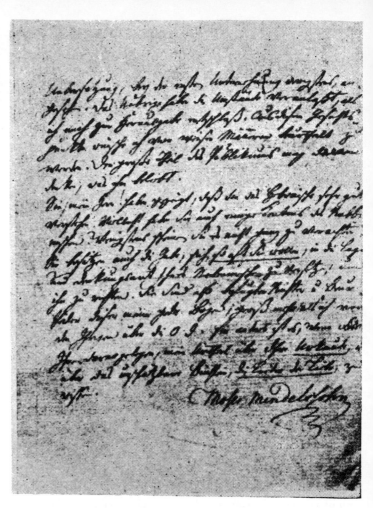

Letter of Mendelssohn to J. G. Herder

*The grave of Mendelssohn in the Old Jewish Cemetery
at Berlin*

MAIMON, SALOMON

MAIMON, SALOMON (1753-1800). Immanuel Kant recognized Maimon as the most acute of all his critics. The famous author of the *Critique of Pure Reason* probably knew what hardships Maimon had endured before he could publish his *Versuch ueber die Transcendentalphilosophie,* in which he successfully dealt with problems not understandable to the great majority of German thinkers of that time. When Maimon, in 1778, left his native village of Nieszwicz, Lithuania, he had been trained in the Heder and Yeshiva, had studied the Talmud, the Cabala and Maimonides, but had had no opportunity to be taught a modern language. Without any teacher he had deciphered the German alphabet by means of adventurous combinations and immense labor; but he could not pronounce a German word correctly when he crossed the borders of Prussia. It took him a long time to learn German thoroughly. It took him even more time to adapt himself to the moderate mentality of his German contemporaries.

Portrait of Salomon Maimon by Arndt

The Tombstone of "Ranak" in Tarnopol, Poland. Nachman Krochmal (1785-1840) was a student of Hegel. In the Guide to the Perplexed of the Age *he set forth his ideas on reconciling essential Judaism with modern thought*

For many years, his violent temper prevented him from concentrating upon the studies he had longed for. He provoked the indignation of his protector Moses Mendelssohn by his radical views and his licentiousness. He perplexed a Protestant minister who was to baptize him by his declaration that he regarded Judaism a religion superior to Christianity. After twelve years of wandering, Maimon anticipated many important views of post-Kantian philosophy, and influenced Fichte particularly. More than a century after Maimon's death, his thoughts became even more influential than during his lifetime. But great as his philosophical thinking had been, his most interesting work is his autobiography which, in 1792, the German psychologist Karl Philipp Moritz edited under the title *Salomon Maimons Eigene Lebensgeschichte*. This book contains a charming description of Jewish life in Lithuania and a courageous vindication of rabbinic Judaism.

Birthplace of Nachman Krochmal in Zolkieve, Poland

41

HESS, MOSES

HESS, MOSES (1812-1875). Hess, who assumed the first name Moses instead of Moritz in order to show his adherence to Judaism, provoked the indignation of his relatives by marrying a prostitute in order to show his contempt of the existing moral standards. He lived with her in happiness until his death. He was, however, a man who willingly obeyed those ethical demands that his thinking recognized as right. He was an early apostle of socialism, and a precursor of Zionism. Because of his participation in the revolution of 1848, Hess was sentenced to death and on escaping had to wander through many countries of Europe before he found refuge in Paris.

In his youth, Hess abounded in ideas. His influence with Karl Marx was considerable. For a time they were closely associated. Later Marx felt himself superior to Hess, and made him smart for his previous ascendancy. Although Hess recognized the importance of economic and social forces, he conceived socialism as a prevalently humanitarian ideal, dissenting from Marx who regarded it as the inevitable result of economic evolution. It was also for the sake of humanity that Hess agitated for the establishment of a Jewish commonwealth in Palestine by publishing his book *Rome and Jerusalem* (1862) and numerous essays in which he expresses Messianic hopes. According to Hess, Judaism has no other dogma but "the teaching of the unity." As already shown by his *Holy Story of Humanity* (1837), he deviated from the Jewish conception of God and called the history of humanity holy because, in his opinion, it is really the history of God, then conceived by him partly in accordance with Spinoza, partly with the Christian doctrine of Trinity. In *European Triarchy* (1841) he outlined a new order of Europe which he claimed was in accordance with "human nature." His socialism is not strictly egalitarian but an effort to satisfy the wants of "human nature," which remained his principal standard of judging human institutions. In his later years he came closer to the views developed in Jewish traditions, but he built his hopes for the settlement of the Jews in the Holy Land upon France, which he regarded as the champion of liberty. After France's defeat in the war of 1870, he admonished the nations of Europe to ally with one another against German militarism.

Moses Hess

Theodor Herzl at the Zionist Congress in Basle, 1901

Theodor Herzl greets Max Nordau at the First Zionist Congress

The Anti-Semitic Trial of Captain Dreyfus, Which Gave Impact to Herzl's Zionism

Abraham Isaac Kook (1865-1935), profound Cabbalist and Talmudist. As rabbi in growing Palestine he greatly influenced the youth of Israel

Courtesy Musaf Lakore Hatzair (Hadoar Weekly)

Hermann Cohen

COHEN, HERMANN

COHEN, HERMANN (1842-1918). The basis of Cohen's philosophy was that God made truth possible. His system of critical idealism dealt with the logic of pure knowledge, the ethics of pure will, and the aesthetics of pure feeling. He emphasized that basically his ethical philosophy was connected with the teachings of Judaism. For many years he was a professor at the University of Marburg. Upon his retirement at the age of seventy, he spent his last years as a teacher of Jewish philosophy at the Institute for the Science of Judaism in Berlin. In addition to educating rabbinical students, he directed discussions each Friday for the benefit of the general public. Many non-Jewish scholars attended these, eager to profit by Cohen's answers to questions concerning the whole range of science and philosophy. His method for teaching the rudiments of philosophy to beginners was greatly admired. He listened patiently to his students, helped them articulate their thoughts and express themselves methodically. He regarded his technique of discussion with beginners as test of his doctrine wherein thought was "pure creation," not the result but the condition of experience. His interpretations of the critiques of Kant, in his early years, gave new direction to the Neo-Kantian movement. The idea of God occupies the central position in his philosophy of critical idealism. The idea contains the connotation of a basic harmony between the structure of the universe and the aspirations of mankind. Cohen's introduction of the idea of God into his philosophy is an attempt to satisfy the longing of men to believe that the ethical ideal is real in a more solid sense than that of an aesthetic ideal. God as an idea is neither alive nor a person. He can be discovered by the process of reason itself. Religion, properly so-called, arises with the emergence of the ethical consciousness. The "function" of God is not to provide prosperity, or even happiness, but to aid the efforts of men to discriminate between right and wrong. Religion alone is capable of producing the ideal of individuality. The conception of sin is in principle applicable to an individual only, not to a social group. The cultivation of intellectual faculties is a religious duty. The religious philosophy of Cohen had idealistic, positivistic, and humanistic elements derived from his intuition concerning the objective validity of ethical experience. (W) THE RELIGION OF REASON FROM THE SOURCES OF JUDAISM; RELIGION IN THE SYSTEM OF PHILOSOPHY.

GINZBERG, ASHER

GINZBERG, ASHER (1856-1927). Best known under his pseudonym, Achad Haam (one of the people), Ginzberg became noted as a philosopher and contributor to the revival of the Hebrew language and Hebrew literature. He also played a significant role in the modern Jewish nationalist movement.

Although his writings deal principally with Jewish affairs, his fundamental ideas are of general interest. Dissatisfied with material evolution, he emphasized the importance of spiritual evolution. He concentrated upon the moral aspects of all problems, rejecting that relationship between ethics and religion where the role of ethics is limited only to the confines of a sociological frame of reference. He regarded ethics as the most important determinant in national character and, for that reason, insisted that the national development of ethical views precedes all political activity. His aim was to harmonize nationalistic sentiments with the necessary sense of responsibility for the future of human civilization. The success of that aim will depend on one's devotion to the ideals of justice enunciated by the prophets of the Old Testament.

His concept of Zionism established him as a genuine philosopher. It is founded upon an original explanation of reality and ideals. For many years he was opposed to political Zionism, advocating, instead, the establishment of a Jewish cultural center in Palestine. This, he hoped, would become a "center of emulation" for Jews dispersed all over the world, effectively raising their cultural standards, and inspiring them to produce a genuine Jewish culture.

Achad-Haam (Asher Ginzberg)

BUBER, MARTIN

BUBER, MARTIN (b. 1878-   ). Martin Buber is one of the leading exponents of Hasidic philosophy. His grandfather, Solomon Buber, was the Hasidic scholar who provided impetus to the mystical movement, and the revival of some of the early tenets and practices of Judaism that resulted in a cultural renaissance among the 18th-century Jews of Eastern Europe.

Martin Buber, a student of the mystical religions of China and India, as well as that of medieval Christianity, maintains that the Judaic experience of divine immanence, as it is expressed in the Talmud and realized in prayer, has a unique importance for all peoples. He accepts the mystical concept of man's communion with God. Religious redemption is the central theme of his spirituality. He believes that the philosophies of religion and sociology have made for greater human cohesiveness.

At the Cradle of Indian Thought

Siva, Vishnu and Krishna

Widow Burning

INDIAN PHILOSOPHY

The beginnings of Indian philosophy are shrouded in uncertainty. There is no doubt, however, that serious philosophical writings in aphoristic form are to be found in the centuries before 1,000 B.C. It is less than 200 years since the West became aware of the importance of Sanskrit, the language of ancient Indian philosophy. Much of the manner of Indian metaphysical speculation has been little understood and never yet standardized.

Indian philosophical beginnings are to be found in the hymns of the Vedas, in the more prosaic Upanishads, and in the Bhagavad Gita. One of the oldest systematic presentations of Indian philosophy is the Sankhya, which is said to have been founded by Kapila, who lived before the great Gautama Buddha. Kapila was an agnostic and op-

posed the Brahman monism of the Upanishads.

A more theistic interpretation of being was offered by the Vaisesika, a system of philosophy founded by Ulaka (Kanada).

Out of this dim past of the various Indian philosophies rose the titanic structure of Buddhism which almost disappeared a thousand years ago from its native India to enchant many neighboring peoples in Burma, China, Japan and spiritually-minded persons throughout the world.

In all the early writings and songs of the Indian philosophers is to be found the dominant theme of the Upanishads: Find Atman and you find Brahman, the divine principle, supreme happiness, the Nirvana of Buddhism. In the ancient scriptures of the Vedas and in the interpretation of the Vedanta (end of the Veda), this, our phe-

Tibetan Wheel of the World, depicting stages of inner development in the Buddhist manner

1   2a   2b   3   4

Forehead Marks of the Four Main Castes of India

Buddha and Eight Scenes from His Life (Stone, Tenth Century)
(Boston Museum of Fine Arts)

nomenal world, appears to be but an illusion; there is only true reality, namely Brahman-Atman, the key to all true wisdom lies in the identity of the soul with Brahma.

The outstanding Vedic commentator was Shankara (800 A.D.).

Much of the philosophy of India was misunderstood, misinterpreted and misused by superstitious beliefs and a fantastic religious misconstruction of metaphysical concepts. Self-denial became self-abuse; pan-animation became childish animal reincarnation; and the holiness of spiritual resignation was turned into a beggar's paradise. But out of the turmoil and the shambles of the contemporary religious scene of Hinduism will forever remain the shining light of Gautama Buddha and the others who evinced profound insight into the Eternal.

BUDDHA, GAUTAMA

BUDDHA, GAUTAMA (c. 563-483 B.C.). The term "Buddha" means the "enlightened one who enlightens" or "the awakened who awakens the sense of truth in his fellow men." Buddhism is conceived of as the possession of perfect wisdom and supernatural powers. According to Buddhist doctrine, there is a line of Buddhas who appear in the course of human history from the time of remote antiquity to the distant future. The man who, in world history, is known as Buddha, was originally named Siddhartha (he who has accomplished his aim) or Sakyamuni (sage of the Sakya tribe). He belonged to the Gautama family, a warrior caste that ruled over the Sakya tribe. According to some scholars, the earliest reports of his life were writ-

46

The young and bitter Buddha, on the road to the bodhi tree, where he is to rise to awareness of the great Enlightenment
(Painting by Liang Kai, Thirteenth Century)

The Great Temple at Bodh Gaya, the birthplace of Buddhism. The bo tree, on the left, is supposed to be a descendant of the one under which Buddha received enlightenment

ten some two hundred to four hundred years after his death. But all these reports undoubtedly are rephrasings of verbal traditions based upon his life which appear in the detailed summaries of his original doctrines. With the exception of a few radical sceptics, most scholars agree that he married his cousin, Yasodhara, at the age of nineteen, and that a son, Rahula, was born of this union. There is no agreement as to the character of his activities.

In all probability, Buddha began to meditate upon the meaning of life in his early years, and became so disturbed by his awareness of human misfortunes and sufferings that he resolved to find the ways by which mankind could be comforted and redeemed. In India, and throughout the East, the path to knowledge that would enable him to rescue humanity, meant a nomadic life in order to obtain the advice of wise men, who themselves were wanderers, and to meditate in isolation. After six years of studying mankind, life, and doctrines, he was convinced that he had discovered Truth, and thereupon devoted the remainder of his lifetime to converting others to his ideas. He renounced his fortune and family and traveled through the valley of the Ganges as a mendicant, surrounded by an ever-increasing host of disciples, who also lived as mendicants, and finally formed an order.

Buddhism teaches four "Noble Truths," namely: Suffering; Knowledge of its cause, explained by the twelvefold Chain of Causation; Getting rid of passions as the means of deliverance from suffering; Truth, the way of removing suffering by a system of moral discipline. Buddha called his truths "noble," because he regarded nobility as moral. Whether rationalist or mystic, Buddha was a teacher of moral behavior. He avoided metaphysics and religion.

Buddhism has spread throughout Eastern Asia, and is the living faith in Ceylon, Japan, China, Indo-China, Siam, Burma, and Tibet, although it has undergone many modifications in these countries. In India, the country where Buddha and Buddhism were born, Buddhism has been all but extinct since 1200 A.D. Modern Hindus are so estranged from Buddhism that Gandhi had to defend himself against the "accusation" of spreading Buddhistic teachings under the guise of Sanatana Hinduism. Gandhi did state, however, that in his "deliberate opinion, the essence of Buddha's teachings now form an integral part of Hinduism."

Maya and the Child Buddha
(An Indian Drawing)

The Buddha, on a Tibetan Banner
(Museum of Natural History)

The central stupa on the Sanchi Hill in Sanghi, where relics of Buddha are said to have been buried 2,300 years ago

The Buddha, in Stone, Second Century
(Metropolitan Museum of Art)

Siddhartha in Meditation (Stone, Sixth Century)
(Boston Museum of Fine Arts)

Daruma, founder of the Zen school of Buddhism. Zen Buddhism (Zen-Shu) takes its name from the Japanese word meaning "meditation"
(Drawing by Fugwei, Seventeenth Century Japanese Priest)

(LEFT TO RIGHT) *D. T. Suzuki, world authority on Zen Buddhism; Abbot Ogata of Chotoko-In; Abbot Daiko Yamasaki of Shokoku-ji, Kyoto*

The Classics of India

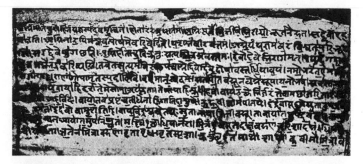

Hymn to Agni in Manuscript of the Rig-Veda

UPANISHADS. The more than 100 philosophic treatises of ancient India. Thirteen of the oldest (Chandogya, Brhadaranyaka, Aitareya, Taittiriya, Katha, Isa, Mundaka, Kausitaki, Kena, Prasna, Svetasvatara, Mandukya, Maitri) antedate, for the most part, the beginnings of Greek philosophy. They are remarkable for their treatment of ontological, metaphysical and ethical problems, and their investigations into the nature of man's soul or self, God, death, immortality, and the symbolic interpretation of ritualistic observances. Many things may be studied in the more archaic Upanishads, including early instances of universal suffrage, philosophic dialogues, celebrated similes and a succession of philosophic teachers.

VEDAS. The ancient, voluminous, sacred literature of India (largely prior to 1000 B.C.), composed of Rig-Veda (hymns to gods), Sama-Veda (priests' chants), Yajur-Veda (sacrificial formulae), and Atharva-Veda (magical chants). Among their theosophical speculations may be found early philosophical insights. Extended and supplemented later by *sutras* and various textbooks on grammar, astronomy, medicine, etc., called *Vedangas* ("members of the Veda"), and philosophical treatises such as the Upanishads.

VEDANTA. Literally, the "end of the Veda," understood in both a temporal and symbolic sense. The term applied to the Upanishads and various systems of thought based on them. Specifically, the doctrine elaborated in the Brahmasutras of Badarayana, reinterpreted and altered by later philosophers, such as Shankara, Ramanuja, Nimbarka, Madhva and Vallabha. The central theme is that found in the Upanishads, of the relation between the world soul and the individual soul. Shankara supposed God and soul identical, Madhva that they were different, Ramanuja that they were different yet identical.

SANKHYA. The oldest Indian philosophic system, pre-Buddhistic and the dominant philosophy of the epic period. Later systems, including the Buddhistic schools, rose in criticism of the Sankhya. The Sankhya came into being as the first synthesis of the Upanishads, which contained two apparently contradictory tenets: the immutability and purity of the self (Atman) and the creation of the world from the self which is the sole reality. To the Sankhya it was axiomatic that what changes cannot be conscious, and what is conscious cannot change. It therefore tried to resolve the contradiction in the Upanishads by sacrificing the sole reality of Atman and by dividing the real into two: the real as changing and the real as unchanging.

YAJNAVALKYA

YAJNAVALKYA (About 600 B.C.). There is no agreement among scholars whether Yajnavalkya was a historical person or the fictitious name for a group of thinkers and teachers. At any rate, this name is connected with the *Brhadaranyaka Upanishad* which does not only belong to the thirteen oldest Upanishads but is considered the most coherent and illuminating of all of them. It is representative of the earliest philosophical development of the Vedic religion, previous to the earliest beginnings of Greek philosophy.

The Upanishads teach the belief in Brahma, the one great reality, as the ground of existence, the belief in transmigration and *karma,* which originally meant sacrificial acts, but later the influence of human action, as the explanation of apparently unjust or incomprehensible distribution of good and evil and the home of liberation of the soul through union of the individual with Brahma. The *Brhadaranyaka Upanishad* presents these tenets in a relatively concentrated form.

Sri Shankaracharya, who gave the earliest extant interpretations of the Upanishads

ISVARAKRSNA

ISVARAKRSNA (Fifth Century A.D.). The name of Isvarakrsna is connected with the *Sankhya Karika,* composed about the middle of the fifth century, and probably the oldest of the six traditional systems of Indian philosophy. Its foundation is attributed to the sage Kapila. Sankhya philosophy inspired Buddha who lived about a century later.

The Sankhya school shares with other systems the belief in the Indian gods, demi-gods and demons, but it conceives them as mortal and subject to transmigration. Contrary to the Brahman concept, there is no place for a universal God in the Sankhya system, which expressly denies the existence of such a god. The Sankhya philosophy is pessimistic, regarding all existence as suffering, and dualistic, insisting on the fundamental difference between soul and matter. Salvation from suffering can be reached by cognitive grasping of the absolute difference between the soul and everything material. It is probable that the Sankhya doctrine influenced Gnosticism and Neo-Platonism.

51

Shankara

Jagatguru ("World Teacher") Sri Shankaracharya Bharati Krishna Tirth of Gowardhan Monastery in Puri, Ecclesiastical Head of most of Contemporary Hindu India and Apostolic Successor of the First Shankaracharya (India's Greatest Philosopher, in the Ninth Century)

SHANKARA

SHANKARA (9th century A.D.). The reports on the life of Shankara, who is considered by some authorities the greatest commentator, even the greatest philosopher of the Hindus, are adorned with myths and legends that ascribe to him superhuman powers and the performance of many miracles. He was revered as a saint and as a scholar whose theoretical and practical teachings became of great consequence. He systematized the philosophy of the Upanishads, and, in his commentaries, elucidated many passages of the Vedanta. He is characterized as a gentle and tolerant reformer and also as an ever-ready controversialist who was eager to refute any doctrine that differed from his own. He denied the relevance of caste and lineage, and denounced the desire for personal separateness as the cause of bondage to conditional existence, birth and death. Devotion is an instrument of emancipation from ignorance and enslavement. Devotion is not to be distinguished from contemplation. Truth is to be understood intellectually, but the highest spiritual intuition leads to the union of the knower, the known and knowledge. Shankara often described the way to that goal as the denial of selfness in thought, feeling and action.

VISHNUISM: (Visnuism) One of the major philosophico-religious groups into which Hinduism has articulated itself. It glorifies Vishnu as the supreme being who creates and maintains the world periodically by means of his *bhuti* and *kriya saktis* or powers of becoming and producing, corresponding to the *causae materialis et efficiens*. The place of man's soul in this development is explained variously, depending on the relation it maintains to the world-ground conceived in Vishnuite fashion.

Sri Madhva, thirteenth century dualistic thinker of India, who held the world soul differs in essence from man's soul

Sri Vallabhacharya, who flourished in the fifteenth century. One of the great students of the Vedanta and Vishnuism. He is the great interpreter of Sat-cit-ananda, *the metaphysics of man's full awareness of himself as part of all reality and reality as part of oneself*

Ramanuja, eminent Indian philosopher of the eleventh century, who restated within the traditions of Vishnuism the doctrines of the Vedanta. The universe and soul are declared by him to be both emanations and transformations of the God Creator, a view close to that of Spinoza

The Practice of Yoga

YOGASUTRAS. Famous work by Patanjali on which is founded Yoga, one of the great systems of Indian philosophy. It is essentially a mental discipline in eight stages for the attainment of spiritual freedom without neglecting physical and moral preparation. In philosophic outlook, the *sutras* and most commentaries on them are allied to the Sankhya, yet not without having theistic leanings.

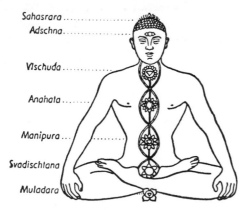

Sahasrara
Adschna
Vischuda
Anahata
Manipura
Svadischtana
Muladara

Typical lotus pose in Yoga. Lotus was the symbol of purity in ancient India

The Ascetic Congregation
(Moghul Painting, Seventeenth Century)

Patanjali, author of the Yogasutras, on which is founded Yoga, one of the great systems of Indian Philosophy

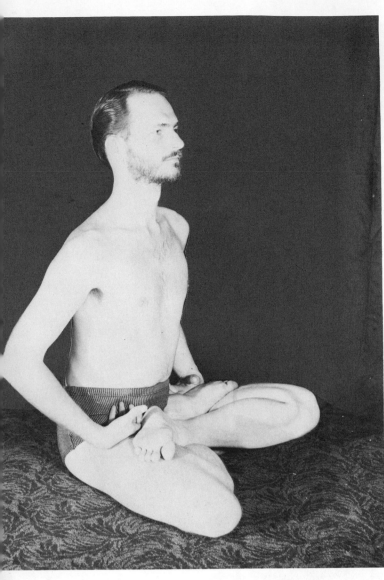

*Padmasana, the Lotus Pose, Favored Position
in Yoga Meditation*

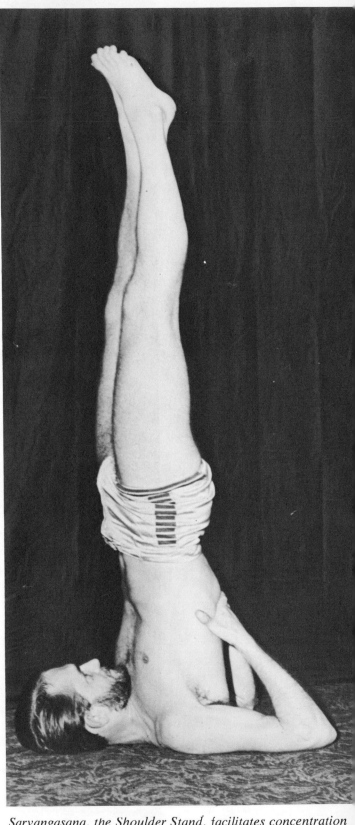

*Sarvangasana, the Shoulder Stand, facilitates concentration
on the opposite view of the world*

Dhanurasana, the Bow Pose

India and the West

Sri Ramakrishna (1836-1886), the most influential of modern thinkers of India. Founded numerous Vedanta study societies in the West. In his interpretation Samadhi, or the final stage of God consciousness, could be reached through Judaism as well as Christianity and Moslemism. His path of universalism in theology was followed by Vivekananda

Panchavati, where Ramakrishna attained divine communion with the Mother of the Universe

The Temple of Dakshineswara

Swami Vivekananda

VIVEKANANDA, SWAMI

VIVEKANANDA, SWAMI (1862-1902). Educated abroad, Swami Vivekananda was an agnostic, whose rationalistic doubts were. dispersed by the teachings of **Ramakrishna Paramahamsa**. His simple belief in the philosophy of the monistic Vedanta of Shankara and the attempt to re-emphasize the unity of all religions made Vivekananda a disciple, who devoted the remainder of his life to the dissemination of his teacher's ideas. He founded the Ramakrishna Mission for humanitarian service, brought to Hinduism an enthusiastic missionary approach, and emphasized the positive aspect of Vedanta: "that all is Brahma, and, therefore, that service of man as God is better than quiescent meditation." His influence has been seen in the works of such philosophers as Radhakrishnan and Aurobindo, in the social service and spread of Hindu ideas throughout the world, and it is even apparent in the political attitude of Mahatma Gandhi.

Swami Vivekananda as a Wandering Monk

Tagore and Helen Keller, 1930, New York

Sri Aurobindo

TAGORE, RABINDRANATH

TAGORE, RABINDRANATH (1861-1941). Rabindranath Tagore, the greatest lyrical poet of modern India, also a successful dramatist and novelist, and a highly respected author of philosophical treatises, was the descendant of an old Brahman family. The great aim of his life was to revive the ideals of ancient India and at the same time to obtain a better understanding between East and West. His attitude was opposed to that of Gandhi, whose methods he held in contempt.

After studying law in England, Tagore managed his family's estate for seventeen years. In 1901 he founded his school, *Abode of Peace,* where pupils were educated in accordance with his principles. When he came to England in 1911, where his poems *Gitanjali* (Song of Offerings) were published in an English version prepared by the author, he was enthusiastically received, and his fame spread over Europe and America. He was the first Asian to receive, in 1913, the Nobel Prize. In 1915, he was knighted. After the massacre of Amritsar he intended to renounce his knightship in order to protest against the British administration of India but instead consented to a compromise.

Tagore's poems have been translated into many languages, and the music of his diction remained charming and strong in most of the versions. The harmonious balance of his personality, which found expression in his writings, never failed to impress everyone he met. His ethics did not tolerate morals of expediency or sanction of means according to their ends. Always ready to protest against injustice and persecution, he was a staunch adversary of German nationalism and Hitler's regime. His philosophy is based on the belief in the progressive realization of the divine in man, and it shows little interest in celestial destiny. He insists that man's perfection shall come in the world in which he is living.

AUROBINDO, SRI

AUROBINDO, SRI (1872-1950). The son of a prominent Bengalese physician, Sri Aurobindo was educated in England, where he was sent at the age of seven. Returning to India at the age of twenty-one, he served the State of Baroda for the next three years in various administrative and teaching capacities; in 1906 he resigned from the Baroda State Service. He anticipated Gandhi in organizing the national action of passive resistance during his next few years of political activity in Bengal. Imprisoned by the government for one year on a false political charge, he left Bengal upon his release in 1910, went to live in French Pondicherry, and from then on devoted his interests exclusively to philosophical writing and teaching.

Two books synthesize his teachings: *The Life Divine,* his philosophy, and *The Synthesis of Yoga,* his system of Yoga. He also completed three volumes of poetry, and from 1914 to 1921, he was the editor of ARYA, a philosophical journal. In 1926, he retired to the *Ashrama,* where he lived in isolation except for a few public appearances during the course of each year.

Mohandas Gandhi

Sri Radhakrishnan, Contemporary Hindu Philosopher

GANDHI, MOHANDAS KARAMCHAND

GANDHI, MOHANDAS KARAMCHAND (1869-1948). Not only the vast majority of Hindus but also many Westerners have accorded to Gandhi the title of "Mahatma," the "great soul," and have revered him as a master of wisdom and saintliness, while also recognizing his political skill and steadfastness. At least in modern times, Gandhi has had no equal in his ability to use spiritual weapons for political aims, in his power to make the resistance of the powerless irresistible. He has been adored as the father of the new State of India. But shortly after he had realized the ideal of a free India, for which he had struggled for nearly half a century, he was assassinated by a fanatical son of his own people.

Gandhi restored the self-reliance of Hinduism after he had been imbued with the spirit of Western civilization and had rejected it. In 1889 he was called to the bar in London. Then, for seventeen years, he was a lawyer in South Africa before becoming the champion of the cause of the Indian settlers in that country. In 1914 he returned to India and in 1919 started the Satyagraha (Truth-seeking movement). From 1920 on he campaigned for non-cooperation with the British government. Devoted to Hinduism as Gandhi was, he was also inspired by Tolstoy's doctrine of non-violence which became his principal battle-cry in the struggle against British domination and was considered by him the panacea for every evil. Non-violence was conceived by him as "conscious suffering," not as meek submission to the will of the evil-doer, but "the putting of one's whole soul against the will of the tyrant." It means the restitution of the ancient Indian law of self-sacrifice. He repeatedly protested against being regarded as a visionary. Instead, he described himself as a "practical idealist" and rightly claimed "to know my millions" and to "recognize no God except the God that is to be found in the hearts of the dumb millions." But he also claimed that he recognized God's presence while the millions could not see it.

The Philosophy of the Celestial People

CHINESE THOUGHT

Among the hundred schools of Chinese metaphysical thought, the two most dominant are Taoism (a hundred years or better before Socrates), and Confucianism, the latter leading strongly to formalistic interpretation.

While Confucianism set cultivation of the good life as the highest principle, Taoism, forever imbued by a deep sense for the mystic and meditative, opened to ancient man the way (Tao) to inner tranquility and enlightenment.

In the Medieval Ages Buddhism, leaving unexplicably its Indian birthplace, found many devoted and devout adherents in China. It was China, too, where first grew the strange flower of Zen, a meditative method of reaching the heart of Buddha through intuition. Zen Buddhism found in Japan and in America numerous friends and believers.

The Three Sages: Buddha, Confucius, and Laotse

The Old Chinese Wall, which was of considerable import in keeping Chinese philosophy isolated

61

A legendary creature bringing to Confucius' mother a message predicting his arrival

The masters of the five powers of change, two dragons and five spirits appear at the birth of Confucius, so the legend goes

CONFUCIUS

CONFUCIUS (556-479 B.C.). Kung Fu Tse, the Grand Master or Confucius, was officially worshipped from 195 B.C. to 1912, but the traditional cult still continues in almost every district of China. Kung lived during a period of cultural decadence, but his teachings and exemplary personal conduct effected a moral and spiritual recovery and cultural renaissance among the people of China. Despite the many foreign influences and internal political conflicts, the stamp of Confucius on Chinese civilization has been more or less permanent.

Kung, a contemporary of Pythagoras and some of the later Hebrew prophets, roamed for some fourteen years throughout China, observing, teaching, and acquiring a steadily increasing number of disciples about him. He taught poetry, history, music, and adherence to tradition. He promulgated an ideal conduct of life, the basis of which was learning, wisdom, moral perfection, and decency in behavior. His doctrine of reciprocity in man's relations with his fellow man paralleled, with almost the same words, the concept of the Golden Rule. He demanded that his followers practice the virtues of sincerity, justice, benevolence, courtesy, respect for older people, and ancestor reverence. He urged them to live in harmony with themselves because that was a requisite condition for harmony between the individual and the universe. He sometimes referred to "Heaven," without, however, expressing belief in a supreme deity. He constantly exhorted that all intellectual and moral energies be channeled for self-perfection, the common good, and social and universal peace.

For a short time he held high office, using his power for reforms, and for the punishment of evil-doers, even when they were mandarins. His services, however, were not adequately appreciated by the ruler.

Confucius

Confucius with his disciple Chü Lu meandering in the hills

Confucius occupied with study on the Book of Changes

Ancient Symbol "Yi" for Confucian "Changes"

Confucius studying the music of the ancients in order to gain insight into their lives, as painted by Ku K'ai Tshi

Confucius with his followers at a stream, pointing out the inconstancy of all things material

Confucius Visiting with Laotse

Page from the Confucian Shi-king *of the Twelfth Century*

MO-TI (About 470-396 B.C.). After Mencius had been successful in discrediting the doctrine of Mo-Ti, it was ignored by Chinese thinkers and the public for twelve centuries. Only Chinese Buddhism retained some of Mo-Ti's tenets. Recently Mohism, as the school of Mo-Ti is called, has been adopted anew by many young Chinese, who regard it as a way to China's salvation from the troubles of the present time. Mo-Ti was a victorious general and an efficient civil servant.

His philosophy combines religious spirituality and utilitarian rationalism. He was also a refined logician and experienced in dialectic. After having adhered to Confucianism he accused Confucius' successors of exaggerated ritualism and rejected his former Master's belief in fate. He set purity of the heart higher than formal correctness in fulfilling ceremonial laws. He pronounced universal love without regard to legal status, and therefore was called "an apostle of human brotherhood." While justifying his doctrine, he declared that universal love was demanded by Heaven, the Supreme Being, as well as by the innermost strivings of the human individual for happiness, and that it would always pay to love his fellow men. His aim was promotion of general welfare by both moral elevation and economic improvement. Devoted to the cause of peace, Mo-Ti allowed defensive war only, and he is credited with having averted several wars.

TZU SSU

TZU SSU (About 335-288 B.C.). Tzu Ssu was a grandson of Confucius. Often he evoked his ancestor's authority; but he also expressed thoughts of his own. Confucius had begun to distinguish between true and supposed knowledge, while Tzu Ssu proceeded to meditations on the relativity of human knowledge of the Universe. He tried to analyze as many types of action as possible, and believed that the reality of the universe can be copied in the character of any wise man who is conscious of his moral and intellectual duties.

HUI SHIH

HUI SHIH (4th century B.C.). Documents of the teachings of Hui Shih are preserved only in the book of Chuang Chou, the brilliant precursor of Taoism, who considered him the worthiest of his adversaries, and evidently esteemed him higher than Confucius. Hui Shih probably was some years older than Chuang Chou and died before the latter had finished his book *Chuang Tzu*. In the aphorisms quoted by Chuang Chou, Hui Shih appears to be a disciple of Confucius' grandson Tzu Ssu, deeply impressed by his awareness of eternal change and fond of pointing out the paradoxical.

MENCIUS (Meng Tzu)

MENCIUS (MENG TZU) (372-289 B.C.). In his efforts to educate kings, Meng Tzu (Master Meng) seems to have been no more successful than his Greek contemporary Aristotle. But to a greater extent than Aristotle, Meng used his personal experiences for the development of his philosophical teachings.

Meng was a disciple of Tzu, who was the grandson of Confucius and himself an influential philosopher, though of lesser importance to the history of Confucianism than his pupil Meng. It was Meng who restored the authority of Confucius by successfully combating deviating opinions such as were advanced by Mo-Ti and Yang Chou, both of whom had become extremely popular and had tried to discredit the cult and doctrine of Confucianism. At the end of his life, Meng composed the book that bears his name and, in the Sung era, was canonized. Extracts from the book became favorite reading in Europe early in the eighteenth century and have continued in their popularity. The book is the fruit of experiences collected during long, extensive travels, and of keen observations of people of all classes from kings down to beggars. Meng declared that man is good by nature but that he has to develop his own nature to the greatest possible perfection. The government, said Meng, must serve the people and promote their welfare. Revolt against bad rulers is permitted. War is branded as a crime. Meng has been quoted more than once by Voltaire and Rousseau. In this way he influenced, at least indirectly, many leaders of the French Revolution.

Mencius

HSUN CHING

HSUN CHING (About 298-238 B.C.). The purely philosophical strain in Confucianism was developed to its highest point by Hsun Ching who, however, was also a great poet and a master of lyrical reflection, penetrating into the secrets of the human soul, inspired by the beauty of nature. Although he adopted views of Mo-Ti and some Taoists, he remained faithful to Confucianism, believing firmly in the necessity of moral order and individual self-perfection, and strongly opposing the belief in fate.

HAN FEI

HAN FEI (died 233 B.C.). Han Fei, a disciple of Hsun Ching and the greatest Chinese philosopher of law, committed suicide because he, as an unofficial adviser of a ruler, had aroused the jealousy of the latter's responsible minister.

Han Fei concentrated upon the problems of government, statecraft, authority and public welfare, and advanced views similar to those of Jeremy Bentham and other British utilitarians. But he also adopted Taoist ideas on essential truth.

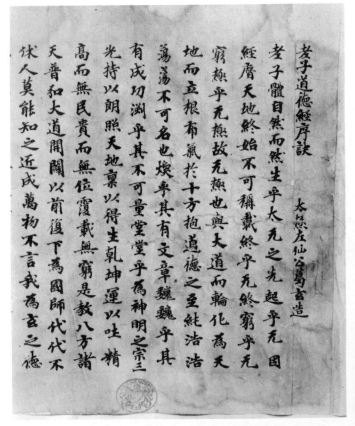

Chuang Chou

CHUANG CHOU

CHUANG CHOU (c. 340-280 B.C.). Modern experts on Chinese philosophy consider Chuang Chou as among the most brilliant of all the Chinese philosophers. He was a scholar, a poet, and a master of dialectic and logic. Aware of the unity of the universe, he longed for "the transcendental bliss" which brought peace of mind and enabled man to live harmoniously with nature. His ability at logic and dialectics made him appear to be a cynical debunker, fond of destroying renowned illusions, but his love of freedom was too great to allow him to deny the values of government and society; he often declined high office in order to retain his personal independence. As a formidable adversary of Confucius, he was frequently and severely criticized by Mencius. If Chuang Chou was not the founder of that which was subsequently called Taoism, certainly he was its precursor, and the extent of his soaring imagination, the profundity of his thought, and the power of his style were never matched by any of the Taoists.

The divine seal of Laotse, used in Taoist magic and as an amulet

Page from Laotse's Tao Te Ching

66

LAOTSE (Lao Tsu)

LAOTSE (LAO TSU) (About the 4th Century B.C.). The traditional assumption that Laotse was a contemporary of Confucius, and, as the author of the book *Tao Te Ching* (Teaching on the Power of the Way), the founder of Taoism, has been disproved by recent scholars. In all probability, the spiritual movement, later called Taoism, started long before the book *Tao* was written, and that book must be considered not so much the creation, as rather a condensation of already current Taoist ideas. It has been said that Lao was a custodian of documents and a priest-teacher. He has been worshipped since the third century A.D.

Tao, the Way, means the cosmic order of Nature that cannot be grasped by human intellects or expressed in words, according to Taoism and contrary to the Confucian meaning of Tao that concerns guidance of moral conduct of life. Taoism is a doctrine of a reality which is different from the world perceptible by the senses. In many regards it is similar to the reality assumed by Plato, and even more so to the Hindu distinction between the world of appearances and true existence. In its later development, Taoism became mixed with ideas of various origin, but it has remained a mystical faith in the unity of Pure Being.

Laotse
(From the Japanese "Miao Tsi T'u Lu")

Laotse Riding a Water Buffalo
(Sung Dynasty)

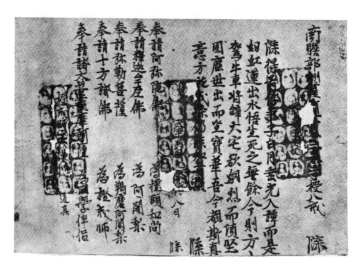

Manuscript of the Tao Te Ching

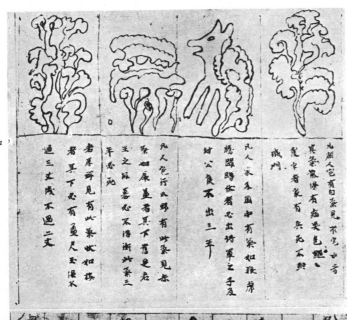

a. *Taoist Text on Divination from Vapors*
b. *Illustration to Taoist Calendar for the Year 978*
(British Museum)

LU WANG (Lu Hsiang-Shan)

LU WANG (LU HSIANG-SHAN) (1139-1192). Confucianism has become most scholastic in the philosophy of Lu Wang, whose thinking was imbued with the spirit of Buddhism although his terminology remained Confucian. He considered mind as the embodiment of reason, and taught training of the mind by "tranquil repose," in which state the essences of truth and goodness will be perceived by intuition, and the individual will be united with the universe. Neo-Confucianism revolted against Lu Wang's metaphysics which regards moral conduct as a mere consequence of intuitive insight into the essences of reality. In recent times, Lu Wang's philosophy was revived by Liang Sou-ming whose book *The Civilization and Philosophy of the East and the West* (1921) was a great sensation in China.

YU-LAN FUNG

YU-LAN FUNG (1895-   ). Professor Yu-Lan Fung, the author of the standard *History of Chinese Philosophy* (1930-33) and *The New Rational Philosophy* (1939), is not only a historian of philosophy but a systematic philosopher whose way of thinking and conceiving reality shows striking analogies to George Santayana's views, though he is firmly rooted in the traditions of Confucianism. He has revived the rational philosophy of the brothers Ch'eng Ming-tao and Ch'eng I Ch'uan (1032-1086 and 1033-1107, respectively) in order to "continue" but not to "follow" them. He distinguishes two realms, that of truth and that of actuality. Reason, according to him, belongs to the realm of truth. It is not in or above the world but rather it is a regulating principle of everything that appears in the actual world. The realm of actuality is not created by reason; it is self-existent. Since reason cannot create, it is a principle which is neither in reason nor in the actual world that brings things into real existence. This principle is called "the Vital Principle of the True Prime Unit." The essences of the realm of truth which are not the causes but the models of the real things can be known only by the objective and systematic studies, by means of inductive method and experimental logic. In this way, Fung has purified Neo-Confucianism from the Buddhist elements which had pervaded it in previous times.

The Glory That Was Greece

The Golden Era of Greece

Homer, the Legendary Author of the Iliad *and* Odyssey, *the Great Classical Epics*

(The Louvre)

Solon (635-559 B.C.), a Great Lawmaker and the First Clear-Cut Philosophical Personality in Athenian History

The various components which made up the early culture of Greece are, to a considerable extent, still in the dark. Recent archæological findings seem to point toward a much greater influence of west-oriental culture upon Greek civilization than was assumed in the past. The similarity between the Greek *alphabet* and the Hebrew *aleph beth* is one of the many issues of evidence of the close acquaintance of the ancient Greeks with the Israelites and their Phoenician trade ambassadors. In addition to these direct and obvious proofs of oriental impact upon Greece, there is a tremendous body of the ethical teachings of the ancient Hebrews, such as the Solomonic wisdom literature, which antedates even the pre-Socratic thinkers of Greece by many hundreds of years; and couldn't possibly have escaped the widely-navigated Greeks.

Heraclitus, Socrates, and Plato appear to have been steeped in the philosophy and ethics of the prophetic Judeans.

The glory of Greece, from Solon to Euclid and from Heraclitus to the schools of the later centuries, the arts and oratory of Euripides and Aeschylus, of Demosthenes and Pindar, the exquisite sculpture and architecture—all that which was the glory of Greece—fell finally before the boots of Rome's conquering Soldateska in the middle of the second century, B.C. Rome made an end to the culture of Greece, as it made an end to the Temple of Jerusalem and the Civilization of Carthage.

Rome levelled the houses of worship as it burned the libraries in Alexandria and elsewhere. It left the *Mediterranean* in ruins; upon which it founded an empire of military law and civil exploitation—all this for the aggrandizement of its Caesarian dictators, from Caligula to Diocletian and from Nero to Commodus.

They also razed to the ground the city of Carthage, founded by pioneering Phoenicians and Semites in the desert of North Africa, and developed into one of the great cultural centers of antiquity. The torch of Rome destroyed in one night the heritage of half a thousand years.

In spite of Roman debaucheries and sanguinary circuses, Greek culture managed to live on, as Hebrew culture did, and finally survive the barbarians.

PERICLES

PERICLES (495-429 B.C.). Pericles' name is inseparably connected with a period that is generally considered the height of ancient Greek civilization. During the time he ruled Athens, the Parthenon was built, sculptors like Phidias, Myron, Polycletus, painters like Zeuxis, Parrhasius and Polygnotus, dramatists like Aeschylus, Sophocles and Euripides, created their immortal works, and Socrates began to meditate about the value of life. Pericles himself was taught philosophy by Anaxagoras. He entrusted to Protagoras an important mission. He developed what in Athens' democracy became of lasting political and humanitarian value, though he could not remove its shortcomings. As a statesman, Pericles has been judged differently. While Thucydides exalts him, Aristotle and Isocrates think that Pericles' policy was not in Athens' best interest. Modern historians hold that his foreign policy was a failure but that he later learned to calculate the forces of Athens' adversaries more rightly. Even his enemies have recognized that Pericles never resorted to the tricks of a demagogue. As a speaker he was regarded by his contemporaries as the most powerful they knew or could even imagine. He was not a frequent orator but when he delivered a speech, his political success was almost certain. Despite all rivalries, he was elected commander-in-chief for fifteen terms. Until his last years his authority in matters of state was supreme.

In 430, at the close of the first year of the Peloponnesian War, which ended with Sparta's victory over Athens, Pericles, in an address celebrating the memory of the citizen-soldiers who were killed in action, defended Athens' democratic way of life.

Pericles

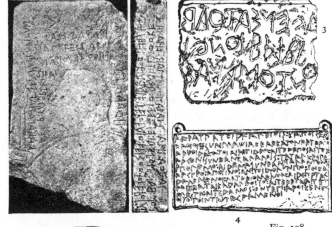

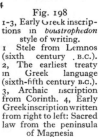

Fig. 198

1-3, Early Greek inscriptions in *boustrophedon* style of writing.
1 Stele from Lemnos (sixth century B.C.).
2, The earliest treaty in Greek language (sixth-fifth century B.C.).
3, Archaic inscription from Corinth. 4, Early Greek inscription written from right to left: Sacred law from the peninsula of Magnesia

Aspasia, Wife of Pericles, Renowned for Her Philosophic Dialogues

Aeschylus (525-456 B.C.), Creator of Greek Tragedy

Euripides, Outstanding Greek Dramatist of the Fifth Century B.C.

Pericles Addressing the Athenians
(Painting by Philipp Foltz)

Demosthenes (384-322). Relentless defender of Athenian freedom against the imperialistic ambitions of ruthless King Philip of Macedonia and his son, Alexander, both students of Aristotle. The Philippics *are a classic of oratory*

THE DEATH OF DEMOSTHENES

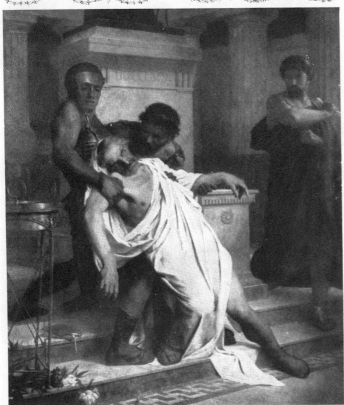

A

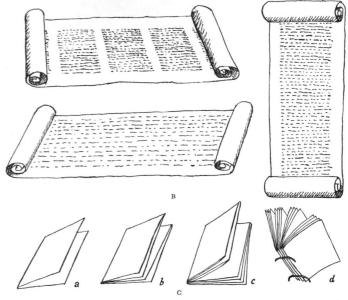

B

A, *The earliest extant Greek literary document on parchment: Oration by Demosthenes; late first century A.D. (British Museum,* Add. MS. 34473). B, *Books in the form of rolls: roll written in page form; roll written longitudinally; and roll written across its width.* C, *Folding of parchment codices: a, folio; b, quarto (quaternion); c, octavo; d, four quaternions stitched together. Drawing by Ella Margules*

MAP OF HERODOTUS

ABOVE: *The world as known to Herodotus; and* (LEFT) *as known to his precursor Hecataeus*

tainly he corrected, amplified, and developed many of the propositions made by predecessors. He gave to mathematics the form which was maintained until the nineteenth century, and he established a standard of scientific exactitude retained by scholars active in all branches of science, even though entirely new concepts of mathematics were current. Philosophers have tried to imitate Euclid's methods of demonstration. The philosophy of Spinoza is the most famous example of the application of Euclid's manner. Euclid was well acquainted with Greek philosophy. His fundamental views were derived from Plato, but he also studied the works of Aristotle and his disciples.

EUCLID

EUCLID (c. 335-275 B.C.). Hippocrates and Euclid were regarded as the most popular scientists of classical antiquity, but no ancient author made note of even the slightest biographical detail of the latter. From Euclid's own statements and from the earliest allusions to his writings by Greek scholars, it may be concluded that he lived during the reign of Ptolemy I of Egypt (305-285 B.C.).

Euclid's *Stoicheia* (Elements) are the basis of the mathematical sciences of both ancient and modern times. He did not perform all, and perhaps not even a large portion of, the discoveries he systematized in his book. But cer-

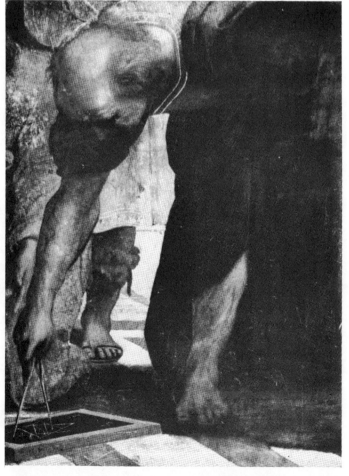

Euclid
(*Raphael, School of Athens, the Vatican*)

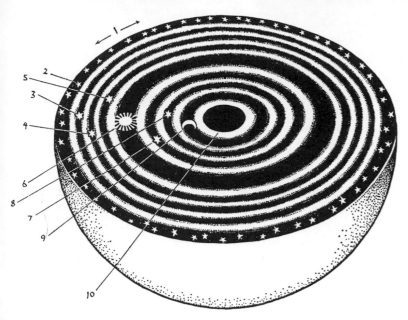

Greek conception of the spherical cosmos: (1) propelling sphere—invisible, immovable; (2) star sphere (carries other spheres with it) period of revolution: 1 day; (3) Saturn sphere—period of revolution: 29 years; (4) Jupiter sphere—period of revolution: 12 years; (5) Mars sphere—period of revolution: 2 years; (6) Sun sphere—period of revolution: 1 year; (7) Venus sphere—period of revolution: 6 years; (8) Mercury sphere—period of revolution: 3 months; (9) Moon sphere—period of revolution: 1 month; (10) Earth sphere—immovable

The death of Archimedes at the hands of a Roman soldier (212 B.C.). Archimedes of Syracuse was the greatest mathematician and physicist of Antiquity

(Mosaic found at Herculaneum)

The Last Days of Ancient Greece: Destruction of Corinth by the Romans

(Painting by Fleury, the Luxembourg)

Pythagoras

PYTHAGORAS

PYTHAGORAS (578?-510? B.C.). Already in the days of Xenophanes and Heraclitus of Ephesus, about 500 B.C., Pythagoras had become a legendary figure, and all the efforts of ancient and modern scholars, to distinguish between fiction and truth or between Pythagoras' own performances and those of his disciples, the Pythagoreans, have resulted only in more or less probable conjectures. But his historical existence cannot be doubted. Some ancient authorities assert that he was born in Syria, but most of them think that he was born on the island of Samos, and that he emigrated to Southern Italy after Polycrates had seized power over his native country in 538 B.C. In Italy, Pythagoras seems to have founded a school which was like a religious and political order, and to have tried to interfere with politics.

There is general agreement that Pythagoras is regarded as the initiator of mathematical demonstration and deduction. Whether he himself or one of his disciples discovered the proposition about right-angled triangles which is named after him, cannot be ascertained. Pythagoras also is credited with having discovered the importance of numbers in music and having laid the fundaments of the theory of that art.

There is also general agreement that Pythagoras combined rational science and religious mysticism, and endeavored to use mathematical concepts and axioms for other-worldly speculations. He influenced Plato and Plotinus, and, through them, many mystics and metaphysicians up to the present day.

Pythagoras
(Capitoline Museum, Rome)

Pythagoras, in whose teachings the demand for purity in life was deeply grounded

Pythagoras Teaching (left foreground)
("School of Athens," Raphael, Vatican)

Pythagoras
(From a Fresco by Raphael)

Pythagoras and the Beautiful Theano. It was Pythagoras who paraphrased the doctrine of the passage of one soul through many bodies, of both men and animals. Among his pupils was a beautiful girl, Theano, the first woman to distinguish herself as a philosopher. She and Pythagoras proved that they were even more man and woman than philosophers by falling desperately in love. Their romance had a happy ending

The Delphic Priestess of Apollo, seated on the Holy Tripod, "the Badge and Symbol of the Sages," adopted by Pythagoras
(By courtesy of the Berlin State Museums)

Pythagoras among Egyptian Priests, on one of his many Travels through the Middle East

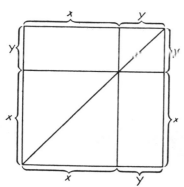

The Pythagorean presentation of the equation
$$(x+y)^2 = x^2+2xy+y^2$$

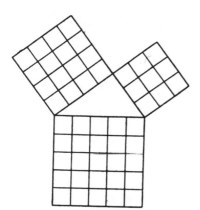

The Theorem of Pythagoras

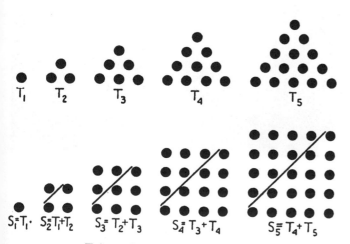

Triangular and square numbers

Hollow bronze statue of Apollo, one of the first Greek figures made by the "subtle method of cire-perdue" which Pythagoras had studied

(The Louvre)

Socrates

SOCRATES

SOCRATES (470-399 B.C.). The Delphic Oracle, regarded as omniscient by great and small and old and young in ancient Greece, used to communicate its knowledge in obscure and equivocal phrases. However, when asked whether there was any man wiser than Socrates, it replied simply and clearly: No one is wiser.

Hearing of this pronouncement, Socrates himself was rather disturbed. For he had steadily disclaimed that he was wise or that he possessed any knowledge. Rather, it was his manner to proceed from the statement that he was an ignorant person, and the only merit he claimed was to be aware of his ignorance. So he went among pretentious people of various professions, particularly rhetoricians and sophists, questioning their knowledge, until he became convinced that they were quite as ignorant as he, but that they did not admit, nor were they even aware of, their ignorance.

Socrates was the son of a stone-cutter and a midwife, and he liked to draw a parallel between his method of making people think and his mother's calling. Before he began to teach, Socrates had served in the army of Athens, his native city, had distinguished himself on the battlefield, and had held offices in the Athenian administration. He owned a house in the city and a modest capital sum, which he was wise enough to entrust for investment to his friend and pupil Crito, an experienced businessman. Socrates, therefore, could afford to teach without demanding fees. While doing so, he embittered other teachers, and aroused suspicion in the minds of influential fellow citizens. His rather eccentric manners, his fondness of jesting, and, above all, his repeated refusal to subordinate his judgment to political party purposes aggravated his situation. Accused of corrupting the youth of Athens by his teaching, Socrates was sentenced to death. On several occasions he could have escaped from jail, but he insisted on his obligation to respect the sentence even though it be wrong. His preparedness to die and his serene fortitude during the last hours of his life gained the admiration of both his contemporaries and posterity.

Socrates did not put his doctrines into writing; he taught orally. His pupils adored him despite his ugliness and slovenliness. Many of them belonged to Athens' aristocracy, while others were humble people. Some of them became outstanding philosophers, like Euclid, Phaedo, Antisthenes, Aristippus, and Plato, the greatest of all of them. All these pupils agree that Socrates insisted on the belief on moral values, on an austere conduct of life, and

on the unity of wisdom, knowledge and virtue. While Plato made him the mouthpiece of the doctrine of ideas, all other philosophers who were close to Socrates were opposed to that doctrine. It is therefore quite probable that Plato went far beyond the philosophical position of his master.

Ruins of the Temple at Delphi

Pythia and the Tripod at Delphi

Athens at the Time of Socrates

Socrates at the Battle of Potidiae, in the Peloponnesian War, where he saved his favorite pupil, Alcibiades

The Acropolis of Athens as it appeared during the city's Golden Age

Socrates Instructing Alcibiades

The Lighter Side of Athenian Life. Woman was represented at Athenian dinner parties only by the hetairai, professional actresses, dancing girls and flute players
(British Museum)

(British Museum)

The Death of Socrates
(Painting by J. L. David, Metropolitan Museum of Art)

Socrates in the Streets of Athens

Xenophon (435-355 B.C.)

Xenophon, warrior and philosopher pupil of Socrates, retreating with the Greek forces of Cyrus to the Black Sea (401 B.C.). Among his writings are the dialogue, Symposium, *relating the table talks of Socrates*

Plato

PLATO

PLATO (427-347 B.C.). For two thousand and three hundred years Plato's work has been a living force that has given to some the firmest certainty while causing creative unrest in the minds of others. Plato's ascendancy over the philosophers of ancient Greco-Roman civilization was immense. It remained great in the Middle Ages, increased in the Renaissance as well as in the eras of Descartes, Berkeley and Hegel, and still today there are outstanding thinkers in America and Europe who adhere to his doctrine. The discussion about its real meaning has not come to an end, and entails re-examinations of the principal methods of modern science and philosophy.

The man whose influence was so deep and lasting is known to posterity by his nickname which means "the Broad." His real name was Aristocles. Belonging to one of the oldest and noblest families of Athens' aristocracy whose members used to take part in governing the state, Plato also felt a leaning toward statesmanship. However, his attempts to play a political role resulted in frustration and disappointment. To these painful experiences Plato reacted by founding and directing his "Academy" which was a University and a center of research as well as a training school for future political leaders. For Plato was convinced that any state must perish if its rulers were not philosophers, and philosophy meant to him the ability to perceive the world of Ideas, immaterial essences, Forms which contain the true and ultimate realities while the world of sensible things is only a vague, transitory and untrustworthy copy. Only the cognition of the Ideas enables man to act with wisdom. The rules of rightful conduct of human life were derived by Plato from the laws that rule the universe. Plato's criteria of human behavior were rooted in his metaphysical conceptions.

Although Plato constantly emphasized his conviction that true knowledge can be obtained only by cognition of the eternal and immutable Ideas or Forms, he by no means neglected the phenomena of change or the imperfect phases of knowledge which are given by sensations or expressed by mere opinions. He was a keen observer of daily life, acquainted with arts and crafts, versed in empirical sciences and literature. He was a tough warrior and sportsman. He even proved to be a clever traveling salesman who dealt in oil when he visited Egypt, and he succeeded well although he found the Egyptians to be extremely shrewd businessmen.

Every work published by Plato is written in the form of a dialogue. Most of them are full of dramatic life. Some are gay comedies. Speech has been given to both historical and fictitious persons but hardly ever to the author himself who attributed most of his own thoughts to his teacher Socrates. The discussions allow representation of various, even opposed, points of view. Their principal means of explanation is the dialectic whose function is to illustrate

Plato among His Students, Depicted in a Pompeian Mosaic
(*National Museum in Naples*)

the logical consequences of a hypothesis. In order to explain ideas difficult to understand, or to elucidate a hypothesis impossible to be proved true, Plato often resorts to the use of a myth which elucidates a thought or truth by means of images.

Plato's doctrine contains the elements of a religion, of positive sciences, of a political system and of legislation. He recognized the complexity of the problems with which he dealt and was aware of the precariousness of the results of his thinking. Until his death he continued to develop his ideas.

Plato and His Students in the Garden of the Academy

Platonic Academy in Bithynia

One of the Famous Platonic Banquets
(By Carstens)

4   6   8   12   20 sides

The five possible regular solids, later known as the "Platonic Bodies," which played considerable part, much of it fanciful, in subsequent philosophical and mathematical speculation

Plato Discoursing with a Student
(From the painting, "Philosophy," by Chavannes, in the Boston Public Library)

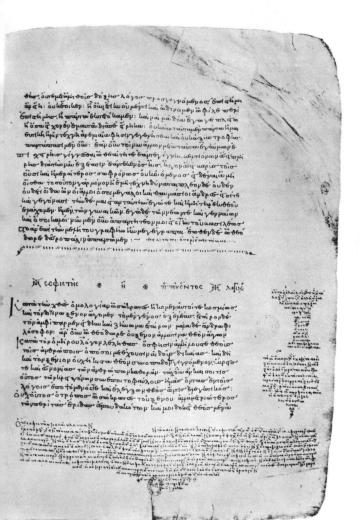

Manuscript of Plato's Dialogue The Sophists
(Manuscript Bodleianus)

Plato and Aristotle
(From "The School of Athens," Raphael, the Vatican)

Aristotle

ARISTOTLE

ARISTOTLE (384-322 B.C.). Still accepted by thousands as the world's leading philosopher, Aristotle possessed one of the few really encyclopedic minds ever produced by the West. His was an unique combination of philosophic insight and keen powers of observation. He was a great thinker, systematic historian, and natural scientist. Although his contributions to the subject matter of physics are important and still used, his subsequent reflections on the causes and principles of physical matter established the field of metaphysics, literally those things beyond or after physics.

The substance of his philosophy, influenced by the highly developed state of Greek art, is that there are two

Aristotle before the Bust of Homer
(Painting by Rembrandt)

Aristotle
(Spada Gallery)

dichotomies: matter and form. Everything is either matter or form. For example, in a brass statue, brass is matter with a variety of potentialities and possibilities; the statue is form, the actuality. It is the form or shape of one of the possibilities of brass. Development is the process by which matter becomes form, and every form the matter for the next highest form. God, the prime mover, is pure form or thought. In man, reason represents the highest form. Entelechy is the formative principle in which purpose and cause unite for a final end.

To Aristotle, man's happiness consisted in virtue—the mean between two extremes. "Even if happiness is not sent by the Gods, but is the result of virtue and of learning of discipline of some kind, it is apparently one of the most divine things in the world; for it would appear that that which is the prize and end of virtue is the supreme good, and in its nature divine and blessed."

He conceived the perfect state to be a democracy in which the masses are restricted and where education is aimed at the development of bodily vigor and the virtues.

Aristotle was born at Stagira, and went to Athens to become a pupil (and later a critic) of Plato. He spent some years in the company of the tyrant, Hermias, whose niece he married. Shortly afterward, he accepted the task of educating the son of Philip of Macedonia, who became known to posterity as Alexander the Great. After the death of Plato, he returned to Athens to found a school. He taught art, politics, physics, systems of natural science, logic, and philosophy at the Lyceum. In his last years, he was condemned as godless and banished from Athens. He died shortly thereafter.

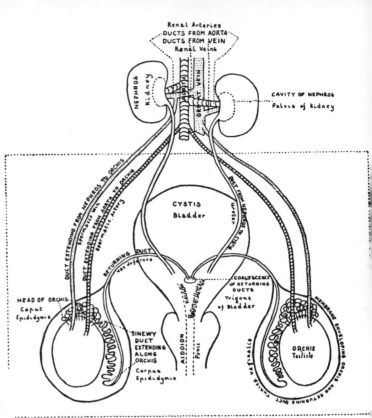

The mammalian urino-genital system as described by Aristotle. (Legends in capitals are the terms employed by Aristotle. The modern equivalents are written in italics.)

Aristotle and his pupil, Alexander, King of Macedonia. His life, like that of his father Philip, was dedicated to ruthless military conquest

The assassination of the imperialistic King Philip of Macedonia, protector of Aristotle, at the hands of a freedom-loving Greek, 336 B.C.

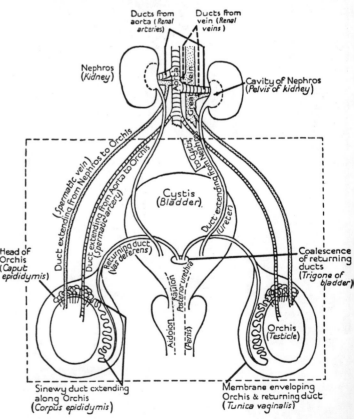

The generative and excretory systems of mammals as described by Aristotle, in his Historia animalium. *(Legends in brackets are modern scientific terms, the others translations of Aristotle's terms.)*

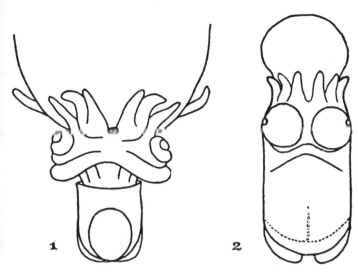

1   2

*Drawing of a Dissection of Development of Sepia
by Aristotle*

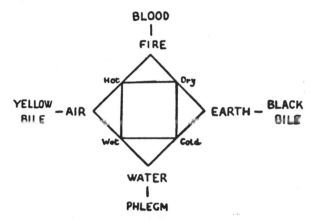

*Scheme of the four qualities, the four elements and the
four humors, according to Aristotle*

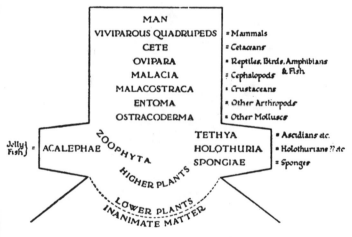

The Scala Naturae *of Aristotle*

Aristotle on the Constitution of Athens
(*British Museum*)

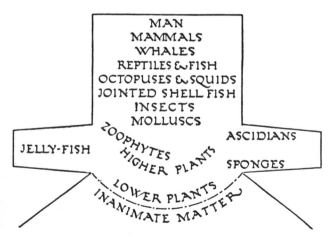

Aristotle's Ladder of Nature

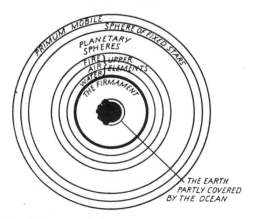

*The Universe of Aristotle as Conceived by a
Medieval Writer*

The Spirit of Athens

THALES

THALES (About 625-545 B.C.). The earliest philosophical school in the history of Western civilization was founded by Thales, a citizen of Miletus in Asia Minor. Although he is unanimously recognized as the initiator of Greek philosophy, he was not of Greek origin but descended from a Semitic (Carian) family, and he owed much of his scientific and technical knowledge to Babylonian and Egyptian influences.

Thales took the initiative in Greek philosophical thinking with his conception of the existing world as the transformation of a single cosmic matter, declaring that water was the fundamental substance and source of all living beings. Although this special hypothesis did not satisfy his successors, his way of distinguishing between the apparent nature and a reality which becomes comprehensible through the unifying and relating functions of reason was of lasting consequence and continued to inspire Greek thinkers.

The whole Greco-Roman antiquity revered Thales as one of the "Seven Sages." He became famous because of his many important inventions and discoveries in the fields of astronomy, geometry, meteorology and navigation, and above all because he predicted the solar eclipse which took place on May 28, 585 B.C., while a great battle was raging between the Lydian and Median armies. He was also a clever businessman who made a fortune by monopolizing the olive trade in years of shortage, which he had foreseen. Thales taught in the Greek language but wrote no books.

Thales

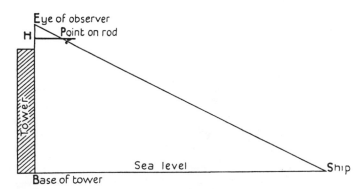

Thales measures distance to ship at sea. Triangle EHP *similar to triangle* EBS. *Therefore* EH *is to* HP *as* EB *is to* BS. *Since* EH, HP, *and* EB *are all measurable* BS *can be calculated*

ANAXIMANDER

ANAXIMANDER (610-c. 547 B.C.). Known as Anaximander of Miletus, he was the earliest Greek philosophical essayist. A pupil of Thales, he was also the first Greek cartographer, and has been credited with the invention of astronomical instruments.

His treatise *On Nature* dealt with the development of matter. In the search of the basic principles from which all things in existence were derived, Anaximander ignored those elements experienced by perception. He upheld the concept of *apeiron,* wherein the universe developed from the infinite by means of rotation.

Neither Anaximander nor his contemporaries analyzed the concept of the infinite. However, he did advance theories concerning infinite space, the infinite possibilities of combinations of qualities, and the infinite power of production.

ONE OF THE FATHERS OF GEOMETRY

Anaximenes

XENOPHANES

XENOPHANES (About 580-485 B.C.). Xenophanes was born in Colophon in Asia Minor. He was the first thinker of Greek culture to present the idea of the one, true, eternal, supreme God in opposition to the ideas of the gods of the poets and the popular cults which, as Xenophanes vigorously declared, were shaped after human images. God, as conceived by Xenophanes, defies all human ways of comprehending. In his ideas on physics, Xenophanes, a contemporary of Pythagoras, relied principally on the Milesian school. Possibly it was because of his religious rigorism that Xenophanes led a migratory life, wandering restlessly after he had left his native country for Italy.

ANAXIMENES

ANAXIMENES (ϵ. 585-525 B.C.). Along with Thales and Anaximander, Anaximenes was one of the triumvirate of important Milesian philosophers. His importance is due to his formulation of the method whereby change is represented as the result of the processes of condensation and rarefication. This theory anticipated the development of physical laws and mechanics and physics.

He also attempted to define the fundamental substance that constitutes the universe. Anaximenes endeavored to synthesize the doctrines of his two Milesian predecessors by stating that the qualities of air were sufficient to explain whatever exists perceptually and intellectually. He maintained that air was as infinite as Anaximander's *apeiron* and as real as the water which Thales considered the fundamental cosmic matter.

Heraclitus of Ephesus
Statue in Museum at Candia from Agora at Gortyna. Work of Second Century A.D. copied from original of Fifth Century B.C.

Inset: Ephesian coin of Fifth Century B.C. showing similar figure

HERACLITUS

HERACLITUS (about 540-480 B.C.). One of the most vigorous thinkers of Greek antiquity, proud and independent, Heraclitus stated with utter candor his opinion of his fellow citizens of Ephesus: They ought to go and hang themselves and hand over the city to juveniles, having expelled Hermodoros, the best among them. So disgusted was he with political intrigue and the wrangles of small minds, that he left the city and sought solace and inspiration in the beauty and grandeur of nature. But for the Ephesians he had a strange wish: Would that their wealth never decline so that their worthlessness might appear to even better advantage!

Himself of noble birth, he disdained the masses. His admirer, Nietzsche, would have concurred in this: "One man to me is worth as much as 10,000, provided he be the best." The masses, he believed, cannot comprehend the divine nature. Indeed, they could not follow Heraclitus in the flight of his spirit, and thus they called him the Dark Philosopher.

From his spiritual height he flayed their idolatry and base thinking, and aligned himself with fate and a divine being for whom all is beautiful, good and just. The world, not created in time but existing from all eternity, he considered as ever in flux, and war as the father of all things. There is a cycle, however, from the eternal fire through want to the manifold of things, and back again through satedness, harmony and peace. Everything is relative— the most beautiful ape is ugly compared to man; illness makes health sweet, evil the good . . . Contentment is achieved by submission to order, reason and wisdom. The soul, a spark of the substance of the stars, is immortal and returns upon death to the all-soul to which it is related.

Heraclitus
(Raphael, "School of Athens," Vatican)

Likeness of Anaxagoras on Old Coin

ANAXAGORAS

ANAXAGORAS (c. 500-428 B.C.). Renowned as the last of the great Ionian philosophers, Anaxagoras was born at Klazomene on the Lydian coast of Asia Minor. A friend of Pericles and a teacher of Thucydides, Euripides, and other noted Greeks, he was the first philosopher to choose Athens as his home. He was held in great reverence until, at the instigation of a bigot, he was accused of blasphemy in speculating that the sun was a red, hot mass of stone and the moon an earthy substance. Although he was condemned to death, his influential friends helped him escape.

Parmenides Eleates philosophus. uixit Olympiade nonagesima.

PARMENIDES

PARMENIDES (About 504-456 B.C.). Down to recent times, philosophy has accepted fundamental concepts from Parmenides, notwithstanding considerable criticisms, modifications and combinations with other ideas. It was Parmenides who initiated the distinction between a sensible and an intelligible world. It was he who first assumed an indestructible *substance* and used it as the basis of his speculations, although he did not formulate its concept. It was he who began to distinguish between scientific truth and popular opinion. In this way, Parmenides influenced Empedocles, Leucippus and Democritus, the Sophists and Plato, while Hegel was not the last philosopher who followed Parmenides by founding metaphysics upon logic.

A principal characteristic of the Greek mind, which is significant not only of Greek philosophy but of Greek art and the Greek feeling of existence, was shaped by Parmenides, the founder of the Eleatic school. This is his preference for unity, composure, and the comprehension of limits and contours. This longing for unity made him suspicious of the senses; this want of composure made him deny change; this need of limits made him conceive the unchanging world as of spherical form and repudiate the idea of the infinite, or the empty space.

Little is known about Parmenides' life. He was born in Elea (Velia) in Southern Italy; probably he was a disciple of Xenophanes and Ameinias, a Pythagorean. In all probability, he resided for some years in Athens where, according to Plato, Socrates met him and learned much from the aged philosopher.

ZENO of ELEA

ZENO of ELEA (About 490-430 B.C.). The subtleties of Zeno of Elea have been endlessly discussed by philosophers and mathematicians, including those of the twentieth century.

Zeno was a scholar and a politician. According to tradition, he combated tyranny and, when a Sicilian tyrant tortured him in order to make him betray his political associates, Zeno cut his own tongue with his teeth, and threw it in the face of the torturer.

Zeno shared his teacher Parmenides' ideas on unity and the impossibility of change. He denied the Pythagorean identification of arithmetical units with geometrical points. His paradoxical arguments against the concept of motion, of which those of Achilles and the tortoise and the flying arrow became famous, were advanced in order to defend the doctrine of Parmenides; they are the crude precursors of the mathematical concepts of continuity and infinity.

Like Parmenides, Zeno resided for some years in Athens. He is said to have invented the art of dialectics which Socrates learned from him.

ZENO

EMPEDOCLES

EMPEDOCLES (c. 490-435 B.C.). Born in Acragas (Agrigentum) on the south coast of Sicily, Empedocles, like his teacher Parmenides, was bred in the Pythagorean tradition. He tried to combine this with the more naturalistic philosophy and science of the Milesians. He did not share Parmenides' distrust of the senses, and like him, composed his philosophy in verse. Fragments of two treatises, one entitled *On Nature* and the other *Purification,* are extant. The term *catharsis,* which became highly important in poetry and aesthetics, was first used in *Purification.* The doctrine of the four elements, water, fire, air, and earth, which dominated the popular. thinking about nature for more than two thousand years, was probably originated by Empedocles. According to him, change was produced by the two fundamental forces, love and strife. The first was the cause of combination; the other of separation. He explained cosmic nature, the functions of the human body, and the activities of the soul as the result of conflicting forces. His philosophy was a blend of mythological imagination and scientific observation. He was an opponent of tyranny and a miracle-worker who claimed to be a God. Hundreds of stories abounded about him throughout ancient Greece and Italy. He was credited with founding the first great medical school. His legendary death is supposed to have taken place by jumping into the crater of Mount Etna; this has been a source of inspiration for many poets, among them: Matthew Arnold and Friedrich Hoelderlin.

Empedocles

Empedocles' Chaos of the Elements

GORGIAS

GORGIAS (About 483-375 B.C.). Next to Protagoras, the most important and respected sophist was Gorgias, born in Leontini in Sicily, who, as leader of an embassy which was sent by his native city to Athens in order to ask for help against Syracusan aggression, succeeded in persuading Athenians who were deeply impressed by his powerful eloquence.

Gorgias has often been mentioned as an example of longevity, and this has been attributed to his great egoism. He did not marry, and was always indifferent to both the sufferings and the happiness of other people. He developed rhetoric as an art whose possibilities are not restricted by anything, least of all by philosophy. To prove this thesis, Gorgias proceeded from Empedocles' theory of perception. He wrote a treatise *On Nature,* a *Technic of Rhetoric,* and several eulogies. Only two small fragments, probably from the treatise *On Nature,* are extant.

PROTAGORAS

PROTAGORAS (About 480-410 B.C.). Professor F. C. Schiller, the founder of the English branch of modern pragmatism, used to call himself a disciple of Protagoras. Possibly he did so because Plato reports a saying of Protagoras, that expressed his disbelief in absolute truth, and maintains that one opinion can be better than another one though it is not true.

For around 2300 years, the Sophists of whom Protagoras is the oldest known in history, have been despised as unscrupulous distorters of facts. It was Friedrich Nietzsche who rehabilitated them, and since then their contribution to philosophy can no longer be disregarded. Plato, who initiated the unfavorable opinion about the Sophists and induced posterity to condemn them without hearing, however, exempted Protagoras from that sentence.

Protagoras was born in Abdera and studied philosophy, if not as a personal disciple of Democritus, yet as a pupil of atomistic materialism. He came to Athens where his conditions seem to have changed more than once. Pericles highly esteemed him and entrusted him with drawing up a constitution for the Attic colony of Thurii. But his books were publicly burned in Athens, and he was persecuted because of blasphemy. In 416, Protagoras was sentenced to death but escaped to his native town.

Several disciples of Socrates had been previously taught by Protagoras. None of them seems to have regarded the change of teachers as a conversion to a very different philosophy. Protagoras, however, insisted on sensation as the only source of knowledge and claimed that the art of the Sophist could modify the sensations of his audience. Any sensation is true as long as it is perceived, and only that is true which is actually sensed. Protagoras was one of the creators of Greek rhetoric, the science of language, and scientific prose. He wrote numerous books, of which only four small fragments are extant.

Metrodorus, Greek Philosopher of Fourth Century B.C., Student of Democritus
(Capitoline Museum, Rome)

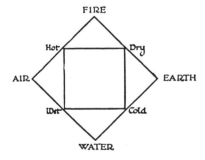

The Four Elements and Four Qualities of Empedocles

LEUCIPPUS

LEUCIPPUS (About 460 B.C.). All modern physicists may be regarded as followers of Leucippus of Miletus, the founder of atomism whose way of thinking has led to immense results in science and practical life. His theory that the Universe is composed of an infinite number of elements which are characterized by quantitative differences has undergone many and important modifications, but it has maintained its validity even after the "indivisible" atoms could be split.

All of Leucippus' works, among which the books *Megas Diakosmos* (the Great Order of the Universe) and *Peri Nou* (On Mind) were most famous, are lost. In the fourth century B.C. his writings were re-edited together with those of his disciple Democritus in one and the same collection. This led Epicurus to deny the historical existence of Leucippus, and some recent scholars have professed the same opinion. But, as Aristotle and Theophrastus remarked, there are differences between the doctrines of Leucippus and Democritus. Although Leucippus created the vocabulary of Greek atomism he remained in many respects more closely connected with the Ionian cosmologists of the older schools, while Democritus proceeded to a strictly scientific view on physical and mental phenomena.

DEMOCRITUS OF ABDERA

DEMOCRITUS OF ABDERA (460-c. 360 B.C.). Although only scarce fragments of the numerous works of Democritus are extant, sufficient pieces have remained to prove that he was one of the greatest of the Greek thinkers; equally outstanding as a scientist and philosopher; a peer of Plato and Aristotle; and a man whose thoughts and feelings were close to the common people. Many legends have been formed about his life. He is said to have traveled from Ethiopia and Egypt to Persia and India. He certainly visited Athens, but no one there took notice of him. Plato, his contemporary, never mentioned Democritus, but Aristotle and Hippocrates quoted him frequently. The legends depicted Democritus as a man easily disposed to laughter; an incurable optimist; moderate, serene, and always prepared to understand the errors and failures of his fellow men.

Democritus conceived the universe to be composed of essential transitory combinations of an infinite number of atoms and their separations as the necessary condition for eternal change; that atomic theory was a working hypothesis which would help explain the experiences of mind and nature; his concepts were comparable to idealistic metaphysics. He was not only an important systematizer of Greek atomism, anticipating the underlying principle of modern physics, but also an acute psychologist; a sage moralist, inspired by humanitarian ideals, without illusions about human nature. He taught that equanimity and fortitude must prevail in all life situations, and that there must be resistance to evil and temptations. He contributed to epistemology, physics, mathematics, and technics. He dealt with logical and musical problems; avoided politics in his writings.

Democritus

ISOCRATES

ISOCRATES (436-338 B.C.). Isocrates, who, despite his delicate health and many misfortunes, lived to be nearly a hundred years old, was considered by the Greeks to be not the most powerful but the most skilled of all orators. After political events had ruined him financially, he established himself as a dealer in speeches and pamphlets which he wrote and sold or prepared on order. He was acquainted with Socrates, though not his disciple. Isocrates attacked the Sophists, as Socrates did, but not for the same reasons. Occasionally, he also attacked, or counter-attacked, Plato and Antisthenes.

Isocrates frequently dealt with political questions. His standpoint was very close to that of Aristotle. Both of them condemned the policy which was inaugurated by Themistocles and developed by Pericles, 'namely, Athens' claim to naval supremacy which, as Isocrates saw it, would provoke an overwhelming alliance of other powers against Athens' ambitions. Isocrates steadily advocated peace among all Greek states. He declared that all Greeks were united, less by blood than by common education and ideals.

ANTISTHENES

ANTISTHENES (c. 445-365 B.C.). Son of a lower-class Athenian father and either a Thracian or Phrygian-slave mother, Antisthenes was the founder of the Cynic school of Greek philosophy. The name of his school was derived from the building in which he taught, the *Cynosarges* (dog's tomb), for Cynic philosophy bears no relation to the modern meaning of cynicism in which human values or moral scruples are held in contempt. He was originally a disciple of Gorgias, the sophist, who came to Athens in 427 B.C. Later he became one of the most faithful pupils of Socrates, tramping five miles each day to the city in order to listen to his master's words. He was present when Socrates drank the cup of hemlock.

Antisthenes was opposed to Plato's doctrine of ideas and to Aristippus' philosophy of pleasure. He interpreted the teachings of Socrates as the doctrine of virtue which can be taught with disregard of feelings, independence of judgment, contempt for conventional opinions, and discrimination between social status, birth and wealth. Later Cynics, exaggerating Antisthenes' statements, were strongly opposed to Stoics and Epicureans.

Antisthenes

Aristippus

ARISTIPPUS

ARISTIPPUS (c. 435-366 B.C.). All the writings of Aristippus are lost, but if the ancient sources about him are not entirely misleading, he seems, of all the disciples of Socrates, to have been the least congenial with his teacher. The only Socratic point in Aristippus' doctrine was the praise of inner freedom and true independence. Unlike Socrates, he denied social responsibility, was indifferent to reason, and conceived of wisdom as that which is concerned with the enjoyment of pleasure and the avoidance of pain. He is said to have been the first disciple of Socrates to request fees for his lessons. When this action aroused Socrates' indignation, he offered his master part of his gain as a royalty.

Aristippus was born in Cyrene, North Africa. Early in life, he settled in Athens to study first with Protagoras and then with Socrates. The little that is known about him through anecdotes reveal him to have been wily, greedy, and ever eager to ridicule Plato. He also seems to have been optimistic, of a serene disposition, and kindly disposed to his fellow-men, except those whom he regarded as his competitors.

97

Diogenes (412-323 B. C.). A pupil of Antisthenes, he moved to Athens where he founded a school of ascetic philosophy known as Cynics (dog like) *because of their attitudes, such as living in a barrel. They developed a type of popular homespun ethics. Many anecdotes surround the life of Diogenes and his fellow Cynics*

Diogenes
(Statue in. the Villa Albani)

98

Diogenes in Search of an Honest Man
(Painting by Salvator Rosa)

Diogenes Throwing away His Bowl on Seeing a Peasant Drink from His Hand
(Painting by Nicolas Poussin, Louvre)

ZENO the STOIC

ZENO the STOIC (About 340-265 B.C.). Stoicism has a long history. It was initiated by Zeno of Citium who was of Phoenician descent, and almost all of its early representatives were not Greeks but Asians. For a time Stoicism was regarded as the last bulwark of Greek paganism. Then it was harmonized with the spirit of Christianity by some Fathers of the Church. Although Stoicism was by no means dormant in the thought of the Middle Ages, the great period of its revival began with the Renaissance and lasted until the beginning of the nineteenth century. Stoic morality inspired Shakespeare, Corneille and Schiller, Spinoza, Immanuel Kant and many leaders of the French Revolution.

Stoicism takes its name from a portico (*stoa*) in Athens, where Zeno, the founder of the school, taught his disciples. He had come to that city from his native town, situated on the island of Cyprus, after having made a fortune as a clever businessman. Fragments of twenty-six books written by him are extant. But more of his works have been lost. His successors often changed the Stoic doctrine and deviated from many original views, or enlarged them, or assumed a considerably more austere attitude toward life. But all of them adhered to the ideal of the sage who endeavors to act in accordance with his self and with nature, indifferent to the vicissitudes of life, and most of them proclaimed the equality of all men, as Zeno did.

Zeno
(National Museum, Naples)

CLEANTHES

CLEANTHES (310-232 B.C.). Noted as a director of the oldest Stoic school for thirty-one years, Cleanthes, an indigent scholar, worked mostly as a porter until finally, at the age of fifty, he was enabled to enter a philosopher's school. He became a devoted disciple of Zeno, the Stoic, studied under his master for nineteen years, and upon Zeno's death, assumed the directorship of the school. Cleanthes slightly modified Zeno's doctrine. He was also famous as a poet; of his forty works, all of them very short, many fragments are extant. A large portion of his most famous poem, *Hymn to Zeus,* has been preserved. Even as head of the school, and despite his advanced years, Cleanthes continually astonished his friends by hoisting heavy loads and earning his living by manual work.

Chrysippus
(British Museum)

Cratylus of Athens, a Heraclitean and first teacher of Plato. Plato's dialogue bearing his name criticizes the Heraclitean theory of language

CHRYSIPPUS

CHRYSIPPUS (c. 280-207 B.C.). The Stoic school of philosophy, established by Zeno, would not have had as lasting an influence had not Chrysippus developed and solidified its concepts. He was born in Soli, Cilicia, Asia Minor, and went to Athens in 260 B.C. There he succeeded Cleanthes as director of the Stoic school. Chrysippus is said to have written some seven hundred books on a variety of topics. Although his literary style was far from masterful, he was a systematic thinker, logician, and tions which were of considerable consequence in later eras. He particularly investigated sentiments and ideas, and tried to obtain through logical and dialectical disquisitions the irrefutable truths upon which his ethics and theology were based. He stated that the essential characteristic of man which distinguished him from the animals was that his judgment became active as soon as his sensations were irritated. In ethics, Chrysippus assumed that a natural impetus operated in all living creatures. This impetus was conscious in man. He did not see any dichotomy between the decision of human will and that of natural impetus. Nature, striving for virtue, made the natural impetus.

EPICURUS

EPICURUS (341-270 B.C.). According to Epicurus, philosophy must be a cure for the mind and soul; it must be a guide to happiness. He taught that pleasure was the beginning and end of the blessed life; that wisdom and culture must be directed toward this end. Contrary to other hedonists, Epicurus regarded the permanent absence of pain as the only true pleasure, rather than joy or debauchery. The pleasure he conceived of demanded self-control; prudence was necessary for the pursuit of happiness. He recommended an extremely frugal life; he himself was ordinarily satisfied with bread and water. The essential part of his philosophy was devoted to ethics and teaching a wise conduct of life. Logic, epistemology, physics, and metaphysics were regarded as helpful toward securing tranquility of soul or disturbing it. He thus concluded that fear of death and religion were the main sources of psychic disorder. He staunchly opposed superstition or any belief in supernatural interference. His concept of nature mainly followed that of Democritus. Although he adopted atomism, he disaffirmed determinism, and established the doctrine of cosmic chance. The latter doctrine has been revived in contemporary times.

In 310 B.C. he founded the oldest sanatorium, in Mytilene, for persons suffering from psychic or nervous disorders, depressions, or the consequences of failure or disappointment. Four years later the sanatorium was removed to Athens. Epicurus, himself, always suffered from diseases of the stomach, bladder, or kidneys. His philosophy en-

Epicurus
(Vatican Museum)

Hermarchos, pupil of Epicurus, who took over after the latter's death (271 B.C.) the direction of his academy

abled him to endure pain and he was able to cure many of the patients in his sanatorium by teaching them his philosophy. Many were indebted to his knowledge whereby psychic disorders could be avoided. Persons of all origins, professions, and social stature were admitted to his sanatorium or school. Neither slaves nor hetaerae were excluded. His teachings, though often distorted, were spread throughout the ancient world. They have had considerable influence through all of history, up to the present time.

101

ARCESILAUS

ARCESILAUS (c. 315-240 B.C.). From 270 to 240 B.C., Arcesilaus directed the Platonic Academy at Athens and helped it to regain its former splendor. During his administration, the doctrine of the Academy turned to a scepticism similar to that of Pyrrho and Timon, although it had developed independently of them and was somewhat milder in form.

Arcesilaus studied mathematics with Autolycus, a predecessor of Euclid at Sardes, Asia Minor. He was also an experienced musician, and a brilliant speaker and teacher. He regarded himself as the true disciple of Plato, haranguing against Speusippus and Xenocrates whom he accused of distorting Plato's doctrines. According to Arcesilaus, the correct understanding of Plato results in doubt, suspension of judgment, and a complete spiritual freedom equivalent to the supreme good. With a vehemence equal to that of other Platonists, Arcesilaus attacked the Stoics, who, in turn, severely criticized him. Epicurus was the only contemporary philosopher he acknowledged. Only a few sayings of Arcesilaus are extant.

Carneades

The Great Library at Alexandria

CARNEADES

CARNEADES (c. 214-129 B.C.). Carneades was born in Cyrene, North Africa. A radical sceptic, he was the first of the philosophers to pronounce the failure of metaphysicians who endeavored to discover rational meanings in religious beliefs. By 159 B.C. he had begun to refute all dogmatic doctrines, particularly Stoicism; nor did he spare the Epicureans as previous sceptics had done. The original theory of probability that he developed was profound and of great consequence. While he attacked the efforts of the Stoics to reconcile popular religions with their philosophical convictions, he also denied the immortality of the gods, their super-human qualities, pantheism, fatalism, and providence. He refused to accept moral values as absolute, although he taught the necessity of learning how to conduct one's life in an artful manner by combining sagacity and reflective thought. In his practical ethics, he professed a moderate Platonism, devoid of all religious or metaphysical elements. He founded the third or New Academy. However, his philosophy had very little in common with Plato, the original founder of the Academy.

PLUTARCH OF CHAERONEA

PLUTARCH OF CHAERONEA (50-120). In the ancient world, Plutarch was considered "the true philanthropist"; in America, Emerson called him the embodiment of the highest ideal of humanity. As a biographer of heroes, as a moralist, as an unorthodox Platonist, Plutarch has been the world's most popular author for many centuries.

His spiritual life was centered in Athens and Delphi, in the Academy, founded by Plato, and in the temple whose priest he was. Plutarch was a pious man, an advocate of general peace and reconciliation. He was a cautious observer of human characters and customs. Notwithstanding his devotion to the old gods, the Fathers of the Church sympathized with him. Among the reformers of the sixteenth century Zwingli and Melanchthon loved him, while Calvin remained cool, and Luther ignored him. Montaigne was called Plutarch's best disciple, and Shakespeare could have been called so. It was only in the nineteenth century, when the historical importance of collective factors was stressed, that Plutarch's influence weakened. But as long as people are interested in individual life, he will be read and re-read, and those who think that history must be conceived as the development of group life, will find in Plutarch's writings highly important information. For he was also one of the greatest folklorists. He wrote on almost everything that could interest, educate or edify his contemporaries, and, in doing so, he amassed a treasury of knowledge, from which modern psychologists, sociologists, educators and students of comparative science of religion may profit as much as historians and philosophers.

PLUTARQUE

Archimedes' Discovery of the Law of the Upthrust of Liquids, according to Plutarch
(Sixteenth Century Etching)

Hipparchus of Alexandria, Greek Astronomer and Mathematician of the Second Century B.C.

Porphyry

PORPHYRY

PORPHYRY (232-304). Porphyry, a Syrian whose original name was Malchos, was one of the last defenders of classical paganism against the Sceptics and Christians. He was a disciple and friend of Plotinus, whose writings he edited. He was also an excellent interpreter of Aristotle.

In his objections to Christianity, Porphyry tried to do justice to the views he fought by informing himself as fully as possible about the history and doctrines of his adversaries, and he took a great many pains to refrain from open hostility. His book *Against the Christians* was considered very dangerous by Christian apologists. Porphyry was convinced that truly religious men do not desire formulas, cults, sacrifices or incantations. But, he said, men of pure heart and wise conduct of life being very rare, people need the images of the gods for their moral discipline and spiritual satisfaction.

LONGINUS, CASSIUS

LONGINUS, CASSIUS (Third century A.D.). The author of the treatise *On the Sublime* has been called "the most modern of all the ancient Greek philosophers" and "next to Aristotle, the greatest literary critic of ancient Greece." All that is known about his personality has been drawn from some passages of his essay, for no other information about him exists. Only this fact is undisputed—that Longinus, the minister of Queen Zenobia of Palmyra, is not the author of the treatise. Longinus, to whom *On the Sublime* has been attributed for centuries, lived from about 213 to 273 A.D., while the treatise must have been written about 50 A.D.

Many authorities agree with Theodor Mommsen that the author probably was a Jew, and those who do not adopt that supposition cannot refute it. For it would have been quite improbable that any gentile author at that time or during the following century and a half could quote from the Old Testament, not even if he were interested, for one reason or another, in the laws and customs of the Jews.

The author surely revered Homer and Moses alike. He speaks of himself as a Greek. But so does Philo whose loyalty to Judaism is beyond doubt. The author, evidently a disciple of Plato and the Stoics, attacks severely another Jew, named Cecilius, who had mordantly criticized Plato in a work that is lost. Cecilius was probably the first to compare Greek, Latin and Hebrew poetry, and his anonymous adversary follows this method.

From Boileau and Milton to Burke and Kant, European aesthetics and literary criticism have been inspired by this anonymous writer. Some of his concepts have been only slightly modified by Hegel and his successors, and even in the twentieth century more than one critic and poet continue to apply the principles of diction which were originally formulated by the unknown Jewish Platonist or perhaps by his fellow-Jew, Cecilius.

PROCLUS

PROCLUS (411-485). Pagan Neo-Platonism reached its last peak in the philosophy of Proclus who was revered as the embodiment of the ideal of the Sage. In accordance with the ideas of late antiquity, Proclus was, at the same time, a refined rationalist, an irresistible logician and dialectician, and a mystic to whom no secret was hidden. His mind is pictured by his contemporaries as the triumph of human reason and the source of superhuman powers. He was the priest of the gods of Greece, Asia Minor and Arabia, and conducted their worship with scientific knowledge and artistic skill. Only Christianity and Judaism were despised and defied by him.

But so great was his fame and the charm of his writings that the Fathers of the Church relied on the commentaries on Plato written by the enemy of Christianity, and Proclus' *Elementa Theologica,* the defense and glorification of paganism, became of basic importance to Christian theology of the Middle Ages. His influence extended even to the thinkers of the Renaissance and Hegelianism.

Jamblicus

JAMBLICUS

JAMBLICUS (About 270-330 A.D.). So far as modern theosophy does not go back to Hindu mysticism, its adherents are using doctrines formulated mostly by Jamblicus, a Syrian and a disciple of Porphyry who tried to systematize the philosophy of Plotinus, wrote commentaries on Plato and about the Greek gods, the doctrines of the Egyptians, Chaldeans and Assyrians. Until the 19th century, Jamblicus was considered one of the great philosophers. In late antiquity his renown was enormous. He was glorified as "posterior to Plato only in time, not in genius," and his devoted disciples did not refrain from forging letters allegedly written by Emperor Julianus, in which Jamblicus was hailed as "Savior of Greece," "Treasury of the Hellenes" or "healer of the souls." For a long time these forgeries enjoyed full credit. For, in fact, Julianus did esteem Jamblicus highly and quoted him frequently in his genuine writings. Jamblicus was revered as a divine being, and many miracles were attributed to him. He attracted many adherents because he promised that the initiation into his philosophy would endow the adept with superhuman powers. Besides, he also promised success in practical life. His thoughts will not impress modern readers except by the eloquence with which they are displayed.

105

Greek Thought in Roman Lands

CICERO, MARCUS TULLIUS

CICERO, MARCUS TULLIUS (106-43 B.C.). The tremendous historical influence of Cicero's philosophical writings cannot be underestimated. It is evident in the works of the Church fathers, Petrarch, Erasmus, and Copernicus. Even Voltaire, among whose many talents the quality of admiration was the least developed, praised two of Cicero's books as "of the noblest works that were ever written." The founding fathers of the United States were equally ardent in their admiration of Cicero. Thomas Jefferson read *De Senectute* (On Old Age) every year; John Adams,

Rome in Cicero's Time

Cicero
(Capitoline Museum, Rome)

the second President of the United States, declared that "all the epochs of world history combined were unable to produce statesman or philosopher as great as Cicero. His authority should have considerable weight." His son, John Quincy Adams, while lecturing at Harvard University, supported Cicero's doctrine that eloquence was the mainstay of liberty. Theodor Mommsen, in his famous *Roman History*, used all his education, ability, and authority to debunk Cicero; for it had become fashionable to abuse and sneer at Cicero as a politician and philosopher. Thadaeus Zielinski, the great Russian philologist, asserted that of all Julius Caesar's achievements none was as important to the history of human civilization as the fact that Caesar, by compelling Cicero to retire to the country, forced the latter to state his philosophy in writing.

It is somewhat difficult to define either Cicero's originality or lack of it, since the works of those Greek philosophers from whom he allegedly borrowed his ideas were lost. One idea was certainly his own: the doctrine that "no war should be undertaken, except to maintain good faith or security."

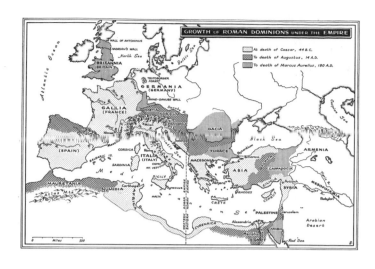

Palimpsest of Cicero's De Republica: *Primary Script, Fourth or Fifth Century; Rewritten in Seventh Century*
(Vatican Library)

Cicero denounces Cataline before the Senate
(Fresco by Maccari, Palace of the Senate, Rome)

LUCRETIUS (Titus Lucretius Carus)

LUCRETIUS (TITUS LUCRETIUS CARUS) (98-55 B.C.). The system of Epicurus was converted into a striking picture of cosmic and human life by Lucretius in his poem *De Rerum Natura* (On the Nature of Things). A tense, electric atmosphere permeates this poem. Much more than a didactic work, it is the confession of a man of violent passions who is longing for equanimity, and, while cleansing his own mind of false ideas, proves to be ready to sacrifice even those illusions that apparently promise peace of mind.

The only extant report of Lucretius' life was written by Jerome, the Father of the Church, who certainly does not approve of the poet's opinions and quite possibly is not an impartial biographer. According to Jerome, Lucretius was afflicted by intermittent insanity, and committed suicide. Some sayings of Lucretius himself indicate that he was threatened by mental disease, and it is probable that he became resolved to die voluntarily when he felt that he had lost the tranquil mind which alone, in his belief, makes life tolerable.

It almost happened that Lucretius' poem was entirely lost. Emperor Augustus, who tried to restitute ancient religion, stigmatized Lucretius, whose memory vanished subsequently, and all but one manuscript of his poems was destroyed. The epoch of the Renaissance meant also the revival of Lucretius, who has since been considered one of the greatest poets of world literature. He was admired by Milton, Shelley and Walt Whitman, whose "Apostrophe to Death" may be traced to his reading of Lucretius. Alfred Tennyson, relying on Jerome, made Lucretius the object of a pathological study.

Posidonius

Lucretius' On the Nature of Things, *in the Vossianus Oblongus Manuscript*

POSIDONIUS

POSIDONIUS (About 135-51 B.C.). The remnants of the works of Posidonius consist of sentences which have been quoted by later authors. In his time and by many succeeding generations, he was esteemed as the most learned scholar who was able to present dry matter in a popular, even picturesque style. Posidonius was born in Syria but taught mostly on the island of Rhodes and at Rome. He traveled through North Africa, Spain, France and Italy and wrote on philosophy, history, geography, physics, and astronomy. Religion played an important part in his thinking. He revered the Greek, Roman, and Oriental gods and rites, and combined the beliefs in the gods and demons with the traditional Stoic pantheism. His picture of the Universe, though preserved in fragments only, influenced many thinkers of the Middle Ages and the Renaissance, and his sayings, which blend reason with mysticism, sober experience with daring conjectures, inspired Leibniz and the romanticists.

SENECA, LUCIUS ANNAEUS

SENECA, LUCIUS ANNAEUS (4 B.C.-65 A.D.). Before Seneca fell into disgrace with Emperor Nero and was forced to commit suicide, he was generally considered, as Elder Pliny said, "the leader in letters and in government"; he was Nero's prime minister. The tragedies he wrote inspired dramatic authors until the days of Queen Elizabeth of England, Louis XIV of France and Napoleon I. Calling himself a Stoic, Seneca wrote treatises on the natural sciences, psychology and moral questions. He was a prominent jurist, and was acknowledged by his contemporaries to be an authority on geology, meteorology and marine zoology. The rise of Christianity was by no means detrimental to Seneca's fame and influence. He was said to have exchanged letters with Paul the Apostle; but these letters, often quoted, were evidently forged. Although the fathers of the Church knew that Seneca was no Christian, they highly appreciated his moral doctrines. So did later Christian philosophers and theologians until Thomas à Kempis. However, it was the age of the Renaissance that enhanced Seneca's importance to Western civilization. His Stoicism penetrated into the minds of Montaigne, Rabelais, Bacon, Shakespeare, Ben Jonson, Corneille and Racine, Milton and Dryden. Even in the 19th century he attracted poets like Wordsworth and thinkers like Emerson.

The Dying Seneca
(Painting by Giordano, Pinakothek, Munich)

Epictetus

EPICTETUS

EPICTETUS (c. 60-110). The son of a slave, himself crippled by a brutal master, Epictetus was legally emancipated and became the example of an upright, independent, free man. Often, when men were afflicted by misfortune, they declined religious consolation and read the *Encheiridion* (Manual) to regain peace of mind. The manual was not written by the Stoic philosopher, Epictetus, but by his faithful disciple Arrian (a military commander and important dignitary of the Roman Empire) who had made notes on his teacher's psychological observations, moral meditations, lectures, and conversations. About half the original manual is extant.

Epictetus was born in Phrygia, Asia Minor. He was sold to one of the retinue of Emperor Nero. He was allowed to attend the lectures of the Stoic philosopher Caius Musonius Rufus whom he greatly admired. From Musonius he learned how to make theoretical discussions personal confessions. When Musonius died (81), Epictetus, who by this time had been freed from slavery, held philosophical lectures in Rome. Emperor Domitian, who disliked freedom of expression, banished Epictetus (90) and all other philosophers from the capital. Epictetus went to Nicopolis, in Epirus, Greece, where among the members of his large audience was the future Emperor Hadrian. He also exerted considerable influence over Emperor Marcus Aurelius; the latter's views almost consistently agreed with those of Epictetus. Epictetus taught that reason governed the world and was identical with God. Sometimes he paralleled Christian doctrines. He mentioned the "Galileans"; praised their courage, but maintained that they were devoid of reason. His work, expressed in simple and frank language, attracted many thinkers of later centuries, notably Montaigne and Kant.

AURELIUS, MARCUS ANTONINUS

AURELIUS, MARCUS ANTONINUS (121-180). While thousands cheered hysterically when the victorious gladiator plunged his sword into his vanquished opponent, a boy in the imperial box buried himself even deeper in a book on moral philosophy. The boy, an adopted son of Antoninus Pius, became Roman emperor in 161 A.D. Ascetic in his ways, his stoical outlook had been carefully nursed by excellent teachers, and he tried to apply it during his reign, turbulent though the times proved to be.

Like his foster father, he believed that no price was too great which might buy peace and good will. Never before in the Western world had a philosopher sat on the throne, none, surely, that had tried so consistently to extol the virtues of the intellect, none that dismissed pleasure and fought with righteous zeal the ignorance which is at the base of the fear, desire and sorrow that constitute the evil in this world. Even the Christians, whom he never understood and who suffered in consequence, acknowledged the saintliness of his character and could not help but admire his half agnostic, half faith-inspired belief in God or gods as the font of wisdom and power.

While the political situation worsened throughout the empire which was no longer protected by Roman armies but by foreign armed bands, while his adoptive brother, Lucius Verus, wasted himself and the empire's opportunities in debauchery in the East, while Rome was gripped in the Oriental plague and the Italian peninsula threatened by the Marcomanni, throughout all this Antoninus remained true to himself. He honored his faithless, scheming wife, Faustina, by consecrating a temple to her at Halala where she died and one at Rome, and by establishing a foundation for poor girls. Her damning letters he nobly burned unread.

His best-known work, the *Meditations,* this emperor-saint wrote on the battlefield. His life and writings show Stoicism at its best although he was judged wanting in ability to cope with empire problems where force was deemed necessary for their successful solution.

Marcus Aurelius with His Wife and Son

Marcus Aurelius
(British Museum)

SEXTUS EMPIRICUS

SEXTUS EMPIRICUS (About 200 A.D.) The writings of Sextus Empiricus are an arsenal of scepticism which has furnished pagan thinkers with weapons to combat Christianity, Christian apologists with arguments to refute paganism, and, in later centuries, philosophers like Montaigne with reasons in defense of the independence of their minds on dogmatism of any kind.

Sextus, a physician by profession, was not so much an original thinker as an informed popularizer, a skilful and vigorous writer, who was able to summarize his thoughts by striking formulas. He attacked not only dogmatic philosophers and theologians but any expert, whether of mathematics or grammar, who claimed infallibility. In this way he has also given highly valuable information about the history of various sciences such as they had developed in his time.

PLOTINUS

PLOTINUS (205-270). Despite careful inquiries and heated controversies, no satisfying answer has been given to the question as to whether or not Plotinus possessed a real knowledge of the religion and philosophy of India to which his own teachings bear surprising analogies. It is, however, certain that Plotinus was eager to study the wisdom of India. For that purpose he participated in Emperor Gordianus' campaign against Persia.

At any rate, Plotinus seems to be nearer to the spirit of India than any other thinker of the Mediterranean civilization. His doctrine that the reality perceived by the senses is a dispersion and degradation of the true Reality, conceived by Plotinus as the Trinity of the One, the *Nous* (Spirit) and the Soul, seems as much of Hindu origin as his advice that asceticism and ecstasy lead to wisdom. But, on the other hand, Saint Augustine was not entirely wrong in saying that Plotinus, in order to become a Christian, would have to change "only a few words." In fact, Christian theology and philosophy of the Middle Ages adopted many of Plotinus' thoughts. So did European mysticism and romanticism up to the present day.

Plotinus, notwithstanding the resemblance to, or affinity with, India and Christianity, persisted in honoring the gods of pagan Greece. Born in Egypt, he was the disciple of Ammonius Saccas who had been converted from Christianity to paganism, and, in all probability, also studied the works of the Jewish philosopher Philo. From 245 until his death, Plotinus taught philosophy in Rome. He was consulted more than once by Emperor Gallienus. His disciples followed him with a religious devotion. Plotinus is also highly esteemed as a keen psychologist and a refined aesthete.

Plotinus

111

Boethius, Epo. I.C.

Philosophy consoles the incarcerated Boethius
(from Thirteenth Century German Musica Aldersbacher)

BOETHIUS

BOETHIUS (475-524). It was while Boethius was rigorously confined to prison, awaiting execution, that he expressed in writing his meditations of his own fate and the destiny of mankind. For years he had served as minister to King Theodoric, the Goth. He fought corruption and, as a result, aroused the hostility of many depraved dignitaries who finally succeeded in making Theodoric believe that Boethius was a traitor in the service of the Byzantine emperor. The false accusations caused Boethius to be sentenced without trial.

The vicissitudes of his life led Boethius to consider the general problem of whether fortune or divine providence governed the world. His *De Consolatione Philosophiae*, which contains his thoughts while imprisoned, has been translated into almost every European language. It asserts that man is superior to the blind forces of nature; that the power of fortune, affecting the practical affairs of mankind, is irrelevant; and that Providence is infinite. Many persons of considerable achievement, such as Dante, Chaucer, and Queen Elizabeth, have found that the writings of Boethius enabled them to face life with courage and renewed confidence whenever they were beset by doubts or alarmed by the mystery of the future.

112

The Beginning of Christianity

CHRISTIANITY IN PHILOSOPHY

Christianity plays not only a major but a dominant role in the philosophy of the Western world. While Western philosophy had its origins in Judaism and Hellenism, only a few hundred years after the beginning of our era it was overtaken and overwhelmed by the power of Christian concepts. To this day Christianity remains the most powerful element in philosophical thought.

The origins of Christianity are historically rather obscure, and we still rely mainly upon the Gospels, especially the synoptics, for Jesus' biography, or shall I rather say, hagiography.

This Jew, Joshua ben Joseph, in Roman-dominated Galilee, preached a wondrous sermon of Jewish revival. He undoubtedly considered himself a prophet of the Lord, come, as he said, to fulfill the Torah and not to destroy it. He was a deeply pious Jew who closely observed the precepts of Moses; and the teachings of Joshua (or as he was later referred to by the Greek equivalent, Jesus) reflect the wisdom of the ancient Hebrew at his best. In the then turbulent Judea, Jesus desired appeasement of the Roman conquerors and dedication to a spiritual unity with God.

Soon many followed the young Jesus whom they considered Messiah, the anointed, or as the Greeks called him, Christos. After his death and the disappearance of

"The Son of Man" ("Temptation in the Wilderness" by Kramskoy)
(American Museum of Photography, Phila.)

his body, the Jew Saul, known as Paul, the Jew Simon, known as Peter, and other Jewish apostles and followers traveled through the Roman realm proclaiming the gospel of the Messiah, the Son of God who took flesh upon himself to save the world from sin and from death through his suffering. They founded the great church which Jesus had proclaimed the depository and guardian of truth eternal.

The main doctrine of Christianity, which is accepted as a dogma not only by all Catholic and Eastern Orthodox Christians, but by the principal Protestant churches, is that God is one in essence but subsists eternally in three equal and perfect persons—Father, Son and Holy Spirit.

While the fundament of Jesus' Messianism was the simple as well as grandiose Mosaic principle, "Thou shalt love thy God with all thy heart, with all thy mind, and all thy soul, and love thy neighbor as thyself," the questions of fundamentalism and heresy have led to multifarious struggles and wars over the past two thousand years. Catholics as well as Protestants have perpetrated inhuman acts of torture upon each other, upon heretics, upon believers, upon infidels, upon doubters, upon deviates, and upon the orthodox.

Based upon the teachings of a man from whose lips came but pearls of wisdom and rubies of kindness, the history of Christianity is a sad book to peruse.

But with this all, in Judaism as well as Christianity, philosophy has found its way to the hearts and minds of great thinkers who, with skill and insight, evolved their philosophical systems within the framework of a dominant faith.

Aramaic, the vernacular in which Jesus preached his sermons

St. Paul Preaching at Athens (Raphael, Tapestry Design)
(Victoria and Albert Museum, London)

Constantine

The legendary conversion of the Talmudic student, Saulus, to belief in Jesus as Messiah of the Hebrews. After his conversion to the new faith, which he at first limited to Jews only, he undertook the gigantic task of proselytizing Messianism (Christianity) throughout the Roman Empire

(Woodcut, 1515)

The battle of 312 between Constantine and Maxentius and other adversaries, in which Constantine won, according to legend, through the miraculous sign of the cross. Himself a convert, in 324 he proclaimed Christianity the state religion of the whole Roman Empire, simultaneously destroying the vestiges of all other faiths

(Raphael)

The Dark Era of Knowledge
Early Christians

Justin Martyr
(Library of Congress)

Clement of Alexandria
(Library of Congress)

JUSTIN MARTYR

JUSTIN MARTYR (About 110-165). The earliest defense of Christianity against paganism using philosophical arguments was written by Justin, who later suffered a martyr's death in Rome. Justin's *Apologies* is also of interest because it describes Christian worship as it was performed in early times, refutes accusations against members of the Christian community and tries to convince pagan philosophers by using their own terms. Justin, who was born in the Samaritan town of Flavia Neapolis, the old Shechem which had been destroyed by Vespasian in 67 A.D. and which is called Nablus today, probably was not of Samaritan but of pagan descent. Evidently he had studied pagan philosophy before his conversion, and acquired, if not profound knowledge, a fluency of style and ability in using philosophical terms. Justin also had a controversy with a Jewish scholar on which he reported in his *Dialogue with Tryphon*. Tryphon probably was a real person, known as Tarfon the Tanna, who was opposed to Christianity, but who died before Justin was grown up.

CLEMENT OF ALEXANDRIA

CLEMENT OF ALEXANDRIA (c. 150-215 A.D.). The pagan philosopher, Celsus, one of the most ardent opponents of Christianity, noticed (c. 150 A.D.) that the dispersed Christian communities were tending toward a closer organization, toward a unified doctrine and common acceptance of a canon of sacred scriptures, and toward a uniformity in their methods of interpretation. What Celsus apprehended was the early formation of a Church that claimed to be Catholic. The first spiritual representative of that Church was Clement. He was also the father of Christian apologetics based upon a faith in divine revelation, but adapted to philosophical concepts. These prevail unto modern days. He adapted the *Philo* (the general concepts of the Jews) to the aims and needs of the nascent Christian Church, although the details of his system of defense of Christianity more closely paralleled the theology of the Stoics. He is principally remembered as the creator of Christian apologetics, but the other doctrines he enunciated were not permanently accepted by the Church.

Origen

Tertullian
(Library of Congress)

TERTULLIAN

Prior to his conversion to Christianity, he traveled extensively through Egypt, Italy, Syria, and Palestine. He was initiated into the mysteries of Eleusis; imbued with the Gnostic spirit, and with the pre-Christian doctrines of salvation which were rooted in Oriental mysticism and integrated with Greek philosophy. He was well acquainted with the books of the Bible, including those which were not incorporated into the canon, and he was well versed in pagan philosophy. His books, *Protrepticus* (Exhortations), *Paidagogus,* and *Stromateis* (Carpet-Bags), were appeals to both educated Christians and pagans. He stated that the simple Christian faith was sufficient for the salvation of man and promised greater knowledge to those who were initiated with Christian philosophy. Logos, not God nor Christ, was the centrifugal point of his teachings. He defined faith as obedience to the reason of Logos. He maintained that philosophy did not make faith a verity but opened the way to complete safety from error, and strengthened the élan toward the deity. He promised pagans deification if they adopted the Christian faith.

TERTULLIAN (About 165-220). At the age of forty, Tertullian, the son of a Roman army officer, was converted to Christianity and became its most ardent apologist. Living during the reigns of emperors Septimius Severus and Caracalla, he courageously protested against the cruelties committed by the magistrates and against the excesses of the mob against Christians, but he was equally prepared to recommend violence against any adversary of his new coreligionists in case persuasion did not help. His works, of which, besides the *Apology,* thirty-three are extant, exhibit fervor, zealotism, knowledge of his times and of past history, and an extremely aggressive spirit. Tertullian was untiring in expressing his contempt of pagan philosophers. To him faith was above reason, and logical contradiction a means to refutation of creed. His saying *Credo quia absurdum est,* however, is often quoted in a sense which its author did not mean. For twenty years, Tertullian intervened in every controversy concerning Christian doctrine. He introduced, in his book *Adversus Praxean,* the term *Trinitas* into the Latin language in order to signify the one God in three persons, although he did not live to see the dogma of the Trinity firmly established. With uncompromising rigor he fought aggressively against Jews, pagans, heretics and secular authorities. He eagerly objected to second marriages and branded Christians who held offices in the imperial administration or did military service. Further, he could not tolerate Christian artists. However in his last years, Tertullian, with ascetic leanings adhering to the sect of Montanists, became himself a heretic.

Origen's Homiliae in Lucam
(Corpus Christi College, Cambridge)

St. Augustine Lecturing on Philosophy
(Painting by Gozzoli)

ORIGEN

ORIGEN (185-253). While Clement of Alexandria is considered the father of Christian apologetics, his pupil Origen has been called the creator of Christian theology. But Origen was not only Clement's disciple; he was also taught by the pagan philosopher Ammonius Saccas, Plotinus' teacher. Origen tried to integrate the Christian faith into a comprehensive explanation of the universe, such as was adopted by Platonism and Stoicism, but he also leaned toward Neo-Platonism which was nascent during his lifetime. He was one of the greatest scholars who ever lived, whose *Hexapla,* the juxtaposition of versions of the Bible in six columns, was of great consequence to the criticism and exegesis of the Bible. He wrote a defense of Christianity *Against Celsus* which, however, was condemned by later orthodox Catholics as containing inadmissible concessions to paganism, and *On Principles,* a treatise on systematic theology which has been preserved in a Latin translation by Rufinus. In the fourth century, the number of Origen's works was estimated at about six thousand.

Origen lived a life of complete asceticism, having castrated himself. While orthodox Catholics continued to suspect him of heresy, the condemnation of his views by the Bishop of Alexandria was more than once confirmed. Protestant theologians and secular historians have always been sympathetically attracted to him whose soul lived in harmony with the course of nature and in confidence in the divine Logos, firm in his unselfish love of God and of his fellow men, longing for the return to the heavenly world of spirit which he conceived, in accordance with Plato, as behind and superior to the temporal world.

Many problems stemming from the doctrine of emanation or the eschatology of the Orphics and various Gnostics have been introduced into Christian thinking by Origen. Some of them became the cause of schism and heresy, while others contributed to the definite formation of the dogma of the Trinity.

St. Augustine Being Entrusted to the Grammarian
(Painting by Gozzoli)

St. Augustine Leaves Rome for Milan
(Painting by Gozzoli)

St. Augustine Reading the Epistles of St. Paul
(Painting by Gozzoli)

St. Augustine Arriving in Italy
(Painting by Gozzoli)

AURELIUS AUGUSTINUS
(Saint Augustine)

AURELIUS AUGUSTINUS (SAINT AUGUSTINE) (354-430). Born in Tagaste, near Carthage, North Africa, Augustine was the son of a pagan father and a pious Christian mother, Monica (who was later canonized). By the time he was thirty-three, he had embraced Christianity, although much earlier he had been an adherent of Manichaeism and scepticism. Shortly after his conversion, he was ordained, and from 395 until his death he served as bishop of Hippo, North Africa. He died when the Vandals besieged his episcopal town.

Living in the period of the disintegration of the Roman Empire, Augustine, through his writings, contributed much to strengthening the position of the Christian church. He defended its established doctrines against heretical attacks, and gave it a philosophy of ethics, metaphysics, and a lasting philosophy of history. His writings show him to have been trained in rhetoric, a sincere confessor, a man of both passion and serenity, and humble, though in an authoritative position.

His works deal with the problems of divine omnipo-

tence, predestination, God, the Trinity, and creation. They consistently affirm that the Catholic Church is the only reliable guide of human reason; that founded by Christ, it practices His teachings. In addition to hundreds of sermons and pamphlets, most of which are devoted to the refutation of heresy, he made world-wide lasting contributions to the history of philosophy and literature. His major works are: *Expositio Fideis Christianae* (397); *De Trinitate* (c. 416); a commentary on *Genesis* the first parts of which were published in 414; *De Civitate Dei;* and *Confessiones.* He spent the years from 410 to 427 in writing *The City of God* (De Civitate Dei). In this work, he enunciated the famous doctrine of the four epochs of human history, a doctrine that was impressed upon the consciousness of Western civilization until the time of Hegel and Comte. However, it is not the originality of his ideas but the profundity of psychological analysis that makes Augustine a great figure in the history of philosophy. His autobiographical *Confessions* has been regarded for many centuries as a manual of self-analysis. His influence, though immeasurable, is especially notable in the teachings of Luther, Pascal, Descartes, and Leibniz.

St. Augustine at Prayer
(Prado Museum)

An Early Edition of The City of God

ALCUIN, FLACCUS ALBINUS

ALCUIN, FLACCUS ALBINUS (c. 735-804). Well-known as a teacher, poet, and monastic, Alcuin achieved his greatest fame as the educator of Charlemagne. The emperor probably met him on his journeys through Italy. Alcuin had returned to Parma from England because of a declining interest in education there, and when Charlemagne invited him to take charge of his court school, the Schola Palatina, he gladly accepted. There, and later at Tours, where he had been given the monastery of St. Martin, Alcuin lived the life of a teacher, always abreast of the literary developments of the period. According to him, he "dispensed the honey of the Holy Scripture, intoxicated his students with the wine of ancient learning, fed them the apples of grammatical refinement, and adorned them with the knowledge of astronomy."

The erudition of Charlemagne is directly traceable to the influence of his versatile teacher. Alcuin was a lover of poetry, and wrote quite acceptable hexameters. But posterity remembers him best as a great letter writer; more than three hundred of his letters have been preserved. Each was written to a distinguished friend, addressed either by some name which characterized the recipient, or a Latin paraphrase of the real name. They are still interesting for their philosophical content as well as for their references to historic events.

120

Alcuin and Charlemagne

Gerbert of Aurillac (Pope Sylvester II) (940?-1003), one of the greatest scholars of his century. A master of the seven liberal arts, he excelled in the knowledge of the quadrivium—logic, mathematics, astronomy and music

ERIUGENA, JOHANNES SCOTUS

ERIUGENA, JOHANNES SCOTUS (c. 815-877). The translator of Pseudo-Dionysius from Greek to Latin adopted Neo-Platonism and tried to reconcile this with Christianity. He regarded Church doctrine as dynamic and therefore attempted an original approach to religion and philosophy. For this heresy, he narrowly escaped persecution.

He asserted that there was only one reality, namely God, who created all things by emanation and to whom all creatures return. In his principal work, *On the Division of Nature,* he stated that God emanates nature in four forms: the highest is God himself, who creates but is not created; then there are those which are created and create; those which are created but do not create, and finally God again, who rests neither created nor creating. Eriugena declined to speculate on God's attributes. He declared: "God is not a *that* but a that." True religion and true philosophy are identical. Both of them rest upon the unity of God who is not subject to necessity but creates by his own free will. Man is a microcosmos with his own unique soul, but in the last analysis "all our souls are but one soul." His concept of the dogma of Trinity is more similar to Plotinus' triad than it is to the doctrine of the Church. Eriugena also wrote about predestination, reducing this concept to a vagueness which makes it little different from free will. Although he never claimed that he was an independent thinker, he actually was. At any rate, he succeeded in fitting what were apparently his personal thoughts within the framework of accepted doctrines. His influence was greater with the mystics than it was with the logicians of the later Middle Ages. An Irish monk, he had mastered Greek and Latin, and was responsible for the revival of philosophical thought which had remained dormant in Western Europe after the death of Boethius. He taught at the royal palace school of Charles the Bald of France and was often entrusted by him to settle theological disputes.

Doctores Scholastici

Anselm, Archbishop of Canterbury

William II of England appoints St. Anselm Archbishop of Canterbury (1093)

ANSELM OF CANTERBURY, SAINT

ANSELM OF CANTERBURY, SAINT (1033-1109). A prominent figure in the struggle for power (in this period) between the secularists and ecclesiastics, Anselm was of even greater importance as a Christian philosopher. Although he was not a Scholastic, this school of church philosophy embodied many of his concepts.

Anselm, first as abbot and later as archbishop, defended the authority of the Pope to William Rufus and Henry I, kings of England. This resulted in his exile. But regardless of whether he was living in poverty or splendor, he always maintained an ascetic existence. His monastic life of contemplation and meditation was frequently interrupted by political activity.

His philosophy, largely a justification of Church practices and dogma, was publicized because he felt its posi-

tion needed strengthening. He was convinced that the comprehension of divine truth was the result of faith, not reason. He stated that believing is a necessary condition of knowledge, and that in order to believe, one need not probe. In his most famous book, *Cur Deus Homo* (Why Did God Become Man), he tried to answer questions concerning the doctrine of man's redemption. He stated that man is created for an immortal life but is frustrated by sin, and that the Messiah has the power of redemption because His virginal birth excludes Him from the inheritance of sin. His theory of atonement and satisfaction has determined Christian thought and piety throughout the centuries. Anselm is held responsible for the ontological argument for the existence of God. This thesis, elaborated in his *Monologium,* was accepted by theologians and such eminent philosophers as Descartes and Leibniz.

Peter Abailard

Abailard installs his mistress Héloïse as abbess of the Convent of the Paraclete

ABAILARD, PETER

ABAILARD, PETER (1079-1142). Abailard's life is a portrait of the triumphs and vicissitudes of philosophy, faith, and love. He was born in a little town in Brittany, and having been ordained as priest, returned there to tutor Héloïse, the niece of Canon Fulbert. His secret love affair with her, and Astrolabius, the son she bore him, caused him considerable misfortune, for when the canon discovered the secret relationship he had the priest physically mutilated. Abailard persuaded Héloïse to take the veil: he himself retired to a quiet place near Troyes.

His disciples, however, sought him out, and once again the handsome, eloquent schoolman attracted students from all over Europe. He established an oratory called the Paraclete. His subtle argumentation persuaded his listeners to found their beliefs on reason. He tabulated the contradictions of the Bible and the Church Fathers for easy reference; he made freedom of the will the basis of all ethics; he opposed the teachings of the famous schoolmen, and expounded those concepts which hold that the Aristotelian precepts, called universals, in scholastic philosophy (such as genus and species), have only intellectual significance.

The story of his "calamities" (he wrote a book by that title) was never-ending. His interpretation of the Trinity was twice condemned as heretical. Finally, weary of the fight, he burned his book on the Trinity and lived out his life, a subdued follower of the faith. Upon his death Héloïse, twenty-one years younger than he, claimed his body and buried him. The ashes of both lovers now rest at the Père-Lachaise in Paris.

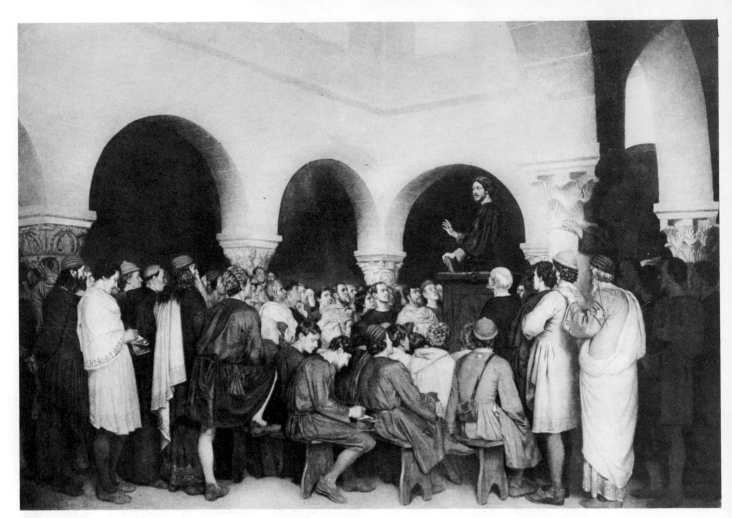

Sermon by Abailard
(Painting by Steinhiel)

ROSCELLIN

ROSCELLIN (About 1050-1120). The war waged by Roscellin against Platonism and every kind of realism is interesting because it induced him to adumbrate a criticism of language which impresses one as most modern. Proceeding from the statement that in nature only individuals exist and species are not things, Roscellin has inquired into the generalizing character of words and language. In 1092 he was accused of adhering to Tritheism, i.e., that he conceived of the Trinity as of three distinct deities. He denied such a doctrine but later returned to it. Roscellin taught at the schools of several French towns. Among his pupils was Abailard who later criticized him. Roscellin's thoughts are known to us only by quotations which his adversaries made. Of all his writings only a letter to Abailard is extant.

LOMBARD, PETER

LOMBARD, PETER (About 1100-1160). For more than two centuries, Peter Lombard's *Four Books of Sentences* has been used as the chief textbook by students of theology. Born in the town of Lumello in Lombardy, Peter became a professor of theology at the Cathedral School of Notre Dame, Paris, and in 1159, he was Bishop of Paris. He was associated with St. Bernard and the teacher of Abailard, his later adversary.

He thought little of logic and epistemology. According to him, human knowledge is bound to remain fragmentary, but true knowledge is higher than faith which, on its part, is higher than opinion. The tenets of metaphysics are to be verified by the study of the Holy Scriptures and thereupon defended by "Catholic reason." In order to offer his pupils a reliable basis for disputations, he compiled his collection of *Sentences* from the Fathers and early teachers of the Church.

St. Bernard of Clairvaux
(Painting by El Greco)

Page from Albertus Magnus' De Animalibus

BERNARD OF CLAIRVAUX, SAINT

BERNARD OF CLAIRVAUX, SAINT (1091-1153). "The visionary of the century" was the way Bernard characterized himself, for he felt that he had been selected by God to guide Christianity along the right paths. He sincerely tried to lead the life of a saint, although he was cognizant of those temptations that led men astray. An objective observer, John of Salisbury, noticed that he often lost his temper and behaved unjustly, and Bishop Otto of Freising, a pious church member, accused him of jealousy and habitual weaknesses. Bernard asserted that his inner life was based on the stages of the ascent of his soul toward God, and upon supernatural grace. His book *De Gradibus Humilitatis et Superbiae* (published c. 1121) established him as the founder of Christian mysticism of the Middle Ages. Here, he condemned the acquisition of knowledge for merely the sake of knowledge. To him knowledge is only justified when it promotes the purification of the soul and leads it toward union with God. Humility is the basic condition for this union, and it, in turn, engenders love. He stated that there are twelve degrees of

humility—the highest constitutes the cognition of truth, and this is identical with union with God. This stage is psychologically characterized as the extinction of all sensitive life, but it does not remove the essential difference between man, a finite being, and God. With this reservation, Bernard's philosophy separates him from the monism of later mystics.

Bernard excelled as an ecclesiastical ruler, as the organizer of a monastic order, as an irresistibly persuasive orator and an experienced administrator. As abbot of the monastery at Clairvaux, he was incapable of imposing his will on popes, kings, and emperors, but his ascendancy over the masses was unfailing. However, shortly before his death, the terrible disasters of the Second Crusade took place. Because he had agitated for this crusade with all his power, its failure aroused doubt and opposition. His abhorrence of knowledge for the sake of knowledge made him a grim adversary of Abailard and Gilbert de la Porée. He succeeded in persecuting the former, but was defeated in his controversy with the latter. Bernard wrote many sermons, epistles, and hymns.

ALBERTVS. MAGNVS.

Page from Works of Albertus Magnus
(Edition of 1477)

ALBERTUS MAGNUS

ALBERTUS MAGNUS (1193-1280). Considered the first representative of humanism during the Middle Ages, Albertus Magnus was born in Germany, a descendant of the Count of Bollstadt in Bavaria. He was educated in Padua and Bologna. Endowed with an encyclopedic mind, he was rightly called "Doctor Universalis."

His reputation as a professor of theology at the University of Paris was known throughout Europe, and he was highly esteemed as a scholar of Arab and Jewish philosophy (studies which had been encouraged under the influence of Emperor Frederick II). In fact, no other Christian scholar of the Middle Ages quoted as many Jewish philosophers as did Albertus. He learned much from Solomon ibn Gabirol's *Fons Vitae* (Source of Life), although he recognized that this book was not in accordance with the accepted precepts of philosophy.

In physics and cosmology, he was a disciple of Maimonides. As a trained scientist he stressed the importance of observation and experiment. Interested in the study of metals and inorganic elements, Albertus is perhaps best remembered as a scientist for his observation of the comet in 1240 and for his contributions to experimental science.

In 1223, Albertus entered the Dominican Order, despite the protestations of his former teachers. He believed in the defense of knowledge for its intrinsic value, and that philosophy was an integral part of that knowledge, rather than an accessory study. He maintained that his essential ideas were best expressed in his theological works. He was more the compiler than the systematic thinker, the commentator rather than the creator of constructive and consistent philosophies. Although he always presented a speculative philosophy with great clarity, he never succeeded in integrating contemporary philosophies into Christian thought.

He taught at Cologne from 1248 to 1254 and after served as Bishop of Ratisbon for two years. His most famous pupil was Thomas Aquinas, and they were devoted friends until Aquinas' death in 1274. One of Albertus' last works was written in defense of his former pupil.

BONAVENTURA, SAINT

BONAVENTURA, SAINT (1221-1274). John Fidanza was born in Tuscany in 1221, and, in 1240, he entered the Order of Franciscans, where he was renamed Fra Bonaventura. He studied with Alexander of Hales in Paris, and later became a teacher of theology. In 1255 he was excluded from the University of Paris because he supported Aquinas in a dispute, but was readmitted in 1257 and elected general of the Franciscan Order. He became a cardinal in 1273, and died in 1274 at the Council of Lyons. Bonaventura, called "Doctor Seraphicus," was canonized in 1482.

A complex personality, Bonaventura was a philosopher, mystic, and dogmatic theologian. He was never a radical thinker, for he was too fond of tradition, too cautious and adverse to controversy, even though he was involved in several. He definitely formulated Franciscan doctrine, but he has been accused of having been greatly influenced by Aquinas and the Dominicans.

Bonaventura's mystical writings were of considerable influence. His central theme concerned the study of God. He stated that man possesses an imperfect but very certain knowledge of the supreme being. His path of thought

St. Bonaventura as a Child Presented to St. Francis
(Painting by Berrera the Elder)

Albertus Preaching in Paris

St. Bonaventura

St. Bonaventura shows St. Thomas the Crucifixion
(*Painting by Zurbarán*)

proceeds from stable faith, to reason,˙ and then to contemplation. Knowledge, derived from human science, is differentiated from mystical knowledge, which is the work of divine grace. His *Itinerarium Mentis* (Journey of the Mind) describes seven stages of ascent, three of which are the result of imagination, reason, and memory; at the fourth stage supernatural grace intervenes. The seventh stage provides knowledge of the Trinity, and is described as a psychological experience of speechless ecstasy. His doctrine of human knowledge is voluntaristic. Knowledge is a spontaneous activity which stems from God and is directed toward God. It beholds the world as a symbol which mirrors divine beauty. Knowledge for its own sake is branded as error. World opinion may consider philosophy great, but in the light of the Christian faith, it is of little value. Bonaventura established the concrete image of the world in accordance with Platonism, corrected by the idea of Biblical omnipotence. He did not consider Plato as the representative of wisdom, nor Aristotle as the representative˙of science. But he viewed Augustine as the manifestation of holy inspiration, and his teachings as the correct guide to human knowledge. The imagery of Bonaventura's prose creates a more lasting impression than does the originality of his thoughts.

St. Thomas Aquinas

Allegory of the Catholic Religion
(Painting by Andrea da Firenza, Metropolitan Museum of Art)

AQUINAS, THOMAS

AQUINAS, THOMAS (1225-1274). Recognized as the leading philosopher of the Roman Catholic Church, Aquinas' authority was officially established by Pope Leo XIII in the encyclical *Aeterni Patris* (1879).

All non-Catholic philosophers and historians regard the doctrines promulgated by Aquinas as the quintessence of the Scholastic spirit of the Middle Ages. He surpassed all Christian predecessors in his ability to deal with the crucial problems of reason and faith by mediating variant tendencies within the Church and systematizing its theology so that it was consistent and precise.

Aquinas subordinated philosophy to theology; natural law to the revelations of Christ; human society to the dogma of the Church. He endeavored to demonstrate that these subordinations benefit philosophy, natural law, and human society, and that the dignity of each of these is reinforced in its subordination to theology. Aquinas tried to show that reality has value because it is created by God. For this reason he opposed Averroism because it rejected the theological control of philosophy; and Platonism because it depreciated the real world. He accepted Aristotelian philosophy because it was compatible with the doctrines of Christianity and met the desires and needs of human society. Many of his pronouncements were directly influenced by Jewish thinkers. His proof for the existence of God was adapted from Maimonides, and one of his proofs for the unity of God was taken from Bahya ibn Pakuda.

He was the son of the Count of Aquino, and a relative of the emperor, Frederick II. He was glorified as the "Doctor Angelicus," and, after his death, canonized as a saint.

Handwriting of Thomas Aquinas
(from Summa contra gentiles, 1262)

Detail of "Allegory of the Catholic Religion"

Medieval Manuscript

Detail of "Allegory of the Catholic Religion"

131

St. Thomas Aquinas in "Allegory of the Catholic Religion"

Duns Scotus

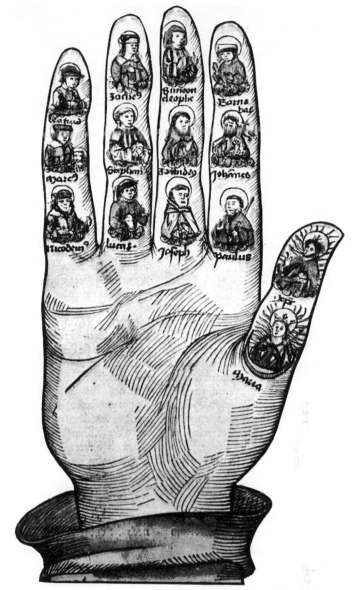

*An Ornamental Credo, from an Incunabula of
Nuremberg, 1491*

DUNS SCOTUS, JOHN

DUNS SCOTUS, JOHN (1270-1308). The popular identification of the words "dunce" and "blockhead," which were sanctioned by Alexander Pope's satiric poem, signifies the age-old contempt in which posterity has held the man who probably was born in the Scottish village of Duns. Although he was so famous and successful as a professor at Oxford that the numerous foreign students could not be accommodated in the town, and although he taught at Paris with even greater success, his name was disparaged by his opponents who, after his premature death, publicly burned his books and distorted the meaning of his doctrine. For Duns Scotus had dared to criticize Augustine and Aquinas, and had attempted to destroy their notions of matter, form and potency, the indispensable resources of Peripatetic philosophers. Victorious Thomism did not pardon this challenge, and imposed its prejudice against Duns Scotus on its opponents, namely, enlightenment.

But, since Charles S. Peirce adopted Duns Scotus' realism, more and more historians have become convinced that Duns Scotus is to be ranked among the great constructive thinkers. In the Middle Ages, Duns Scotus, the inveterate antagonist of Aquinas, was called "Doctor Subtilis." Now he is acknowledged to be not only subtle but vigorous. His insistence on demonstrative proof led him to a demarcation between rationalism and empiricism that has followers among recent philosophers. Instead of matter and form, he established the extremely modern concept of "haecceity," or principle of individuation, which is explained as ontological independence, singularity, or the undefinable quality of ultimate reality, anticipating ways of *Gestalt psychology, Gegenstands theory* and existentialism. Duns Scotus admitted that there is no science of the singular, but he maintained that this indicates only a limit of the human intellect, not of reality. His psychology is essentially voluntaristic. In several of his views, Duns Scotus was inspired by Solomon ibn Gabirol's *Fons Vitae* (Source of Life) which influenced many Franciscans, to whose order Duns Scotus belonged; however, he shows strong originality in their elaboration.

133

William of Ockham

NIKOLAUS VON KUES

DER VERBORGENE GOTT

Ein Gespräch zwischen einem Heiden
und einem Christen

Lateinisch und deutsch

Übertragung und Nachwort von Fritz Stippel

Erich Wewel Verlag · Freiburg im Breisgau

Title Page of The Hidden God *by Nicholas of Cusa, Dialogue Between a Pagan and a Christian*

OCKHAM, WILLIAM OF

OCKHAM, WILLIAM OF (1280-1348). No other Christian thinker of the Middle Ages rejected so many or such important assumptions which were prevalent in his times as did Ockham. His great aim was to teach men to think, and the result of his teachings was the elaboration of laic consciousness in the State, the reduction of the influence of the Church in human society, and the preparation for a new interpretation of the physical world. Although these results were counteracted by men and circumstances, Ockham must be considered as one of the principal agents of the dissolution of the Medieval synthesis of philosophy and theology. In the struggle between Pope John XXII and Emperor Louis of Bavaria, Ockham, collaborating with Marsilius of Padua, defended the rights of secular government against papal claims and contributed to the establishment of the modern political theory of the independence of the state from the church.

In his philosophical works, Ockham proclaimed the primacy of logical method in all disciplines. He rejected all attempts to evade reason but he restricted the range of reason. His epistemology destroyed any relation between knowledge of the universe and knowledge of God. He especially pronounced animosity against all those who claimed to know the psychology of God. He even maintained that monotheism can be derived only from the prime being and not from the prime efficient cause. He rejected Thomist ontology and Augustine's belief in eternal ideas which constitute the archetypes of the universe in the depth of divine essence, and he flatly denied the usefulness and truth of the speculations of all the great Doctors of the Church. He also held ethics to be independent of metaphysics.

In the struggle about universals, Ockham sided with those who held that universality can be attributed only to terms and propositions, not to things. But his interests did not center on this problem. To him, intuition of the singular is the basis of all concepts which are signs of the real. Science has to verify the signs. All existing things depend on God's absolutely free will. All secondary causality is indemonstrable. It is only a fact which science has to interpret. While the will of God is absolutely free, Man has the freedom of alternative choice. Will is an essential attribute of any reasoning creature.

Ockham's diction is very precise but lacks charm. He influenced Wycliffe and Erasmus. Luther borrowed some sentences from him, but would have repudiated his principal doctrines had he known them.

Nicholas of Cusa

CUSA, NICHOLAS OF

CUSA, NICHOLAS OF (1401-1464). Nicholas Krebs, the son of a poor boatman, was born in Cues à Moselle, France. He rose to become bishop and cardinal, and distinguished himself as a mystical theologian, jurist, and diplomat. He was educated by the Brethren of the Common Life at Deventer, Holland, and studied law, mathematics, astronomy, and theology at the Universities of Heidelberg, Padua, Rome and Cologne. He achieved great repute as a scholar and bibliophile, and was especially famous for his large collection of the manuscripts of Augustine and other authors of that period.

Although he was highly respected by the early Italian humanists, he remained, essentially, a scholastic Platonist. To some extent he was also influenced by Arabic and Jewish philosophy. His attempts to integrate metaphysics and mathematics were the result of numerous influences: the theosophical arithmetic of the Jewish Cabala; the *Zohar* or *Book of Splendor;* and the writings of Bonaventura (from whom he borrowed the term *"docta ignorantia").* Although he was interested in astronomy, he maintained that God, not the sun, was the center of the universe. He upheld the Ptolemaic system, even though he had adopted the views of Jewish and Arabic thinkers that the earth really did move.

Cusanus said that there were two directions which enabled the human spirit to arrive at the truth. The first was reason, whose realm was measureable; the second, intel-

Francisco Suarez (1548-1617). Spanish Jesuit theologian, known as Doctor Eximius. He taught philosophy at Avila and Segovia, and as a theologian taught also at Rome, Valladolid, Alcala, Salamanca and Coimbra. As a religious he was firmly devoted to prayer and mortification, and a tireless and humble worker

lect, whose objectives were infinite. Reason was solely a human activity wherein God could only be expressed by antinomies, that is by the coincidence of opposites, so that pure reason was compelled to conceive God, at one and the same time, as both a being and one who was not a being, or as an infinite circle. Intellect was understanding illuminated by faith. This activity had supernatural qualities which enabled God to be viewed as an absolute unity without finite proportions. Since God was infinite, he remained undefinable by the concepts of reason, and therefore generally remained ignored by reason; he was conceived without being comprehended. Cusanus conceived of God as the concentrated unity of all essences; the world as the multiple explications of Divine essences. He used the theory of emanation as the basis for this concept. The essence of God comprised not only all existing creation but all possible creation. Cusanus deviated from one of the principal tenets of Christianity by adopting a statement of William of Ockham that the earth was the peculiar place of death and corruption.

Mystics

Francis of Assisi (1182-1226). A wealthy soldier and bon vivant who became deeply ascetic and meditative after a mystical vision. Dedicated his life to humility and self-denial, sometimes known as "the poor little man"

St. Francis in Ecstasy
(*Painting by Bellini*)

Portrait of St. Francis, Said to Date from 1225
(Convent of Greccio)

Meeting of St. Francis and St. Dominic
(Painting by Fra Angelico, National Gallery, Washington)

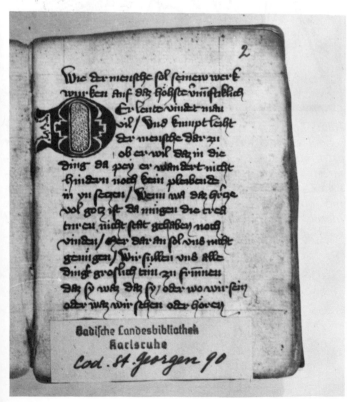

From Talks of the Differentiations, *an Early Eckhart Manuscript*

ECKHART, JOHANNES

ECKHART, JOHANNES (c. 1260-1327). "Wouldst thou be perfect, do not yelp about God." This sentence, uttered by Johannes Eckhart, characterized him as a man of deepest spirituality whose sermons utilized the Bible as an opportunity to lead his listeners to the oneness of God, to make them realize that the approach to God was through the self and silence. A Dominican monk, he rose to high office in the service of the Church. He was prior at Erfurt; vicar-provincial of Thuringia; provincial of Saxony; and vicar-general of Bohemia. A Master of Sacred Theology and Doctor of Divinity, he preached his "sweet doctrine" at the College of St. James, Paris, and in the nunneries of Strassburg and Cologne. Always welcome, he was reverently referred to as the "Holy Master Eckhart."

A "Brother of the Free Spirit," he differed markedly from the schoolmen and their arid teachings. His message paralleled the best of Hindu teachings in *Sankara Acharya*: that God is in every human being; nothing is apart from God, and the complete dissolution of all opposites and self-abandonment to Him constitutes salvation. In the early stages of the Inquisition his mystic teachings and symbolic interpretations were not opposed, but charges were preferred against him in 1327. He was unwilling to recant all his teachings and appealed to Rome. Pope John XXII issued a bull condemning the majority of his propositions as heretical and the rest as "ill-sounding, rash, and probably heretic." It was during that year that Eckhart died; however, official condemnation did not prevent his followers from clinging to his teachings.

Eckhart and Uta
(Figures at the Dome at Naumburg)

John Tauler (1300-1361), a Dominican mystic of the school of Meister Eckhart, whose life as a preacher is associated with the city of Strasbourg. He was mainly interested in the ethical aspects of mysticism and concentrated on an analytical intuition in his endeavor to grasp the imminent reality of God. He was a member of the loosely organized mystical group known as the Friends of God, and his Sermons *have lived on in many translations.*

Peter Canisius, a Jesuit who in 1543 edited the works attributed to Tauler

Birthplace of Henry Suso (c. 1295-1366), Uberlingen, Germany. Also a member of the Friends of God, Suso was a Dominican mystic whose Book of Heavenly Wisdom *interprets the approach of Eckhart in terms of the intensely passionate love lyric of the age of chivalry*

Thomas à Kempis

Skull of Thomas à Kempis

ANONYMOUS

AUTHOR OF THE IMITATION OF CHRIST, AN UN-KNOWN CARTHUSIAN MONK. Carlyle said about this work, "None, except the Bible, is so universally read and loved by Christians of all tongues and sects," a statement confirmed by all lovers of devotional literature. Whoever wrote the book described the trials and temptations, the joys of mystical intercourse with Christ, and the readiness to suffer with him. The debates about the author of this work began around 1430 and have continued up to the present day. For a long time, it was attributed to Thomas à Kempis (1380-1471), who signed a copy of his writing in 1441. But none of his other numerous books is comparable to the *Imitatio,* and the oldest extant manuscript was written in 1383 when Thomas à Kempis was three years old. However, he may be considered as the editor who improved the Latin phraseology. The assumption that the *Imitatio* is based upon the diaries of Gerard Root is also untenable. In all probability, the author was a Carthusian monk who, after many worldly experiences, composed this work, which has been described by Matthew Arnold as "the most exquisite document of Christian spirit after the New Testament."

Loyola Healing the Obsessed
(Painting by Rubens)

Ignatius Loyola (Inigo Lopez de Loyola) (1491-1556), founder of the Society of Jesus, or order of Jesuits, approved by papal bull in 1540. By 1523 his celebrated Spiritual Exercises *were substantially complete, and while a student at the University of Paris he planned the new religious order, mainly to counteract the Protestant Reformation. He governed it until his death in Rome*

Formation of the Society of Jesus
(Painting by Lindenschmidt)

Loyola Returns from Paris
(Stained Glass, Santa Casa, Loyola, Spain)

Conversion on a Sickbed
(Painting by A. Chevalier Tayler, Wimbleton, London)

Jesuits repulse the besiegers of a town

François de Sales (1567-1622), one of the "glad saints" of France and a leader in the Counter Reformation. Author of On the Love of God *and other mystical works*

Jacob Boehme
(Contemporary Painting)

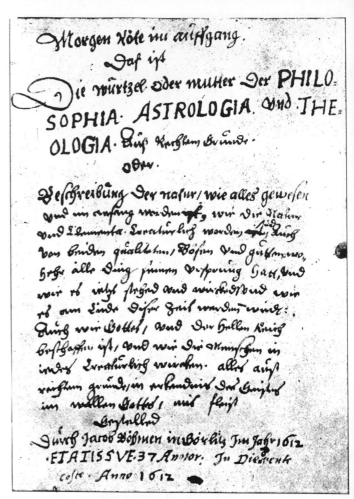

Manuscript of Boehme's Morgenröte, 1612

BOEHME, JACOB

BOEHME, JACOB (1575-1624). One day, Jacob Boehme, a shoemaker, turned from his work and stared at the cupboard, gazing at the reflection of a sunbeam on pewter. He interpreted this as the manifestation of divine truth, revealing the universe as the theater of an eternal conflict between spirit and matter. Boehme regarded matter as an embodiment of evil, but a necessary condition for the existence of all beings. Without its existence, even the divine spirit would evaporate. He thought that contemporary events reiterated and confirmed neo-Platonic and Gnostic ideas. Untiringly he contrasted his vision of the divine order with the reality he saw dominated by evil. His intrepid criticism of church and state, of economic exploitation and political oppression caused the authorities to charge him with heresy in 1612. His *Aurora* and other writings were interdicted. When Boehme tried to penetrate the mysteries of creation and salvation, his unschooled mind often appeared more confused than enlightened. He displayed a powerful originality, but became entangled in fallacies. His descriptions of the anxieties and temptations of the soul have interested many modern readers who dislike his metaphysical speculations. He exerted considerable influence among German romantics and mystics in France, Russia, England, and the United States.

Angelus Silesius (1624-1677), a convert to Catholicism, strongly influenced by Jacob Boehme. Author of numerous religious aphorisms and mystical maxims

Emmanuel Swedenborg

Swedenborg's Cottage, Stockholm

SWEDENBORG, EMANUEL

SWEDENBORG, EMANUEL (1688-1772). Emerson once remarked that it would require "a colony of men" to do justice to Swedenborg's work. Goethe adopted several of Swedenborg's ideas. Balzac founded essential views on human and cosmic nature on Swedenborg's doctrine. So have many modern authors. And today there are thousands of faithful Swedenborgians in Europe and America.

Until his fifty-third year, Swedenborg had been known as a great engineer, a scholar and a scientist. He had written important books on mathematics, mechanics, physiology and astronomy. Then he experienced a grave crisis. As a lad, he had already yearned to know God and had eagerly discussed theological questions with clergymen. In his advanced age he became more and more anxious about his spiritual conditions. He was deeply impressed by dreams in which he had visions. In 1757 he became convinced of having witnessed in one of his visions the Last Judgment. In his *Arcana Coelestia* (in 12 volumes, 1749-56) he offered a mystical interpretation of the first books of the Old Testament which, according to him, was purposely written to prevent profanation, and by exposing their true meaning, he developed his own religious and philosophical system.

Of fundamental importance to Swedenborg's system is his doctrine of correspondence, which, as he asserts, was known to the ancient peoples in Canaan, Chaldea, Syria and Egypt and since had been forgotten. Greek travelers who visited these countries misunderstood the doctrine and changed it into fabulous stories which, however, allow a reconstruction of the true sense. According to this doctrine, everything in our visible, natural or material world corresponds to something in the invisible, spiritual astral world. The total natural world corresponds to the spiritual world not only in general but in particular. Thus, everything in the natural world represents an idea.

Swedenborg distinguishes four styles in the world. The first, the style of the most ancient mankind which extends until Noah and the Flood, has been transcribed by Moses but has an offspring in the third style, the prophetic, while the second, the historic, extends from Abraham to the time of the kings of Judah and Israel. The fourth style, that of David's psalms, is mixed with the prophetic style and common speech. The restitution of the most ancient religion is Swedenborg's purpose. He claims to be sent by God to announce the end of the Christian and the beginning of the New Jerusalem dispensation. He recognizes Jesus Christ as Saviour but rejects the Christian doctrine of Trinity and excludes the Epistles of Paul from the Biblical Canon. God is one, both in essence and person. He is uncreated, eternal, infinite, omnipotent, the union of love and wisdom.

Related with the doctrine of correspondence is Swedenborg's doctrine of degrees. Man is a recipient of three degrees, and capable of thinking analytically and rationally of things within the sphere of nature, and of spiritual and celestial things above the natural sphere. At the highest degree, man may see God.

The Humanists

Marsilio Ficino (1433-1499), central figure of the Floren-
tine Academy. He was a promising Renaissance scholar
chosen by Cosimo de' Medici to head the Platonic cult
founded by Gemisthus Pletho. Ficino sought to use Pla-
tonism to urge the cultivated minds of the Renaissance to
espouse Christianity

Leonardo da Vinci (1452-1519), the dominant figure of
the Italian Renaissance. Student of natural, aesthetic and
scientific phenomena
(Self-portrait)

The Renaissance, or rebirth, of thought and crea-
tivity in the 15th and early 16th centuries in Europe
had an ever-lasting impact upon the western world.
The mainsprings of the new rising stream of cultural
activities are to be found in the influx of scholars and
artists fleeing Constantinople, the capital of the eastern Roman Empire sacked by the Janissaries; and,
on the other end of Europe, in the flight of the Spanish Jews from the terror of the Inquisitions. Within
the short period of less than a century, hundreds of
thousands of banner carriers of Hebrew and Greek
culture intermingled with the stolid, churchbound
population of continental Europe, bringing about a
deepening, as well as widening, of the Western
world's cultural horizon.

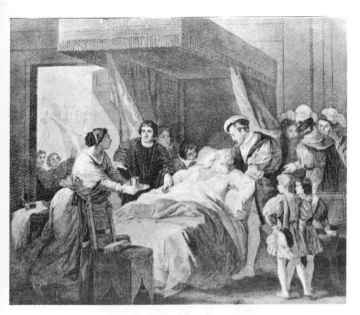

Leonardo's Deathbed, 1519

Niccolò Machiavelli

MACHIAVELLI, NICCOLÒ

MACHIAVELLI, NICCOLÒ (1469-1527). In private life it is never a compliment to anyone of whom it is said that he thinks or acts as a Machiavellian. Statesmen, philosophers of history and historians, on the other hand, have often discussed whether or not Machiavelli's principles are sound and of basic importance for political success, or even for public welfare at all.

Machiavelli's disciples have rarely been frank. King Frederick II of Prussia wrote a book opposing Machiavelli, but he practically adopted his views and acted in accordance with them. Mussolini was a great admirer of Machiavelli, but he would not allow his subjects to read his idol's work, *The Prince,* which was written in 1514 and dedicated to Lorenzo de' Medici, whose daughter, Queen Catherine of France, and one of the earliest disciples of the author, was responsible for the notorious Massacre of St. Bartholomew (1572) where the leaders of French Protestantism were murdered.

The Prince contains advice to sovereigns about how to become successful, how to obtain and maintain power, and, especially, how to render political adversaries harmless and to check a dissatisfied people. This advice was founded upon the author's knowledge of, or ideas on, the possibilities and limitations of human nature. Any moral standard is consciously eliminated. Reality, as Machiavelli saw it, is put above ideals. Success, as the end, has to justify the means. Man, especially the man of genius, was regarded by Machiavelli as an aesthetic phenomenon, and his struggle for existence and power seemed to him like a drama on the stage.

Since Machiavelli professed republicanism in other writings, and since he served the republican government of Florence, his native city, for fourteen years it has often been doubted whether he meant what he said in *The Prince.* Probably he was a republican in principle, but, in the actual situation of Italy at that time, Machiavelli, an ardent Italian patriot, built all his hopes upon a tyrant.

As a statesman, Machiavelli was a failure. As a philosopher, he was, to say the least, disputable. But he was a magnificent writer, and his work is, apart from its great influence, valuable as a document of the spirit, or, at least of a tendency, of the Renaissance.

Raymond Lully

Raymond Lully

LULLY, RAYMOND (Raymundus Lullus)

LULLY, RAYMOND (RAYMUNDUS LULLUS) (1235-1315). Because of his great learning, Lully was called "Doctor Illuminatus." He was born on the island of Majorca, where Christian civilization was in close contact with Jewish and Arabic lore. Lully was the first Christian scholar to study the Cabala, which he regarded as a divine science and a true revelation for the rational soul. He also studied Arabic philosophy but became a sworn adversary of Averröism. In 1275 he published his *Ars Generalis,* intended to serve as a basis for all sciences and as a key to invention and discovery. This work was much admired, even several hundred years later by Giordano Bruno and Leibniz. Lully was a great linguist and in 1311 he obtained the consent of the Council of Vienna for teachers of Hebrew and Arabic to be admitted to the papal schools and the great universities. His great ambition was to convert Moslems to Christianity. He agitated for crusades and travelled alone through Islamic North Africa. Probably he suffered a martyr's death. Lully was also a prolific poet, and is considered to have been a great master of the Catalan language.

The Death of Lully in Tunis

Do leyt der haße.

Johannes Pfefferkozn — Johannes Reuchlyn.

O layd vnnd layd über alle layd
Dye fack haß ich gantz verloren.
Den fack hon ich zu eynem kleyd
Das bewoyß Johannes Pfefferkozn.

*Title Page of the Anti-Jewish Pamphlet against Reuchlin,
by the Convert, Pfefferkorn*

*Johann von Reuchlin (1455-1522), German humanist and
Defender of Sacred Talmudic Scriptures*

Alchemical Allegory: The Philosopher's Egg

Reuchlin Triumphant
(Woodcut, 1519)

Erasmus' Study at Anderlecht

STVLTICIAE LAVS.

Final Page of Praise of Folly, *with Holbein Drawing of Folly Descending from Pulpit*

ERASMUS, DESIDERIUS

ERASMUS, DESIDERIUS (1466-1536). Born in Rotterdam, Erasmus was brought up in the tradition of the Brethren of the Common Life. He believed in Christ and His mission and regarded Christianity not only as a religion and doctrine of salvation, but also as a guide to moral life. He held that philosophy and the arts could also show the right way. In his later years, he conceived of Christianity more as a religion of the spirit based upon confidence in human reason. He stated that all human evils were rooted in ignorance and infatuation and therefore education of humanity was the essential task of his life.

Although he suffered from living in "a century of fury," he endeavored to stem the tide of fanaticism, by complaining and despising religious exaltation and partisanship, thereby exposing himself to the fury of all religious parties. Sometimes referred to as the Voltaire of the Age of Reformation, he was essentially a man of deep religious feeling and conviction; an independent thinker; the greatest philologist of his time and one of the greatest of all times; a staunch defender of human reason, opposed Luther's teachings; a fearless critic of clerical abuses; and a religious reformer who tried to avoid schisms.

Though he disapproved of Luther's theology, of his doctrine of predestination, and his derogation of human reason, he defended Luther only for the sake of freedom of conscience and because he approved of Luther's criticisms of the existing Church, which he himself had severely criticized. In fact, it was Erasmus' courageous intervention that saved Luther's life at the very beginning of the latter's reforming activities. Luther essentially relied on St. Paul; Erasmus maintained that the *Sermon on the Mount* was the principal basis of the Christian religion. He refused to give dogma primary importance, placed piety above tenets, moral righteousness above orthodoxy, and nothing above "true and perfect friendship, dying and living with Christ." Erasmus exerted considerable influence on the spiritual life of England. He died in Basle in 1536.

Erasmus
(Painting by Holbein)

Hourglass Used
by Erasmus

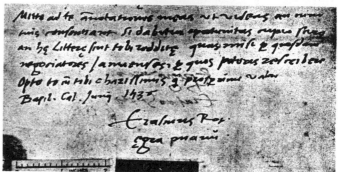

Note Written by Erasmus to an Antwerp Merchant within Six Weeks of His Death

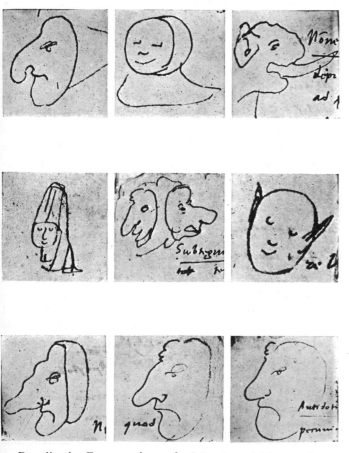

Doodles by Erasmus from the Margins of Manuscripts

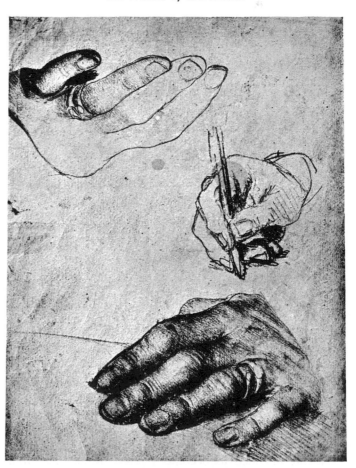

The Hands of Erasmus

Sir Thomas More
(*Painting by Holbein*)

A Drawing of Utopia from More's Classic (1518)

MORE, THOMAS

MORE, THOMAS (1478-1535). Although Thomas More did not live in accordance with the ideas developed in his *Utopia* (1516), he was a man of principles and became a martyr to his convictions.

In the book *Utopia,* after which numerous utopias have been named, More described an imaginary island where a perfectly wise and happy people had established the best imaginable commonwealth by means of ideal institutions, living in peace and abhorring war and oppression of any kind.

More, however, had to live in Tudor England, and, although his spiritual horizon was larger and his moral consciousness was scrupulous, he had to adapt his thoughts and actions to the customs of his contemporary fellow Englishmen and, above all, to the desires of the king. For a time he seemed to be a conformist but when he had to choose between his loyalty to the king and the demands of his conscience, he decided against the royal arbitrary power and faced execution with equanimity.

Having intended to become a priest, More spent four years, from 1499 to 1503, in religious contemplation. Then he suddenly abandoned the idea of ecclesiastical life. Nevertheless, he remained a pious Catholic, although devoted to the "new learning" of humanism. He was an intimate friend of John Colet and Erasmus and participated in their efforts to reform the Catholic Church, to purify religious life and to reconcile religious traditions with the new science of humanism. He wrote poetry, books about English history, a biography of Pico della Mirandola, and protected the painter Hans Holbein and other artists.

After being elected member of Parliament in 1504, he had a brilliant career, was knighted in 1521, and succeeded Cardinal Wolsey as Lord Chancellor of England in 1529. But he was opposed to King Henry VIII's *Act of Supremacy* and *Act of Succession* because the former meant the secession from the Roman Catholic Church, and the latter the nullification of the king's first marriage. The whole of Catholic Europe was startled when it learned that More was executed for his decision to disobey the king. As a prisoner in the Tower, More wrote his *Dialogue of Comfort Against Tribulation* and died as an upright and courageous man.

King Henry VIII

(Portrait by Holbein)

Letter from Sir Thomas More to His Daughter

More and His Daughter Margaret Watching Monks Going to Execution from His Prison Window

(Painting by J. R. Herbert, National Gallery)

More Separated from His Daughter at the Hour of His Execution

The Alchemist. Alchemy was to Paracelsus a constant subject of devoted attention
(Drawing by J. M. Schmidt)

PARACELSUS

PARACELSUS (1493-1541). Theophrastus Bombastus of Hohenheim, called Paracelsus, had been decried as a charlatan, even as a scoundrel, and exalted as a precursor of modern knowledge and a martyr of modern science. In fact, he was an honest man who did wrong only when he was too exasperated by the obstinacy and evil tricks of his adversaries and competitors. He was a self-denying, and certainly also a very efficient physician, who fought routine and prejudices in his special field. But by no means did he attack routine and prejudice with the weapons of modern science, although he anticipated modern views in many ways. He demanded that a physician be an astrologist, an alchemist and a "philosopher," conceiving philosophy as knowledge of the arcana, founded upon a mystical grasp of the forces which work in the Universe. He warned his colleagues against observing the sick patient instead of contemplating the whole of nature, especially the qualities and the degeneration of metals from which he tried to draw conclusions about the sufferings of the

human beings. Anatomy meant to him the astrological structure of the patient. Thus Paracelsus' criticism of medical traditions accepted alchemy, astrology, magic and the Church. "I write as a pagan," he declared, "but I am a Christian." His principal source was the Cabala which he thought proved the truth of Christianity.

But in the midst of his alchemist disquisitions, Paracelsus produced the elements of modern pharmacology. While trying to heal his patients by means of magic spells and sympathetic cures, he proceeded to treatments similar to those of modern psychotherapy, and his philosophy of the Universe led him to the idea of organic life. Although he declined to observe the patient and built his hopes for healing him upon speculation on the mystery of becoming and existence, he arrived at a sound view on the activities of medicine and pharmacology. Disease was considered by him to be a conflict between nature and demonic forces. In this conflict, the physician is "but the helper who furnishes nature with weapons," and the apothecary "the smith who forges the needed weapons.

Paracelsus' Death from Alcohol, His Alleged Elixir of Life

The Alchemist
(Painting by Teniers the Younger)

"The Laboratory of the Alchemist"
(Painting by Brueghel, Metropolitan Museum of Art)

DEBENT IGNARI RES FERRE ET POST OPERARI   QVATVOR INSERTA NATVRIS IN NVBE REFERTA
IVS LAPIDIS CARI VILIS SED DENIQ3 RARI   NVLLA MINERALIS RES EST VBI PRINCIPALIS
VNICA RES CERTA VILIS SED VBIQ3 REPERTA   SED TALIS QVALIS REPERITVR VBIQ3 LOCALIS.

153

Johannes Ludovicus Vives (1492-1540). Born in Spain. Studied Scholasticism in Paris. Befriended Erasmus of Rotterdam. Humanist pathfinder of empirical psychology in his work De Anima et Vita. *Important as pedagogue. Also emphasized the importance of pity and charity rather than doctrine in religion*

Geronimo Cardano (1501-1576). Italian mathematician, astrologer and physician, arrested for heresy, but released and pensioned by Pope Gregory XIII. Author of many works of scientific speculation

TELESIO, BERNARDINO

TELESIO, BERNARDINO (1508-1588). By his refusal to be nominated Archbishop by Pope Paul IV, Telesio renounced a brilliant ecclesiastical career in order to devote his life to independent thought and the study of the sciences. He did not break with the Church, but became one of the initiators of the scientific movement which, though not identical with it, resulted from the spirit of the Renaissance.

Telesio accepted the traditional divisions of psychic life into vegetative, sensitive and intellectual spheres, and he followed the tradition by insisting upon the fundamental difference between the human soul, created by and endowed with the divine spirit, and the animal soul, which is considered a natural formation. But these traditional views allowed him to state numerous physiological and psychical qualities which are common to both man and animals, and to observe that man's psychic life is not sufficiently characterized by the divine origin of his soul but that its description must be completed by a purely empirical study which shows the part played by the animal character in him.

Knowledge is founded, according to Telesio, upon sensation and memory. Essential as sensual perception is considered, an at least equal importance is attributed to the memory of perceiving. Without memory, Telesio said, no formation of thought is possible. While adumbrating a doctrine of psychic atomism, Telesio anticipated both the sensualism and the associationism of later centuries. He also tried to establish the compatibility of psychic and physical motions, as well as relations between time and motion. Physical facts were reduced to contraction and expansion, which are caused by heat and cold.

In his later years, Telesio founded and directed his own academy, the *Academia Telesiana* at Naples, which became instrumental to the propagation and growth of the scientific spirit in Galileo's epoch.

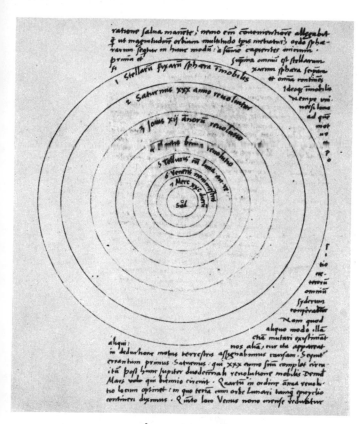

"And there was light"

The Copernican World System

Nicolaus Copernicus (1473-1543), the Polish astronomer who established mathematically that the earth moves around the sun, and is thus not the fixed center of the universe, as held by Ptolemaic astronomy. That the earth moves had, of course, been suggested as early as 250 B.C. But Copernicus, Kepler, Galileo and Newton effected the shift from a teleological to a mathematical way of conceiving nature

RIGHT: *Ancient Concept of the Sun Spiraling around the Earth.* FAR RIGHT: *Opposing Concept of the Sun Revolving around a Revolving Earth*

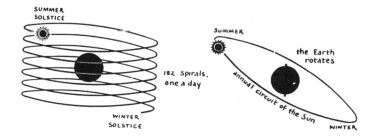

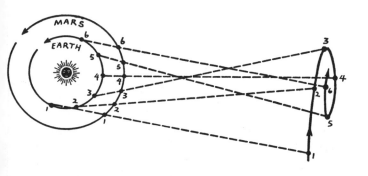

Copernicus' explanation of the planetary loop: As the earth and Mars move around the sun at different speeds, Mars appears to move forward and backward in the loop on the right.

RIGHT: *An early problem for Copernican astronomy: Why does the earth's axis always point in the same direction?*

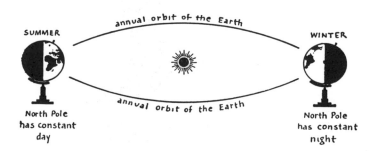

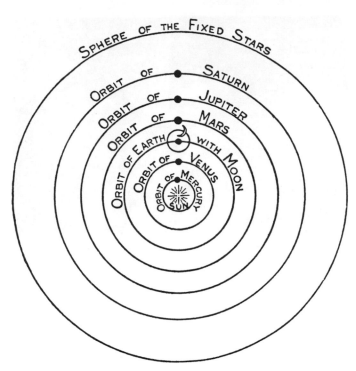

The Copernican World System

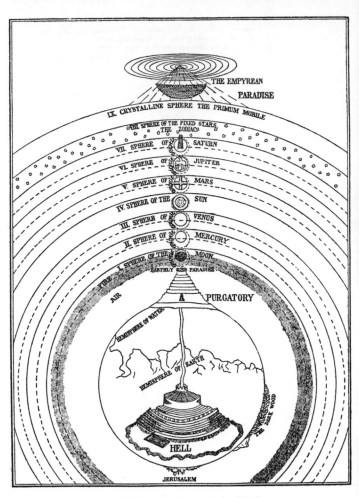

Dante's Conception of the Universe

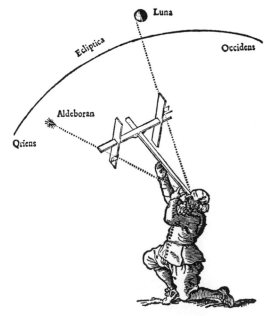

Measurement of angular distance with a cross-staff or
Jacob's staff, an instrument used by Copernicus

Rome in the Sixteenth Century

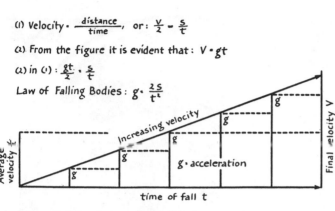

(1) Velocity = $\frac{distance}{time}$, or: $\frac{V}{2} = \frac{s}{t}$

(2) From the figure it is evident that: $V = gt$

(2) in (1): $\frac{gt}{2} = \frac{s}{t}$

Law of Falling Bodies: $g = \frac{2s}{t^2}$

How Galileo Discovered the Law of Falling Bodies
by Graphic Representation

The Moon as Seen by Galileo in 1609

Giordano Bruno
(Navona at Rome)

BRUNO, GIORDANO

BRUNO, GIORDANO (1548-1600). Poet, playwright, philosopher, Bruno is less representative of the development of the modern scientific spirit than he is of the fermentation produced by the contact of Scholastic philosophy with the natural sciences. His enthusiasm for Copernicus' astronomical discovery enabled him to enlarge his cosmic concepts. But instead of thinking empirically, he continued to think in terms of Aristotelian ideas, all the while attacking Aristotle. Bruno was convinced that true philosophy was no different than poetry, music, or painting, since the arts are bound to express divine wisdom. He believed in the infinite perfectibility of knowledge, and conceived of the universe as an imperfect mirror of God's essence in which God's infinity and unity are inadequately depicted.

Throughout his life, Bruno was beset by a restless spirit. He quarreled with the Catholic Church, Calvinists, Lutherans, mathematicians, and physicists. During a fifteen-year period, he lived in Genoa, Venice, Toulouse, Lyons, Paris, Oxford, Wittenberg, and Prague. Wherever he lived he was first admired and then detested for his intolerant attitudes. Like Gabirol, he was both litterateur and philosopher. He wrote many lyrical poems, imbued with an heroic spirit, and ribald comedies—both equally characteristic of the Baroque age. After seven years of imprisonment due to his renunciation of the Dominican Order, he was burned (February 17, 1600) at the stake during the Inquisition in Rome because of his staunch refusal to recant.

157

Galileo Galilei (1564-1642), one of the architects of modern science. Precursor of Newton in mechanics. Embraced the complete range of physics of his time, from the measurement of the speed of light to the weighing of air. His pro-Copernican attitude aroused the sharp displeasure of the Church

Tommaso Campanella

Drawing of Galileo's Idea for a Clock Pendulum

CAMPANELLA, TOMMASO

CAMPANELLA, TOMMASO (1568-1639). A resident of Naples, Campanella was sentenced to lifetime imprisonment during the Spanish rule, for political plotting and heresy. During this time, he wrote a valiant and courageous vindication of Galileo, who had been tried by the Inquisition. After twenty-seven years of incarceration, Campanella succeeded in escaping to France, where he remained for the remainder of his life under the aegis of Cardinal Richelieu. His work was a source of inspiration for Mersenne and other French philosophers; as well as Leibniz. His philosophy was a blend of medieval thought combined with the methods of modern science. A Dominican and partisan of the secular power of the Pope, his communistic utopia, outlined in *City of the Sun,* was ruled by an ideal Pope. He regarded the world as the "living statue of God." Eternal truth is perceptible through the study of nature and the Bible. Many of his ideas are similar to those of modern-day existentialists; for to him, neither the reports of the senses nor the speculations of reason, but only the feelings of one's own existence offer a reliable basis for the knowledge of God, man, and nature. Preservation of existence is the aim of all human activities, and the laws that make for this preservation not only compel man to love God, but also to make him desire to return to Him.

Kepler and Rudolf II

Johann Kepler (1571-1630) is the founder of exact modern science. Both speculatively and mathematically, Kepler believed the evidence of mathematics and astronomy justified the Copernican world scheme. He conceived of God as the creator of the world in accordance with the Pythagorean principle of perfect numbers

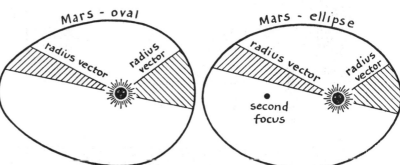

Kepler's law of areas: The radius vector passes over equal areas in equal intervals of time.

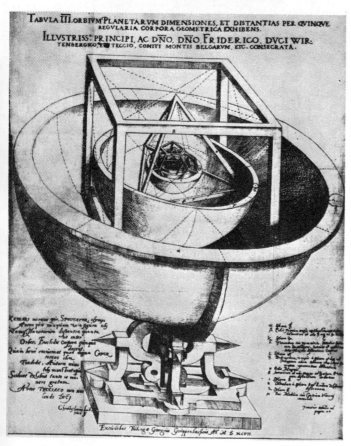

An Illustration from Kepler's Mysterium Cosmographicum, *1596, Showing the Orbits of the Planets*

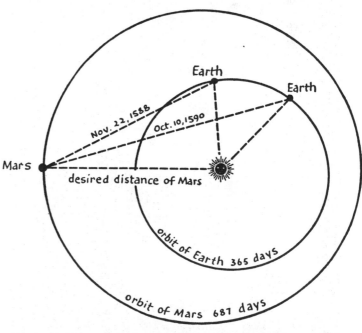

Kepler's calculation of the true orbit of Mars, from the relative distances of Mars from different positions of the earth

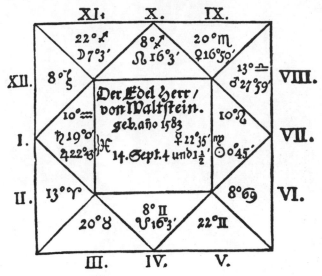

Horoscopium geſtellet durch
Ioannem Kepplerum
1608.

Wallenstein's Horoscope, Cast by Kepler in 1608

Johann Kepler

The Philosopher Derides Magic
(Eighteenth Century Drawing)

The Layman Reads the Luther Bible
(Painting by Karl Ooms)

The Reformation

Martin Luther
(Contemporary Painting)

Luther Nails His 95 Theses to the Church Door

LUTHER, MARTIN

LUTHER, MARTIN (1483-1546) was an Augustinian monk who became the spearhead of Christian Europe's critique and reform of Catholicism. Much of Luther's ideology is found in the anxious meditations of Augustine. Man's only norm can be the Scriptures, his salvation by faith.

Luther was not a systematic theologian, and some of his utterances on German nationalism, irrevocable predestination, Jewish inferiority, and so on estranged such men as Erasmus and Melanchthon.

New reformers set up rigid reconstruction of institutionalism before the flame of Protestantism had reached its full intensity. Ulrich Zwingli (1484-1531) in Switzerland and John Calvin (1509-1564) in France inaugurated the type of Protestantism that for hundreds of years tortured and burned alive heretics, as had the Mother Church in its worst days. In England under John Knox of Scotland (1515-1572) the Reformation took on a political rather than a religious color.

Within the Catholic Church a fervent Counter Reformation caused many of the early abuses to be set right.

161

John Wycliffe (1324-1384). Early English Reformer, who strongly influenced the teachings of John Huss. The first English translation of the Bible is associated with his name

Ulrich von Hutten (1488-1523). His Letters of Obscure Men *and other writings critical of Rome prepared the ground for the Reformation*

Trade in Indulgences in the Early Sixteenth Century

Luther's Study in the Wartburg

Luther and Huss Offering the Holy Meal
(Woodcut by Cranach)

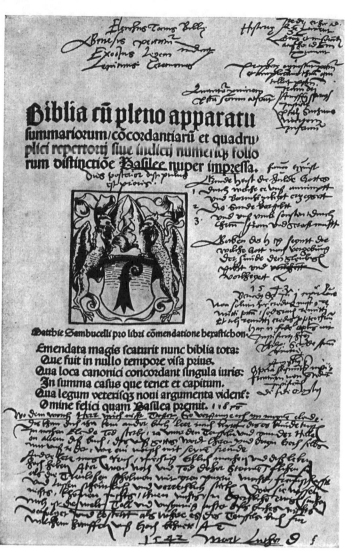

Luther's Annotations to the Latin Bible in His Own Handwriting

Luther, Melanchthon, Pomeranus and Cruciger
(Painting by Labouchère)

Luther Continues His Translation of the Bible with the Assistance of Melanchthon

Ulrich Zwingli (1484-1531)
(Woodcut by Hans Asper)

Ḥer: Ulrich Zwingli leerbiechlein
wie man die Knaben Chriſtlich vnterweyſen
vnd erziehen ſoll / mit kurtzer anzayge
aynes gantzen Chriſtlichen lebens.
M. D. xxiiij

Title Page of Zwingli's Little Manual for Christian Instruction for Youth

View of Basle, 1548

Luther and Zwingli at Marburg, 1529

Calvin and Farel
(by Lugardon)

165

The World of Islam

MOHAMMED

MOHAMMED (570-632). As with every founder of a religion, the life and personality of Mohammed, the founder of Islam, have been transformed by legends which picture him as the only perfect man, the greatest of all saints, the only one worthy of becoming the instrument of divine revelation. Mohammed himself, however, thought otherwise. He said that he was sent by God as a "witness, as a hopeful and warning messenger, as a torch," but he refused to be regarded as an example of virtue. He did not feel that he was a saint, and consciously refrained from performing miracles. He certainly was a fanatic but occasionally he showed a sense of humor, and several of his jokes have been transmitted to posterity.

The original name of Mohammed (The Praised One) was Ubu'l Kassim. He was a merchant in Mecca where plutocracy offended his social feelings, as the idolatry of the whole population offended his reason and piety. Broodings, dreams and visions led him to the belief that he was chosen by God to save the Arabian people from spiritual and moral corruption by announcing the coming judgment of humanity and teaching faith in Allah, the one and omnipotent God.

At the age of 40, Mohammed began his religious mis-

In this miniature the Angel Gabriel appears to Mohammed in a vision, saying, "Thou art the Prophet of God"

sion. The citizens of Mecca sneered at him and forced him to flee. In 622, he came to the city of Jathrib where he was well received and actively supported. Jathrib, therefore, was subsequently renamed Medina (City of the Prophet), and became the base of his power and his religious and military expeditions. The flight of 622 (Hejira) became an event of greatest importance to the history of the world. In Medina, Mohammed, once a lonesome missionary, became a spiritual and military ruler and conqueror, and his religious doctrine was shaped to the religion of Islam, an institution, and, at the same time, a warlike organization. Mohammed subdued Mecca, his native town that had expelled him. But when he died he could not foresee the future expansion of Islam.

166

The basis of Islamic religion is the *Koran* (Recitations), written by Mohammed who claimed to be inspired by Gabriel, the archangel. It consists of 114 sections (Suras), the first third of which was conceived in Mecca and deals with the creation and future fate of the world, the proofs of the omnipotence of Allah and the teachings of a moral conduct of life as a preparation for standing the test on the Day of Judgment. The remainder of the *Koran,* accomplished in Medina, contains polemics against other religious and civil legislation.

Mohammed claimed that he restored the religion of Abraham which, according to him, had been distorted by Judaism and Christianity. Mohammed adopted many of the Judaic and Christian, gnostic, and Babylonian traditions but, the older he grew, the more he stressed the importance of the sword as a means of propagating the right faith. Without Mohammed's *Koran,* the world religion of Islam cannot be understood. However, Islam cannot be understood only by the study of the *Koran.* The moral and dogmatic evolution of Mohammedanism did not stop by any means after Mohammed's death.

The Kaaba at Mecca

Mohammed rededicating the black stone in the wall of the Kaaba at Mecca, sanctifying the pagan relic for Moslem worship

The Apocryphal Sword of Mohammed, Called Sul Fikar

Mohammed with Ali, Husein and Hasan
(Eighteenth Century Miniature)

Mohammed Leading His Hordes on a Holy Conquest
(Painting by Chappel)

Mohammed Preaching His Farewell Sermon

HUNEIN IBN ISHAK

HUNEIN IBN ISHAK (809-873). The *Sayings of the Philosophers,* written by Hunein Ibn Ishak, a Nestorian Christian who was born in Syria and wrote in Syriac and Arabic, has been translated into Hebrew, Spanish and other languages, and became a very popular book among the intellectuals of the early Middle Ages in Europe and the Middle East. This book, however, is highly significant of the deformation of Greek philosophy in the sixth and seventh centuries. Hunein was a learned man. He wrote an *Introduction into the Science of Medicine,* a Syriac-Arabic dictionary and grammar, and many other books. He traveled a great deal and collected Greek manuscripts, which he either translated into Syriac or Arabic, or used as sources for his own books. Without any doubt, Hunein was a careful writer and faithful translator, but the texts of the manuscripts he had at hand were spoiled, because the copyists had been incapable of understanding what they copied, and each succeeding scribe had added new errors to those of his predecessors. Thus Hunein confounded Socrates with Diogenes, or Plato with Bias. Even his own philosophy, whether it consisted of original thoughts or of quotations, is more characteristic of the fate of certain Greek thoughts in a time of spiritual decay.

AL-KINDI

AL-KINDI (died 873 A.D.). The son of a South Arabian governor, Al-Kindi was given the best possible education at Basra and Baghdad. His life was spent in the service of the court as tutor, astrologer, translator and editor of many Greek philosophical works. We possess few of his writings in the original Arabic, probably because, at one time, his extensive library was temporarily confiscated. His optical and astronomical calculations were valued for centuries. He was the first to apply mathematics not only to the physical world but also to Materia Medica where he calculated the effect of medicines from the proportions and qualities represented in the various mixtures.

From Latin translations of his works and literary activities, we learn that his eclecticism was equally characteristic of many Arab philosophers throughout the Middle Ages. He respected Plato, Aristotle and Pythagoras, but remained blind to their essential doctrinal differences. He, thus, shared the tendencies of most Neo-Platonists and Neo-Pythagoreans. In philosophy, he regarded God as the intelligent cause of the universe, the Greek *nous,* that has communicated itself from above through successive emanations of the soul to the sphere in which we live. Through this process, man became free and immortal, though his body remained subject to the influence of the stars.

168

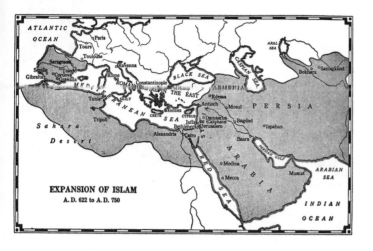

Two of the Thirteen Prescribed Moslem Prayer Positions

AL-FARABI

AL-FARABI (c. 870-950). Born of a Turkish family, educated by a Christian physician at Baghdad, Al-Farabi has been ranked with Aristotle as one of the greatest of all teachers.

A versatile man, his chief occupation was that of philosopher, either by way of comment or original contribution. He is best known for his analyses of the Greek philosophers. Whatever he wrote was syncretistic in nature, for he sought for the compatible concepts of God, soul, time, and space among the diverse philosophies. Thus he found Plato and Aristotle in perfect accord, and historians of philosophy have ever since despaired over his treatise *On the Agreement of the Philosophy of Plato and Aristotle.*

He wrote many works on various aspects of the soul: its intellect, the unity of the soul, its substance, and many of its problems. All his thinking was characterized by an idealism bordering on mysticism.

Al-Farabi was principally influenced by Plotinus whose belief that the materially comprehensive world emanated from God still exerts influence over Moslem scholastic thought, and by Aristotle who assumed there was a Prime Mover of the universe and therefore the world had no beginning in time, that time is relative to motion and could not have preceded God, who himself was the first mover.

Al-Farabi was not only a great philosopher but also a noted musicologist. Dervishes in the East can still be heard singing the chants he composed. He was also a Utopian whose *Model City* envisioned his desires for the heavenly city on this earth.

AVICENNA

AVICENNA (979-1037). Nearly a thousand years have passed and the name of Avicenna is still revered in the East. One of the wisest of physicians, he is referred to in the West as the Galen of the Moslem world. The name Avicenna is the Latinized form of the Hebrew, Aven Sina; or the Arabic, Abu Ali al-Husain ibn Abdullah ibn Sina. While still a youth in his teens, Avicenna was called upon to cure the Sultan of Bokhara. The potentate, in gratitude, opened his library to the young man. This good fortune enabled Avicenna (who had memorized the Koran by the age of ten) to write the *Canon*, the basis of his medical fame, before he had attained his legal majority.

In addition to his medical accomplishments, he studied logic, metaphysics, mathematics, and physics. He studied Aristotelian and neo-Platonic philosophy of Al-Farabi. As a result of this, Avicenna wrote voluminously on Aristotle. He said that cause and effect are simultaneous and therefore God and the world are co-eternal; that God created intelligence or the soul, and these emanate from the heavens and reach the earth in huge chains; that intelligence is sustained by God, and though that is innately eternal, its multiple extensions are not dependent on Him, for He is not concerned with matter.

Avicenna was probably a pantheist. His work *Philosophia Orientalis*, in which his position was apparently clarified, is lost. His mysticism is said to have been derived from Mazdaism. For a time he occupied the office of Vizier at Hamadan.

Avicenna Received by the Governor of Ispahan

Avicenna, "The Persian Galen"

Page from Avicenna's Canon, I, *1474*

ALGHAZZALI, ABU HAMID MOHAMMED IBN GHAZZALI

ALGHAZZALI, ABU HAMID MOHAMMED IBN GHAZZALI (1059-1111). Alghazzali was a Persian philosopher born in the northeastern part of the empire. The greatest teachers of Islam have bestowed upon him innumerable encomiums, among them, "the guide to the True Faith," "the embodiment of religious thought," "the living reaffirmation of Islam." To this day his writings are considered classic throughout the Moslem world.

Alghazzali, never a bigoted orthodox, both advocated and practiced tolerance. He often advised his co-religionists to take the pious Jew as their model in religious reverence. In fact, Jewish philosophers of the Middle Ages soon became aware that Alghazzali's principles and teachings were closely akin to those of Judaism, a fact that has often been confirmed by modern Christian scholars.

Alghazzali was deeply influenced by Sufism despite his faithful study of the Koran. His doctrine of emanation was derived from neo-Platonic writings. He classified those who denied this doctrine as children, for both confuse marionettes or wooden idols with reality. His criticisms of causality pre-dated David Hume's parallel theories by several centuries, and he exerted great influence over William of Ockham and other Christian philosophers. He compared the pursuit of knowledge to the process involved in digging a well: both involved probing; the desired object in both cases was necessary to life.

Magic square for easing childbirth. From Al-Ghazzali's *Deliverance from Error*. The numbers are:

4	9	2
3	5	7
8	1	6

The Moslem Paradise
(From a Persian Drawing, c. 1500)

IBN TUFAIL

IBN TUFAIL (About 1105-1185). The author of "Robinson Crusoe" certainly must have read the English version of Ibn Tufail's book *Hai Ebn Yokdhan* (Alive, Son of Awaken), the imaginary and allegorical story of a man who, living alone on an island, without any intercourse with human beings, discovered truth and conquered nature by reasonable thinking. This book became favorite reading in Europe. It was translated into French, Spanish, German and Dutch, and into English in 1674 and 1708. Its English title is *The Improvement of Human Reason*.

The full name of its author is Abu Bekr Mohammed ben Abd'el Malik ben Mohammed ben Mohammed ben Tufail el-Quaici. His contemporaries also called him El Andaloci, which, at that time, meant Spaniard, or the man of Cordova, or the man of Seville. He was a physician in Granada who then became secretary to the governor and finally the vizier of Sultan Abu Yakub Yusuf, who ruled over Islamic Spain and Morocco. Ibn Tufail distinguished himself in medicine, poetry and astronomy. He criticized the Ptolemaic system as did other Arabic and Jewish thinkers of that period. He was highly respected as a scholar whose wisdom attracted men of all countries. The chronicles of his time also praise him as a Maecenas. Ibn Tufail especially protected Averroës and recommended him to his ruler as his successor when, in 1182, he retired from office. According to contemporary reports, Averroës was inspired to his commentaries on Aristotle by a conversation with Ibn Tufail and the Sultan, who complained that Aristotle was too obscure to him.

St. Thomas Triumphs over Averroës
(Altarpiece by Traini, Sta Catarina, Pisa)

AVENPACE (Ibn Badjdja)

AVENPACE (IBN BADJDJA) (End of 11th Century—1138). Avenpace was a high dignitary in Islamic Spain for twenty years when he was poisoned by his enemies who decried him as an atheist and scorner of the Koran. He was a reputed musician and well acquainted with the natural sciences, mathematics and astronomy. Avenpace wrote commentaries on several works of Aristotle, whom he interpreted in accordance with Neo-Platonism, and treatises among which *The Hermit's Guide* was most famous. It was used by Averroës and the Jewish author Moses of Narbonne, as well as by Albertus Magnus and Aquinas. He distinguished between "animal" and "human" activities, regarded the human intellect as the emanation of the Agens Intellect, the supreme Being, and described their mystical union.

Averroës in Disgrace

Averroës Makes Amends at the Door of the Mosque of Fez

AVERROËS (Ibn Roshd)

AVERROËS (IBN ROSHD) (1126-1198). Due to a mistake made in translating the work of Mohammed ibn Ahmed ibn Mohammed ibn Roshd from the Arabic into Latin, this great Islamic philosopher for about two centuries deeply influenced Christian thinkers, by whom he was known under the name Averroës. In reality, Averroës taught that there is one eternal truth which, according to the various levels of education, can be formulated and comprehended in two ways, namely, the way of revelation, by the Koran, or the way of natural knowledge, with the aid of Aristotle and other philosophers. He maintained on occasion that there is a double truth, and that a proposition may be theologically true and philosophically untrue, and vice versa. Christian Averroism flourished in the thirteenth century, especially at the University of Paris where Siger of Brabant was the leader of that school. In 1277, Averroism was condemned by the Church. Averroës also influenced Jewish philosophers of the Middle Ages.

Apart from his ascendancy over Christian and Jewish philosophy, Averroës has become important as the last great philosopher of Islamic Spain, and as the last and greatest of all Arabian Aristotelians. He studied medicine and jurisprudence, and was a judge in Sevilla and Cordova. Although he was fully acquainted with natural sciences, his approach to philosophy was determined to a great extent by his legal training. As a jurist, Averroës insisted on the literal meaning of religious and secular documents, and was eager to refute misinterpretations, particularly those which were advanced by theologians. In this way, Averroës studied, explained and annotated Aristotle whom he glorified as a "man chosen by God." Violently attacked by the Mohammedan clergy, Averroës' doctrines were condemned and his books burned.

His theories of the evolution of pre-existent forms and of the intellect anticipated modern concepts.

Averroës

173

Classics of France

DESCARTES, RENÉ

DESCARTES, RENÉ (1595-1650). Descartes represented the spirit of the age which rid itself of ancient authority and conventions. His personal life manifested a change from bon vivant to that of recluse. The life-loving, teeming existence of Paris did not deter him. He had been a soldier of fortune with different armies during the Thirty Years' War, a scholar, traveler, pilgrim, and firm adherent to the Catholic faith.

On November 10, 1619, a dream revealed to him the synthetic and analytic method which he was to follow. He never published it in the form he had originally intended because news of the persecution of Galileo, with whom he had sympathized reached him. Like everyone in that age, he doubted everything; even his own existence. The more he doubted, the more certain he became of himself as a thinking being. He tersely couched this insight with the phrase: "I think, therefore I am." His constant intellectual search led him to the idea of an infinite God, which fact he then took as proof that God exists. He argued thus: nothing so great as a divine being could be without a real basis in fact. He stated that the existence of a perfect being was comprised in the idea of it, just as the equality of the three angles to two right ones is comprised in the idea of a triangle. Since God was truthful, he could not be thought of as wishing to deceive man. Hence God guaranteed the truth of whatever is clear and distinct to man's reason and perception.

Thus Descartes, or Cartesius—the Latin form of his name—became the father of modern rationalism. He was also a mechanist, explaining matter by differently shaped

Queen Christina of Sweden, Surrounded by Scholars of Her Time
(Painting by Dumesnil, Versailles)

Detail of Painting Opposite, Showing Descartes on Queen Christina's Left

corpuscles interacting mechanically. He and his disciples maintained that even animals are living automata; that man is also a machine, except for his spirit which represents thinking substance, as distinct from extended substance. Descartes died unhappily in the service of Queen Christina of Sweden who meant to make full use of his talents for philosophy, mathematics, and natural science.

René Descartes

Descartes in the Streets of Paris
(Painting by Chartran)

Pierre Gassendi

Blaise Pascal

GASSENDI, PIERRE

GASSENDI, PIERRE (1592-1655). When, in 1633, Galileo was tormented by his condemnation and was watched narrowly by the Inquisition, many scholars were terrified, and not a few denied any connection with him. But Gassendi, a Catholic priest, known by his writings on astronomy, physics and mathematics, wrote a letter to Galileo that had to pass the censorship of the Inquisition, as Gassendi knew. He comforted Galileo by protesting that the ecclesiastical sentence had nothing to do with the conscience of a scientist, and Galileo had no reason to accuse himself of any moral failure. There were not many savants who acted as frankly as Gassendi did.

Gassendi himself was wise, or at least cautious enough to avoid persecution on the part of the Church, although he professed materialism and criticized Descartes' idealistic views. For Gassendi combined his atomistic materialism with the belief in the Biblical God, and asserted that the atoms, conceived in accordance with the doctrines of Democritus and Epicurus, were created by the Christian God. Gassendi therefore was called the "Christianized Epicurus." Also in his personal life, Gassendi knew how to be a dignified priest, a learned theologian, and how to enjoy the society of witty and gay men, no matter whether they were faithful Christians or libertines.

PASCAL, BLAISE

PASCAL, BLAISE (1623-1662). Scientists honor Pascal as one of the greatest mathematicians and physicists, as one of the founders of hydrodynamics and the mathematical theory of probability, and as a man who also made significant contributions by his investigations of vacuum, and gravity, and by his theory of conic sections. Men of all creeds revere Pascal's piety which was free from bigotry. Historians of literature admire Pascal's prose which contributed to the formation of modern French style. Philosophers highly esteem him as a profound psychologist and a thinker devoted to truth.

Success and fame meant nothing to Pascal. He sought peace of mind. Dissatisfied with abstract science, Pascal turned to the study of man and his spiritual problems. His conviction that self-complacency is the most dangerous obstacle in the way to true knowledge led him to a severe examination of his own inclinations and disinclinations. In his search of truth, Pascal was steadily tormented by his passions and inner conflicts, but he overcame all these obstacles by his honesty of thought. He was equally opposed to those who despise human reason and to those who are overconfident of it. According to him, God enabled man to know religious truth by means of reason, and to feel truth, due to His grace. He protested with energy

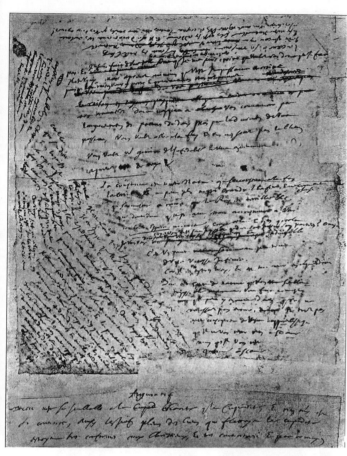

Manuscript Page of Pascal's Pensées

Blaise Pascal

Mathematical Machine Constructed by Pascal When He Was 18

and courage any attempt to convert men to any creed by force. But he fought religious and moral laxity with no less energy, as his *Lettres Provinciales,* masterworks of polemics, have shown. In his *Pensées* (Thoughts), Pascal dealt with the fundamental problems of human existence from the psychological and theological point of view. He regarded truth as the expression of God's will and as a means to know and to love Him.

Marguerite Périer, niece and foster daughter of Pascal, who was healed miraculously from serious illness. Her cure had a deep influence upon the philosopher

Cardinal Richelieu and His Newly Erected Sorbonne, 1642

GEULINCX, ARNOLD

GEULINCX, ARNOLD (1624-1669). For twelve years, Geulincx was professor at the University of Louvain, Belgium, a stronghold of Catholic orthodoxy. Then he was converted to Calvinism, and became professor at the University of Leyden, Holland, at that time the center of learning, and an asylum for scholars who had been persecuted in their native country. He wrote all of his works in Latin, and died before his principal books, namely *Ethica* and *Metaphysica,* could be published.

Although Geulincx often and intensely dealt with metaphysical questions, he was even more interested in ethics, but did not separate one from another. On the contrary, his ethics is founded upon metaphysics, though he also used psychological experience for his argumentation. He summed up his doctrine in the words: *Ita est, ergo ita sit* (So it is, therefore be it so). His view on life is colored with optimistic resignation. His steady confidence in God does

not shut his eyes to the shortcomings of the existing world; if he expressed the idea of what Leibniz, about twenty-five years after Geulincx' death, has called the "pre-established harmony," he did not intend to assert that the existing world was good or the best of all possible but rather that it was good enough for Man who is morally and intellectually far from perfection.

Geulincx was a man of moderation, opposed to any kind of extremism. Following Descartes, he regarded doubt as the force that makes Man ask for truth. He appreciated the educational value of provisional scepticism, but demanded that mature men must believe in God whom he regarded as the first cause of all things, without denying second causes. Geulincx therefore, while adopting the Scholastic term of occasional cause, held that occasionalism was an indispensable hypothesis, apt to explain natural and mental facts, but was far from the radical standpoint of Malebranche who published his views only five years after Geulincx' death.

Nicolas Malebranche

MALEBRANCHE, NICOLAS

MALEBRANCHE, NICOLAS (1638-1715). Malebranche came to philosophy in a way that differs from that of many other philosophers. He began to study it, and, disappointed by its methods and results, turned to theology. He became a member of the Congregation of the Oratory, displayed religious ardor, accepted the doctrines of the Church as unchanging truth, though he was never quite satisfied with the arguments used by traditional theology. In 1664, by chance, he picked up in a bookstore Descartes' treatise *On Man,* and after perusing some pages fugitively, became fascinated by the author's ideas. For the following three years, Malebranche studied Descartes' works, doing nothing else. In 1674, ten years after his haphazard acquaintance with Descartes, he published the first volume of his *Recherche de la Vérité* (Investigation of Truth).

Following Descartes' example, Malebranche looked upon philosophical doubt as his indispensable starting point. But he deviated from his master by conceiving doubt as an act of will, of freedom.

Contrary to Descartes as well as to Bacon, Spinoza and many others, knowledge was not to him of causal determination or explanation. For, according to Malebranche there is no cause in the world but God. All creatures are united with God in an immediate manner. They depend essentially and directly on Him. There is no dependence of one creature or thing on another, since all things are powerless without God's will. All being, all knowing, all acting are produced by God. Man has only the faculties of desire and choice which are constituents of his liberty. As far as he has love of God, he has a will. As far as he has a vision of God, he has reason. What he regards as causal connection of things is not conditional but only apparent, or as Malebranche says, occasional causes.

Since Malebranche reserved all causal acting to God alone, causality was completely abandoned by him as a principle of knowledge. Knowledge was to Malebranche evidence of intuition. He went so far as to declare evidence superior to faith. For faith may change but evidence shall subsist.

By emphasizing evidence, Malebranche influenced Leibniz, Locke, Berkeley and Hume. In modern times, Santayana, Husserl and Scheler adopted similar views.

Julien Lamettrie

"Is man merely an animated machine?"

LAMETTRIE, JULIEN OFFRAY DE

LAMETTRIE, JULIEN OFFRAY DE (1709-1751). This "scapegoat of 18th century materialism," as Friedrich Albert Lange rightly called him, has been blamed and despised by many who had not read a single page of his books. Lamettrie was a physician in the French army. In this capacity he entered into conflict first with medical routine, then with his superiors, and, finally, the government. He was dismissed, and emigrated to Holland. In his books *L'homme machine* and *L'homme plants* (1748), Lamettrie demonstrated by comparative methods the relationship between man and other living beings, and proceeded to a theory of the evolution of organisms. He stated that psychical life is observable already on the lowest level of the evolution. Investigating the functions of the brain, Lamettrie tried to discern various stages of its formation which are of primary importance in the development of mental life. Also, he protested against an evaluation of the moral character of men which depends on the acceptance of religious doctrines. Although Lamettrie was decried as a crude materialist, he also influenced idealist philosophers. To him Goethe owes the inspiration for his botanical ideas.

HELVÉTIUS, CLAUDE ADRIEN

HELVÉTIUS, CLAUDE ADRIEN (1715-1771). Many moralists of many ages have complained that personal interest in the pursuit of happiness is the only efficient principle of human actions. The awareness of this fact has made some of them melancholy, others resigned to that fate, and still others fundamentally pessimistic, or indignant, or hypocritical. There has been no lack of efforts to deny such statements or to change the character of man if the statement were true. Helvétius, contrary to all of these critics of egoism, was the first to draw an optimistic conclusion from the conviction that personal interest was the real rule of human behavior. His book *De l'Esprit* (On the Mind, 1758), in which Helvétius explained his views and founded them upon Condillac's sensualism, was condemned by the Sorbonne and burned in Paris after the judges had declared it dangerous to state and society.

Helvétius was a clever financier by profession. He used his large income for the promotion of literature, philosophy and social welfare. He was one of the first to insist on taking the social environment and economic conditions into consideration before sentencing a defendant. Not this demand but other suggestions advanced by Helvétius were later realized by the legislation of the First French Republic and by Napoleon.

Helvétius' book *On the Mind* was studied by Bentham and, through him, influenced British utilitarianism.

Claude Helvétius

Etienne de Condillac

CONDILLAC, ETIENNE BONNOT DE

CONDILLAC, ETIENNE BONNOT DE (1715-1780). Often referred to as the "philosophers' philosopher," historically, the influence of Condillac is still important, although his prestige has waned. He was an eighteenth century abbot, whose ecclesiastical garment neither hampered his enjoyment of life, nor interfered with his secular thinking.

Condillac professed spiritualism in the area of metaphysics; metaphysics was only loosely connected with his principal interests and occupied a very small part of his writings. In his chief works, *Essai Sur L'Origine des Connaissances Humaines* (An Essay on the Origin of Human Knowledge) (1746) and *Traité des Sensations* (1754) Condillac, like Locke and some of the Cartesians who in some respects deviated from Descartes, denied the usefulness of speculating about the metaphysical nature of the mind. He preferred to study the human mind as a psychologist in order to understand its operations. He thought that the analysis of sensation contained the elements of any judgment connected with the sensation. He regarded the human individual as composed of two egos, that of habit and that of reflection. The ego of habit acted unconsciously: it was capable of the senses of sight, hearing and smell. The ego of reflection was conscious of its acts while performing them. Instinct was derived from the ego of habit, and reason from the habit of reflection. Many of his solutions were considered rash; today, it is recognized that his critics, Kant and Helmholtz among others, were wrong. Condillac was also interested in the psychology of animals, logic and mathematics. His work in economics, *Le Commerce et Le Gouvernement,* deals with ideas and problems very similar to those treated by Adam Smith in his *Wealth of Nations,* both published simultaneously (1776).

Jean Lamarck

LAMARCK, JEAN

LAMARCK, JEAN (1744-1829). The modern theory, called Lamarckism, according to which acquired properties of an organism can become hereditary, has little connection with the thoughts of Jean Lamarck who disregarded the phenomenon of heredity. But he was one of the first scientists to transform the static conception of the universe into an evolutionist one, and was a precursor of modern theories of environment. In doing so, he experienced the truth of Voltaire's saying that it is dangerous to be right while all contemporary authorities are wrong. Cuvier's opposition to and Comte's severe criticism of Lamarck's statements diverted the attention of the scientists from his work for more than one generation. Even Charles Darwin, generally reserved in the expression of his opinion, found in Lamarck's works nothing but "nonsense," "rubbish" or, at best, "uselessness."

During his whole life, Lamarck, the descendant of an impoverished noble family, was a poor man, and in his last two years he lost the modest sum he had saved for his children. His temper revolted against the ecclesiastical life to which he was dedicated in his boyhood. At the age of seventeen he entered the French Army. Discharged after five years of service he became a clerk in a banking house, in order to earn the money he needed to study medicine. Having attained this end, he concentrated upon observing insects and worms, and then proceeded to the investigation of the laws which govern organic and inorganic bod-

ies. In 1776, he wrote *Recherches sur les Causes des Principaux Faits Physiques,* which he could publish only in 1794, and then, as a sincere adherent of the Jacobins, dedicated to the French people while the government of terror was at its height. In 1795, His *Système de la Nature* appeared and, in 1809, his *Philosophie Zoologique.* Lamarck remained a republican under Napoleon and the restored Bourbons.

Lamarck took great care to distinguish between nature and the Supreme Being, and between nature and the physical universe which he regarded as an inactive and powerless mass of substances. To him, the study of nature is the study of motion, and nature a system of laws which rule over life. The motions which are peculiar to beings endowed with life are clearly distinguished from the physical motions. Life is marked by irritability and the faculty to react to the challenge of influences from without. It is this faculty which develops the nervous system. Changes of circumstances cause changes of both needs and faculties. The lower forms of life are moulded by environment. Higher forms, by virtue of their nervous system, tend to modify their environment by active urge or desire. The interaction of urge and environment produces new characters which either become permanent or perish, according to their respective capability of subsisting.

Lamarck combined sober observation with vivid imagination, which enabled him to behold ideal structures and the real characteristics of organic life.

Maine de Biran

MAINE DE BIRAN
(Pierre François Gonthier De Biran)

MAINE DE BIRAN (PIERRE FRANÇOIS GONTHIER
DE BIRAN) (1766-1824). Maine de Biran was a man
of strong moral and metaphysical feelings, but his psychological curiosity was always stronger and sometimes
diverted his thoughts from their initial aims. For years his
military and political activities prevented him from concentrating upon philosophy. He was strictly opposed to Condillac and Cabanis whom he regarded as the representatives of the spirit of the eighteenth century and whom he
accused of evaporating human feelings by their analysis;
but, in fact, as a psychologist, Maine de Biran was closer
to them than he supposed himself to be. Nevertheless,
many of his ideas seem to be anticipations of those of
Whitehead, Santayana, Hocking, Bergson, Scheler and
recent existentialism.

Serving in King Louis XVI's bodyguard, Maine de
Biran was wounded in the fight against the people of Paris
during the early revolutionary days of July 1789. After his
regiment had been disbanded, he turned to mathematics
and philosophy. Despite his ardent royalism and hatred of
the Revolution, he served under the Directory from 1795
on, and was elected a member of the Council of the Five
Hundred in 1797. The coup d'état of Fructidor induced
him to retire into private life until Napoleon, in 1805,
appointed him sub-prefect and member of the Corps Légis-
latif. In 1811, Maine de Biran abandoned the Emperor in
favor of the Bourbons whose return to power he openly
demanded. King Louis XVIII awarded him many honors
but the ultra-reactionary faction accused him of being too
moderate.

From the time of his childhood, Maine de Biran was, as
he said, "astonished while feeling that I exist," and he was
led by an instinct to analyze his consciousness in order "to
know how I can live and be myself." Contrary to Descartes, he conceived man as a willing creature. *Volo, ergo
sum* is his device. Will signifies the constant tension in man
that urges him to act. Will is the primary fact of consciousness that gives man the feeling of being united with a
body and brings him into contact with the outer world and
its resistance to his actions. The knowledge of substance
is derived from observation of the will. In his *New Essays
on Anthropology* which were not finished when he died,
Maine de Biran describes three stages of life. The first is
that of animal life which is dominated by blind passions
which are independent of the will. The second experience
is will, intelligence, the meaning of ideas and words, and
the conflict of wills. The third stage is that of spirit in
which man identifies himself with the eternal source of
power and insight. At its height, man is happy to lose his
ego. At any stage, man needs the support of God.

Maine de Biran claimed to have overcome all difficulties
which are the result of an erroneous tendency to comprehend in abstract or separate terms what is given in relatives
or to divide into sections what really is a running stream.

Robert de Lamennais
(Painting by Pauline Guerin)

École Polytechnique de Paris in the time of Comte

L'Avenir, *political, scientific and literary paper founded by Lamennais in 1830*

LAMENNAIS, ROBERT FÉLICITÉ DE

LAMENNAIS, ROBERT FÉLICITÉ DE (1782-1854). Although Lamennais radically changed his religious and political standpoint at least three times and cursed what he had adored in the preceding period of his life, his mind preserved, despite all shifts, traits of imposing constancy. Lamennais was a keen metaphysician and, at the same time, a passionate sociologist, a thinker whom Schelling, after a long discussion with him, called "the greatest dialectician of the epoch," and an enthusiast whose imagination evidenced dramatic tension and power.

In his early youth, Lamennais, like his father who was a corsair and a descendant of corsairs, was an ardent supporter of the left wing of the French Revolution. In 1804 he abjured all revolutionary ideas and subsequently became a Catholic priest. His *Essai sur l'indifférence en matière de religion* (1817), translated into English, German, Italian and Spanish, maintains that religion is the fundamental principle of human action. Society, therefore, cannot be indifferent to religious doctrines, and must crush atheists, deists and heretics. In 1824, Lamennais reached the zenith of his ultramontanism, displaying more papal-mindedness than the Pope himself, as well as extreme royalism. But, in 1829, he advocated separation of Church and State, admonished the Church to sever its cause from that of the kings, and advocated the alliance between the Catholic Church and democracy, while maintaining the principle of the spiritual leadership of the Pope. Severely rebuked by the Pope, Lamennais, in 1834, published his *Paroles d'un Croyant* (Words of a Believer) of which more than 100,000 copies were sold within a few weeks. He returned to the deism of his youth, and became the herald of "spiritual democracy" and radical republicanism, yet always protesting that without faith in God, human rights and duties must collapse and no civil loyalty can persist.

Lamennais was one of the founders of the Second French Republic, the initiator of Catholic liberalism and Christian socialism.

184

Auguste Comte

Clotilde de Vaux (1814-1846), Comte's Beloved, and Virtual Priestess of His Religious Cult

"The Cured Philosopher"
(Caricature by Dantan)

COMTE, AUGUSTE

COMTE, AUGUSTE (1798-1857). The Utopian socialist, Saint-Simon, influenced Comte in his youth. Comte had little use either for logic or philosophy, but instead advocated the study of phrenology. His object was to show that philosophy was in the stage of being absorbed by science. Theology was the first stage of philosophy, wherein nature was explained by the supernatural; metaphysics constituted the second stage, and philosophy was concerned with such abstractions as purpose, life, and the *a priori;* the third and last stage was positivism, which Comte said implied experiment, observation, and the consequences derived from the laws of phenomena. His best known work, *Cours de Philosophie Positive,* was published (1830-42) in six volumes. He maintained that science had always been experimental and observational, and therefore positivistic; that it never required metaphysics either to help determine its course or its limits. His ethics was based on the factor of egotism. This, he said, would lead to a consideration of others, or altruism, and thence to mankind as the guarantor of a social order that would be beneficial to the individual. In order to insure the effectiveness of this, he formalized this attitude into a religion with saints, holy days, sacraments and prayers, and made himself the high priest of the cult. Although he died in 1857, there still are remnants of sects that uphold the religion he founded.

The personal life of Comte had many unhappy aspects. He was twice committed to an insane asylum: the first time, as a result of his unhappy marriage to a woman of the streets; the second, after the death of Clotilde de Vaux, the wife of a man imprisoned for life. It was Clotilde who served as liaison between the *grand être* (that is, mankind) and its high priest. John Stuart Mill was one of Comte's principal sponsors, helping him to remain solvent, write, and spread his cult. The positivist philosophy was a reaction to the speculative phase that developed in philosophy after Kant.

The French Moralists and Utopists

Michel de Montaigne
(Portrait of Sixteenth Century "French
School," Musée Conce Chantilly)

MONTAIGNE, MICHEL D'EYQUEM DE

MONTAIGNE, MICHEL D'EYQUEM DE (1533-1592). While noblemen used to adorn their coats-of-arms with grandiloquent devices, Montaigne wrote under his own: "Que sais-je?" (What do I know?) His lifetime was a period of constant quarreling between theologians, philosophers and scientists, and a time of bloody religious wars. Montaigne fought for peace and tolerance, using, for that purpose, the weapons of irony and scepticism. Against fanaticism he appealed to clear thinking and considerate reason, and, due to his literary skill, he succeeded in inspiring confidence in the value of reason at least in small circles of men everywhere in Europe, though most of the rulers, politicians and theologians continued to incite the fanaticism of the masses.

Montaigne, born in the castle of Montaigne near Bordeaux, France, was the son of a father who probably was of Jewish descent, and a mother whose family was certainly Jewish. Some of Montaigne's relatives were Marranos, baptized Jews who secretly continued to profess Judaism, and Montaigne knew that. He admired the tenacity with which the Jews held to their faith in the face of persecution, and doubted that any one of them became a true convert to another religion.

Montaigne tried to undermine the position of any orthodoxy and fanaticism by showing the common weaknesses of men in order to make them aware of the possibility that other people might be right and they themselves could be wrong. He declared that arrogance is the natural and characteristic disease of man who, in fact, is the most fragile of all creatures. But his manner of exhorting to humility had nothing in common with that of ecclesiastical sermons. Montaigne completely changed the tone of religious and philosophical discussions. He did not express indignation. He emphasized the personal character of his views and experiences, and did not exclude other people's opinions on the same items. He understood men of genius as well as plain people. He studied Athens' civilization and was interested in the life of American Indians. At those who think that the entire universe is established and moving only for the commodity and the service of human beings he smiled. But while rejecting anthropocentric teleology and opposing any belief in absolute knowledge, Montaigne far from denied the values of human life and character, of nature, beauty, the arts and sciences. The

MICHEL DE MONTAIGNE

Montaigne's Home at Bordeaux

Original Edition of The Book of Reason, *by Montaigne, Displayed at Bordeaux*

relativity of values was to him no proof that there are no values or duties at all. Kindness toward fellow men was presented as an almost absolute value by Montaigne.

For his confessions, Montaigne created a new literary form—namely, the essay. It was used by Bacon, Descartes, Locke, Rousseau, and Voltaire, among others, and has remained popular to the present day. One of Montaigne's most interested readers was William Shakespeare and he was followed by Molière, Laurence Sterne, Anatole France and a host of others.

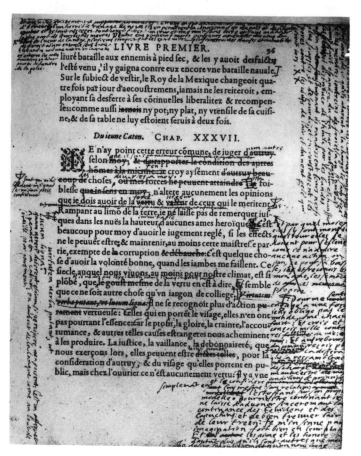

Montaigne's Annotations to a Page of His Essays

La Rochefoucauld

Manuscript Page of Montesquieu's Pensées

LA ROCHEFOUCAULD, FRANÇOIS VI DUC DE
(Prince De Marsillac)

LA ROCHEFOUCAULD, FRANÇOIS VI DUC DE (PRINCE DE MARSILLAC) (1613-1680). The almighty Cardinal Richelieu and his successor, the no less powerful Cardinal Mazarin, were defied by the Duke of La Rochefoucauld who, descending from a family as noble and as old as the Plantagenets, treated the statesmen—virtually absolute rulers over France—as snobs. Fearless on the military and political battlefield, La Rochefoucauld lacked and detested brutality. He was a brilliant soldier, but no warrior. Twice exiled because of his frankness, La Rochefoucauld was more inclined to observation and meditation, and thinking gave him solace for his experiences without mellowing his impressions. His sentiments were benevolent but his eyes and ears were inexorable. He called himself an Epicurean and a sceptic. In fact, La Rochefoucauld, a *grand-seigneur* of the highest rank in the French kingdom, was melancholic. What he had experienced and observed he condensed with admirable artistic skill in his *Maxims* (1665). He had seen the triumph of intrigues, the victory of meanness over generosity, and he had penetrated into the secrets of statesmen and kings, of court-cabals and political plotters. He had participated in foreign and civil wars, and felt himself defeated and disappointed. From all these occurrences he drew the conclusion that egoism is the rule of human actions. His feelings were in constant revolt against this knowledge of his comprehensive mind. The *Maxims* scandalized the society of his time but were eagerly read and translated into many languages, and their resigned wisdom continues to attract philosophers and laymen in France and elsewhere, despite all cultural changes.

Charles de Montesquieu
(Medallion by Dassier)

Montesquieu's Room in the Château de la Brède

MONTESQUIEU, CHARLES DE SECONDAT

MONTESQUIEU, CHARLES DE SECONDAT (1689-1755). The principle of separation of powers, or of checks and balances, which is characteristic of the Constitution of the United States was formulated in such a striking manner by Montesquieu that Jefferson, Hamilton, Adams and Madison and other founders of the United States were deeply impressed by it, and held it more or less clearly in their minds when they gave the Constitution its shape.

Montesquieu was a high judge in France but he was very critical of the regime which he served. In his youth he had been a member of the "First Floor Club" in Paris, a secret society strongly opposed to absolutism and clerical orthodoxy. He remained faithful to the club's principles but became rather moderate in his judgment on the advantages of other political systems. His *Persian Letters* (1721), a thinly veiled satirical criticism of French life, made a great sensation. His *Reflections on the Causes of the Greatness and the Decadence of the Romans* (1734) is considered one of the most important monuments of mod-ern historical literature. The very spirit of Roman civilization is grasped and brilliantly illustrated by Montesquieu, however much scholars of later times may object to his treatment of details. Montesquieu's principal work *The Spirit of the Laws* (1748) was the result of fourteen years of strenuous study into political history and comparative legislation, of reading sources and observing life by traveling through many countries of Europe, and above all, of a stay in England where he arrived on Lord Chesterfield's yacht. Montesquieu admired England, though not uncritically. Its institutions, in his opinion, guaranteed and realized the highest possible degree of freedom, and he derived this view from the application of the principle of checks and balances. This view is not shared by modern constitutional historians or jurists, least of all concerning the England of Montesquieu's days. But his work has been of lasting value to the development of methods of analyzing political, social and legal conditions and their connection. Next to Locke, Montesquieu was the most influential champion of liberalism in the 18th century.

Voltaire
(Painting by Largillière)

Frederick the Great of Prussia, a friend of Voltaire, Playing the Flute at Potsdam

VOLTAIRE, FRANÇOIS MARIE AROUET DE

VOLTAIRE, FRANÇOIS MARIE AROUET DE (1694-1778). W. Somerset Maugham, the well-known novelist and playwright, has declared: "Before I start writing a novel, I read *Candide* over again so that I may have in the back of my mind the touchstone of that lucidity, grace and wit."

Voltaire's *Candide* is, however, not only a literary masterwork that defies the change of time and taste; it is also an attack on Leibniz' *Theodicy*. With mordant irony it castigates the belief that the existing world is the best of all possible ones. Life and studies confirmed Voltaire in his bitter criticism of man and human institutions. Three times imprisoned in the *Bastille* in Paris, Voltaire was then banished from France. As an exile in England, he studied Locke and Newton, and adopted Bolingbroke's deism. The result of these studies, Voltaire's *Lettres philosophiques* (1734), was publicly burned by the hangman in Paris. Dissatisfied with his own time, Voltaire, one of the initiators of modern history of civilization, saw that in the past the triumph of error and injustice had been even more outrageous. But he persisted in teaching that man is capable of shaping the future of humanity in accordance with true morality by making prevail the results of secular science and by resisting arbitrary power and intolerance. Until the last day of his life, Voltaire struggled for liberty of thought and conscience. He, a single man, defeated the

Voltaire reading from his works to King Stanislas of Poland
(Painting by V. de Paredes)

organized power of fanaticism by rehabilitating Jean Calas, the victim of a judicial murder, and by saving his relatives from imprisonment. Voltaire passed the watchword of resistance to fanaticism. It became a battle cry that is heard and echoed in the present time.

190

The Abbé Desfontaines, Literary Critic with Whom Voltaire Conducted His Most Bitter Quarrel
(Engraving by Deorochers)

Voltaire Blessing Benjamin Franklin's Grandson

Arrest of Voltaire and His Niece at Frankfort in 1753 by order of Frederick the Great
(Painting by Jules Girardet)

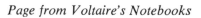

Page from Voltaire's Notebooks

J. J. Rousseau

ROUSSEAU, JEAN JACQUES

ROUSSEAU, JEAN JACQUES (1712-1778). Rousseau was the first to diagnose, from secular aspects, the symptoms of the crisis of modern civilization. Both his approach and many of his conclusions have been exposed to criticism. Nevertheless, he gave us an early and powerful expression of a current of thoughts and sentiments that transformed cultural life and that has not yet come to an end in the age of two world wars.

Both modern civilization and the entire history that shaped its features were condemned by Rousseau as deviation from nature. Rousseau asserted that every man has a unique personality, and that all men are equal. But, in his eyes, state and society are the triumph of oppression, men have become unequal because of artificial conventions, and cultural life is degenerating more and more because vital needs of the human heart are neglected. He demanded a radical reform that does not mean return to primitive barbarism, but rather a restitution of the natural order in which reason and sentiments become harmonized, and in which man meets his fellow man with neither artificial subordination nor any intention of subordinating him, both respecting the general will which is expressed by the majority of citizens.

Rousseau's criticism was determined to a large degree by his sense of justice and his aesthetic sentiments. In this

Rousseau at Madame Basile's

Rousseau's Last Moments
(Painting by Moreau le Jeune)

Rousseau's House at Montmorency

way, he became the precursor of the French Revolution, and caused a literary revolution that started soon after the publication of his principal works. His call "back to nature" was echoed by the masses of oppressed peoples and by individuals who longed for a free development of their faculties. Since Rousseau, sincerity and intensity of feelings and expression, rather than formal perfection, have become the principal criteria of literary and artistic criticism. Rousseau enhanced the effects of his teachings by the charm and vigor of his style and, even more, by the unrestrained exhibition of his inner life, for he was by no means afraid of showing his flaws and vices to the public. His political doctrine emphasizes that the sovereignty belongs to the people. His religious creed is a deism that relies more on feelings than on reason, without excluding rational principles. Rousseau's literary influence remained strong from the times of Goethe and Byron to the days of R. L. Stevenson and D. H. Lawrence. Among the philosophers, his most important disciples, were Kant, Fichte and Hegel and, not the least among them, Karl Marx. In politics, Maximilien Robespierre was Rousseau's most devoted follower. Notwithstanding the excesses of the French Revolution, Rousseau continued to be regarded the apostle of democracy, although it was discovered that some of the aspects of his philosophy favor totalitarian dictatorship.

J. J. Rousseau
(Bust by Houdon, Louvre)

Rousseau's Arrival in the Elysian Fields, Greeted by Plato, Diogenes, Montaigne and Others

Paris in 1750

HOLBACH, PAUL HENRI THIRY BARON D'

HOLBACH, PAUL HENRI THIRY BARON D' (1723-1789). Friends and foes of the French Revolution used to regard Holbach, who died some months before its outbreak, as one of its most important prophets. His writings were deemed responsible for the anti-clerical and anti-Christian excesses which took place. This may be true. But Holbach's atheism was detested by such influential leaders as Robespierre just as by the priests who had been attacked constantly in Holbach's pamphlets and books.

All who knew Holbach personally liked him. He was gentle, generous, ready to help poor writers and scholars, and a brilliant host. Only priests, the Church and religions were hated fanatically by him. His criticism of deism and theism challenged even Voltaire.

Holbach was a German nobleman who settled in Paris and adopted French nationality. He wrote many treatises on political, social and religious questions, generally hiding himself behind a pseudonym. His principal work *The System of Nature* (1770) has been called "the Bible of the atheists." It is something more. Holbach, while dealing with "the laws of the physical and moral world," represented nature not as a creation but as an immense workshop that provides man with tools by means of which he is enabled to give his life a better shape. He developed a philosophy of eternal change, and energetically rejected the assumption that all species have existed all the time or must exist in the future. He sneered at those philosophers or scientists who think nature incapable of giving rise to new organisms hitherto unknown. Man is not exempt from the law of change. Nature is indispensable to man, but man is not indispensable to nature which can continue her eternal course without man. Holbach must be credited for having, in 1770, pronounced evolutionism, declaring "Nature contains no constant forms."

Joseph Joubert
(Drawing by Sophie Joubert)

François Marie Charles Fourier (1772-1835). Utopist who opposed all restrictions on man's path to happiness. Propagated free love and communal living under common ownership of production
(Painting by Gigoux, Louvre)

JOUBERT, JOSEPH

JOUBERT, JOSEPH (1754-1824). With regard to psychological refinement and literary skill, Joubert belongs to that line of French moralists whose outstanding representatives are Montaigne and La Rochefoucauld. However, Joubert differs from them in that he is more interested in psychological curiosities than in truth and morals and he prefers aesthetical enjoyment to knowledge of the facts. In his youth, Joubert was a lay-brother but he left the cloister because he was fond of worldly life and could not renounce his associations with women. He was always sincere when he professed his predilection for the Catholic Church and his hatred of the philosophy, and even more so of the philosophers, of the Enlightenment. He did not conceal that his judgment relied on taste, not on faith. He disliked Diderot and D'Alembert because he considered them "vulgar," and for the same reason, he was horrified by the French Revolution. Under Napoleon, he was appointed inspector-general of the University. But the Emperor's favor entailed the disgrace of the restored Bourbons, and Joubert had always sympathized with royalism.

To Joubert, Plato did not Platonize enough. In fact, Joubert was more akin to Epicureanism, though he felt uneasy while enjoying life. Enjoyment of perfumes, flowers, refined cuisine, precious silk was a vital point to him. But enjoyment could not overcome his feelings of tediousness. Joubert was of very delicate health, but he enjoyed suffering because he believed that sickness made his soul more subtle. As a psychologist of morbidity, Joubert anticipated many psychological discoveries of recent times.

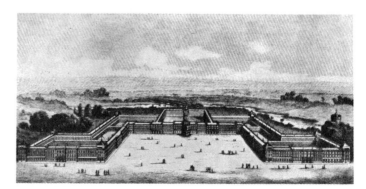

A Utopian Factory designed according to the plans of Fourier. In this institution, living and work facilities were communized, about 400 families to a phalanx

195

Saint-Simon
(Portrait by Guiart-Labille)

SAINT-SIMON, CLAUDE HENRI, COMTE DE

SAINT-SIMON, CLAUDE HENRI, COMTE DE (1760-1825). In Saint-Simon's personality, the mind of a true philosopher was coupled with that of a smart business-man, that of a sincere philanthropist with that of an adventurous schemer. He fought at Yorktown for American independence. He was the first to advocate the building of the canals of Suez and Panama. More than a hundred years before the Young Plan, he demanded the foundation of an international bank, and his most faithful disciples became founders of joint-stock societies and constructors of canals and railroads, which, as Saint-Simon taught them, are necessary for the organization of human welfare and the realization of the ideals of human solidarity. Saint-Simon was the first to denounce "exploitation of men by their fellow men," and to prognosticate the increasing concentration of capital and industry. But he was also one of those "wicked speculators" who were branded by Robespierre, and he narrowly escaped execution. During the French Revolution he amassed a large fortune, but he died in poverty.

Saint-Simon's dominant idea was that the social system must be an application of the philosophical system, and that the function of philosophy is a prevalently social one. After ten years of studies devoted to physics, astronomy and chemistry, he turned to the study of human society and pronounced as its result that philosophical changes cause social changes, and that philosophy, as he conceived of it, must found a new society, a new religion, and a new evaluation of men. He especially emphasized that in modern times the industrial worker had become of far greater importance than the nobleman, the soldier and the priest, and, consequently, that he must occupy a higher social position than the former dignitaries. To industrial workers, scholars, and bankers he entrusted the organization of his new social system, which may be characterized as a kind of technocratic socialism. But the form of government was, in Saint-Simon's opinion, of lesser importance than the problem of administration. Therefore, he was not radically opposed to monarchism. After the publication of his works on the *Reorganization of Europe* (1814), *The Industrial System and Catechism of Industrials* (1821-1824), he wrote *The New Christianity* in the year of his death, 1825, by which he intended to substitute a secular religion of pantheistic and sensualistic color for the Christian faith. A small circle of enthusiastic disciples revered Saint-Simon who lived in obscurity and poverty as the founder of the religion of the future. After his death he became famous the world over, due to the propagandistic ardor of his pupils. He particularly influenced Goethe, Carlyle, Auguste Comte and Karl Marx.

The Encyclopedists

A Reading at Diderot's Home

DIDEROT, DENIS

DIDEROT, DENIS (1713-1784). As a philosopher, Diderot has often been underestimated. His unique versatility of mind was amazing. The journalistic vein (characteristic of his mentality) enabled him to enlarge, rectify, and communicate his philosophical knowledge and his personal concepts of man, nature, life, and moral and cultural values. His arguments were founded upon those recent scientific discoveries whose philosophical consequences he grasped with extraordinary agility.

Diderot, in addition to being the editor of the most influential and famous encyclopedia, was himself a living encyclopedia; well versed in the natural and social sciences, in the history of literature and the arts; in philosophy and religion. He never confined his achievements to the mere summarization of the knowledge of his time; he was an innovator in many fields. He was the first modern

Frontispiece of the Encyclopédie, *Edited by Diderot, D'Alembert and Others*

Diderot and Catherine II of Russia

art critic. He rebelled against the authority of classicism in the literary and artistic life of continental Europe. He criticized the civil and religious institutions of his time and demonstrated the necessity for change. As a dramatist, he pioneered in dealing with social problems and in representing modern middle-class life on the stage.

All of these activities were compatible with his philosophical outlook which conceived of life and spirit as eternal and eternally changing. He stated that the formation of moral values could be traced back to the experiences of early childhood of both the individual and mankind. He made many studies of the blind, mute, and deaf, and proceeded to epistemological, psychological, aesthetic, and sociological points of view that have since had great consequence. His daring spirit caused Diderot to incur royal and papal interdictions and imprisonment.

D'Alembert Delivering a Lecture at the Home of Madame Geoffrin

D'ALEMBERT, JEAN BAPTISTE LE ROND

D'ALEMBERT, JEAN BAPTISTE LE ROND (1717-1783). Considered the father of positivism, and in many ways the progenitor of pragmatism, D'Alembert maintained that truth is hypothetical but useful. In his introduction to the famous encyclopedia that he and Diderot edited, D'Alembert outlined the psychological genesis of knowledge, and the logical order and historical sequence of the sciences. He classed mathematics with natural philosophy, stating that it could be developed into a science of general dimensions contrary to the mathematical theories of Plato and Descartes. One of the most eminent mathematicians of his century, his theory of mathematics was consistent with his perceptual empiricism. He also made valuable contributions to physics, meteorology, and astronomy. In his literary works, he violently opposed all religious organization.

Abandoned as an infant, he was found on November 16, 1717, near the entrance to the Church St. Jean-Le-Rond by a glazier's wife. Brilliant and talented as a child, he achieved membership in the Academy of Sciences at the age of twenty-four. When he had become famous, his real mother, Madame de Tencin, socially important in Paris, recognized him, but he remained attached to his foster mother. He declined the presidency of the Prussian Academy of Sciences, offered him by Frederick II of Prussia, and the offer of Catherine II of Russia who wanted him to become a tutor for her grandson, who later became Czar Paul I.

D'Alembert

"The Ungrateful Son" by Greuze, a Work Much Admired and Discussed by Diderot

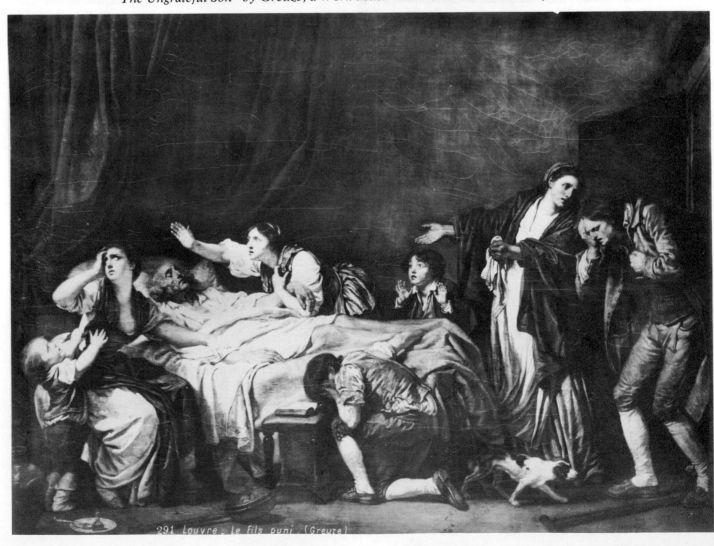

291. Louvre - Le Fils puni. (Greuze)

The French Revolution

The French Revolution (not unlike the Russian *putsch* of Lenin in 1917) began under Danton, Marat and Robespierre as an uprising of a suppressed people against the traditional tyrant on the throne, but soon deteriorated into the military dictatorship of Napoleon Bonaparte, thus in the end replacing a traditional autocracy with a usurpatory one. He made not only himself, but three of his four brothers, kings and the fourth a prince. He made his three sisters a queen, a grand duchess and a princess. Similar nepotism was practiced in our time by the Marxist Stalin and the renegade Socialist, Mussolini.

The wounded Robespierre, about to be moved from the antechamber of the Committee of Public Safety, July 28, 1794

(*Engraving by Berthault after Duplessi-Bertaux*)

Robespierre, in manner typical of so-called Communistic reformers, succumbed easily to the temptation of personal aggrandizement. He permitted the elderly Madame St. Amaranthe to acclaim him as precursor of the coming Messiah

The Execution of Robespierre and His Accomplices

Marat, Writing His L'Ami du Peuple

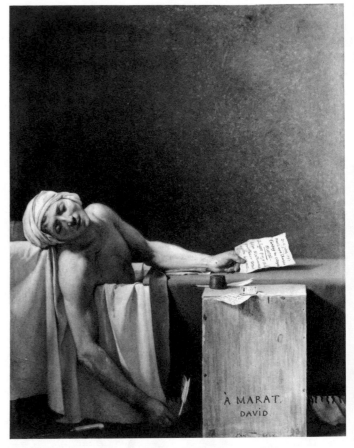

Marat Assassinated by a Disillusioned Citizen

The Body of the Princess de Lamballe at the Mercy of the Mob

Napoleon's troops terrorized Europe from end to end
(Goya, Prado, Madrid)

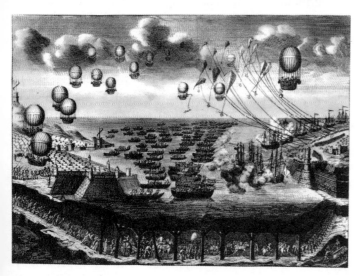

Fantastic Scheme of Napoleonic Days for an Air Attack on England

The final stage of the people's revolt in France, a new monarch replacing the one guillotined

Philosophers of the Third Republic

Victor Cousin

COUSIN, VICTOR

COUSIN, VICTOR (1792-1867). The disrespect largely prevalent for the philosophy of Victor Cousin is based upon his emphasis of *eclecticism,* a term he used to characterize his method, disregarding the pejorative meaning of the word which implied shallowness and dependence. Although Cousin does not belong to that small nucleus of great philosophers, many of his ideas influenced American transcendentalism while others parallel modern American views, and continue to inspire European philosophers.

Cousin was attracted by that which is common to humanity. He was convinced that mankind could not be sceptical; that it needed a common faith (not necessarily a religious faith, but certainty). He maintained that the mission of philosophy was to explain faith, not destroy it. His philosophical studies were principally aimed at the elevation of the soul, not at insight into the mystery of things. His cardinal principle asserted that truth was contained in each of the philosophical systems known throughout historical time; that every major philosopher had made a contribution to the knowledge of truth, and that their composite contributions comprised the whole truth, even though they contained some errors. Modifications of Cousin's concepts are manifest in Wilhelm Dilthey's "doctrine of philosophical types," and Benedetto Croce's identification of philosophy with its history. Cousin believed that he had discovered a method of intellectual distillation whereby the method of essential truth could be extrapolated from the various historical systems. He called this method of critical choice *eclecticism.* It was based upon his belief that spontaneous reason, freed from the control of the will, became pure in its contemplation, and thereby was able to behold essential truth.

As a young man, Cousin adhered to the Scottish school of Thomas Reid; in the period from 1815 to 1833 he was seized by a "metaphysical fever," and studied Hegel and Schelling, both of whom he later came to know personally. In 1840 he returned to the Scottish school of philosophy, and severely criticized his earlier writings. However, it was the writings of his "metaphysical fever" that had the greatest influence on American thought. Cousin was the intermediary whereby the transcendentalists acquainted themselves with German idealism, for his was a more lucid, if not altogether correct, presentation. For a time, James Marsh (the founder of Transcendentalism), Theodore Parker, Charles Sumner, and George Bancroft were his devoted adherents; James Walker and Caleb Henry maintained his views somewhat later. Emerson, too, was indebted to Cousin, although he rightly declared that Cousin's method of "distillation" was the result of optical delusion. Cousin became a peer of France, royal councillor, and minister of public education during the régime of Louis Philippe. He was attacked by the clergy for his defense of the liberty of science, and later by the radical leftists. He became politically obscure after the coup d'état of Napoleon III.

A. A. Cournot

In his early years, Cournot was a tutor in the house of Marshalie Gouvion St. Cyr; later, he became an important dignitary, but regardless of his position, he always led a modest and unpretentious existence. He declined to head a school, and for that reason, his philosophy was neglected for a long time.

Charles Renouvier (1818-1903), a philosopher influenced by Kant and Leibniz. He rejected Kant's thing-in-itself and Leibniz' causal determinism. One of the first modernists to give full consideration to the aspect of contingency in experience, and one of the first to break with the absolutist conception of God, Whom he held to be not in every respect unlimited

COURNOT, ANTOINE AUGUSTINE

COURNOT, ANTOINE AUGUSTINE (1801-1877). Modesty and resignation are the repetitious themes of Cournot's philosophy. His concept of truth was founded upon probability rather than certainty. He renounced those inquiries into what other philosophers termed the essence of truth. He was satisfied with investigating the role of truth in the development of the sciences and determined to find the most adequate expression for that kind of truth instrumental in the promotion of scientific research. His efforts to determine the foundation of human knowledge were not directed to an analysis of general human faculties, but to a study of those principles which make for progress in the positive sciences. The major conclusions of Cournot's reflections were that chance is a positive factor in the sum total of reality; that contingency maintained its position beside order; and that the total continuity of evolution could not be proved. He believed that man could approach truth even though he might not be able to attain it and elaborated this point of view in his books: *Considérations sur la Marche des Idées* (1872) and *Traité de L'Enchanement des Idées Fondamentales dans les Sciences et dans L'Histoire* (A Treatise on the Relationships of the Fundamental Concepts in the Sciences and History, 1881).

Joseph Ernest Renan (1823-1892). Philosopher, theologian, orientalist and historian. Achieved popular fame with the publication of his Vie de Jésus, *in 1863, later expanded to an eight-volume* Histoire des Origines du Christianisme *(1886). Also wrote a five-volume* Histoire du Peuple d'Israel, *as well as many works in philosophy*

Hippolyte Taine (1828-1893). A historian markedly influenced by Comte and John Stuart Mill. Saw the essence of philosophy in the discovery of the underlying laws and principles of causality

BOUTROUX, EMILE

BOUTROUX, EMILE (1845-1921). It is a rare occurrence for European scholars to hail a doctoral thesis in philosophy as a turning point in the history of thought. However, this was the case with Boutroux's thesis published in 1874, *De la Contingence des Lois de la Nature* (On the Contingency of the Laws of Nature). Subsequently he became one of the most influential teachers of philosophy at the Sorbonne in Paris; Henri Bergson was one of his many famous pupils.

He demonstrated that the concept of natural law in all branches of science (from mathematics to biology) is a result rather than a principle, for it does not prove the universal reign of necessity. According to Boutroux, generally the relatively invariable relationship between causes and effects comes about because of an inadequate grasp of such true and profound realities as life and liberty. He encountered the objection that contingency connotes hazard and disorder by stating that necessity implies immutability and death. Many of Boutroux's arguments on the problem of liberty and the extent to which necessity can be admitted have become classic. He always endeavored to strengthen the conviction that man is able to act upon nature. His adherence to the ideas advanced in his first book helped to pave the way for new progress in science. When asked what the good life involved, he replied "a thought conceived in early years and developed in maturity." His opinion was internationally revered as the expression of "Europe's conscience."

POINCARÉ, HENRI

POINCARÉ, HENRI (1854-1912). The name of Poincaré is mostly associated with the person of Raymond Poincaré who was President of the Third French Republic during the First World War. Henri was his first cousin, and outside France he was known in the scientific world only. Eight foreign Universities conferred honorary doctors' degrees upon him; twenty one foreign academies made him their honorary member, not to mention the honors he enjoyed in his native country. Poincaré himself,

however, was more satisfied with the great influence he exercised on succeeding generations through his writings and lectures.

Poincaré made great strides in the history of mathematics, especially by his disquisitions on differential equations and analytical functions. The development of mechanics and astronomy owes to him admirable results concerning the capillarity, the equilibrium of fluid masses and rotating liquids, and, above all, the form of the planets. He made also very important contributions to geography and geodesty. In the field of physics, Poincaré dealt with the problems of vibration and elasticity, electricity and radioactivity, electro-dynamics, and gravitation, and published his views on relativity some months before Albert Einstein made known his famous theory.

Poincaré's philosophical inquiries concerned especially the process of hypothesis making, the relations between the logical and empirical elements of knowledge. From the statement that for any consistent and verifiable hypothesis there is a host of other likewise consistent and verifiable hypotheses, he proceeded to the conclusion that the choice between them is not dictated by logic or observation but by what he called convention. According to Poincaré, the value of science lies not so much in its usefulness as in its intrinsic worth, in the elevation of the soul which the true scientist feels while working. Poincaré was a fighter for human ideals. He courageously and successfully participated in the struggle for Dreyfus by destroying the arguments of the experts who were hired by the French general staff.

DURKHEIM, DAVID ÉMILE

DURKHEIM, DAVID ÉMILE (1858-1917). A founder of the science of sociology, Durkheim regarded sociology neither as a branch of philosophy, psychology, nor biology, though he always stressed the importance of psychological and biological knowledge. Similarly, he was well versed in ethnology and utilized many of its results; but he carefully defined the method and object of sociology as distinct from the former.

Even as a sociologist, Durkheim retained his belief in moral values. He stated that these could not be explained without taking into account the existence of society; that society formed and enlightened the individual; that it was impossible to separate the individual from society, or to regard society as the mere totality of individuals. He conceived of the group mind as a reality distinct from the minds of the individuals who comprised the group.

Durkheim's real starting point was his study of the division of labor. He regarded the division of labor not only as an important social and economic phenomenon but as a proof that the individual was incapable of controlling his life. From this he proceeded to demonstrate that the concepts of causality, space, and time had to be derived from collective sources. He was a man of wide perspectives. His inquiries embraced religion (particularly its elementary forms), law, criminology, ethics, moral data, economics, aesthetics, and the histories of language and the arts. He was particularly interested in education which he viewed as the birth of social man from the embryo of the individual.

All who met Durkheim were deeply impressed by his ascetic appearance. He seemed to be the embodiment of the scientific spirit. His disciples, among whom Lucien Lévy-Bruhl was the outstanding, never forgot the inspiration engendered by Durkheim for methodical investigation. Even his opponents respected the austerity of his devotion to the cause of truth.

David Durkheim

LÉVY-BRUHL, LUCIEN

LÉVY-BRUHL, LUCIEN (1857-1939). When Lévy-Bruhl died, the Sorbonne, the University of Paris, deplored the loss of one of its most brilliant teachers; the French people mourned a staunch defender of human rights and a convinced and active republican and democrat; tens of thousands of political refugees, of human beings persecuted for religious or racial reasons, felt themselves deprived of the moral and material support of a true humanitarian; and experts in sociology, psychology, philosophy, epistemology and many branches of linguistics began to miss the inspiring influence of a scholar whose ideas had offered them new aspects.

Lévy-Bruhl had published solid and significant works on the history of German and French philosophy before he began his important investigations of primitive society. He penetrated into the soul of prelogical man who thought mystically. The philosophical problem that was raised by the results of his inquiries can be formulated as follows: Although all physio-psychological processes of perception of the primitive man are the same as those of modern, logical man—although both have the same structure of brain, the primitive man does not perceive as modern man does. The external world which the primitive man perceives is different from that of modern man, just as the social environments of both are different. Death forced Lévy-Bruhl to commit to his successors the responsibility of drawing further conclusions from his statements.

creative evolution which manifest themselves in organic nature as well as in spiritual life, social processes, and individual actions. He was one of the few modern thinkers convinced of the unlimited progress of humanity.

His international fame was so great that after the collapse of France in 1940, the Vichy government offered him exemption from the Jewish laws, patterned after the Nuremberg Laws. Bergson declined the offer and resigned his professorship at the Collège de France.

Maurice Blondel (1861-1903) is a philosopher in the tradition of Maine de Biran and Boutroux and in his work defends an activistic psychology and metaphysics. His "Philosophy of Action" is an idealistic creed which seeks to find a compromise between the extremes of intellectualism and pragmatism

BERGSON, HENRI

BERGSON, HENRI (1859-1941). When Bergson was asked how a philosopher should state his ideas, his reply was, "There are general problems which interest everybody and must be dealt with in language comprehensible to everybody. The solutions to these problems are frequently subordinated to those questions which interest only scholars. These may be dealt with in technical terms." While he admitted the occasional use of professional terminology, Bergson always wrote with a vocabulary easily comprehensible, inspiring, and exciting to philosophical laymen. When he used or coined technical terms, he was capable of making them popular. His mastery of language and subject matter extended his influence far beyond the realm of philosophy into such areas as the history of poetry, the social sciences, and religion. He also influenced the opinions of many contemporary philosophers.

According to Bergson, philosophy is the conscientious and reflective return to the immediate data of intuition. He classified reason as an impersonal faculty, emphasizing that every philosopher consciously proceeds from a chosen point of view. He regarded the philosopher as a man who faced the essentials of thought in order to discover the conditions for the totality of knowledge. He advocated the concept of duration as contrasted with the mechanistic concept of time. From duration, immediately felt in mental life, he proceeded to the ideas of the vital impetus and

MAETERLINCK, MAURICE

MAETERLINCK, MAURICE (1862-1949). Motoring, canoeing, skating, bicycling, and, in his earlier years, even boxing, were Count Maeterlinck's recreations, even in his advanced age. Perhaps he was the greatest sportsman among poets and thinkers, since the end of the ancient Greek civilization. But, as a poet and thinker, Maeterlinck has conceived of life mostly as a fragile, human existence troubled by indefinite fright or as the presentiment of an inevitable catastrophe. His principal experience is the awareness that the sentiments, instincts and ideas of humanity are incapable of remaining consistent as soon as what he called the Unknown appears in life. He was convinced that no human concept of reality corresponds to the metaphysically Real, and that, when the Unknown and the metaphysically Real interfere with human life, man's habitual connection between his ideas and senses is disrupted. All this drove Maeterlinck to a mysticism, though it did not prevent him from remaining fond of science. He

proved to be an excellent empirical scientist, observing the life of bees, ants and spiders with unsurpassed accuracy. Maeterlinck's mysticism was founded upon pantheism and a sympathy with whatever exists. He felt himself in intimate touch with whatever suffers and desires, and his moral teachings pronounced universal love.

Maeterlinck studied the mystical authors of the Christian Middle Ages, but it was two American authors who influenced him decisively in his formative years. Edgar Allan Poe impressed him by his poetry of horror, and Ralph Waldo Emerson revealed to him the sense of spiritual life, and gave his thinking the direction toward the contemplation of eternity. Maeterlinck also strongly sympathized with Walt Whitman with whom he shared the conviction that nothing can perish definitely. Maeterlinck was no traditionalist. He did not regret any abandonment of a creed, or even the collapse of a civilization that has lost its vitality. In his later years, Maeterlinck turned more and more from mysticism to modern science.

BRUNSCHWICG, LÉON

BRUNSCHWICG, LÉON (1869-1944). When the Germans occupied Paris in 1940, they compelled Léon Brunschwicg to leave his position as professor of philosophy at the Sorbonne, robbed him of his collection of precious books, and destroyed his manuscripts. Even though the Germans knew hardly any of his works, the fact that he was a Jew and that his wife had been an undersecretary in the Popular Front cabinet of Léon Blum was sufficient cause for his removal. Despite all the possible dangers, Brunschwicg refused to leave France and spent the remaining years of his life in complete isolation. During this period, he wrote valuable studies of Montaigne, Descartes, and Pascal which were printed in Switzerland and the United States. For his granddaughter, who was then in her teens, he composed a manual of philosophy, entitled *Héritage de Mots, Héritage d'Idées* (Legacy of Words, Legacy of Ideas) which was published posthumously in 1945 after the liberation of France.

To Brunschwicg, philosophy meant not a system of doctrines, but the expression of an attitude toward the totality of material and spiritual beings. It was essentially a reflection on the activities of the human mind in the fields of mathematics, physics, morality, the arts, and the history of civilization. Brunschwicg energetically emphasized the creative power of the human mind and demonstrated its function in the network of relationships that make up the framework of the universe.

Brunschwicg made highly important contributions to the history of science and philosophy, and at the same time contributed to the understanding and solution of practical problems. His reinterpretation of Descartes has become the foundation for a new idealism. He was a man of universal interests as evidenced by his lectures which criticized newspaper editorials as well as Plato or Kant. He was a friend of Marcel Proust, the novelist, and of Marcel Denis, the painter; a patron of the theater and modern art exhibits; an ardent French patriot, and a fighter for human rights.

MARITAIN, JACQUES

MARITAIN, JACQUES (1882-). Jacques Maritain, one of the most influential contemporary Neo-Thomists, is the descendant of a family of free-thinkers. His mother's father was Jules Favre, one of the founders of the Third French Republic and an ardent adversary of clericalism. Maritain kept himself outside the Catholic Church until he was converted by the mystic and eccentric poet, Léon Bloy, who lived in a world of supranatural symbols but was not at all interested in philosophy. After his conversion, which, in some respects, was prepared by his devotion to Henri Bergson, Maritain went to Heidelberg to study biology with Hans Driesch. Until 1926, Maritain was associated with the *Action Française,* the French royalist shock troop, and, in accordance with its program, he professed strong opposition to republicanism, democracy and liberal ideas. After the *Action Française* was condemned by Pope Pius XI in 1926, Maritain began to profess confidence in a democracy inspired by Christian faith. At the same time, he turned from speculative metaphysics to history and sociology.

Although Maritain has remained a staunch defender of the Catholic Church and Scholasticism, he does not regard the Christian Middle Ages as the obligatory model of hu-

man civilization. Rather, he is inclined to acknowledge the rights of a plurality of civilizations, all of which are guided by Divine providence, and proves his ability to expound historical and contemporary, human and social problems in Thomist terms, which, in his opinion, enable him to discover the relations between historical phenomena and the supratemporal order. Proceeding from these views, Maritain maintains that the value of the human person is rooted in an order which is created by God and strives toward God. The Catholic Church is acknowledged by Maritain as universal, supranational, supraracial and supratemporal, but he is eager to avoid any romanticizing of what he demands to be respected. He insists that the Church is not the home of the elect but the refuge of sinners. On the other hand, he is, on the ground of his conception of the Church, as strongly opposed to Nazism as he is to Bolshevism.

Any contradiction between the Christian faith and modern science is, according to Maritain, due to ontological ambitions on the part of Descartes and Newton, and will vanish after science will have elaborated a thoroughly nonmetaphysical approach. But he does not believe that, even in a distant future, science and faith will cooperate without friction.

GILSON, ETIENNE

GILSON, ETIENNE (1884-). While Jacques Maritain is the outstanding militant exponent of the philosophy of Aquinas in our time, Gilson is its outstanding historian. But, in analyzing Thomism historically, Gilson does not lack the fighting spirit. He defends his master by attacking what is called modern philosophy, and he does so both by special studies and by outlining large aspects, in order to prove that Thomism has not the ambition of achieving philosophy once and for all but rather of keeping philosophical thought alive, and that Thomism is able to offer a basis for relating reality as we know it to the permanent principles in whose light all the changing problems of science, of ethics or of the arts must be solved. To Gilson, Thomism is by no means identical with Scholasticism, but rather a revolt against it. Gilson does not believe in systems of philosophy. He believes firmly in the guidance of such principles which, in the course of the history of philosophy, have become evident as an impersonal necessity for philosophical inquiry and orientation. History of philosophy, therefore, is, for him, by far more a part of philos-

ophy itself than history of science is a part of science. It is possible, he says, to become a competent scientist without knowing much about history of science, but no man can carry very far his own philosophical reflections, unless he first studies the history of philosophy. For Gilson, there have been only three really great metaphysicians, viz., Plato, Aristotle and Aquinas, and none of them had a philosophical system, which would have meant the abolition of philosophy. From the Middle Ages until the present time three great experiments for founding a system have been attempted, and all of them have failed. The medieval, the Cartesian and the modern experiment, represented by Immanuel Kant and Auguste Comte, have broken down. The result, as Gilson sees it, is the reduction of philosophy to science. Its consequences would be the abdication of the right to judge and rule nature, the conception of Man as a mere part of nature, and the green light for the most reckless social adventures to play havoc with human lives and institutions. Gilson is convinced that the revival of the philosophy of Aquinas opens the way out of that zone of danger.

surpassing its rivals in spirituality and psychological refinement.

Romains is no sceptic. He does not believe that human mind is capable of discovering absolute and definite truth. He holds that there will always be an aspect of reality which challenges the dominant one. Reality means change. When man becomes tired of broaching new questions and when he acquiesces in a creed or system, he will lose contact with reality. But he believes that in the course of history man will come closer and closer to truth, although new aspects will be opened which let him see new problems. His "men of good will" respect reason and give experience the last word, though they do not exclude the possibility that intuition, in exceptional cases, may also discover reality.

ROMAINS, JULES

ROMAINS, JULES (1885-   ). At the height of his literary successes as one of the greatest French novelists of our time, Jules Romains has been faithful to the ideal of "unanimism" which has dominated the poetry of his youth, but he has modified it and changed the means of expression.

"Unanimism" originally meant an opposition to individualism, or at least to the exaltation of individual particularities, universal sympathy with life, existence, humanity. In later years, the end of literature has been defined by Romains as "representation of the world without judgment," and his social ideal seems to comprise as well the highest conception of solidarity as the defense of individual rights. In his immense series of novels, *Men of Good Will,* Romains has not limited his task to the invention of characters and events but has also tried to live the lives of his figures with extreme concreteness, to let them think about questions of the day and the universe, about the principal problems of civilization, to let them criticize one another, develop their judgment, and he has indeed succeeded in uniting intellectual force, artistic vision, colorful description, and narrative dynamics. The result is a picture of French cultural life in its stratification, with its fundamental conflicts and common tendencies, on a scale which can be compared only with Balzac and Zola, but

"Alain" (Émile Auguste Chartier) (1868-1951). Philosopher and essayist of aphoristic manner

DE BROGLIE, LOUIS

DE BROGLIE, LOUIS (1892-   ). Albert Einstein evaluated De Broglie's genius and achievements as something which "happens only in large intervals of history." He also expressed great satisfaction with the decision of the Nobel Prize Committee to award the 1929 Nobel Prize to De Broglie.

De Broglie's principal achievement is his formulation of "undulatory mechanics" and "wave mechanics." He overcame the constant antagonism between the theories of emission and undulation by showing the interaction between radiation and matter. The almost-forgotten wave principle of optics was discussed during the seventeenth and eighteenth centuries, and applications of this principle to physics were considered to be completely out of the question. De Broglie's theory assimilates the photons as particulars of light, and the electrons as particulars of matter. These have been confirmed experimentally by noted British and American physicists. De Broglie has always acknowledged that Einstein's theory of relativity was his constant inspiration. He established a relativist mechanics of a more physical character; whereas Einstein's physics is of a more mathematical nature. De Broglie's theory has been stated to be of equal importance with those of Einstein and Planck. It allows for a more rigorous approximation of measurement and a more concrete objectivity of scientific symbolism. It makes for progress in the exactitude of theoretical physics and increasingly reconciles the principles of continuity and discontinuity.

Paul Claudel (1868-1955), poet and philosopher, whose writings make frequent use of Catholic symbolism

Jean Paul Sartre

*Simone de Beauvoir (1908-   ), Existentialist Novelist and
Essayist, Follower of Sartre*

SARTRE, JEAN PAUL

SARTRE, JEAN PAUL (1905-   ). Evidently and avowedly, Sartre, of all younger French authors the one whose
works are most eagerly read in America, has not yet
come to a final formulation of his philosophical thoughts.
In his *Baudelaire* (1947) and in his critical essays *Situations* (1947), he expresses ideas and sentiments which
indicate some changes of viewpoint and standard of evaluation when compared with his principal philosophical
works *Being and Nothingness* (1943) and *Existentialism
Is a Humanism* (1946). Also his drama *The Flies* (1943)
leads to conclusions concerning human destiny which are
not yet theoretically expressed by Sartre.

Sartre, always a man of delicate health, and an orphan
at an early age, was a professor of philosophy at one of
Paris' greatest colleges, after having studied at the Sorbonne and at the German University of Göttingen where
he was a student of Husserl. In World War II he was
made a prisoner but was released from the German pris-
oners' camp because of his sickness. When he returned
to Paris, he became a leader of the resistance.

Sartre's philosophy as far as it has so far developed is
deeply influenced by Heidegger. But Sartre's existentialism
departs from that of Heidegger's by establishing an anti-
theological morale, a phenomenology of the body, and
principles of existential psychoanalysis. While anguish is
Heidegger's fundamental experience, Sartre's is that which
he calls nausea, disgust, revulsion against being, duration
repetition and continuance of life, as well as against the
unending mobility of human existence. Sartre tried to ban-
ish all vagueness while confronting personal existence with
general life but he also tried to find a way to vindicate
freedom and the value of the individual.

Two Spaniards

UNAMUNO Y JUGO, MIGUEL DE

UNAMUNO Y JUGO, MIGUEL DE (1864-1936). Any appraisal of Unamuno's philosophy is incomplete without taking into account his poetry. Unamuno the thinker and Unamuno the poet are one and inseparable. He accepted the word of a French critic, according to which Unamuno, the poet, had written only commentaries, perpetual analyses of his ego, the Spanish people, their dreams and ideals, but he maintained that Homer and Dante equally had written only commentaries. His greatest commentary was devoted to the figure of Don Quixote whom he presents as a fighter for glory, life and survival. The mortal Quixote is a comic character. The immortal, realizing his own comicalness, superimposes himself upon it and triumphs over it without renouncing it. The longing for immortality is the ever-recurring theme of Unamuno's philosophy and poetry. It finds no consolation in reason, which is regarded as a dissolving force, or in the intellect, which means identity and which, on its part, means death. Rather, it relies on faith. But faith is a matter of will, and will needs reason and intellect. Thus faith and reason, or philosophy and religion, are enemies which nevertheless need one another. Neither a purely religious nor a purely rationalistic tradition is possible. This insight leads not to compromise but creates instead the tragic sentiment. The tragic history of human thought is the history of the struggle between veracity and sincerity, between the truth that is thought and the truth that is felt, and no harmony between the two adversaries is possible, although they never cease to need each other.

Unamuno called himself "an incorrigible Spaniard." But his erudition was universal. In a conversation he was able to explain the particular Scotticism in a verse of Robert Burns, or the difference between two German mystics of whom only German specialists had ever heard. He combined a utilitarian mind with the search for God. But he confessed that his idea of God was different each time that he conceived it. Proud of his Basque origin, Unamuno, like Loyola, another Basque, was imbued with stern earnestness and a tragic sense of life. He felt himself as the descendant of saints and mystics. But he loved fools and regarded even Jesus as a divine fool. To him, dreaming meant the essence of life, and systematic thinking the destruction of that essence. He declined any philosophic system, but contemplation of the way of philosophizing was to him a source of profound wisdom. He was indeed the knight errant of the searching spirit.

ORTEGA Y GASSET, JOSÉ

ORTEGA Y GASSET, JOSÉ (1883-   ). Although Ortega y Gasset disagrees with almost every important Spaniard of his time, he is generally acknowledged as the representative thinker of modern Spain. No wonder that he became an exile. He is strongly opposed to Franco's dictatorship; however, he had little sympathy with the government of the Spanish republic and its supporters. As the editor of the *Revista del Occidente,* he acquainted the Spanish public with the spiritual life of the Anglo-Saxon countries, of France and Germany, and he gave readers in foreign countries a striking presentation of the main features of Spanish thought and Spanish cultural tradition. But, above all, he has proved to be an original thinker who, rooted in Spanish civilization, universally cultivated, has developed personal ideas of great consequence.

Ortega y Gasset was educated by the Jesuits and studied at the Central University of Madrid, where he became a professor of metaphysics in 1910. Earlier, he had been a disciple of Hermann Cohen, but he became more interested in the philosophy of Husserl and Dilthey. The final result of his preoccupation with German thought was an opposition to idealism. He adopted Dilthey's concept of historical reason, but tried to avoid his shortcomings and went far beyond Dilthey's views.

He insists that human thinking is much less logical than it is generally supposed to be, that man is born at a definite date, formed by a definite tradition, and that his environment is equally determined by historical factors. Therefore, he concludes, whoever aspires to understand man, must throw overboard all immobile concepts and learn to think in ever-shifting terms. Because human life is radical reality that includes any other reality, history, and not physics, is the highest science.

Concerning the idealistic philosophy that starts from a concept of reality in which the subject, the ego, exists enclosed within itself, within its mental acts and states, he objects that such an existence is the opposite of living, whose meaning is to reach out of oneself, to be devoted to what is called the world. Consciousness is historical but the importance of history is not exhausted with the past. Historical knowledge is valued as a preparation for the future, and this conception involves a new appraisal of thinking. For, to Ortega, action without thought means chaos.

The New Italy

ROSMINI-SERBATI, ANTONIO

ROSMINI-SERBATI, ANTONIO (1797-1855). Even to organize charity and enjoin poverty is not without grave consequences and above suspicion. That is what Rosmini-Serbati had to learn. This thinker who is classed as an ontologist in philosophy, is better known for the world-wide Institutes of Charity, the first of which he established in 1828 on Monte Calvario near Domodossola, Italy. Rosminians have to take vows of absolute poverty, which have been criticized at times as more affective than effective, and they must subscribe in their charitable work to two principles, that of passivity or not seeking out their cases and that of personal indifference or disinterestedness in the performance of their duty.

Rosmini was born at Rovereto in the Austrian Tyrol, studied at Trient and Padua, and in 1823 went to Rome with the avowed intention to resuscitate Catholic philosophy and fortify it against disbelief and doubt, in which purpose Pope Pius VII encouraged him. Deeply influenced by Cartesian thinking, he pored over the philosophy of St. Thomas, modifying it in the direction of an ideological psychologism.

Followers of the Society of Jesus opened a feud lasting for many years until silence was imposed by order of the Pope. Rosmini was devoted to Pius IX, even following him into exile. Still, even these circumstances did not prevent his books from being put on the *Index* at a later date, but, nothing detrimental to the Church being found in them, they were dismissed and thus given a semblance of papal approval. Rosmini lived just long enough to see himself thus partially justified.

GIOBERTI, VINCENZO

GIOBERTI, VINCENZO (1801-1852). The part Gioberti acted in the history of the Italian struggle for national unity is more important than the consequence of his philosophical thoughts. Gioberti was a faithful son of the Catholic Church and a convinced liberal in the sense of early nineteenth-century liberalism. An ordained priest in 1825, he sympathized with the revolutionaries who endeavored to liberate Italy from Austrian domination but differed from them because he intended to entrust the Pope with the task of organizing the country politically. Popes Leo XII, and Pius VIII and Gregory XVI were opposed to any change of both the political and the cultural order, and Gioberti was exiled to France in 1833. When Pius IX was elected Pope in 1846, Gioberti built his hopes upon him, and for a short time, the new Pope seemed to justify Gioberti's expectations. After the outbreak of the revolution in 1848, Gioberti returned to Italy but he was soon disappointed, for the revolution was crushed and Pius IX denied his early liberalism. Gioberti continued in his efforts to reconcile the papacy and political liberalism and to defend the Holy See against reproaches on the part of the liberals. But his strength was broken by his painful experiences, and he died soon after the end of the revolution.

In Gioberti's philosophy there is a conspicuous difference between his fundamental concepts and his method. While his method relied upon immediate intuition of the Absolute, his system was concerned with the dialectical relations between essence and existence. He stated that there is a permanent processus by virtue of which essence creates existence, and existence returns to essence. The individual, whose source is divine, is subject to the same processus. The universal spirit returns to universality after having passed the stages from sensibility to intelligibility.

BOLZANO, BERNARD

BOLZANO, BERNARD (1781-1848). The personal fate of Bolzano affords a dramatic insight into the dangers to which really independent thinkers are exposed when the internal revolutions of a reactionary period are manifest. Bolzano was born shortly prior to the outbreak of the French Revolution and died during the year of multiple European revolutions. Although he was not burned at the stake, he was compelled to live in complete retirement for the last thirty years of his life. Bolzano, whose writings were forbidden publication, was a Catholic priest and professor of philosophy at the University of Prague. However, he continued to work ceaselessly, and some of his friends arranged to have his books published anonymously outside his own country. Half a century after his death, his works were discovered and read eagerly by leading modern philosophers. His consistent distinction between logic and psychology was of great importance to Husserl and his disciples. In a sense, Bolzano anticipated the modern theory of transfinite numbers. He was firmly convinced that human knowledge can be enlarged infinitely and insisted on methodical research, cautioning against wishful thinking.

DE SANCTIS, FRANCESCO

DE SANCTIS, FRANCESCO (1817-1883). In the 1848 revolution in Naples, when the revolutionaries struggled against the king's troops, one barricade, in particular, attracted wide attention. It was led by De Sanctis, then the director of a boys' school, who commanded and organized his pupils as a company of trained soldiers. When the revolution was defeated, De Sanctis was imprisoned for more than four years. He utilized this period of enforced idleness to study the philosophy of Hegel and to translate several German works into Italian. Upon his release, he earned his living as a private tutor and free-lance writer; he later became a professor at Zurich, Switzerland, with the German Hegelian, Friedrich Theodor Vischer, and the historian, Jakob Burckhardt, as his colleagues. When the unified kingdom of Italy was achieved, King Victor Emmanuel II appointed De Sanctis minister of public education (1861), and he was later made professor of comparative literature at the University of Naples (1871). There, De Sanctis had many faithful disciples, among whom Benedetto Croce was the most outstanding.

De Sanctis' chief contribution was to aesthetics. Although he remained a Hegelian, he did not found his aesthetic views upon ideas; instead he concentrated upon form. He stated that living form was the essence of art, rather than the ideal of beauty. He opposed all psychological approaches to the arts, especially poetry, and insisted upon formal analysis. His influence upon Italian literary criticism remained strong up to the present time.

ARDIGO, ROBERTO

ARDIGO, ROBERTO (1828-1920). A former Catholic priest and influential leader of Italian positivism, Ardigo abandoned theology in 1869 and resigned from the Church in 1871. He was appointed a professor of theology at the University of Padua in 1881, and from that time until 1900, when an idealistic reaction had taken place, exerted considerable influence in philosophic circles. His positivism, inspired by Auguste Comte, differed from that of his master. Ardigo considered thought more important than matter and insisted on psychological disquisitions. He stated that thought is dominant in every action, the result of every action, and that it vanishes only in a state of general corruption; according to him, thought is a natural formation, unrelated to an alleged absolute; facts are the contents of consciousness, in which the subjective and objective elements are developed from an originally indistinct state. His principal works are *Psychology As A Positive Science* (1870) and *The Moral of the Positivists* (1879).

PARETO, VILFREDO

PARETO, VILFREDO (1848-1923). At the end of his life, Pareto, a professor of political economy at the University of Lausanne, Switzerland, was honored by Mussolini who had come to power. However, he remained indifferent to all Fascist eulogizers and even hinted that the Fascists misunderstood his thoughts. For a time, Pareto's ideas reached a position of power and prestige in democratic America too. Misunderstanding of Pareto's doctrines is not a little due to the fact, deplored by his most faithful admirers, that he had the habit of mentioning his most important points just casually, or even only in notes. Furthermore, he presented not a close and complete system but, rather, a series of studies. What attracted Fascism to Pareto's ideas was not his doctrine itself, but some passages—namely his great admiration of Machiavelli's *The Prince,* his small respect for ethics, and his contempt for metaphysics and religion.

Pareto was born in Paris. He was the son of an Italian nobleman who was a political refugee, and a French mother. When, in 1858, an amnesty allowed him to return to Italy, Pareto prepared himself for an engineering career and became manager of the railroad in the valley of the Arno River. In 1876, he began to write on economics and established "Pareto's law" which tries to express the relation between the amount of income and the number of its recipients. His *Manual of Political Economics* (1906) was much disputed. Even more controversies were provoked by his *Sociologia Generale* (1916) which was translated into English under the title *The Mind and Society* in 1935.

Pareto claimed to have raised sociology to a logico-experimental science. He stressed and explained the nonlogical factors in human actions by showing the components of social life which he divided into two principal groups—namely, the "residues" or fundamental factors and the derivations which often are erroneous and create myths. By "residues," of which he never gave a sufficient definition, Pareto meant the unexpressed postulates, the things one considers so obvious that they need no explanation, or beliefs which are not formed by logical processes. Social evolution is determined by economic interests, psychic and ideological factors and the "circulation of the elite." Pareto was opposed to "atomistic individualism," and he declared "to be collectively if not a person, at least a unity," and emphasized the importance of social classes.

222

PEANO, GIUSEPPE

PEANO, GIUSEPPE (1858-1932). Modest, simple, kind-hearted, benevolent, affable in his personal behavior, Peano impressed his audiences and readers with the strict precision of his thinking. He was principally a mathematical logician but was also devoted to the idea of the perfection of human relations, international communications, spiritual and technical advance and rapprochement. It was scientific and humanitarian interest that drove him to the problem of universal language or, as he called it, "inter-language" and to the purpose of achieving what Leibniz had planned in his program of a universal characteristic.

After publishing, in 1884, *Differential Calculus and Principles of the Integral Calculus,* and, in 1888, *The Geometrical Calculus,* Peano introduced new concepts and methods into mathematics, whose vocabulary he reduced to three words. He became convinced that, in order to maintain the strict character of mathematics, it was necessary to renounce common language and to shape an instrument of language that renders to thought the same services as the microscope does in biology. The ideography created by Peano uses for logical operations symbols that are shaped differently from algebraic symbols. His system permits writing every proposition of logic in symbols exclusively, in order to emancipate the strictly logical part of reasoning from verbal language and its vagueness and ambiguity. In his *Formulary of Mathematics* (1894-1908) he reduced mathematics to symbolic notation. Besides his efforts to systematize logic as a mathematical science, Peano tried to make the idea of an international language popular and to develop its practical use. As the president of the *Academia pro Interlingua* he was a devoted apostle of this idea.

CROCE, BENEDETTO

CROCE, BENEDETTO (1866-1952). The changing relations between the various forms of the human mind interested Croce far more than the solution of metaphysical problems. According to him, there is nothing that does not represent a manifestation of spirit either in nature or in the realm of science. He is opposed to materialism, naturalism, and the dualism of Kant, and often resorts to a renewal of Scholastic concepts. He considers himself to be a disciple of Plato and De Sanctis in aesthetics; of Herbart in ethics. To read Hegel, is to Croce "a debate within my own consciousness." He never intended to construct a system of philosophy, but, rather, a series of systematizations. He regards all philosophical thoughts as transitional steps, "because philosophy is the history of philosophy."

Croce began with historical studies, became engrossed with records and deeds, and astonished his colleagues with his keen critical faculties. He turned to philosophy around 1893, because his method of examining documents and interpreting historical facts involved an inquiry into the relations between history and the sciences, and an examination of those general concepts from which historical ideas may be derived or with which they may be integrated. The first result of these studies was *Aesthetics* (1902), conceived as the science of expression. Together with three volumes dealing with logic, ethics, and the theory of history, it is a part of his *Philosophy of Spirit* which was completed in 1917.

Croce lost his parents and sister in the earthquake of 1883, and was severely injured himself. However, it was not this experience that made him broach philosophical questions. The news of such events had made Voltaire and Goethe think about metaphysics. Under the Fascist regime of Mussolini, Croce was neither arrested nor compelled to emigrate; he continued to defy the Duce's claims of infallibility within his own country. He was neither intimidated by threats nor lured by promises; continuing to profess idealistic liberalism before, during, and after the reign of terror.

GENTILE, GIOVANNI

GENTILE, GIOVANNI (1875-1944). Gentile was the official philosopher of Italian fascism. After having been a professor of philosophy at the University of Palermo from 1907 to 1914, and later at the University of Pisa, he was Mussolini's minister of Public Education from 1922 to 1924. Then he became senator of the kingdom, and was entrusted with what Mussolini called "reform of the educational system." In this position, he dismissed all teachers who were suspected of being liberals, or democrats; but, since he was not a member of the Fascist Party, Gentile did not satisfy all demands concerning the curriculum. Benedetto Croce protested against Gentile's purge with vigor but without result.

According to Gentile, as he explained it in his principal works *General Theory of the Spirit as Pure Act* (1916) and *Logic as Theory of Knowledge* (1917), philosophy isolated from life and life isolated from philosophy are equally symptoms of cultural bankruptcy. Philosophy must penetrate into human life, govern and mould it. Thought is all-embracing. No one can go out of the sphere of thinking or exceed thought. Reality is not thinkable but in relation to an activity by means of which it becomes thinkable. Every experience occurs between a subject which is one, a center, and of spiritual nature, and a multitude of phenomena which lack such a center. The Real can be thought of only as posing itself, not as being. Reality therefore is spiritual. The spirit is both unity and multitude, and is recognized in the pure act. Gentile added that the "one-multiple" spirit is the same as the ineffable one of the mystics. By this remark, Gentile deviated from Hermann Cohen who characterized thinking as pure creation. Benedetto Croce objected that Gentile's "pure act" is nothing other than Schopenhauer's will. While Gentile followed Hegel, in general he tried to combine the Hegelian phenomenology of the spirit with Berkeley's ideals on perception.

Great Men of Small Countries

Grotius among Friends, by Rubens. Grotius at extreme right, self-portrait of Rubens at extreme left

Hugo Grotius
(Painting by Mierevelt, Rijksmuseum, Amsterdam)

GROTIUS, HUGO (Hugues De Groot)

GROTIUS, HUGO (HUGUES DE GROOT) (1583-1645). At the age of sixteen, Grotius was already a highly successful lawyer in Leyden. He excelled as a jurist, theologian, historian, philologist, poet and diplomat. In 1619, after the defeat of the Dutch republicans, he was tried by the victorious monarchists and sentenced to prison for life, but, in 1621, he escaped to France. Thereafter he lived as an exile, internationally respected as a scholar, and later was recognized by his own country as one of the greatest Dutchmen of all times. For about fifteen years, Grotius was Swedish minister to Paris and accomplished a number of difficult tasks while negotiating with Richelieu.

Grotius was not the first to expound natural law, but he was first to construct a system of international jurisprudence in which the distinction between natural and historical law was essential. According to Grotius, the principle of natural morality is written by God in the hearts and minds of mankind. It is to be ascertained by reason. On the other hand, the existing institutions and laws of the nations are products of human will. The ultimate end of legal development must be the establishment of the supreme command of natural law. For the time being, some minimum demands must be formulated in order to eliminate license in making and conducting war. Grotius' significant work *On the Law of Peace and War* (1625) was directed against arbitrary power policy and radical pacifists, although just wars were admitted. Previously, Grotius, in his *Mare Liberum* (Free Sea, 1609), had tried to secure the rights of neutral ships against ruthless force on the part of Portugal, Spain and England.

Grotius also had a great effect on Old Testament exegesis by his cold lucidity which secured his independence of Christian traditions and enabled him to recognize the historical uniqueness of the Hebrew Bible.

Sören Kierkegaard
(National Historical Museum, Frederiksborg)

Kierkegaard at Chess

KIERKEGAARD, SÖREN

KIERKEGAARD, SÖREN AABY (1813-1855). A little boy of twelve, cold and hungry, tending the sheep on a lonely pasture, suddenly went in despair to the next hillock and there cursed God. This was not our philosopher, it was his father; but this deed hung heavily over the Kierkegaard family, denying the young Sören a happy youth and making him the prophet of anxiety. Only the comfortable income inherited from his father, who after that experience on the heath had gone into the wool business and thrived, his native humor mixed with asceticism and an interest in the sorrows of his fellow men preserved him from insanity. In excessive measure he shared the melancholy so typical of many a Dane; but, artist and poet that he was at heart and in language, he concealed much of it in his virile and colorful style which he devoted to showing that life ever leads to crossroads and demands

decisions that need be made abruptly, by fits or jumps in attitude to tide us between the rational and the irrational. The title of one of his most important works *Either—Or* ironically became his nickname among the "common men" to whom he fled in his daily wanderings through Copenhagen. In a sense, he was the Danish counterpart of Schopenhauer with whom he shared his view of women.

Only recently influential, Kierkegaard, having admired Hegel and Schelling and discarded them, had the avowed intention of creating difficulties instead of solving them. The relation between the knowing mind and eternal truth he considered the great paradox. Truth is attainable only subjectively and subjectivity is truth.

Of Christianity he thought so much that he dissuaded people from joining the church. Having used up his inheritance, spent himself at last in argumentation and written all he wanted to write, he was picked up in the streets and died in a hospital, not yet 43 years of age.

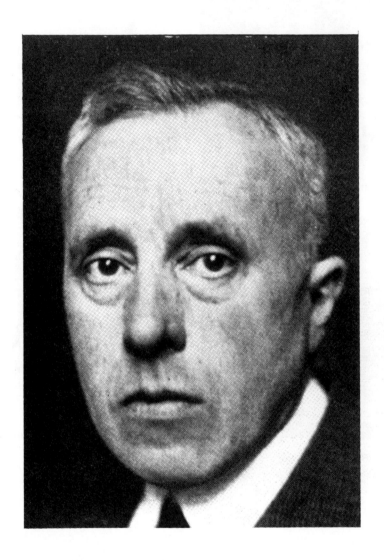

HUIZINGA, JOHAN

HUIZINGA, JOHAN (1872-1945). After Huizinga had become internationally renowned as a historian of the civilization of the later Middle Ages, the Renaissance and Humanism, he began to develop his own philosophy of civilization. His books which deal with problems of contemporary culture, especially his *Shadow of Tomorrow* (1936), show clearly that the historical phenomenon of the *Waning of the Middle Ages,* as his most popular work is entitled, deeply influenced his thoughts about the present and future state of humanity. Although Huizinga regarded history as an irreversible process, he protested his belief in absolute principles of ethics and in eternal truth, which subsist "above the stream of change and evolution," and he regretted the loss of an universal authority, as was represented by the Medieval Church, bound to guide mankind in accordance with unchanging principles.

Culture was defined by Huizinga as cooperation of social life with spiritual productivity. He later abandoned this definition as too narrow, and, while retaining the emphasis on cooperation, tried to introduce the concept of human vocation into it. As the principal symptoms of the present cultural crisis, Huizinga recognized lack of mental concentration, weakening of judgment, renunciation of rationality, worship of life and lack of charity. The last-mentioned symptom became of increasing importance to Huizinga who was induced by the events of contemporary history to lean more and more upon Catholic moral ideology. In a letter to Julien Benda he declared that the doctrine of the seven mortal sins is a better direction for human life than all modern psychology.

British Classics

Roger Bacon
(Statue by Hope-Pinker, Oxford University Museum)

Page of Manuscript by Bacon

BACON, ROGER

BACON, ROGER (c. 1214-1294). A member of the Order of the Franciscans, Roger Bacon was educated at Oxford and Paris. He was known to some as *Doctor mirabilis,* the wonderful doctor; to others as Friar Bacon; and to still others, as a necromancer, feared and respected for the powers he presumably possessed. His ambitions to pry into the secrets of nature, to make physical calculations and experiment with chemicals roused the suspicion and envy of his Brothers who forthwith complained to the Pope. He was denounced as a "sorcerer" for any number of reasons—because he cited the Greeks and Arabs as authorities, made magnifying glasses, investigated the properties of light, discovered a powder similar to gunpowder, enumerated the errors in the Julian calendar, criticized the Schoolmen (he called St. Thomas Aquinas "a teacher yet unschooled"), and attempted to establish ethics as a basis for monastic life. Finally his opponents prevailed upon the Pope to prevent him from teaching. He was confined for ten years with neither books nor instruments. His *Opus Majus* is a defense of himself, but neither this work nor a condensed version, the *Opus Minus,* called forth any notice from Rome. He made a third revision, *Opus Tertium,* with little success. In many ways the struggles of Roger Bacon parallel those of his fellow countryman, Francis Bacon.

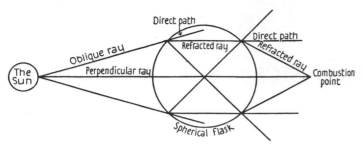

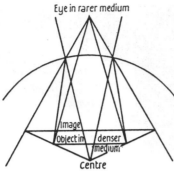

Bacon's diagrams of the paths of rays through spherical glass and through a plano-convex lens

Bacon in His Observatory at Oxford

Roger Bacon

(From a Manuscript of 1450)

Bacon sends the manuscript of his Opus Majus to the Pope from the Franciscan prison in Paris

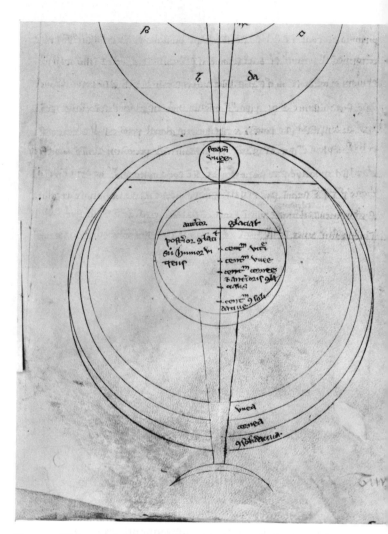

From a Thirteenth Century Manuscript of Roger Bacon

Facsimile Page of Bacon Notebook

Francis Bacon

BACON, FRANCIS

BACON, FRANCIS (1561-1626). The first philosophical work written originally in English was Francis Bacon's *The Advancement of Learning* (1605). Its author was a native of London, son of Nicholas Bacon, Lord Keeper of the Great Seal. Versed, from early age, in political and legal affairs, he advanced to the position of Lord Chancellor. In 1621 he was accused and convicted of accepting bribes from litigants. He subsequently retired from public life and spent his remaining years in scientific research.

Bacon's personal character has been severely condemned by both his contemporaries and posterity. Like many of the men of his time, he placed his career ahead of the public welfare and his personal integrity. But despite his moral shortcomings, Bacon must be credited with his devotion to science, with his sincere efforts to use his power and authority for scientific promotion, and as one of the greatest propagandists for scientific research. He earnestly endeavored to protect scientists against possible Church condemnation, a danger inherent in the very nature of scientific conclusions. He tried to do this by declaring his reverence for orthodox religion, by proclaiming and defending the secularization of science and philosophy, and

by resorting to reason and revelation wherein "double truth" was an acceptable medieval doctrine. Bacon regarded and trusted secularized thought as the instrument for the future improvement of human conditions.

He categorized himself as the "trumpeter of the new age." Actually, he represents an age in transition. Although he emphatically stressed the importance of experiment and the inductive method, he ignored most of the real progress science had made during his lifetime. He was more interested in the effects of knowledge on human behavior than he was in knowledge for its own sake. He asserted that "human knowledge and human power meet

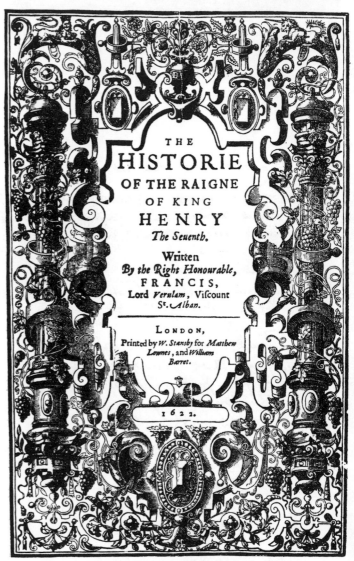

Title Page of Bacon's History of the Reign of Henry VII, *1622*

in one"; therefore, "knowledge is power." He cautioned against the possible abuse of power. Yielding to prejudice or "idols" might result in this. His claim to have permanently established "a true and lawful marriage between the empirical and rational faculty" is a disputable one. However, it is to his incontestable merit that he saw that true philosophy is concerned with "the real business and fortunes of the human race."

Eſſayes.

Religious Meditations.

Places of perſwaſion and diſſwaſion.

Scene and allowed.

At London,
Printed for Humfrey Hooper, and are
to be ſold at the blacke Beare
in Chauncery Lane.
1597.

Title Page of First Edition of Bacon's Essays

Title Page of Bacon's Novum Organum, *1620*

233

Thomas Hobbes

Title Page of Hobbes's Leviathan, *First Edition, 1652*

HOBBES, THOMAS

HOBBES, THOMAS (1588-1679). Born prematurely due to his mother's anxiety over the approach of the Spanish Armada, Hobbes had a streak of timidity in him which did not jibe with the philosophy propounded in his *Leviathan* and *Behemoth*. Influenced by the greatest thinkers of the times—among them Descartes, Gassendi and Galileo, whom he met on the Continent as tutor to Charles II and during an 11-year self-imposed, needless exile—Hobbes professed materialism, seeking to explain everything on mechanical principles. All knowledge comes by way of the senses, he held, and the objects of knowledge are material bodies obeying physical forces. Man too, in his natural state, is "brutish and nasty." Realizing, that if man were to continue as wolf to man, chaos and destruction would result, men have, therefore, entered into a social contract, delegating the control of their fellow men to the state, which is governed and thus insures them a measure of security. In essence, therefore, the state and the kingship is a thing bargained for.

Uninfluenced by Francis Bacon, whose secretary he was for a time, "gaping on mappes" while supposed to be studying at Oxford, reading few books, getting himself into trouble with every publication because either conceptions or Parliament had changed, absorbed in mathematics for which he did not have the talent to make original contributions, and translating Homer and other Greeks, he had attained the age of 89 complaining of having trouble keeping the flies "from pitching on the baldness" of his head. With consistency he had resisted the gains of the Renaissance as well as the resuscitation of scholasticism. His books were condemned by Parliament. Although the clergy hated him as an atheist, he nevertheless played safe by affiliating himself with a church and showing devoutness in the face of death.

Title page of English translation of Hobbes' De Cive.

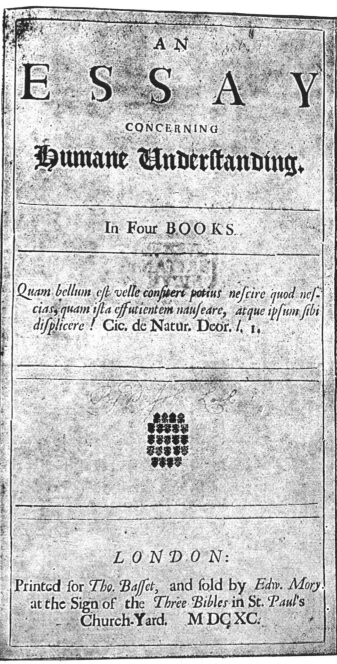

Title Page of Locke's Essay Concerning
Human Understanding

London Bridge in 1616

John Locke

Oates, Home of John Locke

LOCKE, JOHN

LOCKE, JOHN (1632-1704). It is an incontestable fact that the germs of the American Declaration of Independence are contained in the second of John Locke's *Two Treatises on Government,* published in 1690 in order to justify the British Whig Revolution of two years before. It is also generally acknowledged that Locke, by proving, in his *Letter on Toleration* (1689), the necessity of separating Church and State, deeply influenced constitutional and cultural life in the United States. For many decades during the 18th century, Americans could rightly claim to be the true inheritors of Locke's political will, which was neglected in England, the philosopher's home. British liberalism became powerful when it returned to Locke, whose ideas, with Montesquieu and Voltaire as intermediaries, had conquered France, and subsequently imbued the spirit of Holland and Scandinavia.

Locke's political theory was based upon his conception of human nature which was formed by extensive studies and, even more, by the experiences of his life. He had suffered in political persecution, had been active as a diplomat, and engaged in physical, chemical and medical observations before and while he was writing on philosophical subjects. Locke always stressed his conviction that philosophy must be of practical use. He disliked school-dust. He

never consciously forced a fact to fit his theory. He rather risked being accused of inconsistency. Modern historians, however, have stated that Locke was very often more cautious in his wording than his numerous and most famous critics had been.

The great task of an inquiry into the faculties and limits of human mind was accomplished by Locke in his *Essay on Human Understanding* (1690), the result of seventeen years of work. This is an immense topography of the realm of mental activities and, since the problem of knowledge is placed upon a psychological basis, the first comprehensive study in analytical psychology. It inaugurated the age of empiricism, and directed the thoughts of many philosophers in various periods. Still in the 20th century, Alfred North Whitehead, though diverging widely from Locke's main positions, used to extol Locke's "admirable adequacy," and thought that Locke had anticipated the principal points of the philosophy of organism.

When King William III appointed Locke minister to the court of the Hohenzollerns at Berlin, the philosopher, who in his early years had been an attaché there, declined this honor, objecting that hard drinking was indispensable for a minister at that court, and that he, "the soberest man in the kingdom," could not be of any use there. Locke was a sober man not only in the regard mentioned by him on that occasion.

"The Bermuda Group"—Berkeley at extreme right
(Painting by Smibert, Yale University Gallery)

BERKELEY, GEORGE

BERKELEY, GEORGE (1685-1753). A keen thinker and an excellent writer, unafraid of attacking the commonplace, Berkeley's literary style persuaded many antagonistic readers. He was a champion of idealism, or rather of theistic immaterialism. His main purpose was to make evident the existence of God, and to prove that God is the true cause of all things. Proceeding from Locke's examination of the nature and range of human knowledge, Berkeley stressed the distinction between ideas and the mind itself. He conceived of the latter as an active being, distinct from the passivity of its content, and concluded that matter does not exist, that all reality is mental, and that nature is a manifestation of God. The development of his thinking shows the constant influence of Malebranche rather than Plato. In Berkeley's last philosophical works,

he stated that the universe assumes a symbolic character and function. This thesis attracted the interest of Thomas de Quincey, William Blake, and Samuel Taylor Coleridge. His most important philosophical works were *A New Theory of Vision* (1709), *The Principles of Human Knowledge* (1710), and *The Dialogues of Hylas and Philonous* (1713).

Berkeley was born in Ireland. He was a militant apologist for the Anglican Church and subsequently became the Bishop of Cloyne. In 1728, he came to America and resided in Rhode Island for three years. During this period, he helped found the University of Pennsylvania, contributed land and a collection of books to Yale University, and wrote verse in praise of America. His poem, "Verses on . . . America" is chiefly remembered for the line: "westward the course of empire takes its way."

My Good Lord

Cloyne March 9. 1746-7

Your Lordship's letter with which I was favoured last post needed no apology. I wish it may have come time enough to be of use to the patient. Her distemper being of so long continuance, arrived to so great a height, and nature spent and worn out by different courses of medicine, she cannot hope for a perfect recovery without length of time and a more attentive care than people commonly have of their health. I have nevertheless reason to hope she will find in a few months great relief from a constant drinking of tar water joined with a prudent regimen and abstinence from all other medicines.

I would advise that at first her tar water be made by stirring a gallon of water in a quart of tar strongly, with a flat stick, for the space only of two minutes: and that she take of this daily, a pint and a half in six glasses, a quarter of a pint in each glass. She may drink it cold or warm as she best likes upon tryal. But she may drink it still cold, and if they agrees with her, continue it so. It should be drunk night and morning and at an hour's distance at least from her meals I verily think this course and a proper regimen of early hours, light nourishing food, and gentle exercise in good air will by the blessing of God

Facsimile of a Letter by Berkeley

George Berkeley
(Painting by Smibert, National Picture Gallery)

Thomas Reid (1710-1796), a Scottish philosopher who opposed Berkeley and Hume and emphasized the common consciousness of mankind. He was founder of the so-called Common Sense School of philosophy

238

HUME, DAVID

HUME, DAVID (1711-1776). "If one reads Hume's books," Albert Einstein declared, "one is amazed that many sometimes highly esteemed philosophers after him have been able to write so much obscure stuff and even to find grateful readers for it. Hume has permanently influenced the development of the best of philosophers who came after him."

Sometimes, this influence had the very character of a revelation. Immanuel Kant "openly confessed" that Hume awakened him "from my dogmatic slumber and gave my investigation in the field of speculative philosophy quite a new direction." Jeremy Bentham described how, while reading Hume, "I felt as if scales had fallen from my eyes." In modern times, thinkers differing so widely from each other as William James, G. E. Moore, George Santayana and Bertrand Russell, agree in their devotion to Hume, although they have criticized and modified many of his statements.

Hume concentrated upon philosophy in his early years only. Later on he was a soldier, a diplomat, a politician, a member of the Tory party, Under-Secretary of State, and a librarian. He wrote on history, social sciences and religion. But he remained a philosopher, and part of his philosophy must be read out of his later works. Hume called himself a sceptic. Modern philosophers characterize him more rightly as the precursor of positivism. His scepticism was mainly confined to his rejection of the principles of induction. From this position, Hume proceeded to the statement that the concept of causality cannot be gained from material given by the senses. To connect one occurrence with some other by the notions of cause and effect,

Facsimile of a Letter by Hume

is, according to Hume, not the result of rational knowledge but of a habit of expecting the perception of the second after having perceived the first, because that sequence has previously taken place in innumerable cases. This habit is founded upon a belief which can be explained psychologically but cannot be derived by abstraction from either the ideas of the two objects or the impressions of the senses. Hume did not deny that causality works. He only denied that reason is capable of understanding it. Neither did Hume deny the possibility of true knowledge by comprehending resemblance, contrariety, proportions in quantity or degrees in quality. Modern physicists, whose causal laws are elaborated inferences from the observed course of nature, have supported Hume's challenge to the traditional causal connection. Hume has often emphasized that the propensity to believe in the existence of the world and in man's faculty to think and judge is stronger than the awareness of the limits of human reason. Occasionally Hume was depressed by doubts. But his enjoyment of life overcame his melancholy as soon as he recognized that the inadequacy of his reason was natural and common to all men. This insight was to him a cure. By critical examination of facts Hume pioneered in the sciences of political and cultural history, economics, comparative history of religion and sociology.

Shakespeare, Playwright and Humanist

Globe Theater in Shakespeare's London

William Shakespeare (1564-1616), the greatest poet and dramatist in the English language. His understanding of human psychology surpassed by few, his use of language representing the peak of the Elizabethan Age

Queen Elizabeth's Signature
(British Museum)

The Genius of Newton

One of Newton's Inventions, the Reflecting Telescope

Sir Isaac Newton
(Painting by Godfrey Kneller)

NEWTON, SIR ISAAC

SIR ISAAC NEWTON (1642-1727), English philosopher and mathematician. His method of procedure in natural philosophy, especially in his Rules of Reasoning in philosophy (*Mathematical Principles of Natural Philosophy*) is as follows:

"I. We are to admit no more causes of natural things than such as are both true and sufficient to explain their appearances. II. Therefore to the same natural effects we must, as far as possible, assign the same causes. III. The qualities of bodies, which admit neither intension nor remission of degrees, and which are found to belong to all bodies within the reach of our experiments, are to be esteemed the universal qualities of all bodies whatsoever.

IV. In experimental philosophy we are to look upon propositions collected by general induction from phaenomena as accurately or very nearly true, notwithstanding any contrary hypotheses that may be imagined, till such time as other phaenomena occur, by which they may either be made more accurate, or liable to exceptions". To this passage should be appended another statement from the closing pages of the same work: "I do not make hypotheses; for whatever is not deduced from the phaenomena is to be called an hypothesis; and hypotheses, whether metaphysical or physical, whether of occult qualities or mechanical, have no place in experimental philosophy."

He also wrote numerous theological treatises trying to prove intelligent purpose in the cosmos.

Newton Analyzing the Ray of Light

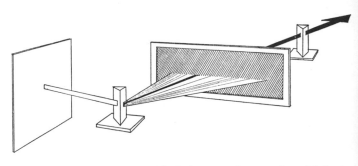

Newton's Experiment with Prisms to Prove that Light in Its Pure Form Is Colored

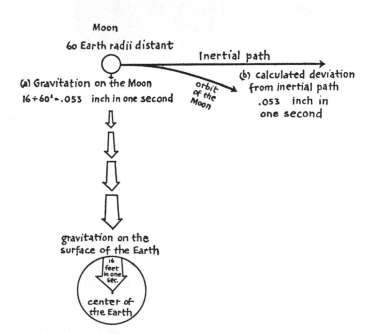

Moon
60 Earth radii distant

Inertial path

(a) Gravitation on the Moon
$16 \div 60^2 = .053$ inch in one second

orbit of the Moon

(b) calculated deviation from inertial path
.053 inch in one second

gravitation on the surface of the Earth

16 feet in one sec.

center of the Earth

Newton's Calculation of the Earth's Gravitational Effect on the Moon

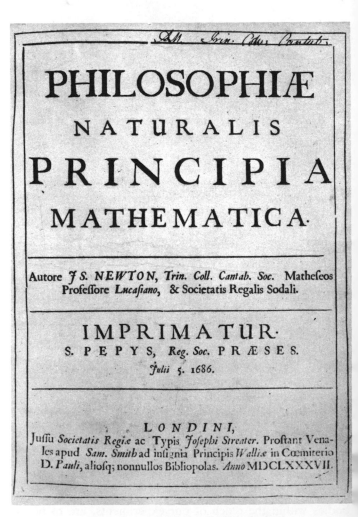

PHILOSOPHIÆ
NATURALIS
PRINCIPIA
MATHEMATICA.

Autore *JS. NEWTON*, Trin. Coll. Cantab. Soc. Matheseos Professore *Lucasiano*, & Societatis Regalis Sodali.

IMPRIMATUR·
S. PEPYS, Reg. Soc. PRÆSES.
Julii 5. 1686.

LONDINI,
Jussu *Societatis Regiæ* ac Typis *Josephi Streater*. Prostant Venales apud *Sam. Smith* ad insignia Principis *Walliæ* in Cœmiterio D. *Pauli*, aliosq; nonnullos Bibliopolas. Anno MDCLXXXVII.

Title Page of Newton's Principia

British Men of God

Sir Thomas Browne (1605-1682), an English physician and scholar, who was interested in esoteric knowledge. His Religio Medici *is celebrated confession of skepticism*

From an Early Edition of Religio Medici

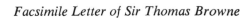

Facsimile Letter of Sir Thomas Browne

R CUDWORTH DD

CUDWORTH, RALPH

CUDWORTH, RALPH (1617-1688). A theologian, Cudworth constantly warned against the over-estimation of dogmatic differences. He was Regius professor of Hebrew at Cambridge University, England, from 1645 to 1688 and while there became known as the leader of the Cambridge Platonists. In his *True Intellectual System of the World* (1678), he concentrated upon the refutation of all the atheistic schools, particularly those of Democritus, Lucretius, and Hobbes. However, he did consider it incumbent upon him to present fairly the disputed doctrines. This caused many critics, among them Dryden, to express apprehension lest readers of these presentations become converts to atheism, and stop reading before perusing Cudworth's refutation. Cudworth maintained that a primitive monotheistic creed could be found even in ancient paganism. In his explanation of the universe, he tried to avoid both the assumption of chance and the hypothesis of a steady interference of God. Therefore, he introduced the concept of "plastic nature" which was to act in a creative manner in accordance with its own laws. This concept, very likely, influenced Spinoza, and the nineteenth century French philosopher, Paul Janet, whose work was based on the idea of "plastic nature."

When the Stuarts resumed their reign of England in 1660, Cudworth encountered some governmental difficulties. They hesitated to reappoint him because he had been an intimate friend of Thurloe, Cromwell's secretary, and Cromwell had consulted Cudworth in 1655 on the question of the readmission of the Jews to England.

(RIGHT) *George Fox (1624-1691), founder of the Society of Friends or Quakers. Having received his mystical "opening" in 1646, he commenced preaching the following year, was repeatedly persecuted for "blasphemy," disturbing the peace, etc., and imprisoned eight times. Led missions to Barbados, Jamaica, Holland and Germany. Fox's mysticism was markedly influenced by the Familists and Boehmists. The success of his movement probably due to his instinctive genius for democratic organization*

(LEFT) *Henry St. John, First Viscount of Bolingbroke (1678-1751). Statesman and orator, and associate of Swift and Pope. Composed the philosophy for Pope's* Essay on Man. *He was hostile to Christianity and resolved all morality into self-love, arguing that it is absurd to deduce moral obligations from the attributes of God, or to pretend to imitate Him in this respect*

John Wesley (1703-1791), founder, with his brother Charles and George Whitefield, of the Methodist movement. Began the Evangelical Revival while at Oxford, c. 1728 in the form of the "Holy Club." In 1735 on a trip to Georgia, came under the influence of Moravians and became impressed with their doctrine of salvation through faith alone. Returning to England, organized prayer meetings, appointed lay preachers, held "love feasts," and eventually formed the society of Methodists, separating sharply from the Church of England

Wesley Preaching in a Private House

Birthplace of John Wesley

Wesley Preaching to the Indians in America

Social Philosophers of England

JOHN OF SALISBURY

JOHN OF SALISBURY (About 1115-1180). The first to personify the type of a cultivated Englishman who combines statesmanship with humanist learning and philosophical mind was John of Salisbury, who played a very important role in the English foreign and ecclesiastical policy of his days, and proved to be an independent thinker and a gifted writer. Numerous pages of his books strike one as most modern. His judgments on people and the state of culture were rather liberal. His descriptions were colorful, and his manner of expression shows a rare combination of humor and dignity, of restraint and acuteness. In 1148, John became secretary to Archbishop Theobald of Canterbury, and, in 1162, he began to serve in the same capacity to Thomas à Becket. He shared Becket's exile and witnessed his murder. He was a friend of Pope Hadrian IV, the only Englishman who ever was crowned with the tiara, and he directed the diplomatic negotiations between Henry II of England and the Holy See on the occasion of the conquest of Ireland.

While secretary to Archbishop Theobald, John wrote the books *Polycraticus* and *Metalogicus*. The first is a theory of the state, defining the rights of the king who, according to him, is limited by religious laws only, but may be killed when he breaks these laws. The second is a defense and criticism of dialectics and refutation of exaggerated realism. John also wrote biographies of St. Anselm and of Thomas à Becket, and, in *Metalogicus,* he inserted his charming autobiography. From 1176 until his death, he was Bishop of Chartres, France, and was associated with the famous school of the cathedral.

Francis Hutcheson (1694-1746), Scottish philosopher who coined the term, "greatest happiness for the greatest nummer," appropriated by Bentham in expounding his utilitarianism. Hutcheson also stressed the "moral sense" or "moral feeling," based on the inborn conscience
(Painting by Ramsay)

Adam Smith (1723-1790). Most famous for his work on economic theory, The Wealth of Nations, *Smith was a professor of logic and ethics and first won his reputation for his* Theory of Moral Sentiments. *In this he affirms sympathy to be the basis of moral consciousness and the test of morality*

David Hartley (1705-1757). Noted as founder of the associationist school of psychology. His theory of the association of ideas influenced the Utilitarians, Bentham and the Mills

Edmund Burke
(Painting by Joshua Reynolds)

William Paley (1743-1805). A theologian whose work, The Principles of Moral and Political Philosophy, *served as a textbook in ethics for many years. He was a Utilitarian, maintaining that it is the beneficial tendency of an action that makes it right. He also wrote works in refutation of the Deists, and arguments for the existence of God*

BURKE, EDMUND

BURKE, EDMUND (1729-1797). The political pamphlets, parliamentary speeches, and essays of Burke proved him to be a genuine philosopher. His contemporaries, regardless of whether they shared his opinions, admired his talent for discerning the basic principles and elucidating the philosophical issues inherent in the disputes and interests of practical matters. Some of his essays, like *The Sublime and the Beautiful,* manifest the influence of Kant, Hegel, and many aestheticians of the eighteenth century. Despite his philosophical attitude toward the events of contemporary politics, Burke was always an ardent partisan, for his theoretical insights blended with his factious spirit and his realism with his romanticism. His morality demanded a rigorous honesty and cautious regard for actual circumstances, traditions, and expediences. He was always prepared to combat imminent dangers and great evil.

For more than three decades, Burke participated in political struggles. An Irishman by birth, and master of the English language, he was one of the greatest orators in the history of the British Parliament. Basically, he was convinced that the human individual is incapable of creating newness; that all useful and legitimate innovations must result from the slow growth of the collective mind in accordance with tradition. He strongly opposed changes in the British Constitution, whose excellent form was dogma to him. He fought for the removal of administrative abuses; opposed corruption, particularly the attempts of King George III to enslave both houses of Parliament. He denounced the French Revolution as a crime because it manifested a break with the past, served as a challenge to true wisdom and experience, and was a threat to liberty and prosperity. With his derision of the theory of the "Rights of Man," Burke became the vanguard of the European counter-revolution.

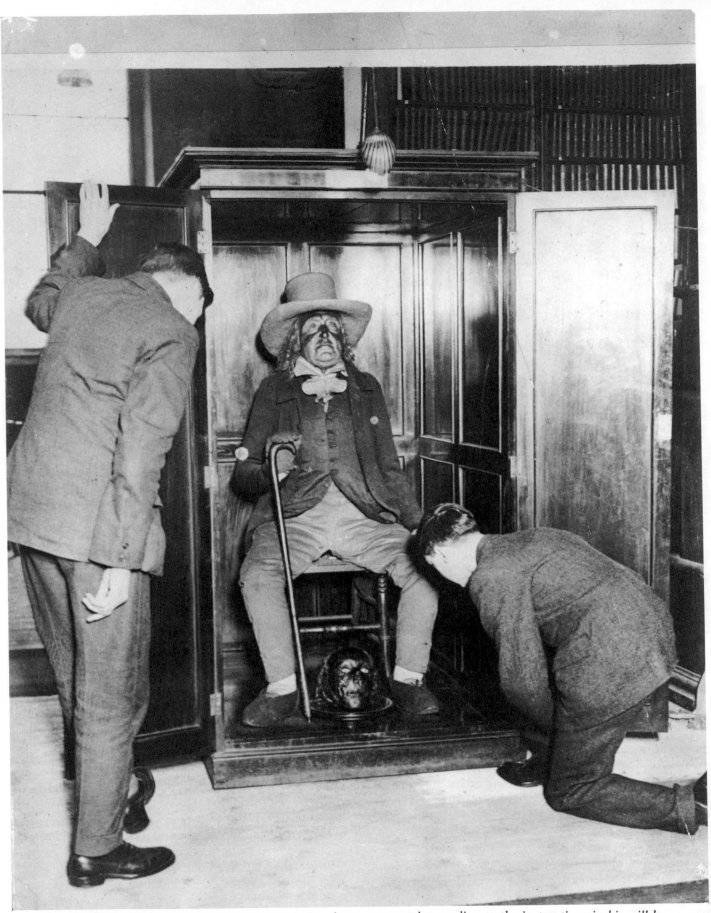

The stuffed and clothed skeleton of Jeremy Bentham, preserved according to the instructions in his will by the University of London. Bentham left his entire estate to the university with the provision that his remains be present at all meetings of the board. The head on the body is wax, but Bentham's actual head rests between his feet, preserved after the manner of South American head hunters

Robert Owen in 1840

BENTHAM, JEREMY

BENTHAM, JEREMY (1748-1832). Noted as an English social philosopher and sympathizer of the American and French revolutions, Bentham's ideas paralleled those of the American founding fathers more closely than those of the French Jacobins. His treatise, *Fragment on Government,* was revised and republished in 1789, the year of the French Revolution, as *An Introduction to the Principles of Morals and Legislation.*

Bentham defined the function of good government as the effort to promote the greatest happiness of the greatest number of citizens and to effect harmony between public and private interests. He declared that the American government was the only good government because it upheld these principles. According to Bentham, happiness is identical with pleasure, and serves as the underlying motivation of human behavior; thus happiness can be the only criterion of morals and legislation. Originally, Bentham called this criterion Utility, but by 1822 he felt that the word did not adequately crystallize his ideas. However, James Mill, a disciple of Bentham, revived the term, Utilitarianism, shortly afterward and henceforth Bentham has been known as the "father of the Utilitarian school."

Bentham had been nicknamed "philosopher" at the age of five.

OWEN, ROBERT

OWEN, ROBERT (1771-1858). It is more by his activities than by his thoughts that Owen influenced the mind and practical life of later ages. He was a man of one idea which he called "socialism" but which rather means "cooperative settlements." He was obsessed by this idea, and not very capable of explaining and developing it in a scientific manner. But he devoted much of his time, energy and fortune to its realization, and influenced British social legislation by his restless insistence on the removal of the most flagrant abuses of the early industrial system.

After being a cotton-twist manufacturer in Manchester, Owen acquired, in 1797, a factory in New Lanark which, under his direction, became a model factory and attracted the curiosity of many thousands of visitors from various countries. Employing 1,700 hands out of the 3,000 inhabitants of the village, Owen refused to employ children under the age of ten, or adults for more than ten and a half hours a day. He provided the families of his workers with schools, a cooperative store, the opportunity to hear music and to take physical exercises. Later he tried to organize cooperative settlements elsewhere in England and in the United States. But he was rather a despotic, though benevolent, ruler, and always a sworn foe of political democracy, educating his adherents to political indifference. In his book *New View of Society* (1813) and in numerous periodicals, he tried to propagate the idea that the existing evils were not due to lack of religion, against which Owen always proclaimed his animosity, but to a wrong distribution of wealth and to a deficient regulation of production which caused economic crises as a consequence of over-production. The rise of the factory system was defended by Owen, who, against Malthus, maintained that the increase of the productive capacity of the human race would be more rapid than the increase of the population. Owen's aim was revolutionary but not his method of realizing it.

View of Robert Owen's Factory Village, New Lanark, 1823

Samuel Taylor Coleridge
(*Portrait by Robert Hancock*)

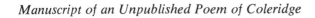

Manuscript of an Unpublished Poem of Coleridge

COLERIDGE, SAMUEL TAYLOR

COLERIDGE, SAMUEL TAYLOR (1772-1834). A gifted poet and leader of the English romantic movement, Coleridge found life a continuous struggle against passion and physical suffering. His unhappy marriage and his love for another married woman caused him grave psychological disturbance and his addiction to opium undermined his physical health. Coleridge did not do justice to his philosophical expositions and often said that he found no comfort "except in the driest speculations." His psychological observations of the activities of the mind under abnormal and morbid conditions are invaluable. The results of his keen self-examination anticipate many of the researches of modern psychopathology. From 1816 to 1834 Coleridge lived in the house of a physician who finally succeeded in curing him, and the last years of the poet were spent in relative psychological security.

Coleridge's philosophy was largely the result of his changing political sentiments. At first an ardent supporter of the French Revolution, he turned to fanatical conservatism and traditionalism. He staunchly opposed almost all of the eighteenth century British philosophers—particularly Locke, Hartley, Hume, and Bentham—and subsequently was converted to German idealism. His *Biographia Literaria,* which developed a theory of literary criticism, influenced British and American aesthetics and philosophy.

David Ricardo

RICARDO, DAVID

RICARDO, DAVID (1772-1823). One of Ricardo's basic convictions, namely, the belief that businessmen are always acting with a full knowledge of all possible consequences of their actions, has been proved to be wrong. Also, some of his other propositions have been definitely refuted. Nevertheless, Ricardo's authority as an acute and informed thinker remains unshattered, and many of his discoveries have become commonplace. Important concepts, formulated by him, have been adopted by economists who defend either private enterprise or socialism.

Ricardo, the son of a Jewish stockbroker who had come to England from Holland, was a financier and member of the London Stock Exchange. He lacked classical education, having attended only an elementary school, but he had learned, as an autodidact, natural sciences and political economics. From 1819 until his death, he was a member of Parliament, and was, despite his radical opinions, revered by both sides of the House as the highest authority in matters of finance and currency. Although Ricardo was a clever businessman, his political and economic demands took no regard of vested interests, not even his own private interests. In his *Principles of Political Economy and Taxation* (1817), Ricardo states an "iron law" in virtue of which rent is always rising while real wages remain stationary, and the profits of the manufacturer and the farmer, kept at the same level by the competition of capital, are constantly declining. In order to change this state of things, Ricardo attempted in vain to ally the rest of the nations against the great landowners. His statements are founded upon exact observations of the economic situation of his own time and the preceding fifty years of British history, but from this reliable knowledge, Ricardo proceeded to rash generalizations. A powerful advocate of free trade, Ricardo was by no means an optimist. He expressed grave apprehensions concerning class struggle. Marx borrowed this and some other formulas from Ricardo but drew different conclusions from them. Bulwer-Lytton's novel *Pelham* and many other literary documents of the second and third decades of the 19th century testify to Ricardo's popularity, although his own style was rather dry. His premature death was mourned by the entire British nation.

John Stuart Mill

"Mill's Logic, or Franchise for Females"
(Cartoon in Punch, March 30, 1867)

MILL, JOHN STUART

MILL, JOHN STUART (1806-1873). Modern progressive pedagogists must be horrified by the methods which were employed for the education of John Stuart Mill by his father, the stern utilitarian James Mill. The latter was not only his son's sole teacher. He was even his sole intercourse, instructing him on walks as well as at home. At the age of three, John Stuart Mill learned Greek. At seven he studied Plato's dialogues. At eight he had to teach his sister Latin. When he was fifteen years old, he was initiated into Bentham's doctrine of the greatest happiness of the greatest number, which struck him as a revelation and made him a convert to utilitarianism for his lifetime.

But far from being an uncritical and orthodox adept of the philosophy which was cherished by his father, John Stuart, recognizing its flaws, became interested in romantic poetry, and, though opposed to Coleridge's political and religious standpoint, praised him as "the awakener of the philosophical spirit in England." Of greater importance, however, was the influence of Comte, Guizot and Tocqueville, to whom Mill owed the enlargement of his historical views and, above all, his awareness of the great social change and its consequences. Mill remained a staunch defender of individual liberty because he was convinced of its social usefulness. But he was ready to sacrifice individual property rights when they endangered the common good. He remained the advocate of represen-tative government, but he considered the social question of increasing importance and became more and more devoted to the cause of the working class, without, however, any intention of idealizing the workers. When he campaigned for a seat in Parliament, he warned his constituents that he would do nothing for their special interests but only what he thought to be right. He also fought for women's suffrage and for the rights of colored people.

Mill's philosophy combined British utilitarianism and French positivism, but, as his last essays prove, would have developed farther if he had lived longer. The main task of his *System of Logic* (1843) is the analysis of inductive proof. His canons of inductive methods for comprehending the causal relations between phenomena are valid under the assumption of the validity of the law of causality; Mill, however, admitted that this law cannot be accepted except on the basis of induction, which, on its part, is fundamentally a matter of enumeration.

Mill was a courageous and considerate fighter for human rights, always trying to understand the fair side of his adversary. During the second half of the 19th century, his ascendancy over the spirit of European philosophy was immense. Since then it has withered. But many of those who used to belittle Mill are, in fact, obligated to him. What he has said of Bentham may be also true of Mill himself: "He was not a great philosopher but a great reformer in philosophy."

254

GREEN, THOMAS HILL

DE MORGAN, AUGUSTUS

DE MORGAN, AUGUSTUS (1806-1871). De Morgan made a number of important contributions to an algebra of logic, and his laws of the propositional calculus have been widely discussed. He is also acknowledged as the founder of the logic of relations. However, the author of *Formal Logic* (1847) never renounced his claims of promoting metaphysics in no lesser degree than he did mathematics and logic. For more than thirty years, De Morgan, as professor at University College in London, acted and taught in accordance with his principle that positive theism must be made the basis of psychological explanation and that, in elucidating mathematical principles, it is necessary to refer to an intelligent and disposed Creator when mental organization is to be dealt with as effect of a cause.

Although a convinced theist, De Morgan never joined a religious congregation. He was a staunch adversary of religious discrimination and was fond of his nonconformism. He renounced his professorship in 1866, when James Martineau was denied a chair at University College because he was a Unitarian. De Morgan, who was admired for his "reading algebra like a novel," was an intimate friend of George Boole who shared his views on mathematics as well as those on religion and ethics.

GREEN, THOMAS HILL

GREEN, THOMAS HILL (1836-1882). "Shut up your Mill and Spencer," Green, professor of moral philosophy at Oxford, admonished his audience, "and open your Kant and Hegel." Green repudiated the whole tradition of British philosophy, especially Locke and Hume, and became the leader of the opposition against positivism and utilitarianism in England. His oratoric power enabled him to convert many British students of philosophy to German idealism. He praised Kant's categories as "the connective tissue of the known world," derived from Kant his conception of self-distinguishing consciousness as a combining agency, and, although he did not adopt Hegel's dialectical method, he did agree with him regarding history and organized society as embodiments of divine will. He flatly rejected Locke's and Hume's assumption that sensations are the raw material of knowledge. According to Green, every experience takes place by forming relations which, consequently, are the real elements of that which is regarded as sensation. Since relations are the work of human mind, reality is characterized as essentially spiritual.

Bitterly opposed as Green was to Darwin, his mind was nevertheless influenced by biological as well as Hegelian evolutionism. He held that an animal organism which has its history in time, gradually becomes the vehicle of an eternally complete consciousness, which, in itself, can have a history of the process by which the animal organism becomes its vehicle. Green even described mystical union as an evolutionary process. He exposed the foundations of his metaphysics and ethics in *Prolegomena to Ethics* (1883).

Darwin and Evolutionism

Charles Darwin

"Dream or Nightmare?"
An allegorical representation of the theory of evolution
(Drawing by J. F. Zalisz)

DARWIN, CHARLES

DARWIN, CHARLES (1809-1882). The age-old dispute between Biblical cosmology and modern natural science was completely overshadowed by Darwin's *Origin of Species* (1859) which resulted in innumerable arguments on evolution. Darwin's earlier book and his *Descent of Man* (1871) revolutionized biology and deeply affected philosophy, historical perspectives, religious controversies, and political, social, and economic criteria.

Darwin, humble, of delicate health, and adverse to publicity, upheld Christian behavior, though he had abandoned theism. He had never intended to provoke religious or philosophical debates. The aim of his special studies, which occupied him for more than twenty-five years, was to show that higher species had come into existence as a

result of the gradual transformation of lower species; that the process of transformation could be explained through the selective effects of the natural environment upon organisms. His theory was based upon the propositions that all organisms and instincts are variable, that the gradual perfection of any organism or instinct is the result of an adaptation to the environment, and that the general struggle for existence (which Darwin considered to be the powerful method of selection) allowed only those organisms which were fit for adaptation to survive. Heredity continued this survival and reproduction of parental and ancestral qualities for many epochs. Darwin stated that although natural selection was the essential factor, it was not the sole factor in transformation. He admitted the possibility of inheriting acquired characteristics; this was denied by later Darwinists. Darwin did not exclude man from his theory that the

"*Darwinism—The Doctrine of Descent from the Ape*"

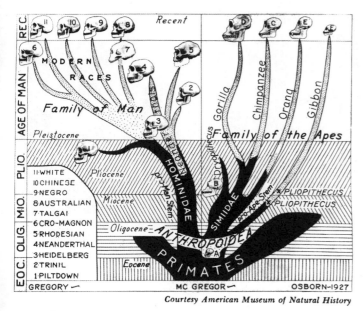

Courtesy American Museum of Natural History

*Evolution of the Human Race, as Visualized by
Henry Fairfield Osborn*

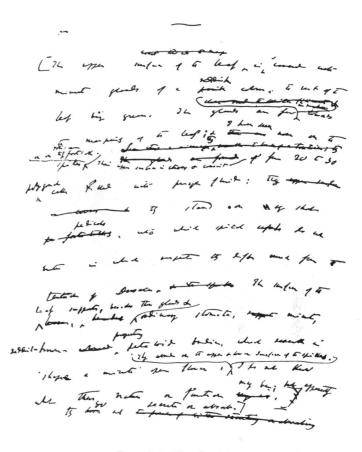

Darwin's Handwriting

higher organisms are the result of long processes of transformation which began with the lowest on the scale.

His work was based upon painstaking observation. His principle of the struggle for existence was not based upon his primary studies of nature. For years, he had sought for a principle by means of which he could arrange the collected facts. Neither his thoughts as a natural scientist nor his observations of nature led him to this. Malthus' *Essay on Population* which Darwin read (1838) clarified for him the entire problem of variation in plants and animals. Malthus maintained that more individuals are born than are able to survive and that the capability of adaptation to the environment is the reason for the survival of the fittest. This principle, borrowed by Darwin from a political economist, has become one of the most disputed portions of his theory.

Since the appearance of the *Origin of Species,* Darwinism and evolutionism have become synonymous. It was Herbert Spencer, to whom Darwin fondly referred as "our philosopher," who characterized Darwin's theory as evolutionism, and to which Darwin agreed. Darwin's concept of evolution is entirely different from other evolutionary theories which assumed a metaphysical entity as the evolving or directing power. Natural selection, regardless of whether it is valid, was conceived and kept by Darwin, free from any metaphysics. Darwin's hypothesis that transformation or evolution proceeds by minute gradations, has been disputed by Thomas Huxley, who, despite this dissension, was an important champion of Darwinism. Most modern biologists share Huxley's views on this question.

257

Herbert Spencer

Drawing by Huxley on the Proof of Spencer's
Principles of Biology

Spencer's Living Quarters at Brighton

SPENCER, HERBERT

SPENCER, HERBERT (1820-1903). An engineer by training, Spencer tried to survey the whole range of human thought with the intention of interpreting "the phenomena of life, mind and society in terms of matter, motion and force." Defining philosophy as "knowledge of the highest degree of generality," he established the formula of evolution as the general law which enabled him to explain all phenomena in the above mentioned terms. Under its simplest and most general aspect, evolution is characterized by Spencer as "the integration of matter and concomitant dissipation of movement: while dissolution is the absorption of motion and concomitant disintegration of matter." To Spencer, evolution was universal and one, dominating the realms of biology, psychology, ethics and sociology. He was the first philosopher to maintain the genetic principle, according to which the more developed thing must be interpreted by the less developed one. He was also the first to use a biological standard for human ethics. He com-

plained that "men do not even know that their sensations are their natural guides and (when not rendered morbid by long-continued disobedience) their most trustworthy guides," because he thought that the senses of man were molded in accordance with the all-embracing law of evolution from a less perfect to a more perfect state. In this way, Spencer identified evolution with progress.

Spencer's notion of evolution has a curious history. At first he borrowed it from Coleridge, and adopted at the same time the latter's idea of social organism, both of which have been conceived of as in opposition to utilitarianism. Later, he came closer to the utilitarian point of view, espoused the cause of rugged individualism, strictly opposed any encroachment upon private enterprise by the state, and became a grim adversary of socialism. He was deeply disappointed when Beatrice Potter, his favorite pupil, married Sidney Webb, the theorist of British labor, and he then cancelled her appointment as his literary executor. At the end of his life, Spencer expressed very pessimistic views about the future of humanity.

Thomas Henry Huxley

Ernst Heinrich Haeckel (1834-1919), the German biologist who popularized Darwinism in Central Europe, and author of The Riddle of the Universe

HUXLEY, THOMAS HENRY

HUXLEY, THOMAS HENRY (1825-1895). Huxley, the son of a poor schoolmaster, attended a regular school for only two years. He described that education as "a pandemonium." Thereafter, from his tenth year on, he had to pursue his studies by himself, which he did with such energy and clear-sightedness that he easily passed the examination for admission to the University. As a surgeon in the British Navy, Huxley was able to study tropical fauna and flora, and he became a pioneer in biology. His contributions to the anatomy of vertebrate and invertebrate animals are regarded as of lasting value. As a professor at London University, Lord Rector of the University of Aberdeen, president of the Royal Society and member of the Privy Council, Huxley used his authority and influence for the promotion of all sciences and the defense of science against detractors of any kind. Not the least of his accomplishments, Huxley was successful in popularizing science and making the working classes acquainted with its principal results. Full of energy and initiative, daring and circumspect in his way of thinking, Huxley was a pugnacious but always courteous critic who was fond of disputing with great authorities in science, in State and Church.

Although Huxley, in his early years, was convinced of the immutability of species, he became, immediately after the publication of Darwin's *Origin of Species,* a brilliant champion of evolutionism. He did not share Darwin's faith in the absolute rule of small variations, and insisted on cases of sudden change observed by himself. But this and other objections did not prevent him from defending and continuously explaining Darwin's theory. As a philosophical thinker, Huxley, a great admirer of Hume, defined his standpoint as *agnosticism,* a strict insistence on the impossibility of knowing anything beyond observation of the senses, indifferent to any theory of reality. Huxley's attitude was not a negative scepticism but rather a plea for sceptical caution in the matter of belief. He was as radically opposed to materialism as to the faith of the Church.

The Flowering of Modern England

Thomas Carlyle
(*Portrait by Whistler*)

CARLYLE, THOMAS

CARLYLE, THOMAS (1795-1881). The writings of Carlyle differ considerably from those of Locke, Hume, Pope, Fielding, Macaulay, and John Stuart Mill. For Carlyle wrote emotionally; his language expressed passion, love, hate, enthusiasm, or scorn; nothing left him unmoved. He was a bitter enemy of the Age of Reason, and detested cold logic, intellectual abstraction, and scientific aloofness.

Although not an orthodox Protestant, he classed himself as a Christian for whom faith was the source of wisdom and the standard of criticism for life and art. Society, as he conceived it, was the brotherhood of men and the union of souls. He categorized political constitution, class distinctions, political parties, and trade unions as the artificial products of human arrogance. He distrusted material progress, opposed the advances of modern civilization, and scoffed at the diseases and misfortunes of modern life. He maintained that the latter were curable, provided mankind was guided by great men. He derided universal suffrage, even though he sympathized with the Chartist movement. He preferred a kind of patriarchal feudalism to the governmental regulation of wages, or the bargaining process between management and labor.

Surely he was not a misanthrope, for he sincerely desired: the improvement of human conditions, a continuing spiritual development, and increased education for the masses. He asserted that great men would serve as the instruments by which those things would be accomplished, that they were the real trustees of the common interests of human happiness and could not be judged by the moral standards of the middle and lower classes. His theories led him to exalt Frederick William I of Prussia, the soldier king, whose principles became the tenets of fascism, and to praise the regime and wars of his son, Frederick II. A great admirer of German poetry and metaphysics, he considered both to be imbued with the true Christian spirit. Until his death he remained an optimist, always hoping for those events which would lead mankind back to a true Christian way of life.

Cardinal John Henry Newman (1808-1890), the Anglican leader of the Oxford Movement in the 1830's. Contributing to the Tracts for the Times, *he aroused a violent controversy with the fateful Tract XC (1841), which opposed religious liberalism, urged Anglican adoption of the doctrine of apostolic succession, and maintained that the 39 Articles were not opposed to Catholicism. Newman was eventually obliged to withdraw from the movement and from the Anglican Church, to become a Catholic*

(Portrait by Emmeline Deane)

BOOLE, GEORGE

BOOLE, GEORGE (1815-1864). Compared with other philosophers, it was relatively late in his lifetime that George Boole began to specialize in the field that ultimately made him famous. At the age of sixteen, he taught school in an English provincial town; by the time he was twenty, he had opened his own school; at thirty, he began to concentrate upon mathematics. In 1847 he published a pamphlet, *The Mathematical Analysis of Logic,* which contained the principal ideas he later developed in his book, *Laws of Thought* (1854). This book marks the beginning of symbolic logic, a new and efficient method of formal logic, designed to avoid the ambiguities of ordinary language. Boole recognized that the canonical forms of Aristotelian syllogism are really symbolical, but less perfect than the symbolism of mathematics. Furthermore, he realized that ordinary language is an inadequate medium for the expression of ideas. He tried to devise a symbolic language, the terms of which would express exactly what he thought. He was less interested in reducing logic to mathematics than in employing symbolic language and notation in a wide generalization of purely logical processes. He organized deductive logic as an algebra, interpretable spatially and proportionally. With this, he paved the way for Frege, Peano, Bertrand Russell, Whitehead, Hilbert, and others.

RUSKIN, JOHN

RUSKIN, JOHN (1819-1900). No understatement can be found in Ruskin's writing which is, as he himself said, as vascillating as his temper, changing from delight into horror, from indignation into enthusiasm. Ruskin was a critic and historian of art, bitterly opposed to the conception of art for art's sake, always considering the artist's work as the test of his moral disposition, acknowledging only those as artists who are recognized as men of a pure heart, and using "sincerity" as the standard of his aesthetic judgment. He limited sincerity to the Gothic style only and upheld it as much on moral as on aesthetical grounds, while he branded the Renaissance, and even the "flamboyant style" of the end of the Gothic period, as moral and artistic decay.

Ruskin was by nature a zealot, even an eccentric. His dislike of modern technics, railroads included, induced him to expensive efforts to become independent of modern means of transportation. Criticism of art was for him a solemn duty, but his moralist aesthetics did not allow him to confine his views to the realm of the arts. He was sensi-

tive to injustice and misery. When, in Venice, he read in the newspaper that a seamstress in London had died of starvation, he became incapable of enjoying his beloved pictures. Ruskin, therefore, by 1860, turned to political economy, and proceeded to regard economic justice, moral and artistic sincerity as one and inseparable. He complained of the substitution of factory work for handicraft, and protested violently against reckless competition. Above all, Ruskin indignantly fought any evaluation of the human individual which identified wealth with worth. Ruskin was one of the first to deny the "economic man."

"In the height of black anger," as Ruskin said, he wrote the first volume of his *Modern Painters* (1842-60) in which he excepted modern landscape painting from his general condemnation of his own time. Another deviation from his general attitude was his defense of British colonial expansion. As a professor at Oxford, he used his lectures on art for converting his audience to imperialism. Among the undergraduates who listened to Ruskin were Cecil Rhodes and Alfred Milner, bound to enlarge the British empire.

Walter Pater

Manuscript of Pater's "Pascal"

PATER, WALTER HORATIO

PATER, WALTER HORATIO (1839-1894). Most of Pater's disciples who pursued his doctrine of thrice-refined hedonism to its extreme consequences finally took refuge in the Church of Rome, and many of those who revolted against Pater's philosophy of life or against his way of criticizing art, after becoming sure of their victory, admitted their personal love of the man whose thoughts and views they had attacked. Pater's belief that nothing which ever has interested mankind can wholly lose its vitality, may be confirmed by the vicissitudes of his literary fame.

Oscar Wilde called Pater's *Renaissance* (1873) his "golden book" and said in *De Profundis* that it had "such a strange influence over my life." George Moore took Pater's *Marius the Epicurean* (1885), which he called his "Bible," as model for his own book *Confessions of a Young Man.* William Butler Yeats and others who later became noted poets and critics founded *The Rhymers' Club* whose program was the cult of Pater's ideas.

Great scholars have praised Pater's principal work *Plato and Platonism* (1893) because of its author's congeniality with the great Greek thinker. But Pater was no Platonist. He called himself an Epicurean, and was perhaps even more influenced by Heraclitus. The essence of what he called his humanism is the conviction that only the sharp apex of the present moment between two hypothetical eternities is secure, and that the art of living consists in the ability of making such passing moments yield the utmost of enjoyment. He tried to show that devotion to enjoyment of beauty gives the soul a strength and austerity which cannot be surpassed even by moral asceticism, and that delicacy of feeling does not exclude purity of thinking. Pater's way of regarding all things and principles as inconsistent did not allow him to acquiesce in any orthodoxy and maintained his curiosity in testing new opinions. But his instincts, which were opposed to academic dullness, let him also recoil from revolutionary excesses.

SIDGWICK, HENRY

SIDGWICK, HENRY (1838-1900). Sidgwick, one of the
founders of the Society for Psychical Research and the
Ethical Society in Cambridge, England, where he was a
professor, gave a number of suggestions which have been
of consequence for the latest development of philosophical
thinking in England and America. A follower of John
Stuart Mill in ethics, politics and economics, Sidgwick
endeavored, especially in his *Methods of Ethics* (1874) to
found utilitarianism anew by resorting to Thomas Reid's
"natural realiarism" and sweeping away all hedonistic theories. His efforts to combine utilitarian ethics with intuition-
ist theory of knowledge did not entirely satisfy Sidgwick,
who was aware of the difficulty of his task and constantly
tried to improve or correct his arguments without abandoning his fundamental position. He recognized that philosophical empiricism was based upon conceptions that
cannot be traced back to experience but declined Kant's
theory of experience. Sidgwick has studied "with reverent
care and patience" what is called the morality of common
sense. For he was convinced that, despite all historical
changes and diversities of thoughts and actions, there is a
large region of broad agreement in the details of morality,
without any attempt to penetrate into the ultimate grounds
upon which principles of moral action may be constructed.
Sidgwick did not only regard this common-sense morality
as the proper starting point for philosophical inquiries into
ethical problems, but he thought that the work of the
philosopher has to be aided, and, in a way, controlled by
the moral judgment of "persons with less philosophy but
more special experience."

BRADLEY, FRANCIS HERBERT

BRADLEY, FRANCIS HERBERT (1846-1924). Noted
for his contribution to English philosophy, Bradley was,
at first, a disciple of Hegel. He lost sympathy with Hegelian
philosophy, and left it ·to revitalize the musty logic of
Mills. Subsequently he opposed utilitarianism and supported the ethics of Kant, by insisting that good will was
a universal principle, as well as a human quality. He
found, by testing the relation of each claim to fundamental
reality, that experience, as such, is nonrelational and contains within itself the essential features of thought which
make for explicit logic. He stated that truth can only reside
in judgment; that not all judgments are true; that when a
subject is circumspect and sufficiently inclusive, then its
judgment is true; and that truth really requires the absolute. Bradley lucidly restated the fundamental idealism
and spiritual monism that form the bases for the analysis
of individual experience. This analysis gradually develops
into the realization of a universal coherent unity, infinite
in character.

In his youth, Bradley accepted a fellowship at Merton
College, Oxford, tenable for life, but terminable at marriage. He enjoyed its benefits for more than half a century.
As an athlete at University College, he contracted typhoid
fever and subsequently suffered from an inflammation of
the kidneys. These illnesses probably resulted in his being
a crotchety recluse. Yet his literary efforts have polish,
style, and even humor. His *Appearance and Reality* (1893)
and *Essays on Truth and Reality* (1914) are philosophical classics.

BOSANQUET, BERNARD

BOSANQUET, BERNARD (1848-1923). The best known (next to Bradley) of the British idealist philosophers, Bosanquet descended from an old Huguenot family. For eleven years he lectured on Greek history and philosophy at University College, Oxford. Then he left this to devote himself to charity and the study of ethics, logic, and aesthetics.

His interests, later shared by his wife, included the London Ethical Society (later known as the London School of Ethics and Social Philosophy) and the Charity Organization Society. This work was not the hobby of a leisure-class gentleman, but the practical application of Bosanquet's philosophy.

His emphasis was on the importance of the individual, the fruition of a cosmoramic view which could only be realized in the individual. Accordingly, he defined the Absolute (and in this he was profoundly influenced by Hegel) not as a personality lacking coherence and unity, but as a whole being. Similarly in his logic, he defined truth as a cohering, comprehensive whole. He perceived ethics as the endeavor towards a unity of pleasure and responsibility, all the while emphasizing the importance of the individual in his relationships with others. His philosophy may be said to bear the stamp of conciliation.

His personal charm, his sympathetic attitudes, and his "critically appreciative powers" were hallmarks of his warm personality. His writings include *Knowledge and Reality, A History of Aesthetic, The Essentials of Logic, The Psychology of the Moral Self,* and *The Philosophic Theory of the State.*

CREIGHTON, JAMES EDWIN

CREIGHTON, JAMES EDWIN (1861-1924). To have his own philosophical system would have been contrary to Creighton's fundamental conviction that human thoughts are never completely the work of an isolated mind. He was an ardent advocate of social cooperation in philosophy, repeatedly pointing to the successes that resulted from cooperation in science. He regarded intellectual life as a form of experience which can be realized only in common with others through participation in a social community. With this point of view, Creighton concluded first, that the philosopher must participate intimately in the mental activities and interests of other people; and second, that he must define the task of philosophy as that of determining the real, stressing the importance of a precise concept of experience. He regarded "concept of experience" as an ambiguous term which was generally appealed to in a very uncritical and too confident fashion. Though he endeavored to define experience as strictly as possible, he was influenced in his earlier years by Kant, Bradley, and Bosanquet. Later, he accepted some views of Windelband and Rickert, without sharing all of their opinions. Creighton differentiated between that which is intelligible in philosophy and that which is intelligible in the natural sciences.

MORGAN, C. LLOYD

MORGAN, C. LLOYD (1852-1936). As a boy, Morgan had an almost exclusively literary education. He was devoted to Byron, Keats, Shelley, Moore and Scott. Then, while in college, the philosophy of Spinoza, Berkeley and Hume had a strong appeal for him. He had intended to become an engineer but, as a student, was drawn by T. H. Huxley to the interpretation of nature by biological studies. His principal interest remained fixed on the borderline of life and mind, and he became more and more convinced that a synthesis of philosophy and science was possible and necessary.

Such a synthesis was, in Morgan's opinion, "bound to take a risk." The risk he took was to acknowledge things, to accept realism. Things were defined by him as "clusters of events," quite in accordance with modern physics. With his principal books *Animal Life and Intelligence* (1891), *Habit and Instinct* (1896) and *Emergent Evolution* (1923), Morgan has inspired biologists, psychologists and philosophers both in England, his homeland, and America. His ideas have also been accepted by outstanding French thinkers. Morgan defined evolution as a constructive scheme which shall provide for a physical realism but also for "something of at least in the same genre as Platonic realism." Emergent evolution was conceived as selective synthesis at certain critical turning points in the course of evolutionary advance. Darwin's conception of evolution as a steady, gradual process was abandoned by Morgan. On a broader basis, he developed T. H. Huxley's and G. H. Lewes's criticism of Darwin's theory and that which is called the theory of mutation. In this way he inspired Henri Bergson and Samuel Alexander, among others, at least by offering them rich material of concrete facts.

SCHILLER, FERDINAND CANNING SCOTT

SCHILLER, FERDINAND CANNING SCOTT (1864-1917). In strong opposition to the Hegelianism prevailing at Oxford University since T. H. Green and strengthened by F. H. Bradley, another professor of that same University, though a namesake of the German idealistic poet Schiller, combated any idealism of German provenience. F. C. S. Schiller called his philosophy *Humanism,* while calling himself a disciple of the sophist Protagoras, who said that man is the measure of all things. Schiller proceeds from the statement that all mental life is purposive to the establishment of a concept of truth whose criteria are given by the consequences of a proposition. This does not mean that truth corresponds to the organic or sentimental needs of the knower. As Schiller says, his humanism is merely the perception that the philosophic problem concerns human beings striving to comprehend a world of human experience by the resources of the human mind. He distinguishes humanism from pragmatism, to which it is in fact akin, by the claim that humanism is of larger range and is able to be applied not only to logic but to ethics, aesthetics, metaphysics and theology, and furthermore by his readiness to acknowledge as many metaphysics as there are tempers, while rejecting any absolute metaphysic. Schiller's principal works about humanism are *Humanism* (1903) and *Studies in Humanism* (1907). He wrote also about the problems of the day. In one of his pamphlets he declared that a government of the world administered by international bankers would by no means be the worst possible.

ALEXANDER, SAMUEL

ALEXANDER, SAMUEL (1859-1938). A teacher at Oxford, Glasgow and Victoria Universities, Alexander's fame rests principally on his book *Space, Time and Deity,* which evolved out of his Gifford Lectures at Glasgow given in 1915. This book has been referred to as the most significant British metaphysical contribution since that of Hobbes. Classed as both idealist and realist, he tended more toward realism as he grew older. In 1889, his prize essay *Moral Order and Progress* (which he disowned some twenty years later) fanned the Anglo-Aristotelian-Hegelian movement in British ethics toward the direction of a sophisticated evolutionary theory.

RUSSELL, BERTRAND (1872-   ). As late as 1940, the appointment of Bertrand Russell as professor of philosophy at the College of the City of New York has roused the fury of bigots of all denominations. It was denounced as "the establishment of a chair of indecency" and withdrawn by the Board of Education after a trial had ended with Russell's condemnation as "immoral" and a danger to the youth of the city.

The victim of this persecution has been accustomed to making sacrifices for his convictions. During World War I he had been imprisoned because of his radical pacifism. He had also been accustomed to having his opinions explained by radical leftists as being determined by his connection with the British aristocracy. His grandfather, Lord John Russell, who had been Prime Minister and Foreign Secretary, had tried to defend European solidarity against Bismarck's national egoism, and had brought about the repeal of the Test and Corporation Act which barred from public office anyone not belonging to the established Church of England.

Russell is regarded as the most controversial figure of modern Anglo-Saxon philosophy, even by those who recognize him as one of the greatest thinkers of the twentieth century and who agree with Albert Einstein who has confessed that he owes "innumerable happiness to the reading of Russell's works." Russell's mind is uncompromising, not afraid of running risks, yet always ready to change and to admit errors. He always has maintained the independence of his thought and judgment although he underwent many influences. Russell is a prolific writer who attributes the clarity and fluency of his style to his absence from the influence of public school education. Conspicuous qualities of his books are the firm direction of the course of ideas, his ability to continue or check a discussion according to his principal intention, and particularly his easy humor and his devastating irony.

Russell has taken an outstanding part in the foundation of modern mathematical logic. Together with Alfred North Whitehead he has written *Principia Mathematica* (1910-13), one of the most comprehensive systems of mathematics. At first, Russell regarded mathematics as the ideal of philosophy. Then, abandoning Platonism, he thought of mathematics as an instrument of science, and finally de-

Bertrand Russell

Bertrand Russell with Members of His Family in California

clared that logic is not a part of philosophy but of a general theory of science.

To Russell, philosophy is a conception of life and the world which is the product of two factors. The one consists of inherited religious and ethical concepts, the other of investigations which may be called scientific. Philosophy is regarded as something intermediate between theology and science. Like theology it is concerned with speculations on matters concerning which knowledge has been unascertainable. Like science it appeals to human reason rather than to authority. Russell holds that all human knowledge remains uncertain, inexact and partial, and that scepticism, while logically faultless, is psychologically impossible. To obtain some results which may be useful for humanity, philosophy should take its problems from natural sciences, not from theology or ethics.

At least in its broad outline, scientific knowledge is to be accepted. But, against traditional concepts, Russell maintains that knowledge is an intimate, almost mystical contact between subject and object by perception. Although perception is far more complicated than is generally supposed, common-sense realism comes closer to truth than idealism. Subjectivism is justified to ask how knowledge of the world is obtained but not to say what sort of world exists in which we live. Kant's claim to have effected a "Copernican revolution" is refuted by Russell who declares that Kant rather achieved a "Ptolemaic counter-revolution." Knowledge is characterized as a sub-class of true belief, but not every true belief is to be recognized as knowledge. In *Human Knowledge* (1948) Russell deals with the problem of the relation between individual experience and the general body of scientific knowledge, and arrives at the result that science cannot be wholly interpreted in terms of experience. He demands that the description of the world be kept free from influences derived from the nature of human knowledge, and declares that "cosmically and causally, knowledge is an unimportant feature of the universe." Like Whitehead, he holds that the distinction between mind and body is a dubious one. It will be better to speak of organism, leaving the division of its activities between the mind and the body undetermined. What is true or false is a state of organism. But it is true or false in general, in virtue of occurrences outside the organism.

Joseph Stalin, the chief architect of Russian imperialism, who by admission of his own lieutenants executed three and a half million Russian peasants and thousands of his personal coworkers.

On frequent occasion Bertrand Russell deviated from his philosophical work into the realm of social idiosyncrasy and anti-American platitudes. He delighted in attacking the United States as a monger of atomic warfare, advocating a general acceptance of Soviet Russian world dominance

MOORE, GEORGE EDWARD

MOORE, GEORGE EDWARD (1873-). There has been a debate between G. E. Moore and Bertrand Russell which is quite different from the usual disputes recorded in the history of philosophy. Russell declared in the preface to *Principia Mathematica,* "On fundamental questions of philosophy my position in all of its chief features is derived from G. E. Moore." But Moore, on his part, protested that if there were a question concerning who had learned from whom, then Russell was the teacher and himself the disciple. Literally, Moore was right but in reality Russell was right. It was Moore who started the movement of British New Realism by publishing his essay *Refutation of Idealism in Mind* in 1903. He holds that knowing means apprehension of the objectively real because in the mental act the object becomes transparent. A sense datum, therefore, is not the subjective image of the mind of something corresponding to it in the outer world but it is the object itself which immediately enters into the mind which looks through it. This view has been, with more or less modification, accepted by a great number of British philosophers of recent time. It has led to a partial rehabilitation of common sense.

Moore has also, especially in his *Principia Ethica* (1903), made a considerable contribution to axiology. Moore principally fought what he called the "naturalistic fallacy." He demonstrated the failure of any attempt to derive value from existent things or to define value in terms of relations between existing things. But together with evolutionary naturalism and utilitarianism he also refutes all metaphysical foundations of value, accusing all of them of trying in vain to derive the "ought" from the "is." He is also opposed to any subjectivist theory of value. According to Moore, value is not subjective but depends on intrinsic properties which, however, cannot be defined. "Good is good, and that is the end of the matter," says Moore. Good is not identical with being willed. Right and wrong are not names of the characteristic of values. They are emotive, not cognitive expressions, meaning only approval or disapproval, and do not mean any metaphysical or natural property.

Moore's method is called "microscopic." It concentrates on isolating and questioning, and most of its results lead to new questions.

James Hopwood Jeans

Arthur Stanley Eddington (1882-1944), British Astronomer and Philosopher of Science

JEANS, JAMES HOPWOOD

JEANS, JAMES HOPWOOD (1877-1946). Jeans, one of the most eminent savants and an international authority in mathematics, theoretical physics and astronomy, has also been called "the Edgar Wallace of cosmology." Very few scientists of his rank have ever had his talents for combining profundity with a colorful, popular style. While his earlier books *The Dynamical Theory of Gases* (1904), *Theoretical Mechanics* (1906), *Mathematical Theory of Electricity and Magnetism* (1908) and numerous learned papers were written for experts, his later works *The Stars in Their Courses* (1931), *The New Background of Science* (1933) and *Through Space and Time* (1934) have been admired by tens of thousands of readers who were not prepared to read other scientific books. Jeans himself

was fond of fiction and detective stories, and he knew how to charm the public, although he never made a confession to his readers which he could not justify before his scientific conscience.

Towards the end of his life, Jeans became more and more convinced that the scientific viewpoint was synonymous with that of the astronomer. Human life was to be seen as a chain of causes and effects. The problems of the day were to be set against a background of time into which the whole of human history shrinks to the twinkling of an eye. Abstract problems of philosophy did not trouble him. Nor did he feel a need for seeking a rational basis for morals. According to Jeans, neither science nor philosophy has a voice in the region of moral acting. This is left to the Christian religion only.

William Temple

dialectical realism. He adopted Marxian dialectics and subscribed to many points of the socialist program, especially those concerning public ownership; but the most radical realization of socialist ideas seemed to him insufficient for the thorough reform of human conditions. He remained convinced that only Christian faith can fulfil this task and that Christianity is necessary for the completion of human thought and life, as well as for the cultural progress in which he firmly believed.

While in philosophy Temple turned from idealism to realism, in theology he turned from liberalism to orthodoxy. But just as he could say that, while being a liberal, he never for a moment had doubted the divinity of Christ, Temple, while an orthodox theologian, retained a liberal and tolerant attitude in questions of religious convictions. He defended discussion and believed in democracy, vital need for which is discussion. Temple never faced doubt as a personal problem. He was as happy as he was pious, and as simple and good-humored as he was dignified. The energetic manner in which he insisted on the close connection between faith and life revealed his judgment on mystical religion. Temple would not deny that the mystical experience might be the purest and intensest of all religious experiences. But just for the reason that it claims to be the most detached from nonreligious interests, he held that it is the most representative and least important of all religious forms. He declared that any philosophy that arrives at theism arrives at the study of the real world which is created and explained by God.

TEMPLE, WILLIAM

TEMPLE, WILLIAM (1881-1944). When William Temple, who had been Archbishop of York since 1929, became in 1942, Archbishop of Canterbury and in this way succeeded his father, Frederick Temple, the event was considered unheard of in the history of the English Church. But even greater astonishment was caused by the fact that the new Archbishop, the highest ecclesiastical dignitary of the British kingdom, was an avowed student of Karl Marx. Temple had had a thorough classical education, combined with training in logic, ethics, metaphysics and the history of philosophy. His tutor, Edward Caird, had initiated him in the philosophy of Plato and Hegel, but he also read with admiration Aristotle and Aquinas, and finally two such different thinkers as Bergson and Marx induced him to break with traditional idealism and to adopt a kind of

RAMSEY, FRANK PLUMPTON

RAMSEY, FRANK PLUMPTON (1903-1930). The premature death of Ramsey at the age of twenty-six has been felt as a heavy loss by leading thinkers in the field of philosophy, mathematical logic, and theory of economics.

Ramsey tried to tackle problems at the point where Bertrand Russell and Ludwig Wittgenstein had left them. He makes a fundamental distinction between *human logic,* which deals with useful mental habits and is applicable to the logic of probability, and *formal logic,* which is concerned with the rules of consistent thought. Against John Maynard Keynes he holds that probability is concerned not with objective relations between propositions but with degrees of belief. Keynes partly yielded to Ramsey without abandoning his efforts to make induction an application of mathematical probability.

German Poets, Thinkers, Scientists

THE LITERARY TRADITION

Sebastian Brant (1458-1520), German humanistic satirist, author of The Ship of Fools, *which traversed his Europe from end to end*

The Ship of Fools
(Woodcut, 1494)

Johann Joachim Winckelmann (1717-1768), Eminent Historian and Critic of the Art of Antiquity

Gotthold Ephraim Lessing

LESSING, GOTTHOLD EPHRAIM

LESSING, GOTTHOLD EPHRAIM (1729-1781). The idea of religious tolerance has been given its noblest poetic symbolization in Lessing's drama *Nathan the Wise* (1779), which also became the model for Goethe's and Schiller's classical dramas. For admonishing the German people to love their fellow men without prejudice, Lessing was hated by German zealots of religious, political and racial orthodoxy, and considered to be not a genuine German but of Slavic origin.

Poet, dramatist, critic of art and literature, archæologist, historian and theologian, Lessing was the first man of letters in Germany who dared to earn his living as a freelance writer. Living among people who recoiled from activities involving personal responsibility, Lessing valued independent thinking and feeling, criticism and knowledge as the highest energies of life and mind, and endeavored to awaken the spirit of responsibility among the German people. He rehabilitated wrongly depreciated or condemned thinkers of the past, he struggled against wrong authorities of his time, he tried to secure liberty of expression for a German literature that did not yet exist when he wrote his principal works. But he was not satisfied with his success in combating prejudices and narrowing rules. He also tried to establish standards of judgment and principles of poetic and artistic creation. This he did in his *Hamburgische Dramaturgie* and *Laokoon* (1766-67). Open revolt against the absolutist regime, in particular that of Frederick II of Prussia, was considered hopeless by Lessing, who limited his political criticism to some sporadic bitter remarks in his printed works but branded the political and social conditions of Germany with mordant sarcasm in his correspondence. At the end of his life, Lessing concentrated upon the theological disquisitions and defending himself against attacks on the part of orthodox clergymen. In this struggle that threatened his civil existence, Lessing proclaimed that he put striving for truth above possession of truth.

Nathan the Wise
(from a contemporary drawing)

Lessing's Birthplace

Hamburg Theater, Often Frequented by Lessing

*"The Laocoon," Subject of Lessing's Famous Essay
on Aesthetics*

HAMANN, JOHANN GEORG

HAMANN, JOHANN GEORG (1730-1788). During a stay in London, where he was bound to become acquainted with British business methods, Hamann, a native of Königsberg, Prussia, had a mystical experience which made him a grim adversary of rationalism and the spirit of enlightenment that fascinated most of his contemporaries. With the aid of allegorical interpretation, Hamann regarded the Bible as the fundamental book of all possible knowledge, including that of nature. Allegory and symbol gave Hamann truer knowledge than notions. Myths and poetry were to him of greater validity than scientific research and logical conclusions. Language was the key that opens the door to reality. Hamann was a past master in sensing the unconscious tendencies of speech. But in his style there are no consequences, no development of ideas. He tried to grasp the flux of life, but, according to his own avowal, often forgot the meaning of the similes he had used and to which he alluded in later pages of the same treatise. His fugitive associations, therefore, are of greater value than his efforts to express his intentions elaborately. Devout and coquettish, excessive in his piety and repentance of transgressions with which his imagination remained fascinated, Hamann tried to embrace spirit and sensuality, sometimes illuminating their relations, sometimes becoming hopelessly confused. His writings were inspired by sublime earnestness and brilliant irony. He accused the rationalistic spirit of his age of ignoring God and nature, human genius, creative action and the enjoyment of real life. His views deeply impressed Herder, Goethe, Friedrich Heinrich Jacobi, Hegel and Kierkegaard.

NICOLAI, FRIEDRICH

NICOLAI, FRIEDRICH (1733-1811). The world record in being vilified by the greatest number of his most illustrious contemporaries can hardly be disputed to be held by Nicolai, who was a bookseller, publisher, editor of reviews, novelist, and theological and philosophical writer. For about a decade (1755-1765), Nicolai's good reputation was not attacked. He was the friend of Gotthold Ephraim Lessing and Moses Mendelssohn, and was considered a man of sound ideas, a fighter for the Enlightenment that flourished in Germany during that period. But then, for more than forty-five years, Nicolai was the object of satires, polemical pamphlets, literary assaults and expressions of indignation and contempt. Among Nicolai's most violent enemies were Immanuel Kant and Fichte, Goethe and Schiller, the poets of the movement of Storm and Stress and the leaders of German romanticism.

After Lessing's and Mendelssohn's deaths, Nicolai, almost alone, answered the attacks directed against him, sometimes with humor, sometimes with serious arguments, always with equanimity, though not always adequately. It cannot be denied that he was inferior to Kant, and that most of his debates with Kant resulted in his defeat. It cannot be denied that his devotion to the ideas of the Enlightenment was stiffened by a sort of orthodoxy. Nicolai was a fanatic adversary of sentimentalism, superstition, of obscurantism of any kind. He was a champion of common sense, and therefore became suspicious of Kant's criticism and Fichte's idealism. The poetry of Goethe, especially his *Werther,* was accused by him of favoring exaggeration of sentiments, and romanticism was, to him, identical with a return to the Middle Ages in politics, thought and religion. In all these struggles, the German public acclaimed Nicolai's adversaries. He was not discouraged nor afraid of replying to the romanticist Friedrich Schlegel, who exalted Fichte's doctrine of science, concerning which he, Nicolai, thought the introduction of planting potatoes was of greater importance to humanity. Nicolai's novels contain some interesting descriptions. His *Sebaldus Nothanker* (1773) gives a clear picture of Berlin under Frederick II.

German historians and philosophers still continue to sneer at Nicolai who defended common sense and felt that the German spirit took a dangerous route.

Friedrich Heinrich Jacobi

JACOBI, FRIEDRICH HEINRICH

JACOBI, FRIEDRICH HEINRICH (1743-1819). As far as Jacobi's philosophy enjoyed any authority during his lifetime, it seemed to be definitely destroyed by the devastating criticism of Kant, Fichte, Schelling and Hegel. Jacobi died a defeated man. Today, however, he is regarded as a precursor of existentialism.

Jacobi called himself an aphoristic thinker. He was aware of his incapability to overcome all the contradictions which prevented him from being consistent. His principal propositions are presented in the form of novels. The first *Allwill* (1775) was intended as an encomium of Goethe, who was his friend, but it finally became a warning against the man of genius. Jacobi blamed contemporary civilization for its lack of original and immediate feelings, of natural behavior, for the decay of heart and intellect, and he exalted the morals of the man of genius who is independent of traditional ethical standards, whose life is dominated by passion which means confidence in life. Nevertheless, he recognized that surrendering to passion entails individual and social dangers. The second novel *Woldemar* (1777) is essentially the author's self-criticism.

It was Jacobi's principal intention to present "humanity as it is," no matter whether it be conceivable or inconceivable. He was inclined to attribute to life an absolute value but he was also aware of the ambiguity of life. He insisted that feeling, not knowledge, constitutes the contact between the ego and the external world, and that what cannot be proved by reason, can be comprehended by feeling; but he did not question traditional logic which secures experience in creating steadiness. Only when steadiness degenerates into rigidity does it become a danger. According to Jacobi, the only philosophical system that is logically irrefutable is that of Spinoza which, however, he rejected as metaphysically wrong. Jacobi's God, different from the pantheistic deity, is also different from the Christian God. But, personally, Jacobi sympathized with Christian piety, and his conception of man is essentially Christian. Faith is, he said, intellectual evidence of logical principles as well as divination of Truth, imperfect knowledge as well as immediateness of feeling. The faithful disposition is the condition of any knowledge of truth and secures permanent certainty and peace of mind.

From this position, Jacobi proceeded to a severe criticism of the German idealists who replied with a roughness unheard of until then in the history of German controversies.

Georg Christoph Lichtenberg

Johann Gottfried Herder

LICHTENBERG, GEORG CHRISTOPH

LICHTENBERG, GEORG CHRISTOPH (1742-1799). Aphorism is a form of literary art that corresponds to the character of Lichtenberg, the ironic sceptic of German enlightenment. He liked to collect observations of daily life, curiosities, oddities, psychological experiences, and to shape them into short and easy sentences which mirrored his general philosophical outlook. Lichtenberg, professor of mathematics and natural sciences at the University of Göttingen, had a high idea of spiritual freedom, and he was not afraid to defend it. He particularly liked to ridicule orthodoxy and missionary zeal. Combining common sense and refinement of feeling, Lichtenberg remained lonely among German writers and thinkers.

HERDER, JOHANN GOTTFRIED

HERDER, JOHANN GOTTFRIED (1744-1803). It would not be incorrect to derive the growth, if not the origin, of modern German nationalism from Herder's writings. But it would not do justice to him to ignore his humanitarian cosmopolitanism. In fact, Slavic national feelings have been equally strengthened by Herder who spoke and wrote German but was a descendant from Germanized Lithuanians. More than once, Herder not only expressed his fondness of Slavic literature but protested against German oppression of the Baltic Slavs. He attributed a high value to nationality as a medium of human civilization. But he denied any claim to superiority.

To Herder, love of the historical past was a cultural force, a way to psychic renovation. He believed that acquaintance with the poetry of the Bible, with Homer, Shakespeare and medieval folk songs would refresh and

278

Title Page of Ideen zur Philosophie der Geschichte der Menschheit, *First Edition*

Herder and His Wife at Breakfast

Herder House in Weimar

enhance the sentiments of modern humanity. But he was an enthusiast of history because he was no less an enthusiast of the future of civilization, and he was firmly convinced that humanitarian ideals were the manifestations of God's will. In his *Ideen zur Philosophie der Geschichte der Menschheit* (Ideas on the Philosophy of History of Humanity, 1784-91), Herder combined biological, ethnological and literary studies with the ideas of Spinoza, Leibniz, Shaftesbury, Montesquieu and Voltaire. His work began with the stars, among which earth is one of many others, and described the influence of climate, geography, customs and individual fates on the history of mankind. Change, growth, and development were of basic importance to Herder's image of the world.

Originally a disciple of Kant, Herder, in his later years, opposed his teacher, especially his ideas concerning the "depraved nature" of man, as a consequence of original sin. He also tried to refute Kant's Critiques.

Party given by the Duchess Amalia von Weimar. Goethe is third from left, Herder third from right
(Painting by Kraus)

279

Johann Wolfgang von Goethe

Poem of Goethe in Manuscript

GOETHE, JOHANN WOLFGANG VON

GOETHE, JOHANN WOLFGANG VON (1749-1832).
Goethe often expressed his resentment when he was hailed
and exalted as the author of *Faust, Werther* and so many
other dramatic, epic and lyrical poems but ignored as a
scientist. In his later years, he constantly declared that no
adequate appraisal of his work was possible without taking into account the importance of his contributions to
anatomy, mineralogy, meteorology, botany, zoology, optics, and most modern scientists agree with his biographers
that Goethe was right. It is true, Goethe's theory of colors
is disputed, but in all the other fields, his scientific activities, especially concerning comparative morphology, are
acknowledged as of high value. Moreover, there is today
an almost general agreement that Goethe's life and personality cannot be comprehensively understood and appreciated without due regard to his studies on natural sciences. It was science to which Goethe devoted most of his
time during many years, even decades, and it was his scientific activities that formed a conspicuous strain in his
character and mind.

To Goethe, science meant exact observation of the phenomena, inquiry into their conditions, effects, coherence
and variety. His methods were both analytical and syn-
thetical, study of the characteristics of the individual and
of general laws of formation. But, as far as science is concerned with measuring and counting, with mathematical
methods, Goethe did not like it. The instrument he regarded as the most sure and precious was the human eye,
and he passionately protested confidence in sensory experience.

The Earth Spirit Appears
(Drawing by Goethe)

Faust and Mephisto Galloping in the Night
(Delacroix, Metropolitan Museum of Art)

Goethe's science and poetry were founded upon general views of philosophical character, although he remained distrustful of any technical philosophy. The only philosopher he admired without reserve was Spinoza. He adopted his pantheism but not his determinism. Or, more precisely, he adopted his determinism to a certain extent but did not believe that life and the universe are totally determined. He even did not believe in the general validity of causality. Goethe repeatedly declared that freedom is blended, in a mysterious manner, with necessity, and that law and arbitrary forces rule the universe, working side by side. It was for these reasons that Goethe regarded man as both subject to necessity and capable of free will. In his autobiography *Fiction and Truth,* in his studies on French literature and on oriental poetry, he tried to penetrate into the realm of necessity, by inquiring into historical factors that condition the existence of the individual, but he felt himself obliged to state that all knowable factors of historical development are not sufficient to explain the peculiarity of the human individual. On the other hand, he repeatedly warned against miscalculation or neglect of historical, social and natural conditions which limit the freedom of the individual.

Goethe's philosophy spells serene resignation. But it does not mean easy acquiescence in the fact that human knowledge is limited. He constantly admonished mankind to inquire as far as possible and not to give up too quickly. It is quite another thing, said Goethe, to resign near the boundaries of human thought, than to rest within one's narrow-minded ego. What he regarded as the greatest happiness of thinking man was "to have explored whatever is explorable, and to revere silently what is inexplorable."

281

Wilhelm von Humboldt

Wilhelm von Humboldt

HUMBOLDT, WILHELM VON

HUMBOLDT, WILHELM VON (1767-1835). As a contemporary observer remarked, Humboldt was not young at the age of sixteen and not old at the age of sixty. Although Humboldt did not disagree with that statement, he claimed that his independence from change was the result of his self-education and striving and of the organization and economy of his living energies. Even if this assumption was incorrect, it is true that Humboldt endeavored, from his early years till his death, to construct his character in accordance with his ideals of human perfection and, although he persisted in wearing such a mask, his behavior was considered natural by men like Goethe and Schiller, his friends. This mask helped him, sensitive and sensual as he actually was, to appear serene and imperturbable. But he was by no means a hypocrite. He was deeply convinced that character was not a natural human quality but the result of will.

Humboldt was a man of highest culture and wide interests. He was a great linguist, a pioneer in studying the languages of American aborigines, of Sanskrit and Basque; in philosophy, an independent disciple of Kant and Schelling, not abandoning, however, the ideas of enlightenment; a historian; and a statesman who was an excellent minister of public education in Prussia, but was defeated when he struggled against routine and reaction and for a moderate liberalism.

In his early writings, Humboldt was an extreme individualist. Later he was interested in investigating the relations between the individual and the great movements of history, but he maintained, in opposition to Hegel, that the individual and the so-called spirit of the epoch or nation are incommensurable. He became convinced of the coherence of the spiritual life of all times and nations but his principal interest remained devoted to the individual. To him the diversity of men, times and nations constituted no objection to the establishment of a universal ideal of human education and perfection, and he constantly endeavored to give this ideal a telling, characteristic, concrete content.

Friedrich von Schlegel

Jean Paul Friedrich Richter (1763-1825),
Whimsical Essayist and Humanist

SCHLEGEL, FRIEDRICH VON

SCHLEGEL, FRIEDRICH VON (1772-1829). Friedrich Schlegel is one of the most characteristic representatives of German romanticism whose principal trait is the longing for a reality different from that which is determined by natural laws and historical circumstances. Dissatisfied with the civilization of his own time, Schlegel at first exalted the French Revolution, then the Middle Ages, and finally, considering the Roman Catholic Church as the keeper of the medieval mind, he was converted to it, and became a champion of political and cultural reaction. He began as an admirer and pupil of Kant, Fichte and Goethe, and later turned to Metternich and Joseph de Maistre who asserted the superiority of tradition over reason, and proclaimed papacy as the one legitimate ruler over humanity.

Schlegel was a poor poet. His novel *Lucinde,* although it scandalized middle-class morals, proved to be unreadable. His tragedy *Alarcos,* produced by Goethe in Weimar, fell flat. But in his early aphorisms and essays,

Schlegel refined the understanding of poetry and evoked the sense of personality in every kind of spiritual activity, be it poetic, scientific, philosophical or religious. In his later works, Schlegel stiffened his opposition to Enlightenment, natural law, democracy and liberalism, but, despite his turn to traditionalism, he preserved a revolutionary strain of which he was conscious. He defined it as his faculty to perceive historical changes without sympathizing with them, and to combat the revolution with what he called "revolutionary spirit in a valid sense but different from the common conception." He therefore was as distrusted by Catholics as he was blamed by Protestants.

For many years, Schlegel led a destitute life for he was rather indolent. He would have perished without the help of his wife Dorothea, Moses Mendelssohn's daughter with whom he had eloped from the house of her husband Simon Veit. Dorothea, the "child of enlightenment," nine years older than Schlegel, followed him from folly to folly and, at the same time, provided him with money by writing novels and articles with untiring energy.

The Classics of Germany

Queen Sophie Charlotte of Prussia Receives Leibniz

Leibniz House in Hannover

LEIBNIZ, GOTTFRIED WILHELM

LEIBNIZ, GOTTFRIED WILHELM (1646-1716). Born at the end of the Thirty Years' War, Leibniz constantly longed for peace and the reconciliation of warring parties. He was by nature one of the greatest mediators in the history of mankind. As a diplomat, he endeavored to unite the nations of Europe. As a theologian, he devoted much of his energy to a plan for the revision of the Christian Churches. As a philosopher, he tried, according to his own words, to connect Plato with Democritus, Aristotle with Descartes, the Scholastics with modern physicists, theology with reason. His philosophical conception of the Universe united aesthetical and mathematical, historical and logical, psychological and biological points of view with metaphysical feelings which were inspired by his confidence in God, the creator of the best of possible worlds. The elements of this world are called *monads* by Leibniz. They are characterized by him as the "true atoms," as metaphysical beings. They are not agglomerations of qualita-

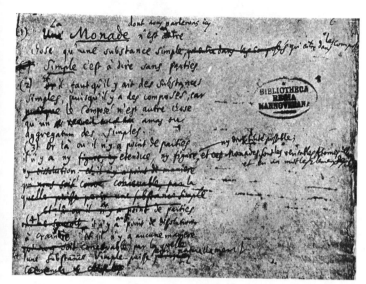

Beginning of Leibniz' Monadology in His Own Hand
(Niedersächs, Landesbibliothek)

Queen Sophie Charlotte of Prussia Entertaining Leibniz

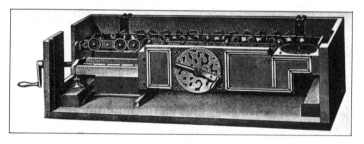

Mathematical Machine Constructed by Leibniz

tively undistinguishable particles but individual centers of force, endowed with the faculty of perception and appetition. Insisting upon their immaterial, metaphysical essence, Leibniz denied the possibility of any physical interaction between them. Their coexistence and intercourse are regulated by the "pre-established harmony" which is the work of God.

Before Leibniz began to construct his philosophical system, he had, in 1684, discovered the differential calculus which, as he expected, would make the analytical method of mathematics applicable to all objects of science.

The belief in the intrinsic value of an infinite variety of individual beings, which he refused to regard as modifications of but one substance, made Leibniz the first modern pluralist. At the end of the 19th century, pluralism seemed to be definitely defeated. But it has been restored, particularly in America, by thinkers like William James, F. J. E. Woodbridge and John Dewey.

WOLFF, CHRISTIAN

WOLFF, CHRISTIAN (1679-1754). Frederick William I, the "soldier king" of Prussia, dismissed Wolff, in 1723, from his post as professor at the University of Halle, forced him to leave the kingdom within forty-eight hours, and, some years later, decreed that everyone who used a book of Wolff's should be sentenced to wheelbarrow labor. What incited the fury of the King was an address given by Wolff in which he had praised the ethical teachings of Confucius, and had added that a man could be happy and good without the Divine grace of revelation. Furthermore, the king was impressed by the apprehension, expressed by some of his generals, that Wolff, as an adherent of determinism, might endanger the discipline of the Prussian army.

Wolff's international fame was enhanced by the King's measures. Other governments offered him a professorship. Learned societies in France and England awarded him degrees and honors. However, the University of Halle suffered from the consequences of Wolff's expulsion, so that the King, reluctantly, invited Wolff to come back. Before the negotiations were completed, Frederick William I died, and his successor Frederick II used Wolff's final reappointment to exhibit himself as a tolerant ruler.

Wolff was a disciple of Leibniz, but he completed the latter's system, or, as Leibniz saw it, deformed it, by concessions to Aquinas, Descartes, and even to Locke. Despite different opinions, Leibniz remained friendly to Wolff, and continued to recommend and advise him. For Leibniz was aware that Wolff had a faculty of clear expression and systematization which he himself lacked. Wolff's authority and influence with the German Enlightenment were immense until Kant shook the fundamentals of Wolff's system. But even Kant revered him as "the most powerful representative of dogmatic rationalism, of the standpoint of pure, unshaken confidence in the strength of reason."

Immanuel Kant

KANT, IMMANUEL

KANT, IMMANUEL (1724-1804). The ancestors of Immanuel Kant on his father's side were Scotch. Had he kept the original spelling of Cant, the citizens of Königsberg would have pronounced his name "Zand." His entire well-ordered life, with the exception of a negligible period, was spent in that East Prussian city whose burghers used to set their watches when he passed under their windows on his daily walks. After mature reflection, Kant decided to stay single. From theological student he rose to Privatdozent and full professor of philosophy, and with his epoch-making answer to the problems posed by David Hume, he became not only Germany's greatest philosopher, but one of the greatest philosophers of all times.

In his famous *Critique of Pure Reason* he showed that knowledge *a priori* is possible, which means that by virtue of the forms and categories of the mind, like space, time and causality, man possesses the presuppositions for coherent and intelligible experience. To be sure, we know only appearances, colors, sounds and the like, never the

Title Page of First Edition of Critique of Pure Reason

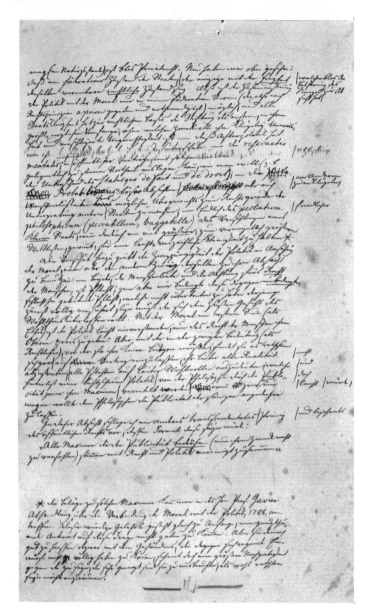

Manuscript Page from Toward Eternal Peace

thing-in-itself. Kant maintained that true knowledge cannot transcend or go beyond experience. Still, for the sake of religion and morality, we need such concepts as God, soul, freedom and immortality. To satisfy these demands of human nature, Kant wrote the *Critique of Practical Reason,* in which he acknowledged the necessity and validity of these values.

In the categorical imperative Kant laid a solid foundation for morality by enjoining man to act in such a way that the maxim of his will may at the same time be raised into a principle of universal law. Religionists called him the all-devourer, but they failed to recognize his deep piety expressed in these lines: "Two things fill the soul with ever new and increasing wonder and reverence the oftener and the more fervently reflection ponders on it: The starry heavens above and the moral law within." Scientists know him as the co-author of the Kant-Laplace theory of the heavens. And lovers of freedom are inspired by his treatise on eternal peace. All modern philosophy must orient itself to Kant.

United Nations Headquarters, New York. The UN Charter was based on Kant's Toward Eternal Peace

Kant's House

UN Palais des Nations at Geneva

Kant and His Friends

Johann Gottlieb Fichte
(Schiller-Nationalmuseum)

Fichte as a Member of the Home Defense

FICHTE, JOHANN GOTTLIEB

FICHTE, JOHANN GOTTLIEB (1762-1814). Fichte, a German philosopher, studied at Meissen, Pforta, Jena and Leipzig to be a theologian. Shortly thereafter, he accepted a tutoring position in Switzerland, but dissatisfied with it, he intended to accept one in Poland. En route there he met Kant whose moral and religious doctrines attracted him and caused him to change all his plans. Forthwith he wrote *An Essay Towards A Critique of All Revelation*. For some unaccountable reason, the publisher neglected to place Fichte's name on the title page; everyone hailed the essay as a new work of Kant. When the real author became known, Fichte, overnight, was recognized as a first-rate philosopher and was called to Jena to lecture on the vocation of the scholar.

Fichte lost his position because he regarded God as the moral order of the universe; he went to Berlin, and lectured on occasion at the University of Erlangen. When the French occupied Berlin, (1806) Fichte left. He returned the following year and devoted himself wholeheartedly to freeing Prussia of foreign domination. As rector of the new Berlin university, he fired his listeners with enthusiasm. His addresses to the German nation are still famous. His view of the state was socialistic, and he had visions of a league of peoples united in a moral endeavor and in true culture.

As a philosopher, he was a transcendental subjective idealist; his system reversed the idea of I, the non-I or the world, and their synthesis in experience. In his *Science of Knowledge,* he sought a complete system of reason. His life was devoted to ideals and he exemplified his thesis that the world is but the occasion for man to exercise his moral duty. "The system of freedom satisfies my heart; the opposite system destroys and annihilates it. To stand cold and unmoved, amid the current of events, a passive mirror of fugitive and passing phenomena—this existence is impossible for me. I scorn and detest it. I will love; I will lose myself in sympathy; I will know the joy and grief of life."

BAADER, FRANCIS XAVIER VON

BAADER, FRANCIS XAVIER VON (1765-1841). An expert on mints and mining, and consultant in both these fields, Baader was also a writer, a Catholic layman whose works were read by both Protestant and Catholic philosophers. The latter found him stimulating if unorthodox, particularly in view of the fact that he once stated that should the devil appear on earth, it would be in the garb of a professor of moral philosophy. During a five-year sojourn in England, Baader acquainted himself with the opposing ideologies of David Hartley, the sensualist, David Hume, the sceptic, and Jacob Boehme, the mystic. His writings, as a result of these influences, contained many unpredictable flashes of insight and startling affirmations. Mysticism influenced him more than did philosophies. Baader never strove for a system, but aimed at the deep and profound; he frequently appeared paradoxical. Rationalism was abhorrent to him; human knowledge required the greater wisdom of God, whom he viewed as the real spontaneity in all forms of knowledge. The phrase *con-scientia* symbolized to him man's participation in God's knowledge. He disapproved of some aspects of the papacy, but, nonetheless, elected to stay within the fold, striving, in his lectures, for a philosophic rationale of Catholicism, and making the love of God and neighbor the mainstay of his sociology, which also incorporated his ideas of liberty and equality. In 1826 he was called to assume the chair of professor of speculative dogmatics at the University of Munich, his native city. However, he was compelled in 1838 to exchange this for a chair in anthropology because he was barred from lecturing on the philosophy of religion for the reason that he was a layman.

SCHELLING, FRIEDRICH WILHELM JOSEPH VON

SCHELLING, FRIEDRICH WILHELM JOSEPH VON (1775-1854). Schelling has been called the Proteus among philosophers. His mind was as changeable as it was impressible. In his early years, Schelling fascinated everyone he met. He was overflowing with ideas, versatile, and apt in understanding men and problems. Goethe considered him the most congenial philosopher he knew, and it was Schelling who inspired Hegel, although the latter would not admit it.

Schelling created the philosophy of identity by asserting that nature is not essentially different from mind; his way of representing the various forms of existence as the work of an unconsciously creating activity which is the same in shaping nature and mind, influenced not only his German contemporaries but English and French thinkers as well, and not the least among them—Bergson.

The aged Schelling was rigid in his attitude toward man and the universe. He recanted his earlier pantheistic belief in the identity of nature and mind and repudiated transcendental idealism, even idealism and judgments *a priori* at all. The "positive philosophy" of Schelling's last years considered empiricism the lesser evil compared with any kind of rational deduction. Originally an admirer of Epicurus and Spinoza, he had become the defender of Protestant and Catholic orthodoxy and the champion of political reaction. But he could not prevent liberals from referring to his words, spoken in earlier days, which extolled eternal change.

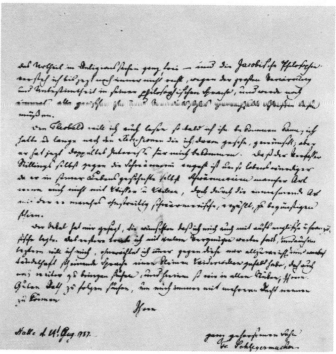

Facsimile letter from Schleiermacher

SCHLEIERMACHER, FRIEDRICH DANIEL

SCHLEIERMACHER, FRIEDRICH DANIEL (1768-1834). The life, theology and philosophy of Schleiermacher may be characterized as a steady concordance of contraries. He was a minister of the Reformed Church, devoted to the spiritual welfare of his community and an influential professor of theology, but he shocked faithful Christians by his close association with Friedrich Schlegel when this romanticist author was an avowed libertine and defied Christian morality with his lascivious novel *Lucinde,* which Schleiermacher defended against general indignation. He offended not only the members of his congregation by his intimate friendship with the Jewess, Henriette Herz, but, even more so, by his love of a married woman, which was the talk of the town. Wilhelm Dilthey, his biographer, destroyed much of Schleiermacher's correspondence in order to remove, as he said, "ugly spots" from his memory. Yet all this could not, and cannot, cause us to question the sincerity of Schleiermacher's religious feelings, his spiritual dignity and the originality of his thinking.

Schleiermacher became known by his book *On Religion* (1799), in which he defended religion "against its educated scorners." He intended to found an eternal covenant between the Christian faith and independent science. He professed firm confidence that no rational criticism could destroy Christian religion, which he conceived as the "feeling of absolute dependence," indispensable to human life but not closely connected with thought, knowledge and will. Personally convinced of the truth of Christianity, Schleiermacher nevertheless denied its claim "to be universal and to rule alone over mankind as the sole religion." He was strongly opposed to uniformity, and, above all, to uniformity in religion. He was an ardent defender of the rights of each person to have a religion of his own that corresponds to the uniqueness of his individuality. But Schleiermacher, who, in theology and philosophy, vindicated the cause of the individual, regarded him always as a link in the chain of history. As a historically minded thinker and as a philosopher of religion he refused to identify the infinite value of the individual, whom he acknowledged, with his independence from historical tradition and present society, and regarded this standpoint as justification of his activities as a churchman. Theology was to him no rational science but a compound of knowledge and rules which are needed for the maintenance and direction of the Christian community, and individual faith, valuable as it remains, requires emotional response and moral support on the part of a community of voluntary and devoted members. In the history of the Church, Schleiermacher achieved a notable success by effecting the union between Lutheranism and Calvinism in Prussia.

In his philosophical writings, Schleiermacher also insisted on the value of the individual, whom he regarded in his connection with nature and history. Fichte sneered at him and Hegel hated him, but Schleiermacher retaliated shrewdly. In his frequent quarrels with his fellow professors he did not rely on the teachings of the Sermon on the Mount.

Berlin toward the End of the Eighteenth Century

University of Berlin, 1810

Hegel in His Study

HEGEL, GEORG WILHELM FRIEDRICH

HEGEL, GEORG WILHELM FRIEDRICH (1770-1831). Long after Hegel lost his once immense authority, many of his intellectual formulas continued to attract the philosophers of various schools in various countries. Hegel's philosophy is often regarded as typically German, and certainly some of its main features represent the very characteristics of the German way of reacting to reality. Numerous great philosophers in England and America, in Italy and France, and in other countries have testified that they owed to Hegel not only an increase of knowledge but the fundamental principles of their own thinking. Outstanding Hegelians in England were T. H. Green, Edward and John Caird, F. H. Bradley and Bernard Bosanquet, and in America, W. T. Harris, Royce, Creighton and Calkins. John Dewey said that "acquaintance with Hegel has left a permanent deposit in my thinking."

Hegel's philosophy has often been despised as abstract speculation. Yet soon after his death it became evident that his thoughts could offer an ideological basis to political parties which were radically opposed to each other. Bismarck and the Prussian Junkers adopted Hegel's view on the state. So did Fascism and National Socialism, while Marx, and after him, Lenin, adapted Hegel's dialectical method to give reasons for the doctrine of the dictatorship of the proletariat. And even staunch defenders of liberalism and democracy have appealed to Hegel's philosophy of history.

In a similar way, the champions of religious orthodoxy and liberalism have used Hegel's ideas to justify their respective positions. King Frederick William III of Prussia and his minister of public education favored Hegelianism as the firmest bulwark of Christianity, while King Frederick William IV of Prussia and his minister of public education persecuted the Hegelians whom they accused of undermining the Christian faith.

Hegel has been glorified and vilified as the protector of reactionary conservatism and as the prophet of revolution-

Hegel Writing Die Phänomenologie des Geistes *During the Battle of Jena, October 14, 1806*

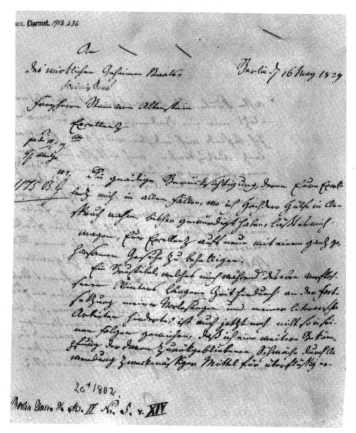

Facsimile of Hegel Letter

ary change because his system tries to synthesize antagonistic tendencies. On the one hand, he put becoming above being, and conceived of the world as an eternally evolutionary process; on the other hand, he claimed to have laid the groundwork for definite knowledge and for the understanding of timeless perfection.

In a lecture on the history of philosophy, Hegel, from his chair at the University of Berlin, called to his audience: "Man cannot over-estimate the greatness and power of his mind." For he regarded human mind as one of the manifestations of the Absolute which he defined as spirit. The world, Hegel stated, is penetrable to thought which is, on its part, a description of the Absolute. Cosmic reason operates within the soul of man, whose consciousness is the area of the subjective spirit, while the objective spirit becomes manifest in cultural and social institutions like law and morality, and the absolute spirit can be grasped in the arts, in religion and philosophy. Human history and social life, culminating in the state, represent the highest

level of a gradation that rises from inorganic nature to human genius, from "mere existence" to consciousness, knowledge of truth and action in accordance with recognized duties. The history of the world means the progressive realization of freedom which can be demonstrated by purely logical development. For Hegel does not acknowledge any other cause of historical change than the movement of thought by integrating a thesis and its antithesis into a synthesis which, on its part, provokes a new antithesis with which it becomes integrated into a new synthesis. These succeeding syntheses will bring the world to reason. Hegel thought that he had found the pattern for both human and cosmic reason in this conflict of thesis and antithesis which he called the dialectics. For becoming was regarded by Hegel as the modification of a being by factors which he defined as the negation of the being to be modified. In this way, evolution was conceived by Hegel as a purely logical procedure for which he claimed the acknowledgment of real necessity.

The Young Schopenhauer
(Copper Cut by Ludwig Ruhl)

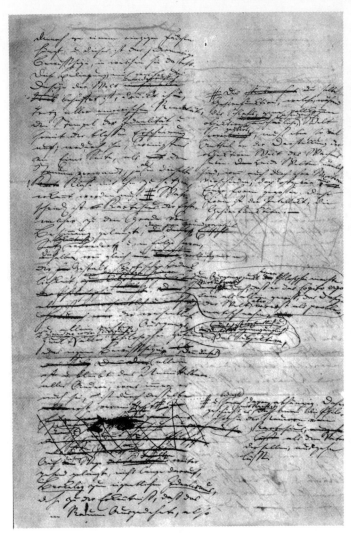

Manuscript Page from Die Welt als Wille und Vorstellung

SCHOPENHAUER, ARTHUR

SCHOPENHAUER, ARTHUR (1788-1860). Schopenhauer almost became an Englishman when his father, a citizen of Danzig, then in Poland, fearing the annexation of his native town by Prussia (which in fact was imminent), intended to take his wife, who was expecting a baby, to England, so that his son would not be a subject of the hated Prussian monarchy. However, the son was born before the parents could reach the land of their hope.

Arthur Schopenhauer did not share his father's predilection for England or his opposition to Prussian despotism. But he nevertheless adopted some English habits, read the *London Times* regularly, and remained aloof from any political movement in Germany, indifferent to nationalism, yet hating democracy, Judaism and Christianity. He pre-

ferred animals to his fellow men, and particularly he disliked women. British empiricism did not satisfy him, and his German contemporaries, Fichte, Schelling and Hegel, were branded by him as humbugs. He respected Kant from whose criticism he proceeded to his own philosophy. The wisdom and religion of India, the Vedas, Upanishads and Buddhism, aroused his enthusiasm, and he untiringly proclaimed the superiority of Indian thought to the European mind.

Although to his father's satisfaction, Schopenhauer had forgotten the German language during his stay in Paris and London, and had had to learn it again, when, at the age of seventeen, he returned to Germany, he became one of the greatest masters of German prose style. His clear and well-organized sentences proved able to captivate

Schopenhauer with His Poodle

Daguerreotype of Schopenhauer at Time of Completion of Volume II of Die Welt als Wille und Vorstellung

readers who recoil from the language of most of the German philosophers. Goethe, whom Schopenhauer knew personally and highly esteemed both as a poet and thinker, wrote in Schopenhauer's album an epigram, saying: "If you will enjoy the value of your own personality you must enjoy the value of the world." Nothing could be more contrary to Schopenhauer's doctrine, for, according to it, the world is fundamentally evil. Its reality cannot be grasped by reason which is only capable of perceiving delusive appearances of the real things. The only real, metaphysical, cosmic being is the will which comprises both mental acts of the human individual and the drive, urge or instinctive force of the entire organic world. Even the crystallization of the diamond, or the turning of the magnet to the pole, or chemical affinities are regarded by Schopenhauer as utterances of the will which is essentially

one. The fact that man takes cognizance of his body as much by way of reason as by immediate feeling, enables him to become aware of the will that works within his organism, and thus of the cosmic will which is identical with the former. To Schopenhauer this procedure offers the key to the understanding of the real world.

But, while the world of appearances or ideas is delusive, the world of the will is fundamentally evil. Will is the source of crime and suffering. The only salvation available to mankind is mortification of the will, complete resignation, extinction of the self.

Schopenhauer's pessimism had many followers. Of even greater influence was his doctrine of the superiority of instinct, the will, the unconscious drive to reason and knowledge, after Nietzsche had dissolved its connection with pessimism.

FEUERBACH, LUDWIG

FEUERBACH, LUDWIG (1804-1872). Modern existentialists ought to recognize Feuerbach as well as Kierkegaard as their forerunners, instead of regarding the former as a mere materialist. It is true that Feuerbach, while opposing Hegel's idealism, professed materialistic views, but materialism, to him, meant only a part of the truth, not its entirety. He defined philosophy as "the science of reality in its truth and totality." To find the total truth, he resorted to a concept of anthropology which included theology. He did not deny the existence of God, but explained the formation of the idea of God as the result of the longing of sensual man to reconcile the apparent contradictions of life. He accused the idealist philosophers of having deprived man of his feelings of immediateness and existence. According to Feuerbach, man was nothing without the world of objects with which he was connected: existence was defined as the abundance of relations; sensuality was the criterion of existence, but not its only characteristic. He maintained that the cooperation of physical and psychic elements made for the unity of man. He denied the possibility of reducing mental phenomena to the physical level or deriving God from nature. The antinomy between mind and nature was described by Feuerbach with ironic humor. He enjoined his fellow men not to ignore the contradictions of life, and to concentrate upon the tasks of the present day.

LANGE, FRIEDRICH ALBERT

LANGE, FRIEDRICH ALBERT (1828-1875). Germany has produced very few philosophers who are as lucid, judicious and sincere as Lange, whose *History of Materialism* (1866) has maintained its value as a standard work and an example of philosophical historiography despite the change of time and the increase of knowledge. Lange, a leader of Neo-Kantianism, demonstrated materialism but, on the other hand, he taught us to appreciate the materialistic philosophers whose independence of idealistic traditions has often obtained sound results and has been directed by true critical insight. Above all, Lange destroyed the not uncommon prejudice that the adoption of idealistic views on metaphysics would guarantee higher moral standards than could be achieved by the conduct of life of those who professed materialism in metaphysics.

Before Lange published his history of materialism, his book *Die Arbeiterfrage* (The Workers' Question, 1865) created quite a stir in German social politics. Lange, a professor at the University of Marburg, energetically defended the interests of the workers and their political and economic demands, and he was eager to improve their educational and cultural conditions. He often debated with the earliest leaders of German socialism, and quite as often supported them, speaking at meetings arranged by them. Lange honestly tried to ally German democrats and socialists. His premature death was mourned by intellectuals and workers alike.

STIRNER, MAX

STIRNER, MAX (1806-1856). In the daytime, Herr Kaspar Schmidt was a teacher at a young ladies' school, a respectable citizen of Berlin and a loyal subject of his king, Frederick William IV of Prussia. In the evening, he drank wine in a restaurant where he met some writers of left-wing Hegelianism and discussed with them philosophical problems. More often than not, these debates and the wine fired the imagination of the speakers who competed one with another in exalting, both earnestly and parodistically, their personal mission as radical revolutionaries. Some members of that company later became notorious as political adventurers, others became more or less prominent socialists. Kaspar Schmidt, after coming home, worked, late in the night, at a manuscript which he published under the title *Der Einzige und sein Eigentum* (The Ego and his Own, 1845). The author of this book, calling himself Max Stirner, is generally considered as the founder of theoretical anarchism and the most radical individualist in the history of philosophy. While most of his contemporaries conceived the individual as determined by collective factors of various kinds, Stirner proclaimed the uniqueness and absolute independence of his ego. For even the notion of the individual is in Stirner's opinion a useless concession to collectivism. He leaves it to other egos to claim the same uniqueness for themselves. While establishing the ego as the sole reality and the sole value, Stirner emphasizes his opposition against society, against the state, against reactionary and revolutionary parties, against liberalism and socialism, against any legislation and social conventions. For Stirner, the negation of all values except the ego means the only guarantee of personal freedom and the sole way of constructing a philosophical system by independent thinking. His motto is, "I am dependent on nothing," and his cardinal principle is, "For me there is nothing like myself." Whatever other people regard as value, ideas, notions, tenets or laws, are dealt with by Stirner as spectres which haunt unenlightened men. While trying to exorcise these spectres by exposing their unreality, Stirner becomes a mythologist on his own. He was severely attacked by Marx and Engels; however, his book remained practically ignored during his lifetime. Stirner gave his adventurous spirit a free course only in his inward life. What later became known as political anarchism would have terrified him, and he would have opposed it as contrary to his cult of the ego.

STRAUSS, DAVID FRIEDRICH

STRAUSS, DAVID FRIEDRICH (1808-1874). Before Strauss published his *Life of Jesus* (1835), it seemed that the authority of the Christian faith was defended in Germany far more efficiently than it had been during the preceding century. Hegel and Schleiermacher, bitterly opposed one to another, had produced a synthesis of Christian religion and modern thought that was supposed to satisfy all spiritual needs of German intellectuals, not to mention that pressure was exercised by more orthodox theologians who used to denounce really or allegedly un-Christian opinions, and by the governments which were always ready to punish the expression of such opinions. The appearance of Strauss' book had the effect of a bombshell and changed the situation completely. It made Germany the arena of a religious struggle whose violence was unheard of since the end of the Thirty Years' War.

Strauss, without denying the historical existence of Jesus, inexorably criticized the sources of the New Testament, proved their inner contradictions in principal and minor points, and demonstrated that many reports on the life of Jesus, narrated in the Gospels, were entirely unreliable, products of, as he said, "mythical" literature which, to a large extent, was patterned on tales and sayings of the Old Testament. The synthesis of theology and science was destroyed, and could not be saved either by orthodox theologians who called for the police or by rightist Hegelians who protested that Strauss had misunderstood their master.

The book that made Strauss famous, destroyed his happiness. He was not a fighter, and the permanent hostilities which culminated in an open revolt of the people of Zurich, where he had been appointed professor, undermined his health. But his sense of truth remained unshattered. In his *Doctrine of the Christian Faith* (1840), Strauss definitely broke with Christian theology and Christianity completely. His frankness surpassed that of the most daring thinkers in Germany previous to him. He maintained his standpoint in his later works, especially in his *The Old Faith and the New* (1872), while flatly answering "No" to the question "Can we still be Christians?", and trying to harmonize the doctrine of Ludwig Feuerbach with Darwinism. Certainly, this last work of a tired, constantly persecuted and physically suffering man has many weak points. But it did not deserve the violent attack made by Friedrich Nietzsche who ignored that Strauss, at least in his early writings, had accomplished that which Nietzsche himself demanded from a valiant thinker.

Nietzsche and His Mother
(Louis Held, Weimar)

NIETZSCHE, FRIEDRICH

NIETZSCHE, FRIEDRICH (1844-1900). The fact that Nietzsche was insane for the last twelve years of his life has often been exploited by unfair adversaries who embarrassed serious critics of his doctrines.

Before Nietzsche took his Ph.D. degree, he had already been appointed a full professor of classical philology at the University of Basel in 1869. But scholarship, which promised him a brilliant career, did not satisfy him. The aim of his life was a philosophy that would comprise both cool analysis and enthusiastic vision, a synthesis of a new religious creed and merciless criticism. Apollo, the god of lucid wisdom, and Dionysos, the god of orgiastic mysticism, were taken for its symbols.

Nietzsche is acknowledged, even by most of his opponents, as a great psychologist who, particularly by using the concept of "resentment," succeeded in unmasking hypocrisy, in exposing delusions, perversion of feeling and judgment or intellectual timidity, and opened new ways by his much-disputed inquiry into the formation of morality.

But the view of the philosopher, as Nietzsche conceived it, is not confined to things past and present. His task is not so much to take care of the well-being of his contemporary fellow men as rather to pave the way for the future development which will change man into a higher type, the superman. For the sake of the future, Nietzsche violently fought against Christianity, whose ethics were depreciated by him as "slave morality," and he pronounced the necessity of a general "trans-valuation of values." Nietzsche's ideal of human personality meant the union of physical strength and mental energy. It combined the virtues of the warrior and the independent thinker. It was founded upon his conviction that the "will to power" is the ruling principle of all life, and that life on earth has an absolute value. Nietzsche's ethics, however, does not preach self-indulgence or regard suffering as an evil. It demands fearlessness, not love of pleasure. It prefers the dangerous life to the comfortable one.

While endeavoring to grasp the essential features of cosmic life or to predict a far future, Nietzsche constantly kept his eye upon the cultural situation of his own time, foreboding a terrible catastrophe. Nihilism and decadence seemed to him the greatest dangers that threaten European civilization. He was equally opposed to democracy, socialism and nationalism, and most of all, to the national aspirations and pride of the Germans. He proclaimed the ideal of a "good European."

No philosopher has raged as vehemently against his own soul as Nietzsche did by glorifying physical strength and the will to power. In reality, he was gentle, always in poor health, hating noise and trying to avoid quarrels.

"Glory and Eternity"

Nietzsche as a Young Man

The Nietzsche House in Sils-Maria

Richard Wagner and His Wife Cosima

300

Elizabeth Foerster-Nietzsche, the Philosopher's Sister

THE NIETZSCHE SCANDAL

For decades the life and some of the later works of Nietzsche were suspect to the initiated and scandalized by the ignorant. It is only during the last few years that, largely through the efforts of Dr. Karl Schlechta, the truth has come to the foreground. The ill and helpless Nietzsche had been systematically victimized by an unscrupulous, ambitious and avaricious younger sister who, as early as 1894, appropriated the rights to all his manuscripts and papers, and for six years at the home of her mother in Naumberg, established a Nietzsche Archive—where, on proper occasion, she presented the mentally disturbed philosopher clothed in white toga as the living center of the house.

Elizabeth Nietzsche, being the only person with legal access to the Nietzsche papers, published among others, spurious, aphoristic material under the title *The Will to Power*, in which she interpolated bizarre pan-Germanistic and anti-Semitic outbursts of her lover (and later, husband), the high school teacher, Bernhard Foerster. These were attributed to the Nietzsche who had repeatedly authored such sentences as: "The word anti-Semite is not much more than a synonym for failure. . . . I pity the European brain if we were to abstract from it the Jewish mind. . . . The self-admiration of the German race-consciousness is almost criminal. . . . Anti-Semitism is the disease of this century. . . . I have a simple rule of life—to have no traffic with any of these lying race swindlers."

Mr. Foerster prevailed upon Nietzsche's sister to go with him to Paraguay in order to found there a new Germany (Nueva Germania), in which they could live out with congenial kinsmen their Wagnerian ideas.

Irrefutable evidence has been produced by Professor Schlechta and others that Nietzsche's sister erased and even singed out letters addressed to her mother, replacing the original name with her own, and of course changing the signature from "Your loving son, Fritz" to "Your loving brother, Fritz." Naturally, letters addressed by a sick man to his old mother acquired a different meaning when they were read as epistles to a young and attractive sister, giving rise thereby to ugly suspicions of sexual connotation. But such was the character of the "Lama," or "sheep"—which, significantly, Nietzsche called his sister—that she preferred those suspicions to the truth, which would have been disastrous for her, not only socially but also money-wise—a woman whom Nietzsche, except in the obviously forged correspondence, considered an ignorant and cunning person.

The pseudo-Nietzschean maxims of the Beyreuth Circle, led by Mr. Foerster, found, in Adolf Hitler and his clique, devout admirers.

Hitler Admiring a Bust of Nietzsche

Psychologists and Educators

Johann Amos Comenius

August Hermann Francke (1663-1727), charitable and pietistic pedagogue, responsible for widespread educational activities in German cities

COMENIUS, JOHANN AMOS

COMENIUS, JOHANN AMOS (1592-1670). A bishop of the Bohemian Brethren and the first great democrat among Christian educational philosophers, Comenius fled from Czechoslovakia in 1628 when that country lost its liberty and its national culture was threatened with extinction by the Hapsburg emperor. He roamed throughout Europe working untiringly for the salvation of his nation and the realization of his educational, political, and scientific projects. Despite his misfortunes and precarious existence, Comenius never lost confidence in the rational mind or in human progress.

His ultimate aim was universal peace. He recognized that the necessary steps preliminary to the attainment of this goal involved the unification of rival Christian denominations, fundamental reforms in education, and a new approach to natural science. It was largely the result of his initiative that scientific societies promoting research were founded throughout Europe during the seventeenth century. He insisted that education should be free, universally available, and compulsory for every child; that automatic memorization should be replaced by teaching words with perceptual objects; and that the sensual faculties of school children should be taken into consideration. Comenius

A page from Lavater's Physiognomics, *describing the four characters of man: the phlegmatic, the choleric, the sanguine and the melancholic*

Lavater in His Study

LAVATER, JOHANN KASPAR

LAVATER, JOHANN KASPAR (1741-1801). Protestant orthodoxy and pietism, formerly opposed to each other, became allied in the mind of Lavater, whose complicated character made him sometimes obstinate, sometimes humble. He always tried to realize, by his thinking and conduct of life, the ideal of Christian humanity. He also tried to combine belief in miracles with the modern cult of poetic genius. Trained in psychological self-analysis, he was, nevertheless, a helpless illusionist, whose extreme gullibility exposed him to the suspicion of being insincere. A staunch adversary of rationalism, Lavater was often the victim of fanatics, charlatans and crooks who exploited his longing for miracles and the manifestation of supernatural forces. Notwithstanding his attempts to reach simple faith, an unsophisticated belief in the Word of the Bible, he was never satisfied with plain truth, and was always ready to take divination for knowledge and phantoms for reality because they stirred his imagination more than did reason. But when he was not occupied with the propaganda for his ideas, Lavater always proved to be a noble-minded and charitable man. However, it was not his theological writings that made him famous but his *Physiognomics* (1774-78), which was translated into several languages. This work contains a wealth of material and has inspired psychologists and poets, but it lacks scientific method. Lavater, who collected and interpreted a great number of historical or artistic portraits, was convinced that his physiognomical studies would promote not only a knowledge of man but also a mutual love of men.

stands as a transitional figure in the area of science—halfway between the medieval Aristotelianism and modern empiricism. He believed that independent study and observation offered greater intellectual rewards than did constant reliance upon Aristotle or Pliny. His textbooks, translated into more than seventeen languages, were used in the early years of Harvard University, and throughout the seventeenth century schools of New England, Asia, and Europe. His principal works were: *The Gates of Unlocked Tongues* (1631); *The Way of Light* (1642); *Patterns of Universal Knowledge* (1651); and *The Great Didactic* (1657).

Johann Heinrich Pestalozzi

From Pestalozzi's book, Lienhard und Gertrud
(Eighteenth Century Woodcut)

PESTALOZZI, JOHANN HEINRICH

PESTALOZZI, JOHANN HEINRICH (1746-1827). Pestalozzi is generally regarded as the father of modern European pedagogics. Born in Switzerland, an ardent Swiss patriot, he not only influenced the educational system of his own country and of Germany, but also inspired French and Scandinavian educators, and men like Horace Mann and Henry Barnard in the United States.

It is true, Pestalozzi could never heed to order in his own house or in his enterprises, and neglected his appearance to a degree no progressive educator could approve if one of his pupils did so. But he was an extraordinarily gifted leader of young people. He thoroughly knew and loved children, and also knew and loved humanity. His educational ideas are imbedded in a totality of ideas on the perfection of Man. Indignant of individual wickedness and terrified by events of contemporary history, Pestalozzi never lost confidence in what he considered true human nature. His pedagogical skill was founded upon a large experience. He had been not only a teacher of children and a teacher of teachers, but also a trustee of orphans, and it was from the observation of abandoned children that he learned the most.

Educational ardor made Pestalozzi write philosophical

treatises, as it also caused him to write novels, the best known of which is *Lienhard and Gertrude,* which was widely read. By no means did he claim to be a philosopher. He was neither a rationalist nor an intellectual, and he declared that his whole work was a work of the heart, not of understanding. He even felt uneasy while writing on philosophical problems. But he thought it necessary in order to explain his aims and methods which are conditional on broad views on the destiny of humanity. He considered man as an animal, a member of society and an ethical power. After trying to outline the course of nature in the development of humanity, he proceeded to the establishment of an ethical humanism which has to dominate the education of children and the conduct of adults —their economic, political and spiritual life. Development of the mind, the heart and manual work were the principal points of Pestalozzi's education. He did not ignore the fact that any political community is threatened by inner contradictions; but he hoped to overcome many difficulties by pedagogical care.

Pestalozzi and His Beloved Pupils

Jakob Friedrich Fries (1773-1843). Professor of philosophy. Confused Kantian metaphysics with Platonic and romantic ideologies. Considered human minds capable of apprehending directly the transcendental reality of the Ideas by means of "feeling" (Ahnung). Suggested that all Jewish newborn infants be thrown into the rivers, as a simple solution to the Jewish problem

HERBART, JOHANN FRIEDRICH

HERBART, JOHANN FRIEDRICH (1776-1841). American thinking was influenced by Herbart during the two decades which preceded the First World War. But even those who declined to follow him thereafter could not but acknowledge that Herbart was a pioneer in psychological research and pedagogics.

Herbart, who occupied Immanuel Kant's chair at the University of Königsberg for many years, was regarded by Fichte, Schelling and Hegel as their most formidable adversary. In some regards, Herbart maintained the Kantian tradition but more often he relied upon Leibniz, Hume and British associationism. He was an excellent musician, a master of the piano, the violin, the violoncello and the harp, and liked to explain psychological laws by examples taken from the theory of harmony.

Contrary to Fichte, Schelling and Hegel, Herbart always took great care to tally his thoughts with the results of the empirical sciences. To him, philosophy was the reflection upon the conceptions which are commonly used in experience, both daily and scientific. The philosopher must ask what is it that in reality corresponds to the empirical conceptions which are called substance and causality. While German idealists proceeded from the individual knower, the subject, to the metaphysics of nature and mind, Herbart regarded the subject as the highest metaphysical problem. At the same time, the subject was known to him as the changing product of ideas, and, therefore, was explorable by means of psychological research. Psychology, to Herbart, was founded upon experience, metaphysics and mathematics. He followed Locke and Hume by trying to conceive complex psychic phenomena in terms of simple ideas, each of which was supposed to have a certain degree of strength. His great dream was a future psychodynamics determined by mathematical laws.

306

Friedrich Fröbel (1782-1852) continued Pestalozzi's theories of education. Significant in the development of the kindergarten and visual education

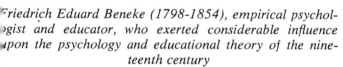

Friedrich Eduard Beneke (1798-1854), empirical psychologist and educator, who exerted considerable influence upon the psychology and educational theory of the nineteenth century

Gustav Theodor Fechner

FECHNER, GUSTAV THEODOR

FECHNER, GUSTAV THEODOR (1801-1887). When Fechner studied medicine, he regarded the world from a mechanistic point of view and almost became an atheist. Then he read Lorenz Oken's *Philosophy of Nature*. This disciple of Schelling influenced him to become a firm theist. Fechner called his philosophy an "offshoot from the tree of Schelling, though growing far away from the mother tree." He ignored Kant completely. As a professor of physics and chemistry, he contended that the natural sciences can only offer partial knowledge and demand completion by a metaphysical-idealistic interpretation of nature. But he also proved to be a staunch empiricist by founding psycho-physics and experimental aesthetics. He was a native of Lusatia, whose population was largely composed of Slavs, who were inclined toward mysticism. Fechner himself turned for a while from empiricism to speculations about the supernatural, but then returned again to empiricism.

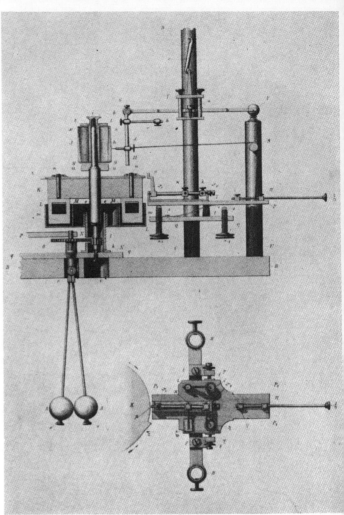

Apparatus used by Helmholtz to time muscle contractions under electrical stimulus, and thus measure the speed of nerve impulses

HELMHOLTZ, HERMANN VON

HELMHOLTZ, HERMANN VON (1821-1894). When Helmholtz, in 1847, delivered his lecture on the conservation of energy, he was prepared to be reproached by the authorities of his time for talking about old stuff. Instead he was hailed by some as a discoverer, and blamed by others as a fanciful speculative philosopher. Most of the physicists had ignored the principle of persistence of energy. Helmholtz knew better. He did not claim to have discovered it. His intention was rather to demonstrate what it means to physical phenomena and to what numerical consequences it leads everywhere.

The universality of Helmholtz' mind is proved by the mere fact that he was successively appointed full professor of physiology, anatomy and physics at the greatest universities of Germany. He promoted optics and acoustics, mechanics, the general theory of electricity, thermodynamics, hydrodynamics, electrodynamics, geometry and the theory of numbers. In 1850 he invented the ophthalmoscope, and received no other material profit from his invention than about fifteen dollars as honorarium for the treatise in which he communicated it.

Helmholtz was also interested in philosophy which, according to him, is concerned with the inquiry into the cognitive faculties and performances of man. He charac-

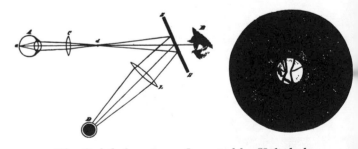

The Ophthalmoscope, Invented by Helmholtz

terized sensation as a symbol, not an image of the external world, and the world of these symbols as the mirror of the real world. If man learns to read the symbols correctly, he becomes able to arrange his actions in a way that the effects correspond to the aims. Helmholtz conceded the theoretical possibility of interpreting the facts in terms of subjective idealism but held that the realist interpretation is the simpler one. Helmholtz, one of whose maternal ancestors was William Penn, was respected internationally not only because of his scientific performances but as the very incarnation of the dignity and probity of science.

WUNDT, WILHELM

WUNDT, WILHELM (1832-1920). The first psychological laboratory was founded in 1879 at Leipzig by Wundt who was a professor at that University from 1875 until his death, and who attracted to his lectures and demonstrations not only young students but scholars who had distinguished themselves, from almost all countries. Wundt developed physiological psychology by experimental methods, measuring reactions to physical and physiological changes, effects, stimulations. But, to him, physiological psychology covers only part of psychology. It is to be completed by introspective analysis of "internal experience," founded upon a philosophical system and integrated into the general doctrine of science. Wundt's introspective psychology is characterized by his conviction that will, together with the emotional states closely connected with it, is the constituent of psychological experience, and is far more important than sensations and ideas; all the other psychical processes must be conceived of by analogy to the experience of will. To him, the soul is a subject but no substance. It is event, activity, evolution.

Wundt's philosophical system is described by himself as a synthesis of Hegelianism and positivism, though he intended to avoid the one-sidedness of each. The fundamental principle of his metaphysics maintained that all material and mechanical things are but the outer shell behind which spiritual activities and strivings are hidden. According to Wundt, the world is the purposive evolution of the spirit. To this extent, Wundt agreed with Hegel. However, he tried to found his philosophy upon a thorough study of the empirical sciences.

Oswald Külpe (1865-1915), founder of the Würzburg school of experimental psychology. He initiated the experimental investigation of thought processes, and continued Fechner's experimental study of aesthetics

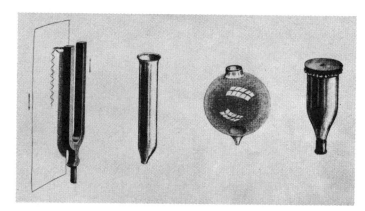

Instruments used by Helmholtz to study the physics of sound: tuning fork and glass resonators for analyzing complex musical tones

Freud and Coworkers in Berlin, 1922. LEFT TO RIGHT:
*Otto Rank, Freud, Karl Abraham, Max Eitingon, Sandor
Ferenczi, Ernest Jones, Hanns Sachs*

Alfred Adler

*Hebrew Inscription in Bible Presented to Freud
by His Father*

FREUD, SIGMUND

FREUD, SIGMUND (1856-1939). Main philosophic
theme: love of an ideal is no more than sublimation of
sexual desire. Freud's system of therapeutic psychoanalysis
made a tremendous impact on the mind of the mid-century
West, especially in the United States and England. The
Soviet countries prohibit its advocacy as fraud.

ADLER, ALFRED

ADLER, ALFRED (1870-1937). Adler is important for
his formulation of the theory of "individual psychology,"
the most widely accepted technique (next to psychoanalysis,
founded by Sigmund Freud) in the treatment of neuroses.
This concept is largely based upon the general
theory of psychology and human character. Because "individual
psychology" is based on medical practice as well
as philosophy, it is easily distinguishable from the various
social psychologies.

Adler, a disciple and collaborator of Freud, is said to
have influenced his teacher in some ways. Like Freud,
Adler attributed primary importance to infantile experiences.
But, whereas Freud considered sexuality or its
repression as the formative force of character and the
cause of certain types of neuroses, Adler stated that the
formative force is the desire of the individual to secure
authority in the social milieu. Neurosis, according to
Adler, is the effect of inferior feelings that result from the
individual's failure to gain superiority or dominance. Inferior
feelings may be caused either by physical or mental
shortcomings. Consequently, the individual tends to com-

Carl Gustav Jung

JUNG, CARL GUSTAV

JUNG, CARL GUSTAV (1875-   ). From 1906 to 1913, Jung was one of the most enthusiastic adherents and disciples of Sigmund Freud. He was the editor of the *Annual for Psychoanalytic Research,* and, at Freud's suggestion, was appointed the first president of the International Psychoanalytical Association. His separation from Freud hurt the latter a great deal, and Freud subsequently criticized Jung's own theories with animosity, which was paid back in kind by Jung.

Jung started as a clinical psychiatrist but, at the same time he showed great sympathy for spiritism, and has retained in his late years a special interest in occult forces and mystical experiences. In addition to his temporary devotion to Freud's psychoanalysis, Jung has also been a student of the philosopher Heinrich Rickert, whose distinction between the methods of natural and social sciences he adopted.

Jung called his own doctrine "analytical psychology" at first and then "complex psychology." To him psychical is the true reality, and all conflicts between mind and nature are of no fundamental importance but are derived from the difference of origin of psychic contents. He conceives the psychic as of both individual and general character. The conscious personality is the focus of psychic processes. Without such a focus, no organized ego, no continuity of experience is possible. But the contents of psychic experience, Jung insists, reach beyond the range of individual consciousness. The individual is in a state of fusion with his environment, with the social group to which he belongs, with his nation and race. This fusion is taking place in the realm of the unconscious which completes and compensates the conscious in man. Any psychical structure of the human individual is shaped by the tension between the conscious and the unconscious, and the extension of the unconscious to the psychic life of the group, nation and race is of fundamental importance for the psychology of the individual. Its attitude toward the objects is determined by the tendency to either introversion or extraversion, one which is predominant and forms the humane type. This classification of men has aroused general interest and is the most frequently mentioned part of Jung's doctrine. However, according to Jung, the aim of mature man must be totality of the psychic, harmony between the cultivation of the self and the devotion to the outer world. He regards progress of culture as conditioned by the enlargement of the realm of consciousness. Both the progress of culture and the development of the individual are placed and kept in motion by what Jung calls energy, but which he tries to differentiate from physical energy.

Despite secession and mutual polemics, Jung has retained many of Freud's conceptions. However, Jung has substituted a general principle of energy for Freud's sexual drive as the moving cause of human life and destiny, and his interpretation of dreams and their symbols is different from the methods used by the founder of psychoanalysis. While Freud, notwithstanding his interest in instinctual drives, is essentially a rationalist, Jung, although proclaiming the increase of consciousness as the cultural goal, is, by nature, a romanticist.

pensate or even over-compensate. He assumes superior attitudes which cause abnormal behavior patterns.

Freud endeavored to discover the sexual components of the healthy or neurotic personality, while Adler deviated from this overemphasis of sexuality. He maintained that no component could be evaluated accurately without regard for the unity of character which manifests itself in the individual's "style of life." The weak individual, unable to overcome his shortcomings or to discipline himself, adopts a "style of life" which enables him to enjoy illusions of superiority. He expects social prestige because of his imagined superiority instead of actual efficiency. Consequently he becomes a stranger to reality, pursuing "fictive goals." The function of the psychologist, according to Adler, is to induce the patient (whose fundamental "style of life" cannot be changed after early childhood) to avoid conflicts with society by recognizing its dangers, to act in accordance with reality and abstain from a reversion to delusions. Because of the emphasis on early childhood, Adler and his disciples were interested in educational reform.

His principal works are *The Neurotic Constitution* (1912) and *Individual Psychology* (1924).

Max Dessoir (1867-1947). Psychologist and aesthete. Student of parapsychological phenomena. Numerous writings on the ego and transcendentalism

STERN, WILLIAM

STERN, WILLIAM (1871-1938). When William Stern, in 1927, wrote his autobiography, he summarized his external life in two lines by naming three cities: Berlin where he was born and had studied philosophy, and Breslau and Hamburg where he had been, and was then, a professor. He had no idea that six years later Hitler would oust him, notwithstanding all his merits, and that he would thus come to teach at Duke University and Harvard.

Stern became famous as a pioneer in applied psychology. His contributions to the psychology of deposition created a sensation among jurists, and his investigations of the psychology of childhood attracted the attention of educators. Of equal importance were Stern's concept of the intelligence quotient and other studies on intelligence testing.

This successful psychologist also became a highly respected and influential philosopher. According to Stern, psychology and philosophy must follow the strategic principle of "marching separately and battling commonly."

Stern was strongly opposed to what he called "scientification of psychology" because its result was "mechaniza-

tion of spiritual life." His philosophy of critical personalism tries to overcome the antagonism between common sense, which believes in separate persons, gods, or vital forces, and impersonal science, which regards the whole world as a system of elementary units and all individuals as physico-chemical aggregates. Stern declared that the person is the primordial and most pervasive unity in the range of the experimental world. Any attempt to dissect it, to typify or to reduce it to notions or principles he rejected as distortion of facts. Stern's concept of person is larger than that of the human individual. It comprises also groups. The person is to be distinguished from the thing. The person is a whole, individuality, quality, while the thing is an aggregate, quantity, comparable with other things. Personal development is no mechanical interchange between the person and his environment. It involves a constant, though not necessarily conscious, readiness to realize values which are suggested by environment. Stern's concept of history denies both biological evolution and the dialectical process, and also Rickert's reference to general values. Stern's personalism begins as ontology and proceeds to "axiosophy."

312

HAEBERLIN, PAUL

HAEBERLIN, PAUL (1878-   ). The evolution of Haeberlin's thinking has proceeded from the religious belief of a Protestant minister to idealism, returned to a prevalently religious attitude, then approached a purely theoretical standpoint, and returned again to the view that religious experience, and not philosophical knowledge, is able to master the problems of life and to comprehend the meaning of existence. Haeberlin assigns a very important task to philosophy but he does not give it the last word. Haeberlin maintains that life and existence are essentially problematical, and concludes that knowledge also is necessarily problematical. The human mind is characterized by him as the constant protest against this inevitable fact which remains a mystery to man but is not a mystery to God. Man is capable of becoming aware of his real situation only by assuming a religious attitude. Philosophy, provided it recognizes its true functions, can help man to obtain knowledge of his real situation.

Haeberlin has made valuable contributions to psychology, characterology, pedagogics and psychotherapeutics. He was especially successful in treating psychopathic children and young people in their teens. Since 1922 he has been a full professor of philosophy, psychology and pedagogics at the University of Basel. His principal works are: *The Object of Psychology* (1921), *Aesthetics* (1929), *The Essence of Philosophy* (1934) and *Possibilities and Limits of Education* (1936).

WERTHEIMER, MAX

WERTHEIMER, MAX (1880-1943). Wertheimer's article *Experimental Studies on the Vision of Movement*, published in *Zeitschrift für Psychologie* (1912), led to the development of *Gestalt* theory which has been formulated at first psychologically, and then enlarged into a philosophical conception of physical, biological and social facts. Wertheimer broke away from the purely summative theory of sensory experience. Instead he held that the phenomena must be considered autonomous unities, coherent wholes, that the existence of each element of such a unity is dependent on the latter's structure, and that the knowledge of the whole cannot be derived from that of its elements. Neither psychologically nor physiologically is the element anterior to the whole.

In his *Productive Thinking,* published posthumously in 1945, Wertheimer defined thinking as "envisaging, realizing structural features, structural requirements, proceeding in accordance with, and determined by, these requirements; thereby changing the situation in the direction of structural improvement." He claimed that *Gestalt* theory had started scientific study of the problems of thinking, clarified them theoretically, and that it tried to form appropriate tools for dealing with the facts and laws involved in them in a scientific manner.

Wolfgang Köhler (1877-　　), associate of Wertheimer at Frankfort, and one of the cofounders of Gestalt *psychology*

Eduard Spranger (1882-　　), with Karl Jaspers, the chief living exponent of Verstehende Psychologie, *originated by Wilhelm Dilthey. The method of the school consists in the postulating of ideal types, representing ultimate and coherent patterns of value, unifying any personality capable of following one of them consistently. The value directions for Spranger are the religious, the aesthetic, the theoretical, the economic, the social and the political. The individual is viewed as striving to fit himself into the objective spirit which embodies these values*

The Era of Prolificity

"Maria im Kapitol in Köln," Drawing in Burckhardt's Sketchbook

BURCKHARDT, JAKOB

BURCKHARDT, JAKOB (1818-1897). Burckhardt taught history and lived quietly, frugally, undisturbed, and independent of the good and evil of modern civilization in his native town of Basle. His *Kultur der Renaissance* (1860) made him famous in all civilized countries, but his dislike for publicity was so great, that even though he continued to study and collect ample material to fill many more volumes, he refrained from publishing any further works during his lifetime. His skill as a teacher, his gift for narrating facts and events and integrating them with all branches of knowledge and cultural activity as part of a continuous evolutionary pattern attracted students from many countries. After his death, his lectures were edited, and those entitled *Reflections on History* have been acknowledged as a major contribution to modern historiography.

Burckhardt, the historian, was an austere judge of morality. He often condemned morally that which he admired aesthetically. He regarded history as the best means for ridding the world of its illusion, for though he saw beyond the superficial veil, nevertheless he loved and admired its fallacious charm. His sympathy was always with defeated minorities; their defeat confirmed his conviction that success had little to do with merit insofar as active life was concerned. However, he did admit that in poetry and art, greatness and success were often identical. His disapproval of results never prevented him from studying their causes.

315

LOTZE, RUDOLPH HERMANN

LOTZE, RUDOLPH HERMANN (1817-1881). Lotze dealt with the principal problems of his philosophy three times and each time somewhat differently. At the age of 24, he published his first *Metaphysics,* and two years later, in 1843, his first *Logic.* He developed his views on metaphysics, logic, ethics and other topics in his *Microcosmos* (1856-1864), and wrote a third *Logic* (1874) and a third *Metaphysics* (1879). Death prevented him from revising his Ethics and other disquisitions. Although his *Microcosmos* was not meant as his last word, his name remains connected with this work which is regarded as one of the most important documents of modern German philosophy, and has influenced many great thinkers in foreign countries, not least of all America. Before the publication of *Microcosmos,* Lotze was regarded as a physiologist rather than a philosopher. He had studied and taught medicine and physiology, and had become known by his theory of "local signs," an attempt to establish relations between sensory affections and areas of the brain, and even more by his rigorous criticism of the concept of "vital force," by demonstrating that physiological processes can and must be explained by strictly mechanistic terms. In his first *Logic,* he protested against any blending of logic with metaphysics. In his first *Metaphysics* he severely criticized German idealism. Lotze's *Microcosmos* is of anthropocentric character, and in this work the effort to reconcile philosophy and religion, philosophy and science, knowledge and the needs of human nature is conspicuous. Maintaining his conviction of the mutual affection of mind and body, Lotze proceeds to a monism which he characterizes as teleological idealism, sometimes as panpsychism. The mechanistic interpretation of nature is considered unavoidable, but Lotze insists that there are ideal interests, values and duties which are not to be rejected as phantoms because they cannot be proved mechanically, and that psychic life cannot be compared with external, natural occurrences. All concepts of the cosmic order are reduced to a consciousness of truth, facts and values. Evidently inspired by Malebranche, Lotze assumes God as the ultimate cause of all events, all. becoming, and the condition of the possible.

In his third stage, Lotze tried to formulate his ideas more precisely. He abandoned panpsychism. Always devoted to modern humanism, Lotze abhorred the idea of revolution, and did not like democracy.

Ludwig Büchner (1824-1899), through his book, Power and Matter, *made materialism a popular attitude in Central Europe. In philosophy he opposed dualism, believing the soul is merely a function of the brain*

316

Kuno Fischer (1824-1907), one of the more eminent his-torians inspired by Hegel's theory of history. He also joined in the revival of Kantianism in opposition to the growth of materialism

Gustav Teichmüller (1832-1888). Influenced by Leibniz and Lotze, Teichmüller regarded the "I" of immediate experience as real, and the world of ideas as a projection of its determination (perspectivism). Reality is interpreted monadologically

DILTHEY, WILHELM

DILTHEY, WILHELM (1833-1911). Wilhelm Dilthey was born two years after Hegel's death. He devoted much of his energy to the task of investigating the structure of the human mind and in writing its history. This had been Hegel's purpose, but Dilthey was strongly opposed to the Hegelian system, as well as to any metaphysical inquiry into the realm of the supernatural.

Hegel regarded the human mind as one of the manifestations of the cosmic spirit, and when he wrote the history of the human mind, he believed that he had recognized and defined the essence of mind. Dilthey, on the other hand, relied upon empiricism: historical facts, biographies, the extant works of great personalities, documents on the currents of cultural life, religious traditions, and social institutions supplied the answer to the question of what man really is. Dilthey, the historian of the human mind, stated that philosophical definitions were the historical documents which informed him about the mental situation of an epoch; poems, laws, and customs of that epoch did the same.

He saw history as a means of comprehending man as a thinking, feeling, willing, creating being who lived in the historical stream of life. His total activities were designed to elaborate "a critique of historical reason," as necessary for the completion of Kant's three critiques. It was to be founded upon an "understanding and analyzing psychology" whose starting point was the analysis of consciousness, and whose development was necessary for understanding the way of civilization and its functional relation to the totality of spontaneous impulses, which he considered to be the stream of life.

Dilthey left great and important fragments of his projected work. His academic career was extremely brilliant, but his real influence was felt only after he died.

MACH, ERNST

MACH, ERNST (1838-1916). Mach made important discoveries and wrote a number of standard works in the fields of mechanics, theory of heat, optics and acoustics. He was also an academic teacher to whom his audience was enthusiastically devoted. While he refused to be called a philosopher, he did accept acknowledgment as a methodologist of science and a psychologist of knowledge. In fact, he formulated positivism anew, differing from Comte in attributing an equal importance to psychic as to physical facts. His aim was to attain a standpoint entirely free from metaphysics, and to eliminate all hypotheses which cannot be controlled by experience, to create an epistemology which preserves all advantages of empiricism without any ontological implication, be it idealistic or materialistic. Trying to avoid all anthropomorphical conceptions in science, he even regarded causality as a remainder of primitive religion, and would only admit functional dependence, as it is used in mathematical terminology. To him, laws of nature were only more and more improved propositions of experience. The ordinary conception of things was criticized by Mach's statement that language signifies them by the same proper names even when they change. Instead, things were characterized by Mach as symbols for a complex of sensations, such as sounds, colors, smells, pressures, temperature, spatial and temporal impressions. Consequently, the ego, as far as it is scientifically cognizable, is reduced to a bundle of changing sensations, and no fundamental difference between the psychic and physical world is admitted. However, Mach insisted that there are no isolated acts of sensing, feeling, willing and thinking, and that psychic life is not only receptive but also active, although his investigation concentrated upon its receptive side. Mach explained his theories in *Analysis of Sensations* (1886) and *Knowledge and Error* (1905).

BRENTANO, FRANZ

BRENTANO, FRANZ (1838-1917). The intellectual milieu of his early background is not manifest in Franz Brentano's writings. He was uninterested in literature and politics, and declined to exploit the influence of his relatives. He was educated by his father, Christian, a devout Catholic and religious author. Franz became a Catholic priest, but after nine years, he abandoned the Catholic Church in 1873. He then became a professor at Wuerzburg and Vienna, and spent the remaining twenty years of his life in Italy and Switzerland. He maintained friendly relations only with his brother, Lujo Brentano, who was noted as a political economist and champion of free trade.

Brentano's chief contributions were in the fields of epistemology, logic, axiology, and psychology. He declared that psychology was the basis of philosophy and the path to metaphysics. He did not believe in metaphysical systems, but believed that reliable metaphysical knowledge was possible. He thought that constant change might lead to increasing perfection. Resolutely opposed to German idealism, he stated that the natural sciences were the true method of philosophic thought. He was disdainful of the "physiological psychology" of Wilhelm Wundt and others who tried to found a psychology based upon experimental methods. Brentano revived those concepts of Scholasticism that deal with the intentional relation of the consciousness to the object. He considered this to be the essential character of psychological experience. He also made great efforts to demonstrate that psychological analysis was not the way to achieve knowledge of an object. He stressed the fundamental differences between judgment and presentation—two completely different means by which the consciousness of an object is perceived. His energetic rejection of the attempts to reduce logic to psychology was of great importance to his disciples: Husserl, Stumpf, Marty, Meinong, Kraus, and Ehrenfels.

Brentano's exemplary character and sincerity of thought enabled him to proceed courageously and independently in his defiance of religious and secular authority. He never yielded to a need for popular approval, or paid much attention to ideas merely because they were the current vogue.

Eduard von Hartmann

HARTMANN, EDUARD VON

HARTMANN, EDUARD VON (1842-1906). An officer in the Prussian army, Eduard von Hartmann became disabled, suffering from a nervous disease that forced him to lie on his back. After quitting military service, he studied philosophy, and soon became famous because of the great success of his *Philosophie des Unbewussten* (Philosophy of the Unconscious, 1869). Later, he published many other books, none of which attracted as much attention as his first work.

By no means was Hartmann a precursor of modern investigation of unconscious or subconscious activities. He is rather to be regarded as one of the last constructors of systems, each of whom was immediately inspired by Schelling. Avowedly Hartmann tried to form a synthesis of Leibniz, Schelling, Hegel, Schopenhauer and the results of modern natural sciences. What he called the Unconscious combines the qualities of Hegel's absolute spirit and Schopenhauer's blind will. It is proclaimed as the "thing in itself," the origin of the cosmic order and the mental life of the human individual. Hartmann called his system "transcendental realism" and claimed to have constructed the reliable bridge to metaphysics and, at the same time, "the only possible bridge to natural science."

AVENARIUS, RICHARD

AVENARIUS, RICHARD (1843-1896). Empirio-criticism was a radical positivist doctrine formulated by Avenarius. He maintained that scientific philosophy must be confined to the descriptive, generalized definitions of experience; that pure experience must be kept free of metaphysics or materialism. This doctrine assumes that there is a constancy in the mutual relationship between the ego and its environment; that only parts of our environment constitute pure experience; that those occasions where experience is said to transcend the environment must be regarded and repudiated as an extraneous element or invention of the mind. Substance and causality are such inventions. Avenarius accepted a parallelism between brain changes and states of consciousness, but emphasized that neither thoughts nor sensations are to be explained as functions of the brain. He stated that since men are equal, the experience of each ego has equal validity, provided that individual variations are recognized; that the experience of each ego can be used to construct a natural concept of the world. His opposition to the materialist assertions of Karl Vogt resulted in a violent attack upon empirio-criticism by Lenin. Avenarius, whose principal works are *Critique of Pure Experience* (1888-90) and *The Human Concept of the World* (1891) influenced Ernst Mach and, to some extent, William James.

HÖFFDING, HARALD

HÖFFDING, HARALD (1843-1931). After a long, difficult struggle, Höffding resolved to renounce theology and to devote his life to philosophy. It was his great esteem for Kierkegaard, the adversary of the established church and inquirer into the mystery of personal faith, that fortified Höffding in his decision. He became Denmark's most important modern philosopher, and his works have also been read and highly appreciated in France, England and Germany.

Höffding was more interested in philosophical problems than in systems. Asked which philosopher was his personal ideal, Höffding answered Spinoza. But he rejected Spinoza's system. He only loved and revered his personality. Höffding called himself a critical positivist. He held that experience is of decisive importance to all a philosopher might think, but declared that experience is a problem that defies the efforts of all philosophers. To Höffding, philosophy alone frees human mind from habits, prejudices and traditions. It enlarges the spiritual horizon in such a manner as no special science can.

EUCKEN, RUDOLF (1846-1926). The core of Eucken's philosophy was that the concept of life manifests its mere existence through sensual experience, activity, and in a world of relationships comprehensible to the spirit. He explained the history of the world as a blending of reason and blind necessity. Throughout the course of history, spiritual life was evolved as a new level of reality. It was not the human individual, nor the sum of individuals, who created the new order of things and relationships, but the motion of the universe. Eucken thought that his concept corresponded more to the nature of man than that of Fichte, Schelling, or Hegel who overestimated the range of the human mind. Eucken accused positivism, materialism, and naturalism of ignoring the faculties of the mind.

His colleagues, professors of philosophy at the German universities, were surprised when he was awarded the Nobel Prize (1908); they felt that the selection of candidates for the prize should be made more carefully. Eucken, however, maintained that German philosophers were indifferent to his writings; that he was popular in England, America, and China before he even began to attract attention in Germany. During World War I, Eucken professed aggressive German nationalism, and this new attitude increased the number of his German adherents.

WINDELBAND, WILHELM

WINDELBAND, WILHELM (1848-1915). As a historian of philosophy and as the founder of the "South-West-German school of philosophy," Windelband exercised considerable influence. In both activities, he emphasized that philosophy must reflect on civilization and its historical evolution. Windelband belongs to those German philosophers who proceed from Kant's criticism, but he protested against other neo-Kantians who mainly confined their thinking to a renewal of Kant's epistemology, and he stressed the importance of his inquiries into ethics, aesthetics, and philosophy of law and religion. Windelband's program, however, maintained that "to understand Kant rightly means to go beyond him." While Kant considered only mathematics and natural sciences, founded upon mathematics, as real sciences, Windelband held that history in the broadest sense of the word, comprising views on all kinds of human activities, must be acknowledged as a true science. He distinguished between the natural sciences, which are concerned with the establishment of laws, and the historical sciences, which try to grasp, to describe and explain individual facts. The methods of the natural sciences are characterized as being of a generalizing, nomothetic character, those of the historical sciences as "idiographic." From this distinction, Windel-

JODL, FRIEDRICH

JODL, FRIEDRICH (1848-1914) followed the Positivists, John Stuart Mill, Feuerbach and Comte. He upheld the humanistic formula and projected a new religion of national culture.

band proceeded to a sharp opposition to epistemological naturalism, and broached the question, of whether the nomothetic or the idiographic sciences are of more essential importance to philosophy. He decided in favor of the historical sciences, because, according to him, philosophy must interpret spiritual life and explain values, and the sense of values is rooted in the sense of the individual.

In his efforts to "go beyond Kant," Windelband relied on Hegel, Herbart and Lotze. Closely associated with Windelband was Heinrich Rickert. Among Windelband's disciples were not only noted philosophers but sociologists like Max Weber and theologians like Ernst Troeltsch.

FREGE, FRIEDRICH LUDWIG GOTTLOB

FREGE, FRIEDRICH LUDWIG GOTTLOB (1848-1925), a mathematician and logician largely unknown or misunderstood by his contemporaries. After Boole, he is the second founder of symbolic logic, the essential steps in the passage from the algebra of logic to the logistic method. The culmination of his work is his *Grundlagen der Arithmetik,* in which he derives arithmetic from logic.

REHMCKE, JOHANNES

REHMCKE, JOHANNES (1848-1930), teacher of religion and philosophy, who struggled to surmount the antithesis of materialism-idealism. God was for him the all-comprehensive psychic and spiritual individuality, the subject of the whole of the given. Opposed to pantheism, he felt that God was the real as such, and as God and man influence each other, divine and human communion is real. A philosophy with a concept of God must place theology upon sure ground.

STUMPF, KARL

STUMPF, KARL (1848-1936), a lifelong Platonist, who made notable contributions to the psychology of tone and music, and in musicology.

VOLKELT, JOHANNES

VOLKELT, JOHANNES (1848-1930), strongly influenced by German idealism, insisted that reality is "trans-subjective"—that is, consists neither of mere objects nor of mere data, but is rather a synthesis of both elements of existence. His major work lay in this analysis of knowledge.

MEINONG, ALEXIUS VON

MEINONG, ALEXIUS VON (1853-1920). When Meinong expressed opinions about political facts, he was convinced of being just and right. As a philosopher, however, he remained conscious that to err means to be a human being. He thought that scientists could not obtain definite results, save some fortunate exceptions that prove the rule, and that one might be satisfied with exploring more favorable starting points to broach old questions.

It is true that Meinong did not claim to have found definite truth. But he claimed to have established a new science, namely—the *Theory of Objects,* which, as he said, was bound to fill a gap which had been left by epistemology, metaphysics and psychology. His theory of objects differs from psychology because it does not envisage the psychic acts but the objects. It differs from metaphysics since it also comprises the non-real. It differs from ontology by stressing the experience of resistance to the experiencing subject on the part of the object. It was developed by its founder to a new doctrine of perception and of value and valuing. Ethics is regarded as a part of the theory of values, and ethical values comprise moral as well as nonmoral values.

Meinong, who first studied history and philology, came to philosophy, as he said, by chance and as an autodidact. He was encouraged by Franz Brentano, who later rejected many of Meinong's statements. Meinong was rather surprised when he was appointed a professor by the Austrian government. He had numerous disciples, some of whom modified Meinong's theory and brought it close to phenomenology.

VAIHINGER, HANS

VAIHINGER, HANS (1852-1933), an idealistic positivist, for whom religious ideas were beautiful myths and useful fictions, even though knowledge as such has no real truth value. His "as if" viewpoint triumphed particularly in religious philosophy, and offered a solution to those who felt pressed by the inert formulas of rigid orthodoxy.

(*Drawing by Dolbin*)

NATORP, PAUL

NATORP, PAUL (1854-1924). Until his late years, Natorp was a faithful follower of Hermann Cohen. It was due to the excitement of the war years, 1914-1918, that he deviated slightly from his master's tenets and became more inclined to exalt the German national character and civilization in his book *Deutscher Weltberuf* (*Germany's Vocation in the World,* 1918). Natorp's interpretation of Plato's doctrine of ideas was much discussed. So was his *General Psychology* (1912). More successful was his *Socialpaedagogik* (1899) which was re-edited several times. According to Natorp, education must influence all social and economic activities as well as schools and universities in order to realize national solidarity and social peace.

WAHLE, RICHARD

WAHLE, RICHARD (1857-1935). Proceeding from extreme positivism, Wahle, once a professor of philosophy at the Universities of Czernovitz and Vienna, pronounced in his *Tragicomedy of Wisdom* (2nd edition, 1925) his death sentence on philosophy. He acknowledged only "definite, agnostic, absolute critique of knowledge" and psychology as surviving, or rather he maintained that critiques of knowledge, logic and psychology have nothing to do with philosophy. As a consequence of his fundamental attitude, Wahle did not recognize the ego as a nucleus of forces but only as a changing whirl or as some stitches in the texture of the universe. But in his *Formation of Character* (2nd edition, 1928) he made important contributions to modern characterology. Wahle's devastating criticism of philosophers has spared only very few such as Spinoza, Hume and Herbart, whose works he praised as useful.

rooted by the events of war and revolution, were forced to renounce philosophy altogether, or turned to radical Marxism or nationalism, both of which were contrary to Simmel's mind which, despite all changes, maintained a relativist attitude.

Simmel's talents for psychological analysis are unsurpassed, and he always succeeded in elucidating psychological insight by philosophical aspects, no matter whether he dealt with Platonic ideas or fashions, Schopenhauer's pessimism or the flirt, the effects of money lending or the question of theistic faith. He interpreted Kant's *a priori,* which he himself adopted, psychologically and as supporting relativism. Later he developed, independently of American thinkers, a kind of pragmatism. Likewise, he was independent of Bergson when he tried to overcome his relativism by a belief in the self-transcendence of life. From a purely descriptive ethics he proceeded to one of valid values. He always remained an unorthodox Kantian, stressing the antagonism between immediate experience and the elaboration of this experience by the creative human spirit, insisting that the natural sciences as well as history offer only an image of reality that is transformed by the theoretical or historical *a priori.* According to Simmel, sociology does not belong to philosophy. Sociology and philosophy offer two different aspects of the situation of man in the world. They are two autonomous interpretations of mental life. Simmel started with studies *On Social Differentiation* (1890), then published his *Philosophy of Money* (1900) and *Sociology* (1908). A thorough student of Marx, he admitted the influence of economic facts on intellectual attitudes but insisted that the effects of intellectual patterns on economics act likewise. He maintained that the decisive factor of human attitudes is antecedent to changes of social or economic institutions. Sociology is conceived by Simmel as the doctrine of the forms of the relations between individuals, independent of spiritual contents which are subject to historical change. It is the "geometry of social life."

Religion and the arts represent to Simmel autonomous worlds which are independent of science but accessible to the philosopher, provided he does not disregard their autonomous foundations. In his monographs on *Goethe* (1913) and *Rembrandt* (1916), Simmel tried to show that the poet and artist while forming his own image of life, although determined by the historical situation of his lifetime, transcends historical conditions and testifies that life always hints beyond itself. The principal problem of culture is formulated by Simmel as the difficulty to seize life without violating it.

SIMMEL, GEORG

SIMMEL, GEORG (1858-1918). From about 1900 to the outbreak of the First World War, Simmel was considered one of the greatest contemporary philosophers. Not favored by the Prussian government, Simmel was a lecturer, then an associate professor at the University of Berlin, and only a few years before his death he was appointed full professor at the University of Strasbourg. As long as he lectured in Berlin, his audience was composed mostly of students from Russia and Central and Southern Europe where his fame was even greater than in Germany. Nevertheless, he did not form a school. Many of his former pupils died on the battlefield, others, up-

HUSSERL, EDMUND

HUSSERL, EDMUND (1859-1938). More than fifty years of strenuous work had to pass between the beginning and the accomplishment of Husserl's philosophy. At its completion he expressed his confidence in having established philosophy as a "rigorous science," as an "absolute discipline," and he classified all precedent philosophies as either superficial or poor, vague or sterile. In his early days, however, Husserl was tormented by doubts that his own talents were adequate to his aspirations, and that philosophy in itself could satisfy them. It was his teacher, Franz Brentano, who not only encouraged Husserl to devote his life to philosophy but gave him certainty that philosophy could clear up any doubt. Husserl did not find the way to Brentano spontaneously. He was brought into contact with him by his friend Thomas G. Masaryk, who was to become the founder and first president of the Czechoslovakian republic.

Brentano taught Husserl the importance of three points which remained characteristic of Husserl's own thinking, notwithstanding the modifications or even radical changes his philosophy underwent in the course of time. At first, he taught him to distinguish between logical laws and the laws of psychic facts which involved opposition to "psychologism," to any concept of logical notions as psychic formations apt to be explained by their genesis. Secondly, Husserl took from Brentano the Scholastic distinction between essence and existence, and, furthermore, the term of "intentionality" of thought, which means that thought is always directed toward things different from itself.

From this basis, Husserl proceeded to the foundations of phenomenology, which, before him, had been used as a theory of appearances, and, through him, became a full-fledged philosophy. It deals with insight into essences without regard to the empirical conditions of their perceptibility, even without regard to existence. Intuitive evidence is the criterion of truth. It is not to be confounded with certainty or proof of reality. Husserl would not deal with metaphysical considerations of any kind but he was convinced that his phenomenology could provide answers to any "legitimate" metaphysical question, and he maintained that recognition and pursuit of phenomenological analysis, as developed by him, would produce true knowledge quite independently of the adherence of the analyzer to any philosopher in other regard. Husserl claimed to have established a doctrine of ideal conditions of the possibility of science, and to have served truth in a safer way than any philosophical system.

Max Planck

David Hilbert (1862-1943), one of the great mathematicians of his generation. His work on the foundations of Euclidean geometry is found in his Grundlagen der Geometrie

PLANCK, MAX

PLANCK, MAX (1858-1947). The first revolutionary novelty since Newton was introduced into the science of physics by Planck, the founder of the quantum theory. Before Planck, physical thinking rested on the assumption that all causal interactions are continuous. Planck, after studying entropy and radiation, showed that in a light or heat wave of frequency, the energy of the wave does not vary continuously, and established an "elementary quantum of action" of a definite numerical value as the unit of these variations. Quantum theory has made an inroad upon the concept of mass but it is most important in the regular occurrences of all atomic processes.

Planck's elementary quantum of action could not be welded in the framework of classical physics. All theoretical difficulties were removed by Einstein's special theory of relativity which was published in 1905, five years after Planck had established his quantum theory. Through the cooperation of Planck and Einstein a new picture of the world emerged. Its elements are no longer chemical atoms but electrons and protons whose mutual interactions are governed by the velocity of light and the elementary quantum of action.

Planck regarded the quanta as the building blocks of the universe and as proof of the existence in nature of something real and independent of every human measurement. He rejected positivism and believed in the possibility of reconciling natural science and religion.

Goetheanum, Free University for Culture at Dornach, Switzerland

Rudolf Steiner

STEINER, RUDOLF

STEINER, RUDOLF (1861-1925). By 1900, Rudolf Steiner, then at the age of forty, surprised his friends by a complete change of personality. He had been a faithful disciple of Ernst Haeckel and a devoted adherent of evolutionist materialism, when he suddenly became a mystic. He had been a Bohemian, and suddenly became a saint. He had been nonchalant, and suddenly proved to be a fanatic. Only his admiration of Goethe did not change; but now Steiner interpreted his works in a new way, claiming that his understanding of Goethe was the only correct and congenial one, and that it was, at the same time, a justification of his new creed. Dissatisfied with natural sciences, Steiner became devoted to theosophy which he regarded as the legitimate and consequent continuance of biology and psychology. For a time he adopted the doctrine of Annie Besant, and was its enthusiastic

progagator in Germany, winning influential adherents among the industrialists, army officers, even clergymen and poets. But when he tried to graft European ideas upon the "ancient wisdom," he and his followers were excluded from the Theosophical Society. Thereupon Steiner founded the "Anthroposophical Society" whose center was in Dornach, Switzerland. Steiner, who regarded himself an occult scientist rather than a mystic, taught that moral purification, emancipation from egoistic drives, and training in meditation developed spiritual qualities which enabled him and his followers to know realms of human and cosmic existence which otherwise remain hidden to the profane mind. Steiner was also interested in rhythmics, dancing, social questions and medicine. In 1917 he advanced a program for general peace. He exposed his doctrine in *Vom Menschenraetsel* (On the Riddle of Man, 1916) and *Von Seelenraetseln* (On the Riddles of the Soul, 1917).

RICKERT, HEINRICH

RICKERT, HEINRICH (1863-1936). Closely associated with Wilhelm Windelband and his successor as professor of philosophy at the University of Heidelberg, Rickert was also a leader of the "South-West-German school of philosophy" and fought, as Windelband did, against a concept of science that comprises natural sciences only. His early works were concerned with the demonstration of the limits of the formation of concepts which natural sciences cannot extend, or with the thesis that natural sciences envisage only part of nature, leaving it to other sciences, namely historical sciences, to deal with the neglected aspects of reality.

In his later years, Rickert, without abandoning the views he shared with Windelband, concentrated more and more upon the problem of values. While declaring that the values of civilization are the real object of philosophy, Rickert refuted the doctrines according to which life in itself is the supreme value. Contrary to philosophers like Nietzsche and Bergson, Rickert emphasized that values demand a distance from life, and that what Bergson, Dilthey or Simmel called "vital values" were not true values. For Rickert, the connection between value and life was secured by the realm of meaning. While reality is to be explained and values are to be understood, meanings are to be interpreted. According to Rickert, the meaning of life can be interpreted only by understanding the value of civilization, even if civilization might be recognized as of no value.

WEBER, MAX (1864-1920). Very few scholars have been so severely tormented by the conflict between their scientific convictions and their vital instincts as was Max Weber, and hardly any other one has, in his writings and teachings, so sternly disciplined himself as did he. His penetrating analysis of social formations, of the economic factor in history, of the relations between religion and economics and the general trends of human civilization, proceeds from and results in the statement that the victory of rational impersonality over irrational impulses is inevitable and historically justified. But Weber himself, a man of impulsive vehemence, afflicted by psychic tensions and disturbances, bitterly resented any loss of irrational privacy which was imposed on him by the development of depersonalizing tendencies, although his insight forced him to accept it. His constant endeavor was not to betray personal feelings in his teachings and to keep his statements and characteristics of the objects of his science free from intrinsic value judgments. According to him, science has to give only technical knowledge which may be useful for the domination of things and human beings. Social science is defined by him as a method of interpreting social action and of explaining its course and its effects by the quest for its intention and the means of its accomplishment, without any regard to its desirability.

Only on the occasion of literary feuds and political debates did Weber allow eruptions of his feelings. He was a formidable controversialist, capable of knocking down his

adversaries with ice-cold irony or with truculent impetuosity. He was an ardent German nationalist but, for the greater part of his life, believed that democracy was more efficient than any authoritarian regime, and therefore he advocated Germany's democratization. Still opposed to the Treaty of Versailles, Weber, at the end of his life, came closer to nationalist extremists whom he had energetically combated during the war.

SCHELER, MAX

SCHELER, MAX (1874-1928) was originally a disciple of Rudolf Eucken, then joined the Husserl circle of phenomenologists, to become one of its leading exponents. He was the psychologist, ethicist, and religious and social philosopher of the phenomenological movement. His ultimate position might be called a synthesis of phenomenology and Catholic philosophy, sociological dynamism and ideorealistic humanism. His unique contribution lies in his interpretation of the value qualities of experience, especially love, as the key to the revelation of being; and his working out of a philosophical anthropology which shows man's position in and toward the whole of being.

DRIESCH, HANS

DRIESCH, HANS (1867-1941). A discovery made in 1895 by Hans Driesch attracted international attention and firmly placed him among the important figures in the history of biology. Driesch, by experiment, demonstrated that it was possible to remove large pieces from eggs; shuffle the blastomeres at will; take several blastomeres away; interfere in many ways, and yet not affect the resulting embryo. The fact that despite such operations, a normal, though small-sized embryo emerged was taken as proof that any single monad in the original egg cell was capable of forming any part of the completed embryo. This discovery made Driesch internationally famous as a zoologist. Until then he had been a disciple and adherent of Ernest Haeckel, but the success of the experiments led him to abandon the mechanistic point of view and to profess a renovated vitalism. At this time, he turned from biology to philosophy.

His system was comprised of three parts: the first dealt with causality and consciousness; the second with logic, which he called "a doctrine of order"; the third was a doctrine of reality. Driesch was converted to vitalism because he believed that physical laws were insufficient to explain his discovery, which he declared to be beyond the powers of any machine ever constructed by man. Thus far, he encountered no objections. When he tried to prove the autonomy of life by introducing a nonphysical cause: entelechy (using Aristotle), he met with violent opposition. This opposition held for all other arguments that he advanced. Until his death, Driesch energetically continued to defend his views. Though he was an unscholarly thinker, his style was animated and colorful.

KLAGES, LUDWIG

KLAGES, LUDWIG (1872-   ). Between the two world wars, Klages was one of the most influential harbingers of German anti-intellectualism, and his latest utterances seem to indicate that, even after Germany's catastrophe, he is not prepared to recant. He has remained a rabid sympathizer with Nazism, although he preferred to live in democratic Switzerland and to admire the house Hitler built without moving in. But even after the end of World War II, Klages continued to express hostility toward democracy, Western civilization, reason and logic, while enjoying the indulgence of a democratic government.

In his youth, Klages associated with the German poet Stefan George who, inspired by Baudelaire and Mallarmé, adhered to the theory of art for art's sake but declared that the cult of artistic form realized the highest ideals of human beings. Devoted to Roman Catholic traditionalism George

and his circle detested the principal tendencies of 19th century civilization, especially positivism, naturalism, materialism and rationalism. From this position, Klages, after a period of graphological and characterological studies, proceeded to extreme anti-intellectualism, denouncing thinking consciousness as a destroying force. In his principal work *Spirit, the Adversary of Soul,* Klages holds that body and soul form the natural unity of human existence in which spirit has invaded from outside in order to split this unity and in this way to kill the foundation of life. While the soul, directed by instincts, feelings and traditions, forms a sensually colorful world, spirit analyzes this world into abstract atoms, in order to subject nature to human will. This is condemned by Klages as sacrilege. While combating natural science as the main representative of the destructive spirit, Klages denies the value and right of any conscious and voluntary knowledge. Return to unconscious life is regarded by him as the way to salvation.

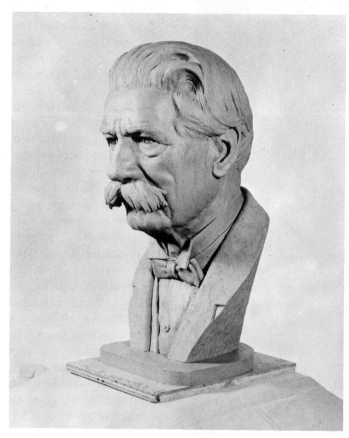

(Bust by Upton Ewing)

SCHWEITZER, ALBERT

SCHWEITZER, ALBERT (1875-   ). The greatest and most famous Universities of the world have offered to Albert Schweitzer a professorship endowed with all possible advantages. As the historian of *The Quest of the Historical Jesus* (Geschichte der Leben Jesu Forschung, 1906; English edition, 1910), of *Paul and His Interpreters* (1912), and *The Mysticism of Paul the Apostle* (1931); as the authoritative biographer of *Johann Sebastian Bach* (1904); as the author of *Civilization and Ethics* (1929) and *The Philosophy of Civilization* (1932), Schweitzer could have made his own choice whether to become a professor of theology or of philosophy, of musicology or of history, in America, England, France or Germany. But he declined the most promising offers. Sacrificing a brilliant academic career in order to study medicine, he became a missionary-physician in Lambarene, French West Africa. Since 1913, Schweitzer has lived in that plague-stricken area, devoting himself to the medical treatment and spiritual education of the Negroes. He travelled to Europe and, in 1949, to America to deliver lectures, to do research for his books, and to gather funds for the maintenance of his activities in Africa.

In the wilderness, Schweitzer remained a man of widest interests and original views on life, science, philosophy and religion. He interprets the teachings of Jesus as determined by the expectation of the imminent end of the world. Although far from Europe, he warned against Hitler's savageness, but was not heeded. The fundamental idea of Schweitzer's ethics and philosophy is "reverence for life," which involves sympathy with and respect for all creatures, as well as human solidarity and devotion to spiritual progress. While most other philosophers of life are somewhat inclined to exalt egoism, will to power or sensualism, to Schweitzer the cult of life means altruism, love of mankind without regard to origin, creed or color. Further, altruism does not mean resignation but rather enhanced activity on behalf of humanity.

HARTMANN, NICOLAI

HARTMANN, NICOLAI (1882-1950). Born and educated in Tsarist Russia, Hartmann, shortly after 1900, emigrated to Germany where he became naturalized. During World War I, he fought in the German army. In his adopted country, Hartmann was at first a follower of Hermann Cohen, but later became an adversary of Neo-Kantianism. Since this change, Hartmann has developed his philosophical views with progressive consistency.

Hartmann emphasizes the necessity that the philosopher must take into account the fact that no one begins with his own thinking, but rather meets a historically conditioned situation in which ideas and problems, already developed by previous thinkers, or expressed in various spiritual creations of the time, direct the way a beginner selects the questions which interest him, and formulate his problems and principles. From this standpoint, Hartmann proceeds to the establishment of the science of ontology, which, to him, is at least equally as important as epistemology. According to Hartmann, the realm of reason covers only a sector of reality. It is impossible to solve the metaphysical problem because irrational remainders always defy reason. But, if metaphysics is impossible in the form of any system, it remains the principal business of the philosopher to mark the boundary between the rational and the irrational and to recognize the metaphysical elements in all branches of philosophy. His inquiry results in the statement that epistemology, ethics, and aesthetics can offer partial solutions only, and that the notions of logic are subject to historical change, although their ideal structure remains unalterable. The history of the notions forms the center of the history of philosophy and science. As to ethics and axiology, Hartmann tries to harmonize the absolute character of the moral duty with the historical variety of evaluations.

CASSIRER, ERNST

CASSIRER, ERNST (1874-1945). Cassirer's philosophy proceeds from the basic conviction that historical investigation and systematic order do not contradict each other, but rather are conditional and mutually support one another. Their result is the demonstration of the "immanent logic of history," based upon the critical examination of abundant empirical materials. Cassirer's works contributed to historical development of epistemology. In *Philosophie der Symbolischen Formen* (1924), he dealt with the functions of linguistic and mythical thinking, coordinating the world of pure knowledge with religious, mythical, and artistic ideas. Cassirer was firmly convinced that the different approaches to reality cooperate in the formation of a totality of meaning.

During the Kaiser's reign in Germany, he was denied appointment as a professor and tolerated only as a lecturer. Under the Hitler regime, he was compelled to emigrate—first, to Sweden, where he was a professor at the University of Goetenborg, then to the United States.

NEURATH, OTTO

NEURATH, OTTO (1882-1945), one of the founders of the Viennese Circle School of Logical Empiricism led by Moritz Schlick.

SCHLICK, MORITZ

SCHLICK, MORITZ (1882-1936). When, in 1936 a lunatic murdered Professor Schlick, many of the numerous admirers of the assassinated scholar considered it a particularly tragic irony that this nonsensical misdeed put an end to a life that was devoted to the inquiry into the meaning of life.

Schlick's aim was not the construction of a system of ideas or thoughts but the investigation of the way of philosophizing that satisfies the demands of the most scrupulous scientific conscience. This task involved skill in seeing through wrongly set problems and in surveying the consequences of wrong approaches to them, and Schlick himself was never afraid of abandoning previously elaborated views when, in the course of his development, he recognized their falsehood.

The principal results of Schlick's thinking are: a distinct demarcation between experience which is immediate and knowledge which is no vision but rather calculation and organization by means of concepts and symbols, and, furthermore, a new foundation of empiricism, which leans upon Berkeley and Hume but profits from modern logic. Reality is defined as happening in time. Every Real has a definite place in time. The task of science is to obtain knowledge of reality, and the true achievements of science can neither be destroyed nor altered by philosophy. But the aim of philosophy is to interpret these achievements correctly and to expound their deepest meaning.

Schlick was fundamentally a man who preferred aesthetic contemplation to exact science. But as a thinker he was convinced of the unique philosophical significance of natural science, and he branded it as a grave mistake to believe that the arts and cultural sciences are in any way equivalent to natural science.

WITTGENSTEIN, LUDWIG

WITTGENSTEIN, LUDWIG (1889-1951). For a time, Wittgenstein was preoccupied with architecture and only intermittently interested in philosophy. But his *Tractatus Logico-Philosophicus* (1922) became of great consequence to the development of logical positivism or scientific empiricism, while its author, then about thirty years old, inspired older thinkers like Moritz Schlick, Bertrand Russell and Alfred Whitehead.

In this treatise, Wittgenstein offers a general way of removing philosophical difficulties by investigating the logical structure of language. Incapability of seeing through the logic of language, or at least neglect of its importance, is the cause of apparently or really insoluble philosophical problems. Wittgenstein insists that whatever can be said, can be said clearly. Philosophy is not a doctrine but, rather, an activity. Its result is not new propositions but classification of propositions. Philosophy will mean the inexpressible by presenting the expressible as clearly as possible.

Some years after the publication of his treatise, Wittgenstein concentrated upon his philosophical studies, and was called to Cambridge, England, where later he was appointed successor to G. E. Moore.

REICHENBACH, HANS

REICHENBACH, HANS (1891-1953). Reichenbach belongs to a generation of scientists who began to study after most of their teachers had already abandoned the concepts of classical physics; thus they were able to start with ideas and modes of thought found by their predecessors after much hardship, trial and error. Reichenbach, however, has actively participated in the further advance of science and philosophy. His contributions have been discussed by the greatest contemporary scientists and philosophers with respect if not with general consent, and are recognized either as real contributions or at least as working hypotheses or useful suggestions.

At first, Reichenbach was preoccupied with the clarification of the concepts of space and time, their relations, and the way of assimilating one to another. As a theorist of knowledge, Reichenbach comes in his own way closer to the methods of the Vienna Circle, but he even more vigorously insists that all our knowledge is only probable. The doctrine of probability, advanced by R. von Mises and Reichenbach, is based on the concept of "frequency," a statistical concept. Every definition of induction is involved in this doctrine. Induction is described as a process of predicting future events with the aid of propositions of probability which serve as instruments of indication. Reichenbach objects to classical logic that it classifies propositions according to their truth or falsity instead of lower or higher degrees of probability. He holds that true logic is probability logic, and has presented his views in *Wahrscheinlichkeitslehre* (Doctrine of Probability, 1935) and *Experience and Prediction* (1938).

In his *Elements of Symbolic Logic* (1947), Reichenbach acknowledges classical logic as the "mother of all logics" and admits that it can be carried through in the sense of approximation, even if refined analysis demands probability logic.

JASPERS, KARL

JASPERS, KARL (1883-   ). Since Germany's unconditional surrender, Jaspers has been the most respected, if not the most influential, philosopher in that country. His prestige had already been great during the time of the Weimar Republic. He disliked Nazism and did not abandon his Jewish wife, but neither had he felt a predilection for the pre-Hitlerian republic and he cannot be considered a convert to parliamentarian democracy. Jaspers began his career as a psychiatrist. His *General Psychopathology* (1913), in which he offered a new classification of mental illnesses, has been of great consequence for the diagnosis of psychoses and neuroses. It was from the viewpoint of a psychiatrist that Jaspers first studied the philosophy of Friedrich Nietzsche and then the works of Kierkegaard, whose habits interested the student of abnormalities. As his *Psychology of Weltanschauungen* (1919) shows, Jaspers became more and more interested in inquiring into the relations between a philosopher's personality and his doctrine. The results of these studies remained valid to him when he exposed his own philosophy in *Principles of Philosophy* (1932), *Existenzphilosophie* (1938) and *The Perennial Scope of Philosophy* (1949). Despite all changes, Jaspers maintained the principle that philosophy is more than cogent intellectual knowledge and fundamentally different from, yet not opposite to, science. The distinguishing feature of the philosophical mind, in contradistinction to the scientific mind, is characterized as personal faith. Though always allied with knowledge, philosophical faith transcends object cognition. Philosophical faith is neither grounded in any concept of anything objective or finite in the world nor subordinated to it. The truth of philosophical faith is not universal but both eternal and historical, a dynamism acting in time and longing for transcending time. The true value of man is seen by Jaspers not in the species or type but in the historical individual, and the situation of this individual—the conditions of his existence—is one of the principal problems of Jaspers' disquisitions.

Jaspers is one of the earliest contemporary existentialists. He belongs neither to the Christian nor to the atheistic group, and differs from most of them because he adopts Kant's idea of the phenomenality with its division into subject and object, and because he regards reason an indispensable element of philosophical faith, bluntly declining irrationalism.

The religious trend and the theistic conviction have become most conspicuous in Jaspers' latest works. He praises the values of the Old and New Testament but thinks that Judaism and Christianity are wrong in claiming absolute truth. According to Jaspers, the aim of philosophy is at all times to achieve the independence of man as an individual. To him independence is attachment to transcendence, and awareness of true being is identical with certainty of God. In his earlier works Jaspers stated that philosophy and religion will be in constant struggle with each other. Now he says that in all philosophical efforts lies a tendency to aid religious institutions whose practical values are affirmed by philosophy although philosophers cannot participate directly in them.

HEIDEGGER, MARTIN

HEIDEGGER, MARTIN (1889-   ). Heidegger is a modern German philosopher who has a considerable French following despite the fact that he had leanings toward the socio-political views of the Third Reich. As a keen analyst of being, Being, existence being present and thus-being (even the French speak of *le Sosein* and *le Dasein*) he has no equal and the fine distinctions which he draws have earned him derision and the charge of mental acrobatics among those incapable of following him. Yet he is no more abstruse than his teacher Husserl, and in his philosophy he is continually reaching down into the very core of personality in which he discovers grave guilt, anxiety and fear which make our existence one for death. Man is lost in utter loneliness, he is totally isolated. Only against the background of historical fate does his present existence attain value.

Heidegger himself is conscious of the difficult style in which his main work *Sein und Zeit* and all the others are written, and he is now clarifying his position, controversial on that account, by occupying himself with the problem of language and communication. He accepted the rectorship at the University offered by Hitler's regime in 1933, and for years idolized Hitler as the great protagonist of a new European culture.

Hitler's elite guard with flamethrowers driving Jewish women and children out of their ghetto hiding places in Warsaw

Russia's Great Century

KIREYEVSKI, IVAN

KIREYEVSKI, IVAN (1806-1856), philosopher, critic and journalist, one of the leading Slavophiles of nineteenth century Russia. Believing the West to be decadent and placing too great a reliance on reason, he emphasized faith in the Orthodox Church and envisioned Russia as the coming nation of dominance, culturally and spiritually.

BELINSKI, VISSARION

BELINSKI, VISSARION (1811-1848), literary critic, political theorist and philosopher, whose lack of reverence for traditional judgments marks the end of the domination of Russian literature by the aristocracy, and the rise of a new class, the so-called intelligentsia. Largely self-educated, he was influenced by German idealism, particularly Fichte, Hegel and Feuerbach. His famous letter to Gogol, upbraiding him for what he imagined was the novelist's defection to the camp of reaction, became famous among the radical thinkers of his day, its publication outlawed in Russia. He died from tuberculosis before the state police could contrive the martyrdom which might otherwise have been his lot.

BAKUNIN, MICHAEL

BAKUNIN, MICHAEL (1814-1876). For nearly thirty years, he was an active participant in all European revolutions. Neither failure nor defeat could discourage his anarchistic spirit. To him, revolution meant the destruction of a corrupt and doomed society, and the desire for destruction served as a creative outlet for him. He detested the quiet life and often reiterated: "We need a tempestuous lawlessness to secure a free world."

A lawless world seemed both possible and good to Bakunin. It would produce "the free initiative of free individuals within free groups." It would destroy the uniformity of the social order (which to him meant death) and create the variety which he considered identical with the life spirit. He was a grim adversary of all contemporary governments and of the socialism advocated by Karl Marx.

Bakunin, the prophet of destruction, who exalted radicals as the most honorable enemies of decadent institutions, was a nobleman and former officer of the Tsar's imperial guard.

HERZEN, ALEXANDER

HERZEN, ALEXANDER (1812-1870), leading Russian revolutionary thinker and philosopher of the mid-nineteenth century. Arrested for belonging to a socialist circle, he was exiled and spent most of his remaining life in Paris and London. Embittered by his personal misfortunes, he developed a philosophy of history in which the improvisations of chance played the major role. Yet, like Belinski, he believed that a possibility for human progress lay in the creative freedom of the individual. His influence in Russia was great. The Populists were largely his followers, and after them the Socialist Revolutionary party of the early twentieth century. He came to regard Russia as primarily an agrarian country, in which socialism would develop out of existing peasant institutions. He is perhaps the most honored of all Russian nineteenth-century political thinkers.

LEONTIEV, KONSTANTIN

CHERNYSHEVSKY, NICOLAI GAVRILOVICH

CHERNYSHEVSKY, NICOLAI GAVRILOVICH (1828-1889). After the assassination of Czar Alexander II of Russia, the secret police, in order to avoid a similar recurrence on the occasion of the coronation of the new Czar, affected a compromise with the revolutionary groups. The latter demanded the liberation of Chernyshevsky as the principal condition for their refraining from an attempt on the Czar's life.

Chernyshevsky did not belong to any revolutionary organization or party. He had been sentenced, after two years of imprisonment in a fortress, to seven years' hard labor and lifelong banishment to Siberia.

The son of an orthodox priest, educated in the spirit of Russian orthodoxy, he adopted the views of Feuerbach, Fourier, Proudhon, and John Stuart Mill, whose *Principles of Political Economy* he had translated into Russian. His interpretation and critical notes on Mill's work not only proved Chernyshevsky's independent mind, but also pointed up the social problems of Russia. As a member of the staff of the influential periodical, *Sovremennik* (Contemporary), he introduced the spirit of Western civilization into Russia and defended the interests of the peasants against the great landowners before and after the emancipation of the serfs. He believed that philosophical materialism was the basis for social progress, but that ethics of self-discipline and altruism were also needed. As

LEONTIEV, KONSTANTIN (1831-1891), famous anti-democrat and reactionary, whose fear and hatred of the masses won him the title of the Russian Nietzsche. Critic and novelist, he was also employed as a censor and in the consular service. At the end of his life he took monastic vows. He emphasized the fear of God as the origin of true morality, and declared man's purpose in life is not to be happy, but to fulfill God's will in history. Unyielding and isolated, Leontiev was never a popular thinker, but he exerted a marked influence on such men as Soloviev and Berdyaev.

prisoner in the Peter and Paul fortress, he wrote the novel, *What Is To Be Done,* (1863) which was a source of inspiration to Russian youth until the First World War.

Chernyshevsky returned to St. Petersburg in 1881, his health undermined, forced to live in isolation, and dependent upon translating as a means of livelihood. Until the 1905 Russian revolution, censorship did not permit any mention of his name. His works were printed anonymously, but the Russian people recognized him as the author, and revered him as the martyr of free thought.

Tolstoy in His Study

TOLSTOY, LEO

TOLSTOY, LEO (1828-1910). In *Resurrection* (1899), the third of Tolstoy's great novels, the author summarized the experiences of his life by asserting his conviction that in every human being a spiritual and altruistic principle is working against an animal and egoistic one "which is ready to sacrifice the well-being of the whole world to one's own comfort." The defeat of the animal in man by the spirit, which was identified by Tolstoy with conscience, is the underlying principle in all Tolstoy's works, as well as the aim of his life. The antagonism between spirit and animal is the standard of valuing which Tolstoy applied to modern humanity and civilization, and he has not concealed that he himself could not stand its test. Tolstoy was a rigorous moralist but he far from simplified the things his moral judgment condemned. His art penetrated into the inner secrets of a society and of persons despised by him. He knew what was important to an officer of the imperial bodyguard, what troubled the nerves of a lady of fashion, what lured the ambition of an official, and he showed the vanity of their hopes and apprehensions with such a power that the outstanding critics of all civilized nations agree with William Dean Howells who said that "Tolstoy's imag-

ination leaves all tricks of fancy, all effects of art immeasurably behind."

Yet it was Tolstoy's moralism that turned against his own art. Though in his youth he had been very fond of the power of literary imagination, in his later years he rejected every kind of power, not the least of which being the power of art. He had conquered the world with his novel *War and Peace* (1869), and he seemed to have secured this conquest by his novel *Anna Karenina* (1877). But in *My Confession* (1882) he declared: "When I had ended *Anna Karenina* my despair reached such a height that I could do nothing but think of the horrible condition in which I found myself. I saw only one thing, Death. Everything else was a lie."

Tolstoy saw only one way out of his crisis, namely the strict obeyance to the Sermon on the Mount which, according to him, involves social repentance, religious purification, radical opposition to the interests and institutions of the world, rejection of property, power, war, oath and political statutes. He fought the Church, because, while ruling the world, it was dominated by the world. He revered Christ, but did not look back to the events narrated in the New Testament. He was looking forward, expecting the coming kingdom of God and the end of the rule of earthly power.

Tolstoy Revered by the Serfs of His Native Russia
(*From* The Power of Darkness)

Tolstoy at Work in the Fields
(*Painting by Repin*)

Nicolai Dobrolyubov

Every philosophy was to Tolstoy an evil in so far as it tried to form a system, an artificial order of thoughts. But he was interested in the efforts of some philosophers—especially Descartes, Leibniz, Rousseau, Kant, Schopenhauer and African Spir—to deal with the power of evil or to know God, although he protested that no philosopher had given more than a vague idea of God. Tolstoy himself conceived of God not as a person in the proper sense of the word but rather through man's relation to God as comparable with personal loyalty, and the feeling of God as the source of love and moral law. He regarded the uneducated, poor, enslaved Russian peasant as the most reliable guide to the way to God and as the true representative of humanity.

DOBROLYUBOV, NICOLAI

DOBROLYUBOV, NICOLAI (1836-1861), a leading radical critic of his time, regarded by some as an originator of revolutionary activity in Russia. A critic who was interested mainly in social commentary, his major contribution was his discovery of social types in Russian literature, and their importance in an analysis of Russian society—particularly the so-called "superfluous man," as in Goncharov's Oblomov. He believed that the liberal nobility were impotent as leaders, and characterized the life of the reactionary Russian merchant class as the "Kingdom of Darkness."

Nicolai Mikhailovski

MIKHAILOVSKI, NICOLAI

MIKHAILOVSKI, NICOLAI (1842-1904), political thinker, sociologist and critic, who devoted his life to radical journalism, but refrained from taking any actual part in political activities lest he be deprived of the right to publish. Coming from an impoverished noble family, he was one of those familiar "repentant noblemen" who are motivated by a sense of guilt and the need to right the wrongs committed by their serf-holding forebears. He conceived of sociology as a science which should be used to serve human progress, and believed socialism would bring man happiness by destroying the contradictions between man and society, thus releasing potentially creative energies otherwise suppressed. Mikhailovski's influence was particularly great on those radicals who rejected Marxism, since his emphasis was upon ethical values and individualism rather than collectivism.

KROPOTKIN, PRINCE PETER

KROPOTKIN, PRINCE PETER (1842-1921). Administrative experience and Utopian vision became confused in the mind of Prince Kropotkin, the founder of communist, or, more precisely, communalist anarchism. For free communities are the political form which he thought social revolution should assume.

At the age of 19, Kropotkin, who had attended the Imperial Military School for Pages, became an officer of the Cossacks, and went with his regiment to Transbaikalia and Manchuria. In this capacity, he undertook numerous exploring expeditions and was also entrusted with administrative tasks. It was in this latter activity that he became imbued with animosity toward centralized government. Although he was decorated by the Tsar for his exploration and governmental services, Kropotkin became an ardent revolutionary. He professed socialist views, but was as opposed to the centralist systems of Saint-Simon and Marx as he was to centralist Tsarism. In 1874, Kropotkin was arrested by the Russian police because of his revolutionary activities. However, in 1876, he escaped to England. After a stay in Switzerland, he was expelled from that country at the request of the Tsarist police. In 1883 he was imprisoned in France, also at the instigation of the Russian police, but was released in 1886 at the personal order of President Jules Grévy. Thereafter he lived in England. Kropotkin made valuable contributions to geology, geography, chemistry, economics, sociology and history. Without systematic erudition, he proved to have vision in all fields of his scientific activities. He especially succeeded in elucidating important stages of the French Revolution in his book *The Great Revolution* (1909). His social system is explained in his book *Mutual Aid—A Factor in Evolution* (1902). The First World War isolated Kropotkin, who sided with the Western Allies against Germany and his anarchist followers. In 1917, he supported Kerensky against the Bolshevists.

AXELROD, PAVEL BORISSOVICH

AXELROD, PAVEL BORISSOVICH (1850-1928). Brought up in a small provincial town in Russia, the son of a poor Jewish innkeeper, Axelrod realized that his quest for knowledge was inseparable from the struggle for human progress; that his desire for self-education was only an aspect of his desire to educate the masses of the people.

In his youth he was a disciple of Bakunin, and he remained an idealist even after adopting the Marxist concept of historical materialism. With his lifelong friend, Plekhanov, he became one of the founders of the Russian Social Democratic Party. Plekhanov was the leading theorist of the movement, and Axelrod directed its propaganda and applied the theories to practical politics. It was largely due to his efforts that the labor movement of Russia participated in the political struggle against Tsarist absolutism instead of concentrating their activities upon economic improvement. He took a leading part in directing and formulating the policies of the Menshevist Party, and was elected a member of the executive committee of the Second Internationale. One of the principal aims of his activities was to organize the Russian worker and make him as politically active as his Western European counterpart. He was often referred to as the great Westerner among the Russian Socialists. From 1903 until his death, he and Plekhanov combatted Lenin and the Bolshevists.

Vladimir Soloviev

SOLOVIEV, VLADIMIR

SOLOVIEV, VLADIMIR (1853-1900). Soloviev has been called "the Russian Newman" or "the Russian Carlyle," and he could easily be called "the Russian Kierkegaard" with equal, or even more justice. For the struggle against the established Church, against the alliance between Church and State, which, in his opinion, meant domination of the Church by the State, and the effort to take the doctrine of Christ seriously was Soloviev's great purpose just as it was Kierkegaard's. Soloviev protested against the division of mankind into a Church which claimed to possess divine truth and to represent the will of God, and all the rest. This division, as it has been developed in the history of Christianity, was deplored by Soloviev and regarded by him as seducing the Church to abuse its lust of power. Deeply convinced of the truth of Christianity, Soloviev asserted the idea of "Godmanhood," bequeathed to humanity, and the ideal of universal theocracy, which he conceived as absolutely incompatible with the claims of the Orthodox Church.

Soloviev was the son of the noted Russian historian Sergius Soloviev, who was devoted to Tsarism, the Orthodox Church and Slavophile ideas. His career promised to become brilliant, but he renounced it, in 1881, after the assassination of Tsar Alexander II, when he publicly asked for mercy for the assassins. He always was a strong adversary of capital punishment. Then retired to private life, Soloviev became one of the greatest Russian philosophers of religion.

It is not so much the originality of Soloviev's ideas that makes his works important as rather their connection with fundamental trends of Russian thought, and his view of the crisis of European civilization. Soloviev's hostility against nationalism, especially Russian nationalism, is no less ardent than his opposition to the claims of the Orthodox Church. At the end of his life, he recognized Rome as the center of Christianity, without, however, converting to the Roman Church. His positive doctrine culminated in the "justification of the good," founded upon a psychology of human conscience and upon his strong belief that man cannot be entirely wicked. He was a man who lived in accordance with his ideas, and was revered as a saint by people of all classes. His tombstone became a place of pilgrimage.

Ivan Pavlov (1849-1936). Eminent experimental psychologist and physiologist of pre-Soviet Russia. Renowned for his studies of the reflex reaction in man and animal. Strong opponent of the Freudian interpretation of neuroses
(Painting by Mikhail Nesterov)

BERDYAEV, NICHOLAS

BERDYAEV, NICHOLAS (1874-1948). Berdyaev was educated in the military school of the Tsarist cadet corps. Later he became a Marxist, was arrested in 1898 for his socialist activities, and banished to the north of Russia for three years. Around 1905 he reverted to the Christian faith, but was accused, in 1914, of insulting the Holy Synod. His trial in 1917 was ended by the Russian Revolution. The Bolshevist government had him arrested in 1920 and then again in 1922. He was expelled from the Soviet Union because of his persistent support of faithful Christians. His remaining years were spent in France.

He regarded himself as the prophet of a new world about to be born; the eventide of history whose means of research, adequate as they might appear for the sun-lit day of rationalism, would be completely inadequate for the new era. He predicted a "New Middle Ages" which would spell the end of humanism, individualism, formal liberalism, nationalism, socialism, and communism. It would be the beginning of a new religious collectivity, which would not be ruled by an ecclesiastic hierarchy, but would imbue knowledge, morality, art, and economic and political institutions with a religious spirit free from external constraint. Berdyaev's philosophy conceives of man as the conjunction of the natural and divine world. Man, created by a creator, must necessarily continue the creative process in order to prove the creative character of his cognitive faculties and use them for the perfection of true civilization. Berdyaev arrived at this point of view after considerable changes in his personal philosophy.

The Communist Planners

MARX, KARL (1818-1883). To the impact of Marx's doctrine on political and social ideas and the subsequent changes of social structure there is no parallel in the whole history of philosophy. Only religious reformers have produced similar changes. What distinguishes Marx from other philosophers who more or less deeply influenced political and social ideas is the simple fact that his teachings directly affected the mind of the masses of working people in various nations, not only by appealing to their material interests but even more so by imbuing them with an apparently imperturbable confidence in the absolute truth of his statements and predictions. In his *Theses on Feuerbach* (1845), Marx, who had turned from the political radicalism of the Left Hegelians to what he then called communism and later scientific socialism, declared that the question of absolute truth is not one of theory but a practical one, and that the reality and power of thought must be demonstrated in practice by both interpreting and changing the world. But he always insisted that a vigorous theory is as indispensable to the destruction of a corrupted society and the construction of a new one as is drastically disciplined action. When, in his *Critique of Political Economics* (1859), Marx called his method empirical, he did so in order to mark his opposition to abstract spiritualism. But he continued to sneer at pure empiricists. He turned Hegel's dialectic upside down because he thought that Hegel's way of proceeding from the abstract to the concrete, from the ideal to the real, never could reach reality, and that Hegel's conception of the dialectical motion as the development of consciousness was bound to miss human totality. But when Marx declared in opposition to Hegel that it is not consciousness that determines the existence of man but that the social existence of man determines his consciousness, he nevertheless was regarding dialectic as the only infallible method of scientific thinking to which all empirical knowledge of facts is subordinated. He reproached Feuerbach for having abandoned not only idealism, of which he approved, but also dialectics of history which, to Marx, meant renouncing scientific exactness. In the same way, although he applied his theory mainly to economic and social life, and devoted much of his energy to the direction of political movements, Marx remained the philosopher of the dialectical movement who retained both Hegel's conviction that the real is rational and Hegel's dialectical concept of becoming. He continued to agree with Hegel that reality is a process, that life means itself and its contradiction, and that as soon as contradiction ceases to act, life will come to an end.

The fundamental characteristic of Marx's doctrine is not his theory of the concentration of wealth in the hands of a few powerful capitalists, or the condemnation of the "exploitation of man by his fellow-man." These views are borrowed from Saint-Simon, Sismondi and Constantin Pecqueur. Nor is it his theory of class struggle, borrowed from French historians of his time, or his theory of surplus

Karl Marx and the Communist Manifesto, *Authored by Himself and Engels*

value, owed to English economists. What really dominates the unity of his thinking is his conception of history, according to which the forms of economic production determine the formation of human society and the consciousness of its members so that ideas, moral values, aesthetic standards, political and social concepts, educational and religious systems are to be conceived as produced by the economic situation. As long as the "ideological superstructure" remains in accordance with the conditions of economic production, civilization is healthy. But, since these conditions are changing more rapidly than the superstructure, cultural crises are unavoidable, and, when people, incapable of understanding the laws of history, resist the changes dictated by it, revolution becomes necessary. In his principal work *Das Kapital* (1867 and later) Marx developed his philosophy by applying it to modern eco-

The Manchester Mills of the Nineteenth Century Industrial Revolution

Although, in his later years, Marx became more and more reluctant to define concepts, because he was afraid lest he should admit in this way any fixed existence, he maintained his belief in the dynamics of economic change as the prime mover of historic life. He presented this conviction as an eternally valid law of nature, as the highest tribunal from which no appeal to another court is possible. He did it by an inexorable diction, fond of disillusioning and with dry irony, sneering at moralists, utopians, reformers who, as he said, tried in vain to escape the compulsion dictated by historical laws, such as are revealed by the right use of dialectics. He, on his part, claimed to teach how to cooperate with the due course of historical evolution. When each science will have become perfect, philosophy will be useless except formal logic and dialectic. Of these two disciplines, dialectic is declared superior, as a method of advancing from the known to the unknown. According to Marx, dialectic forces the way beyond the narrow horizon of formal logic, because it contains the germ of a more developed view of the world. He was fond of dialectic because he conceived of it as of constant fermentation. Marx's search for the causation and end of the historical process, which assumes that men, while producing the means of material existence, enter human relations independently of their will and change these human relations independently of their will when the way of production changes, has been much disputed. But many philosophers, historians and sociologists who contradict him are ready to admit that he has created a working hypothesis.

Adolph Hitler, who was strongly influenced in the making of the National Socialist party by the anti-Semitic writings of Karl Marx, who frequently pleaded for the extermination of what he called Jewish Capitalism

nomic life, demonstrating by a historico-sociological analysis of economics that that which he calls the *bourgeoisie* has accomplished its historical task by great performances but that it is not capable any longer of adapting itself to the changed conditions of production and must give room to the proletariat.

Marx tried to regard phenomena as incessantly changing, life as continual movement of growth and destruction, so that nothing immutable remains except movement itself. For that reason, said his intimate friend and collaborator Friedrich Engels, Marx refrained from offering in his principal work any fixed and universally applicable definition. Marx even criticized the German Social Democratic Party which, in its program of 1875, mentioned the "present-day State." Marx maintained the "present-day State" to be a fiction since it differed from one country to another.

Marx's gigantic stature was considerably dented by his anti-Semitic tendencies. Although himself a converted Jew, he persisted in publicly identifying Jews with money, banking, usury and materialism. In his pamphlet, *Zur Judenfrage*, he permits himself such statements as: "The basis of Judaism is selfishness. The only bond that ties Jews is the conservation of their property and their egotism." "The secular culture of the Jew is usury, his god—money. The emancipation from usury and money—that is, from realistic Judaism—would constitute the liberation of our time." This anti-Semitism blackened the socialistic movement of Europe from Proudhon to Stalin, and unfortunately has not yet ceased.

German Social Democrats at Zurich. (FROM LEFT TO RIGHT: 3. *Von Links;* 4. *Engels;* 6. *August Bebel;* 9. *Eduard Bernstein)*

LASSALLE, FERDINAND

ENGELS, FRIEDRICH

ENGELS, FRIEDRICH (1820-1895). As long as Karl Marx lived, Engels was his intimate friend, collaborator, and supporter. Though he remained in the background, were it not for Engels' money, moral encouragement, and innumerable other services, Marx would have perished. Several of the writings were the collaboration of both; Engels was always ready to recognize Marx as his superior. After Marx died, Engels edited the second and third volumes of Marx's *Capital;* when socialists disagreed about the meaning of the work, or adversaries distorted it, Engels untiringly interpreted his late friend's meaning.

Engels was the descendant of a dynasty of German industrialists who adhered to religious orthodoxy and political conservatism. He had planned, in his youth, to become a poet, for he was an enthusiast of German romanticism, the historical past and beauty and nature in art. When a new Oriental crisis threatened to cause war between France and Germany (1840), Engels, still an excited nationalist, dreamed of German military victories. A sojourn in London and military service in the Prussian army made him revise his beliefs. He abandoned German nationalism, and all prospects of succeeding his father in his well-to-do business. Thereafter, he devoted his life to the fight for the rights of the working class and for the realization of Marx's plans. In 1845 Engels published his pamphlet, *On The Situation of The Working Class,* in England. He was greatly indebted for this to Constantin Pecqueur, who also wrote a pamphlet dealing with the same subject. Engels' subsequent collaboration with Marx was so close that it is impossible to define his part in it with exactness. In his later years, Engels blended dialectical materialism (as Marx had conceived of it) with philosophical materialism. He also tried to expand the meaning of Marx's terminology. He developed a great interest in ethnology in order to attack social conventions with arguments that demonstrated the relativity of social values. Until his death, he remained the executor of Marx's will.

LASSALLE, FERDINAND (1825-1864). It was one of the many paradoxes in Ferdinand Lassalle's life that he was mortally wounded in a duel, although he constantly struggled against obsolete institutions and conventions. He often perplexed both his admirers and his adversaries by the contradictory traits in his character. But it was just his inner contrasts that were the main constituents of the brilliancy and fascinating power of his personality.

August Boeckh, one of the most famous philologists and historians of that time, worded the epitaph of Lassalle's tombstone in the Breslau Jewish cemetery: "Here rests what was mortal of Ferdinand Lassalle, the thinker and fighter." Lassalle, when engaged in a conflict, fought recklessly and with relentless audacity. As a thinker he destroyed illusions but not ideals. While vindicating the rights of the working people, he appealed to the brutal facts of economic and political power as well as to humanitarian ideas. He was a profound scholar, whose work on Heraclitus is still consulted by students ninety years after its appearance, and whose *System der Erworbenen Rechte* (1861) contains remarks of great consequence for the philosophy of law. He was also a great organizer who created the first political party of workers in Germany, and a popular leader whose oratorical campaigns enraptured the masses. Adolf Hitler, despite his rabid anti-Semitism, studied Lassalle's public speeches, and tried to imitate some of their effects. But Hitler could grasp only the passionate, hypnotizing power of Lassalle's behavior. He was incapable of understanding Lassalle's clarity and mental culture, and his steady endeavor to raise the intellectual level of his audiences.

Proudhon and His Children
(Painting by Courbet)

PROUDHON, PIERRE JOSEPH

PROUDHON, PIERRE JOSEPH (1809-1865). Of all socialist theorists of the 19th century, Proudhon was the most abounding in ideas but the least capable of mastering them. He was a vigorous but poorly trained thinker, often very original and independent, but sometimes haunted by prejudices and whims. To him philosophy was only a means of changing the thoughts of men. Karl Marx, who met Proudhon in Paris, and admired him greatly though he shortly thereafter vilified him, adopted Proudhon's view that the philosopher has not only to interpret the world but to alter it. Marx learned much more from Proudhon, and gave him information about Hegel that confused Proudhon rather than inspired him. Proudhon, as Marx did after him, criticized his socialist predecessors with no lesser severity than the classical economists. He rejected any Utopian system and also communism as forms of government. He was fundamentally not a revolutionary but a reformer who intended to improve the existing methods of production and distribution instead of overthrowing them. His often quoted saying *La propriété c'est le vol* ("Property is theft") is not meant as a definition of property but as a condemnation of what he considers an abuse of it—namely, the power to provide unearned income. Apart from the right of escheat and lending on interest, private property, the disposal of the results of labor and savings, was declared by Proudhon as the essence of liberty and a necessary stimulant to labor and energy.

Proudhon's philosophy maintains that solidarity is a natural and original characteristic of human beings, and egoism the result of a deviation from natural conditions. Man must be guided back from his present isolation to a community in which the equilibrium between the rights of the individual and "public" or "collective" reason must be established anew, and too great inequality of wealth must be prohibited. He was opposed to the assumption that ideas of justice and morality are dependent on economic or social conditions. In this regard he professed to be a Platonist.

Proudhon was the son of a poor cooper who had not the means to give his children a higher education, and who died in misery because he refused to earn more than the medieval theory of the "just price" allowed. Proudhon therefore had to earn his living as a printer, compositor and proofreader before he became a free-lance writer. The first studies he made as an economist concerned his father's fate. From it he drew the conclusion that the world must be altered although he maintained his father's belief that no one should be permitted to earn beyond the "just price."

PLEKHANOV, GEORGE

PLEKHANOV, GEORGE (1857-1918). Although for many years, from 1904 until his death, Plekhanov strongly opposed Lenin and the Bolshevists, and was arrested by them after their victory in 1917, Lenin did not deny his spiritual indebtedness to his adversary and the rulers of Soviet Russia acknowledged the value of Plekhanov's works and permitted them to be re-edited by the Marx-Engels-Institute.

Plekhanov was the founder of the Russian Social-Democratic party which was subsequently divided into the Menshevik and Bolshevik parties.

He was the son of a noble, but not wealthy, landowner who treated his serfs ruthlessly. When, after his father's death, his mother tried to cheat her peasants, the son prevented her from doing so by threatening to set fire to the paternal home.

As a student, Plekhanov joined the Narodniki (Friends of the People) who advocated immediate socialization of Russia. But in 1880 he was converted to Marxism, and, on the ground of his interpretation of this doctrine, he opposed the Narodniki by arguing that Russian economic conditions had to ripen before socialism could be introduced into that country. Because of his revolutionary activities, Plekhanov went into exile. In the following year he founded the "Union for Emancipation of Labor," the germ-cell of the Social-Democratic Party of Russia, whose program was elaborated by him. At the request of the German Social Democrats, he wrote *Anarchism and Socialism* (1894); in the following year he wrote against the Narodniki in *On the Question of the Development of the Monist View in History;* and in 1896 his *Essay on the History of Materialism* was published, which, like his *Fundamental Problems of Marxism* (1908), was generally acknowledged to be an authoritative interpretation of Marxism. Plekhanov fought the socialist revisionists in Germany and France but sided, in 1904, with the Russian Mensheviks against Lenin. When Plekhanov returned to Russia after the overthrow of Tsarism, he was hopelessly suffering from tuberculosis but struggled against Bolshevism to his last gasp.

The Prophets of Communism: Marx, Engels, Lenin and Stalin

LENIN, V. I.

LENIN, V. I. (1870-1924). When, under the leadership of Lenin, the Bolshevik party seized political power in Russia on November 7, 1917, a new chapter was opened in the history not only of Russia but of the whole world. The character and effects of the Bolshevist revolution and of that party's regime are a matter of endless dispute. There is, furthermore, no agreement concerning Lenin's personality and the part played by him in the Russian revolution. But there is one fact that seems to be certain—that without Lenin, Marxian socialism in its rigid shape would not have been established and maintained as the exclusively ruling creed in Russia. Whether or not the governmental practice of the Bolshevist State has remained in accordance with the official creed is another question. However, it was Lenin, and he alone, who was responsible for the inauguration and continuance of a governmental course which, although in practice is sometimes ready to accept compromises or deviations, insists on the exclusive authority of socialism of the Marxian stamp and suppresses any attempt to express, let alone to practice, heterodox views. For this reason, Lenin is frequently considered, even by non-Bolshevists,

*Leninists Massacring the Opposing Moderate
Democratic Socialists*

*Lenin Urging the Troops of Russia to Desert
and Go Home*

as the greatest thinker of the Russian revolution. But his undisputed authority as leader of his party and as ruler over his country does not mean that he was equally superior in the realm of thought.

It is true that Lenin had spent about twenty years in preparing a theoretical and organizational basis for the Bolshevist revolution, and, undisturbed by delays and reverses, he had elaborated the main features of his governmental program when the moment came for seizing power. Lenin, whose original name was Vladimir Ilyich Ulianov, had studied the strategy of civil war, the tactics of sabotage, the weak points of dissenting groups, and the malleability of the mass of the Russian people. But, in his general ideas, he depended upon Marx. According to Lenin, Marx had sufficiently explained the world, and left to him the task of changing this world. He was not even interested in the philosophical foundation of Marxism. Lacking intellectual curiosity, Lenin was unwilling to indulge in thinking activity for its own sake. *Materialism and Empiro-Criticism* (1909), Lenin's only work on philosophical principles, abounds in misunderstandings. Its aim is to deter socialists from reading Avenarius or Mach rather than to refute their arguments. Lenin's book on *Imperial-*

ism (1916) is not an original analysis of political, economic or sociological facts, but it is, instead, a collection of comments on quotations from the German socialist Rudolph Hilferding's *Finanzkapital*. In his numerous disputes with dissenting socialists, Lenin contented himself with producing a text from Marx or Engels in order to crush his adversaries. This confidence in his masters was a source of strength for Lenin, the party leader and statesman. Apart from his Marxian orthodoxy, Lenin remained versatile and resourceful, not in the least because of his lack of philosophical interest. On the other hand, he was far from considering any of his collaborators as efficient if the latter was only an orthodox Marxian. Noncommunist foreigners were often impressed by Lenin's sarcastic remarks on incapable communist zealots, and took his frankness as a proof of his freedom from prejudice. But, although he judged men and their faculties with acuteness and almost without any bias, he remained fanatically devoted to his creed, and he was aware that he owed his leadership not to his theoretical thinking or his practical ability but to his fervor, his energy, his commanding glance, his educational talents and his skill in maintaining discipline.

The Rise of the New World

The American Divines

PENN, WILLIAM

PENN, WILLIAM (1644-1718). The part that William Penn played in making freedom of conscience prevail in America is of primary importance, even granted that many other men and groups of people have struggled for the same cause. As soon as he had been converted to Quakerism, he gave powerful expression to his longing for freedom of worship and his opposition to religious intolerance. He was ready to sacrifice his own liberty for his faith, and while in prison, he told his jailer that he "scorned that religion which is not worth suffering for, and able to sustain those that are afflicted for it." But when he himself became the ruler over a territory that now is a state of the Union, third in its population, he provided that no one should be obliged "to frequent or maintain any religious worship, place or ministry contrary" to his conscience. Many of his provisions became basic to corresponding articles in the Constitution of the United States.

A curious combination of circumstances enabled Penn to undertake what he called "a holy experiment" and to establish a "theocratic democracy," different from all the other great British colonies in America. The inheritance of a claim for money advanced to the Crown by his father, Admiral Sir William Penn, gave him the opportunity of acquiring the territory of Pennsylvania and of founding there a state in accordance with his religious and political ideas. Without this opportunity, Penn would have been no more than an agitator, however influential and self-denying, confined to an environment which did not promise great success, or else merely the author of a Utopian scheme. He could not secure permanent realization of his ideal, but he established and maintained his government "without ever drawing a sword." His treaties with the Indians aroused even the admiration of Voltaire, who praised them because they were "not ratified by an oath and were never infringed."

Penn was a religious perfectionist and a man of the world. He wrote with great clarity of his religious experiences, but his interests were not limited to religion and theology. Many of his works reveal great erudition. Religious tolerance was the cornerstone of his political system, in which fundamental and circumstantial laws are distinguished. He repeatedly emphasized that "the political union of loyal citizens does not depend upon unity of belief."

William Penn

Penn's Treaty with the Indians
(*Painting by Benjamin West*)

George Fox (1624-1691), Founder of the Society of Friends (Quakers) in protest against religious and social insincerities in the England of his time

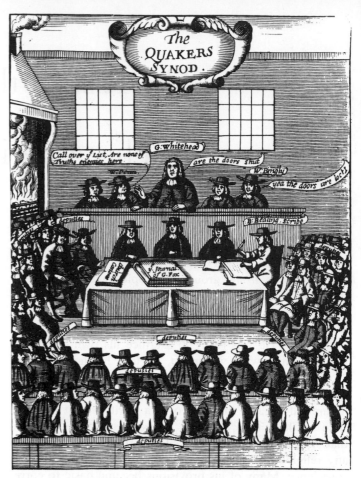

Yearly Meeting of Quakers, 1696

The seekers after religious freedom carry on the tradition of religious persecution. Quakers being whipped in the Colony of Massachusetts

Cotton Mather (1663-1728), an early and influential divine in New England. At first supported witchcraft persecutions, but later opposed trials as unfair. Author of many religious books and a monumental history of colonial times

EDWARDS, JONATHAN

EDWARDS, JONATHAN (1703-1758). Until the very end of the nineteenth century, Jonathan Edwards was considered America's greatest philosopher. Only in later manuals of philosophy published in the United States were men like Charles Peirce and William James hesitantly acknowledged as his equals. Outside of the United States Edwards' philosophy remains virtually unknown; his name is mentioned only in the histories of American religious life.

Edwards, who, in his early years, admired Locke and adopted the ideas of Cudworth and other Cambridge Platonists, lost interest in theoretical philosophy after he was ordained minister (1726) in the church at Northampton. A persuasive preacher and devoted spiritual leader of his congregation, he was also very influential as the author of religious and theological treatises. His sermon *Justification by Faith* (1734) marked the beginning of "New England Theology" which dominated the congregationalism of New England until 1880. Edwards had revolted against Calvinism in his youth and initiated what has been called "Consistent Calvinism," "Strict Calvinism," or the "New Divinity." He defended its fundamental doctrines against Arminians and deists, and preached the

Jonathan Edwards
(Painting by Joseph Badger, Yale University Gallery)

The Trial of George Jacobs for Witchcraft in 1692 by Matteson

doctrine of divine immanence and divine initiative. He denied the freedom of human will and affirmed election by predestination. His congregation was the starting point of the "Great Awakening" of New England. Edwards was not only the theologian of this movement, but also its historian and psychologist. His *Treatise Concerning Religious Affections* (1746) tried to distinguish between sincere religious emotion, genuine conversion, hysteria, false sentimentality, and enthusiastic exaggeration. William James praised Edwards' descriptions as "admirably rich and delicate."

Unfortunately, the life of piety and purity to which Edwards tried to convert his people was beyond their comprehension. He was dismissed in 1750 by his parishioners when he excluded from full communion those members of the congregation who did not correspond to his ideal. He turned to missionary work among the Indians and wrote voluminous works on topics he had previously dealt with in shorter form. In 1757 he was elected president of the College of New Jersey, later to become Princeton University.

Theodore Parker (1810-1860), Nineteenth Century Congregationalist Minister who strongly influenced Unitarianism. The liberality of his sermons aroused strong criticism, and he took leading part in antislavery agitation

Bowdoin, James (1726-1790). American statesman and Revolutionary leader. Member of the Constitutional Convention and later Governor of Massachusetts. A learned man, he received many honors and was influential not only in the dissemination of ideas of liberty, leading to the American Revolution, but in the profession of his Christian principles

The Founding Fathers

Ethan Allen rescuing lost children in the White Mountains. Many of his deeds of heroism became legendary

Allen in the Provost Prison

ALLEN, ETHAN

ALLEN, ETHAN (1738-1789). Ten years prior to the publication of Thomas Paine's *Age of Reason,* Ethan Allen's book, *Reason The Only Oracle of Man* (1784), enunciated the principles of deism operative in American life. Condemned by the clergy and New England universities, it was admiringly referred to by freethinkers as "Ethan's Bible." When a fire at the publishing house destroyed the stock of copies, the orthodox welcomed the incident as "an act of God."

Though Allen was a contemplative man, he led an active life, engaging in farming, mining, manufacturing, and real-estate transactions. He was a soldier during the French and Indian War, and, during the War for Independence, he commanded the Green Mountain Boys of Vermont and captured from the British Fort Ticonderoga, the main approach to Canada. He was a pioneer in the development of American economic life and built a blast furnace in the Litchfield Hills of Connecticut, his native state. Vermont was his adopted state, and he vociferously defended its boundary and land claims against those of New York and New Hampshire.

Allen was reared in Arminianism. This religious belief, though tolerant of Calvinist orthodoxy, emphasized human duties more than theological speculation. Allen rebelled against any accepted dogma, publicly protesting that he was not a Christian but a deist. He opposed authority of all kinds and declared that tradition was fallible, reason the highest gift of God, and faith less reliable and unimportant. He viewed human beings as "the most selfish, oddest, and most cunning medley of beings of that size in the universe." And though his opinions of contemporary human conditions were equally pessimistic, he was confident that the ultimate victory of virtue would make for human progress. He was convinced that the existence of Man was necessary for the maintenance of the world created by God and, therefore, there "can be no ultimate failure." He held that the future was beyond human comprehension and that goodness and happiness would prevail in the last stage of human development, for so had God ordained.

Allen's Grave near Burlington, Vermont

Bust of Paine by John Wesley Jarvis
(New York Historical Society)

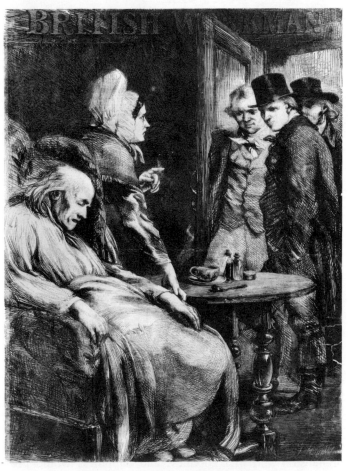

The Last Moments of Tom Paine
(Drawing by John Gilbert)

PAINE, THOMAS

PAINE, THOMAS (1737-1809). Contemporaries used to speak of Paine only in superlatives either of enthusiasm or contempt. Jefferson and Hamilton, though differing on so many points, agreed that Paine was a man to be avoided or distrusted. England, his native country, outlawed him. Jacobin France, where Paine at first had been made an honorary citizen and had been elected a member of the National Convention although he did not speak French, imprisoned him because he had agitated against the execution of the king. When Paine died, he had been poor, sick and ostracized for many years. A century after his death, Theodore Roosevelt sneered at him as a "filthy little atheist."

But independent historians have recognized that Paine, by his pamphlet *Common Sense* (1776) and by untiring agitation, convinced influential but hesitating Americans that independence should be declared because it was the only way to save the colonies. It was also Paine who insisted on the gathering of the Continental Congress, for the purpose of framing a Continental charter. Furthermore, it was Paine who earlier than any other proclaimed America's mission to be the defense of freedom and democracy by presenting to the whole world the example of a republic of free men.

Without any doubt, America and humanity in general owe him a grateful memory, although he was not free from vanity and his education was incomplete. But Paine was not a man to serve only one country. He defended

The famous kite episode. At Franklin's feet is his famous electrical machine

The Franklin Desk

Swivel-armed writing chair, invented by Franklin

363

ADAMS, JOHN

ADAMS, JOHN (1735-1826). The second president of the United States regarded himself as "one of those Protestants who do not believe in anything." He repudiated Platonism, the doctrines of the Christian churches, deism, materialism, and scoffed at the belief in the perfectability of human nature and the progressive development of the human intellect. An austere, cynical, selfless, and stubborn man, he opposed democracy because he distrusted the people, yet he devoted himself to the welfare of the entire nation. He maintained that an aristocratic class could provide for the interests of the poor more adequately than the masses of plain people whose very interests might be at stake.

Adams was a political philosopher despite his contemptuous attitude toward philosophy. His concepts of government were based upon the arguments of Aristotle and Montesquieu. He admired the ideas of these men, even though they were philosophers, and in the same way, he revered Bolingbroke, Hume and Voltaire as "comets" of thought. He staunchly defended the governmental system of checks and balances against the demands for centralized power or an extension of democracy.

Adams played a leading part in the opposition to the Stamp Act of 1765 and in the organization of the War of Independence; but he remained a Tory in his persistent sympathy for the British form of government. Thus the constitution for the State of Massachusetts, written by him, was very conservative. As President, Adams resisted Alexander Hamilton's requests for a declaration of war against France and the negation of the lower-class demands. Adams' domestic policy of taking the middle course was a failure; his Presidential experiences reinforced his feelings of detached cynicism. After he left the Capitol, he declared that "a fine load of manure was a fair exchange for the honors and virtues of the world."

Harvard College in 1751, at time John Adams taught Latin grammar there
(Engraving by William Burgis, Library of Congress)

John Adams
(Painting by John Singleton Copley, Library of Congress)

Jefferson Writing the Declaration
(Painting by Howard Pyle)

The U.S. Capitol in 1800, at the time John Adams was President
(Library of Congress)

JEFFERSON, THOMAS

JEFFERSON, THOMAS (1743-1826). In accordance with Jefferson's own will, his tombstone reads:

Here was buried Thomas Jefferson
Author of the Declaration of American Independence
Of the Statute of Virginia for religious freedom
And Father of the University of Virginia.

Jefferson did not want to have mentioned that he had been Governor of Virginia, member of Congress, Minister to France, Secretary of State, Vice-President and third President of the United States. Jefferson often protested that he disliked politics and preferred the peaceful life on his farm and among his books. Undoubtedly these declarations were sincere. His was a meditative mind. He was not a man of action. But for decades he was involved in political struggles because they concerned not so much his material interests as his philosophy, and it was his philosophy, at least its broad outline, which caused a great political upheaval, resulting in Jefferson's victory over men of action, and his election to the Presidency.

Jefferson's political philosophy was founded upon his ideas on human nature. His motto was, "I cannot act as if all men were unfaithful because some are so. . . . I had rather be the victim of occasional infidelities than relinquish my general confidence in the honesty of man." His confidence disregarded differences of education, wealth, social position. The aim of his political activity was a life of freedom in which every individual would be able to develop his moral and intellectual nature and pursue his happiness. He was also confident that the common man would give authority to good and wise leaders. He firmly believed that Providence created man for society and endowed him with a sense of right and wrong so that an orderly society could subsist.

Jefferson, who in his youth had been engaged in "dancing, junketing and high jinks," was a man of solid studies in various fields. He was a profound jurist, versed in mathematics, botany and meteorology, interested in zoology, astronomy and ethnology, mechanics and architecture, well-read in classical and modern literature, a talented musician and a model farmer. He was opposed to Calvinist orthodoxy, advocated religious tolerance, emancipation of slaves and public education. Among modern political economists there are some who think it fashionable to deride Jefferson as "a petty bourgeois liberal." It is true, Jefferson, the leader of small farmers, shopkeepers and artisans, disliked big business and large-scale industrialization. But his philosophy was anything but the expression of his material interests or of his prejudices.

"Declaration of Independence," by John Trumbull

Jefferson's Garden Book

Interview with the Lafayettes in the prison of Olmutz
(Wide World)

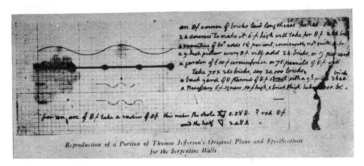

*Reproduction of a Portion of Thomas Jefferson's Original
Plans and Specifications for the Serpentine Walls*

*Outacite, Cherokee Chief admired by Jefferson for his
eloquence as an orator*

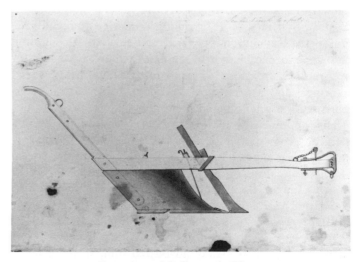

Drawing of Jefferson's Plow

RUSH, BENJAMIN

RUSH, BENJAMIN (1745-1813). Rush Medical College, now affiliated with the University of Chicago, was so named in honor of Benjamin Rush, one of the most successful physicians of 18th century America, surgeon general in the Revolutionary War, a signer of the Declaration of Independence, author of the first textbook on chemistry in America, treasurer of the United States Mint, social reformer, and a prolific writer on medicine, social problems, natural sciences and philosophy.

His approach to philosophy was determined by his medical profession, especially his experiences in psychiatry. He was mainly interested in investigating the effects of physical causes on the mind and the effects of psychic changes on the body. His *Inquiry Upon Physical Causes Upon the Moral Faculty* (1786) and *Medical Inquiries and Observations Upon the Diseases of the Mind* (1812) were for a long time considered standard works on psychiatry. Rush energetically advocated human understanding of mentally ill people, and he also advocated human treatment of criminals. He demanded abolition of capital punishment and slavery. However, his philanthropy did not imply any laxity in moral principles. Rush was firmly convinced that science and religion are in harmony, that ethics is founded upon the Christian faith, and he untiringly protested against any materialistic interpretation of the results of his psychological research. It was on religious grounds that Rush became an ardent American patriot, a revolutionary fighter, and a defender of popular government. He was an intimate friend of Thomas Paine who owed the title of his pamphlet *Common Sense* to Rush's suggestion. Rush was no deist but a Christian who was politically closely allied with Paine, together with whom he even challenged the authority of George Washington. His religious and political ideas made Rush a supporter of the advancement of learning and the improvement of public education. He actively participated in the foundation of colleges and elementary schools, always confident that the increase of knowledge would strengthen democracy and religious belief.

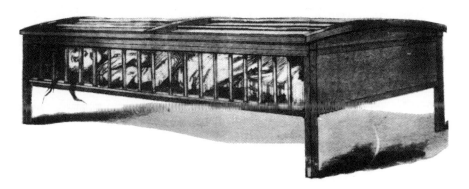

Locking the insane in a crib was a common treatment in the eighteenth century

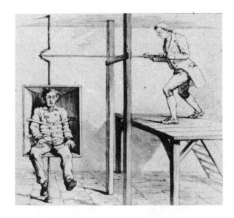

A gyrator, whirling a hundred times a minute, was device used "to calm cases of torpid madness"

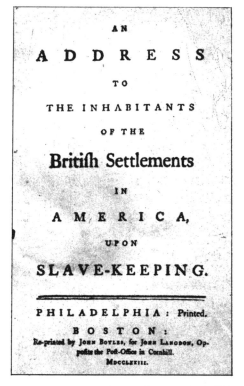

AN

ADDRESS

TO

THE INHABITANTS

OF THE

British Settlements

IN

AMERICA,

UPON

SLAVE-KEEPING.

PHILADELPHIA: Printed.
BOSTON:
Re-printed by JOHN BOYLES, for JOHN LANGDON, Op-
posite the Post-Office in Cornhill.
MDCCLXXIII.

Antislavery Address by Rush, 1773

Rush suggested this kind of tranquilizing treatment to restrain violent patients

Lincoln, Sage and Seer

LINCOLN, ABRAHAM

LINCOLN, ABRAHAM (1809-1865). Compared with Abraham Lincoln, many great figures in the history of the world, many really great leaders of nations, seem to be actors playing the roles of great men. There was nothing of the actor in Lincoln. His behavior was so simple that not only his adversaries but his political followers and many of his subordinates could not imagine that he was a hero. As Emerson said in his funeral discourse, Lincoln was a plain man of the people, a middle-class president, "yes, in manners and sympathies, but not in powers for his powers were superior." Lincoln never lost the characteristics of a small-town lawyer, indulging often in the jocular talk in which he relished and in which he was a past master. But through the atmosphere of jocularity flashed the brilliance of his hard thinking and tragic earnestness, the flame of his devotion to the nation. To that which Lincoln considered identical with the spirit of the nation—the cause of popular government—his name remains inseparably connected. Little by little Lincoln's sagacity, his valor and patience, his sense of justice and his generosity were recognized, at first by the people of the Union, and thereafter by the whole world. He was recognized as a good and wise man whose wisdom was the result of strenuous life, self-education and appreciation of the apparently unimportant events and accidents in the lives of small people, of enjoyment and resignation. Even his famous Gettysburg Address, from which his expression of confidence in the "government of the people, by the people and for the people" has been and will be quoted again and again, did not immediately work up his audience. It took time before the public was moved by Lincoln's words, but then the deep impression lasted. Lincoln possessed the art of making simple words meaningful and of coining sentences which have become proverbial wisdom in almost all languages. He appealed to the intelligence not to the brute instincts of the public, and he knew how to make difficult decisions and questions understandable to the untrained mind.

NEGROES FOR SALE.

I will sell by Public Auction, on Tuesday of next Court, being the 29th of November, *Eight Valuable Family Servants*, consisting of one Negro Man, a first-rate field hand, one No. 1 Boy, 17 years o' age, a trusty house servant, one excellent Cook, one House-Maid, and one Seamstress. The balance are under 12 years of age. They are sold for no fault, but in consequence of my going to reside North. Also a quantity of Household and Kitchen Furniture, Stable Lot, &c. Terms accommodating, and made known on day of sale.

Jacob August.
P. J. TURNBULL, *Auctioneer.*

Warrenton, October 28, 1859.

Printed at the *News* office, Warrenton, North Carolina.

Announcement of Slave Auction, 1859

"The Last Moments of John Brown"
(Painting by Thomas Hovenden, Metropolitan Museum of Art)

RAFFLE

Mr. Joseph Jennings respectfully informs his friends and the public that, at the request of many acquaintances, he has been induced to purchase from Mr. Osborne, of Missouri, the celebrated

DARK BAY HORSE, "STAR,"

Aged five years, square trotter and warranted sound; with a new light Trotting Buggy and Harness also, the dark, stout

MULATTO GIRL, "SARAH,"

Aged about twenty years, general house servant, valued at *nine hundred dollars*, and guaranteed, and

Will be Raffled for

At 4 o'clock P. M., February first, at the selection hotel of the subscribers. The above is as represented and those persons who may wish to engage in the usual practice of raffling, will, I assure them, be perfectly satisfied with their destiny in this affair.
The whole is valued at its just worth, fifteen hundred dollars; fifteen hundred

CHANCES AT ONE DOLLAR EACH.

The Raffle will be conducted by gentlemen selected by the interested subscribers present. Five nights will be allowed to complete the Raffle. BOTH OF THE ABOVE DESCRIBED CAN BE SEEN AT MY STORE, No. 78 Common St., second door from Camp, at from 9 o'clock A. M. to 2 P. M.
Highest throw to take the first choice; the lowest throw the remaining prize, and the fortunate winners will pay twenty dollars each for the refreshments furnished on the occasion.
N. B. No chances recognized unless paid for previous to the commencement.

JOSEPH JENNINGS.

Typical Description of Negro Slaves Being Put up for Sale

America's Coming of Age

The Alcott House, Concord, Massachusetts

ALCOTT, AMOS BRONSON

ALCOTT, AMOS BRONSON (1799-1888). Alcott is frequently referred to as a dreamer because of his unsystematic, deeply veiled philosophy. Yet, like his friend, Emerson, he is truly representative of the New England transcendentalist movement. He was best received at small gatherings, where people listened patiently to his rambling ideas, eager to catch the secret meaning of his orthodoxy. His critics like to dwell upon his personal oddities with the result that his virtues and thoughts are little known. However, many of his lectures throughout the East and Middle West were published in *The Dial*. He is also the author of *Orphic Sayings, Tablets,* and *Concord Days*. Principally a distributor of ideas, a reiterator of previously formulated concepts, he was a teacher by conversation rather than indoctrination. He established several schools based upon these ideas, and was a member of the short-lived Utopian experiment at Fruitlands. Through his solid friendships with Ralph Waldo Emerson and William T. Harris, he was able to realize his dream of a school of philosophy at Concord, Massachusetts.

It is frequently said, despite his contributions to American letters and philosophy, that his life was a failure—largely because his household larder was empty most of the time. This in no way detracted from his family's allegiance to him. His daughter, Louisa May Alcott, portrayed him as the grandfather in *Little Women*. In spite of his critics, this peripatetic lover of wisdom remains one of New England's most lovable sons.

Alcott in His Home

EMERSON, RALPH WALDO

EMERSON, RALPH WALDO (1803-1882). William James pointed out that there were two Emersons: one was the instinctive New Englander whose sharp eyes penetrated the defects of the American republic without despairing of it; the other was the Platonizing Emerson who exalted the Over-Soul, and before whom revelations of time, space, and nature shrank away. Emerson was often aware of the fact that his readiness to perceive various phenomena and to expand his spiritual interests could lead his mind in disparate directions. The elder Henry James asserted that Emerson "had no conscience, in fact he lived by perception." Emerson looked upon consistency as the hob-goblin of little minds. In *Self-Reliance,* he stated: "With consistency a great soul has simply nothing to do." In *History,* he declared: "It is the fault of our rhetoric that we cannot state one fact without seeming to belie some other."

When Emerson spoke of the realm of the soul which embraced the mind and the spirit, it was with certainty and strong conviction, not theoretical knowledge. He distinguished between philosophers like Spinoza, Kant, and Coleridge and others like Locke, Paley, Mackintosh, and Stewart. He held that the former spoke from within or from experience as parties to or possessors of the fact; while the others spoke from without, as spectators whose acquaintance with the fact came from the evidence of third persons. He treated the latter and their doctrines contemptuously, and characterized them as coarse translators of things into conscience, ignorant of the relationship of the soul to the divine spirit. The latter relationship was the only thing that mattered to Emerson, for him no facts as such were sacred; none unworthy but which became instantly important when they indicated or symbolized the history of the living soul, regardless of whether they voiced a mythical imagination, history, law, customs, proverbial wisdom, the creative spirit of artists and poets, the contemplation of a saint, the decision of a hero, or the conversation of ordinary persons. He believed that the worth of any individual man was derived from the universe which contained all human life and was therefore mysterious. He regarded every man as the entrance to the universal mind, capable of feeling and comprehending that which at any time befell any man.

Emerson's Study

The Emerson House, Concord

"Emerson Feels the Gravity of Books"
(*A Cartoon from* The American Scholar)

The Thoreau House, Concord

Thoreau's Room

Henry Thoreau
(From the Rowse Sketch)

Thoreau Felling Wood at Walden Pond

THOREAU, HENRY DAVID

THOREAU, HENRY DAVID (1817-1862). Thoreau was not satisfied merely to entertain an opinion and to enjoy it; he was resolved to live it. For himself and for any individual he claimed the right of revolution against bad government, and he regarded the authority of good government still an impure one, defended civil disobedience, and refused to pay taxes after facing and suffering imprisonment. "Under a government," Thoreau wrote, "which imprisons any unjustly, the true place for a just man is also a prison." The spirit of revolt, the impulse to isolation, the ideal to live alone with thought, nature and God, as well as practical considerations, caused him to retreat to Walden Pond (1845-46) where he contemplated nature and meditated upon it.

Thoreau was a scholar and poet, an eccentric and a shrewd realist. His *Walden* (1854), the work of a great naturalist and an even greater poet of nature, has been translated into many languages.

"To be a philosopher," says Thoreau, "is not merely to have subtle thought, or even to found a school but so to love wisdom as to live, according to its dictates, a life of simplicity, independence, magnanimity and trust." No serene sage, Thoreau's ferocity often disturbed his most faithful friends, and estranged from him Emerson with whom he had been, for a time, closely associated. His temperament committed him to action, his faith to contemplation. Until 1850, Thoreau was an enthusiast of community life. Thereafter he became a staunch opponent of popular movements.

The essential life meant to him life in nature. To him, the burden of the civilization of his age was not caused by mere defects in industrial organization and distribution, but rather by the domination of industry itself over human interests. Against a cultural evolution which he condemned as resulting in the neglect of human values, Thoreau was resolved to live his own time by his own terms.

BEECHER, HENRY WARD

BEECHER, HENRY WARD (1813-1887). One of the outstanding public figures of American life and a brilliantly persuasive preacher, Henry Ward Beecher was regarded, in his youth, as unusually stupid by his parents, teachers, and playmates. He decided to study navigation and become a sailor, for he felt unsuited for other occupations. A great change took place in him during his sojourn at Mount Pleasant Classical Institute, Amherst, Massachusetts; his extraordinary vitality broke through. He became active in sports, read omnivorously, and resolved to become a preacher. He subsequently continued his studies at Lane Theological Seminary in Cincinnati. Here, he revolted against Calvinism and professed independent Presbyterianism in the name of life and the beauty of nature.

Beecher was not a man of original thought; he started no new movement, but he succeeded in attracting and educating Church people, and helped them to develop the power to withstand life's tests and conflicts. He used his sermons to advocate social reforms; he was strongly opposed to slavery despite his dislike for radical abolitionists. He taught a disbelief of hell; defended evolution, and advocated that of which he was so terribly fond, the outdoor life. Despite their great success, his sermons did not satisfy him. He carefully scrutinized and adhered to the methods of Jonathan Edwards, the leader of the "Great Awakening" in New England, and those of the Apostles as they are described in the book of *Acts*. His last years were troubled by a highly publicized trial in which charges of adultery were brought against him. The jury could not agree and an ecclesiastical council acquitted him. Beecher was minister, from 1847 until his death, at Plymouth Church, Brooklyn, New York. Though often ranged on the side of unpopular causes, Beecher's powers of persuasion were such that his sermons gained nation-wide hearing and swayed popular opinion.

Henry Ward Beecher

Beecher on Trial for Adultery

The Cottage in Brooklyn, where Whitman Worked on Leaves of Grass

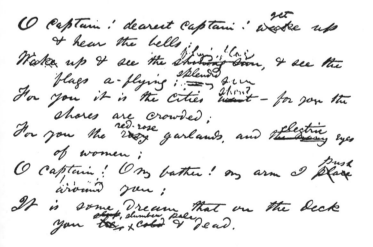

Manuscript of "O Captain! My Captain!"

WHITMAN, WALT

WHITMAN, WALT (1819-1892). Not only in America but also in England, France, Germany and other countries, Whitman has been celebrated as the prophet of the age of democracy, a title which the poet himself relished. The new technique of lyrical expression and description which he initiated has been adopted by outstanding French poets and by many minor poets in several languages.

The function of poetry was conceived by Whitman as not only enjoying but leading and teaching mankind, and in many of his poems he attempted to answer philosophical questions. Whitman also dealt with philosophical problems in his notebooks. In 1847 he did not believe himself to have become a great philosopher, and in 1860 he wrote, in a similar mood, that he had not founded a philosophical school. In a way, he even repudiated philosophy as a bond of thinking, and exclaimed: "I leave all free, I charge you to leave all free." But he also claimed that the poet of the cosmos "advances through all interpositions, coverings and turmoils and stratagems to first principles." In *Passage to India* he declared that the poet fuses nature and man who were diffused before. In fact, Whitman was devoted to a philosophy which combined pantheism with a strong belief in human action, which unites the human soul with cosmic life but stresses the uniqueness of human personality and human relations. His civil, democratic, human consciousness was rooted in an all-embracing feeling of cosmic solidarity, and he was anxious to avoid any attenuation, and not to be deterred by psychic transmigration to the remotest objects. There is a tension between Whitman's firmness of conviction and his universal receptivity for impressions, sensations, ideas and phenomena, between his feelings of being a missionary of democracy and his mythical imagination. But this same tension strengthened his poetical power and did not endanger the unity of his character. From cosmic vagaries he always found the way back to simple truth and common sense.

George Holmes Howison

William Torrey Harris

HOWISON, GEORGE HOLMES

HOWISON, GEORGE HOLMES (1834-1916). One of America's most inspiring teachers of philosophy, who taught at Massachusetts Institute of Technology, Michigan University and University of California. Howison's philosophy, which he termed "Personal Idealism," is an original, theistic personalism, with God representing the Perfect Person, Final Cause and Center of a Republic of persons. He opposed absolute idealism or cosmic theism as a thoroughgoing monism because of its destruction of the implications of experience, its reduction to solipsism and its resolution into pantheism.

HARRIS, WILLIAM TORREY

HARRIS, WILLIAM TORREY (1835-1909). When passions ran high at the beginning of the Civil War, a group met together in St. Louis and calmly interpreted the events as part of a universal plan, the working out of an eternal dialectic which Hegel had explained in all his works, particularly his *Philosophy of History*. One of the key men of that philosophical society was Harris who rose from teacher in the public schools to the superintendency and the United States Commissionership of Education, which post he held for 17 years, longer than any other incumbent. He might be termed the idealist in education in that he organized all phases of it on the principles of a philosophical pedagogy in which the German idealists Hegel, Kant, Fichte and Goethe were his principal teachers, apart from Froebel, Pestalozzi and the rest.

Harris founded and edited the first philosophical periodical in America, the *Journal of Speculative Philosophy,* in which men like William James, Josiah Royce and John Dewey first spread their wings. He initiated, with Brokmeyer, the St. Louis Movement in Philosophy which had far-reaching influence. Together with Amos Bronson Alcott and with the support of Emerson, he revived New England transcendentalism but gave it a more logical, metaphysical twist. Lecturing from coast to coast as one of America's most popular educators, he made his hearers realize the importance of philosophy, of having objectives in an education for democracy, and of viewing things in their whole.

Far from being a dreamer, he was practical in his activities. As editor-in-chief of Webster's, he originated the divided page. He expanded the functions of the Bureau of Education; represented the United States in graphic exhibits at many an international exposition; incorporated the first kindergarten into an American public school system, and was responsible for introducing the reindeer into Alaska as a condition for educating the natives who were thus supplied with an industry and a livelihood which the whalers and trappers had brought to the verge of extinction.

GEORGE, HENRY

GEORGE, HENRY (1839-1897). John Dewey called Henry George "one of the world's great social philosophers, certainly the greatest which our country has produced." Dewey's appraisal of George has not been shared by many Americans. The great majority of American economists have severely criticized George's insistence on nationalization of land and on the "single tax," the two principal tenets of his system. In 1941, George R. Geiger stated that Henry George was neglected and even ignored in liberal and progressive circles and that he had been forgotten by his conservative critics. But the statement is true for America only. In England and Germany the doctrine of Henry George always had greater influence than in his homeland, and it still has many adherents there. His *Progress and Poverty* (1880) became of special consequence for British socialism, as well as for the *Socialist League,* led by William Morris, and the *Fabian Society,* the great training school for labor leaders.

George regarded political economy as justified only when directed by moral principles and social consciousness. He founded his movement for abolition of private landed property upon both religious and political grounds. Land, he said, is the creation of God; it therefore must be common property for all people. Land, he also argued, is the physical foundation of the entire economic process. Therefore, he concluded, no democracy is secure as long as it is in private hands.

George repudiated materialism and evolutionism. He vigorously attacked Herbert Spencer because he had, in 1850, declared that property in land was wrong and in 1882 recanted what George considered the fundamental truth.

Henry George

FISKE, JOHN

FISKE, JOHN (1842-1901). An American historian noted also for his attempts to show that evolutionary theory and religion are compatible. According to Fiske, the events of the evolutionary process are the results of the imminent causality of the living God, "the infinite and eternal Power that is manifested in every pulsation of the universe." Since the evolutionary process has progressively tended toward the highest ethical and spiritual qualities of man, we recognize the essential kinship of the human soul with God and we affirm as a reasonable faith the "quasi-personal" and moral character of God, the imminently operating Cause.

John Fiske

Peirce at the Age of Twenty

PEIRCE, CHARLES SAUNDERS

PEIRCE, CHARLES SAUNDERS (1839-1914). Until William James turned to philosophy and made pragmatism popular, his life-long friend, Peirce, the initiator of this movement, had been almost unknown. Peirce had lectured at Harvard during the periods 1864-65 and 1869-70 and at Johns Hopkins during 1879-84. He had contributed to scientific and general reviews, but no University was induced by his publications to appoint him a professor. For thirty years he had been associated with the United States Coast and Geodetic Survey. He had had no time to complete a book, except his *Grand Logic* which, however, was published after his death, together with other works he had left.

Before men like James and Dewey made Peirce's name famous, he could state: "I am a man of whom critics never found anything good to say." But once he was rather happy to be blamed by a malicious critic who reproached him for not being sure of his own conclusions. Peirce regarded this reproof as a praise. For to him any truth is provisional. In any proposition there must be taken account of coefficient of probability. This theory, called by Peirce "fallibilism," is a substitute for scepticism, and a constituent of his philosophical system, of no lesser importance than pragmatism, which he substitutes for positivism.

Peirce was the son of the great mathematician, Benja-

min Peirce, and himself a mathematician who pioneered in various fields. Before he concentrated upon philosophical studies, he had worked for ten years in chemical laboratories, and had been devoted to exact sciences. He was, by nature, a logician, and it was his interest in logic that made him a philosopher. His conception of pragmatism was not a metaphysical but a logical theory. After studying German and English philosophies, Peirce declared that the Germans acquainted him with "a rich mine of suggestions," which were "of little argumentative weight," while the results of the British were "meager but more accurate."

Peirce's pragmatism, though a logical theory, interprets thought in terms of operation and control. Its striking feature is the inseparable connection between rational cognition and rational purpose. The whole function of thinking, says Peirce, is but one step in the production of habits of action. His statement of the close relation between thought and human conduct has often been misunderstood as though Peirce had proclaimed subordination of reason to action, or even to profit and particular interests. In fact, Peirce defined the meaning of a concept or proposition as that form which is most directly applicable to self-control in any situation and to any purpose. To him, the rational meaning of every proposition lies in the future which is regarded as the ultimate test of what truth means.

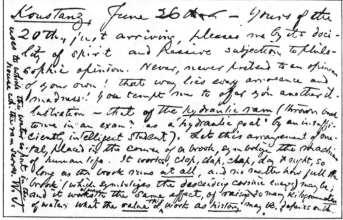

A Postcard from James to Henry Adams

William James (c. 1895)

JAMES, WILLIAM

JAMES, WILLIAM (1842-1910). William James is generally considered not only the most influential of all American philosophers but the very representative of American thought. However, the results of his thinking are by no means confined to his native country, and his background is anything but exclusively American. Very few American families maintained such intimate contact with Europe as did Henry James, Senior, a theologian and philosophical writer, and a great amateur of wide culture, and his sons William and Henry, the great novelist, who, on his part, was more at home in France and England than in the land of his birth. William James often visited Europe where he became acquainted with Alexander Bain, Herbert Spencer, Wilhelm Wundt and Hermann von Helmholtz, whose works he appreciated as sources of information but whose principles he rejected. He became an intimate friend of James Ward and Carl Stumpf and felt himself much indebted to Charles Renouvier whose personality he revered.

In his youth, William James desired to become known as a painter. But, while living with art, he learned that he could live without art, and turned to medicine and the natural sciences. However, his early study of painting was no labor lost. On the contrary, James derived from it his pictorial manner of philosophizing, which does not involve picturesqueness of style but rather his talents for conveying the present aspect of a situation, for finding immediate joy in the variety of appearances from which he proceeded

to enjoy the various psychic experiences, while being capable of describing them in scientific terms, coined afresh, without much regard to traditional terminology. Such blending of scientific sagacity with artistic sensibility, such psychological perspicacity, enriched and refined by his previous study of art, and disciplined by scientific training, are characteristic of James' brilliant lectures and writing, and the cause of his great success. His gifts became known to the public in 1890 when his *Principles of Psychology* appeared, marking a new period in this special branch of science and foreshadowing his turn to philosophy.

It was the latent artist in James that made his treatment of moral, epistemological, and metaphysical problems a revolt of the spirit of immediate concrete experience against the intellectualistic idealism. James' radical empiricism maintains the plurality of the real units of which, according to him, experience consists, against any harmonizing or simplifying monism. Pragmatism, as James defines his empiricism, has become of immense consequence in modern thinking. James surpasses Hume by denying consciousness. He acknowledges a stream of experiences but not a stream of conscious experiences. Therewith he denies that in knowledge the relation between the knowing subject and the object to be known is fundamental, which almost all modern philosophers had taken for granted. This denial has induced many contemporary philosophers, though opposed to James' views, to reconsider the bases and starting points of their own thoughts.

381

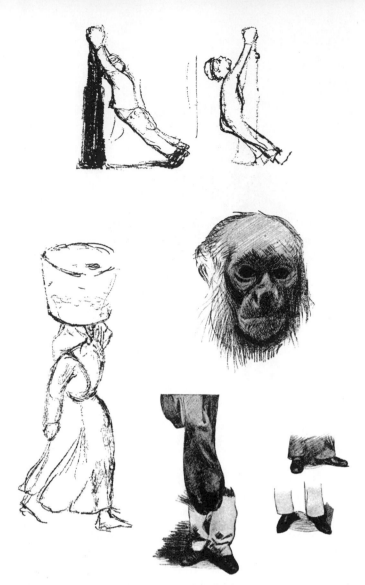

Josiah Royce

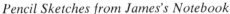

Pencil Sketches from James's Notebook

ROYCE, JOSIAH

ROYCE, JOSIAH (1855-1916). Royce was born in Grass Valley, Nevada County, California, a mining town which was about five years older than himself. Living among rough-handed pioneer people, the sensitive, timid boy who lacked physical strength and skill very early became aware of the value of an established social order because his environment was devoid of it. When his sixtieth birthday was celebrated, Royce, reviewing his mental development, expressed his strong feeling that his deepest motives and problems had centered about the idea of a community, although this idea had come only gradually to his clear consciousness. A platonist vein in his mind caused him to base the idea of human community upon a theory of life and upon a conception of the nature of truth and reality. Idealistic metaphysics was to him the guarantee not only for absolute certainty, but also for a rule over the whole life by right judgment, directed by the sense of absolute truth. Royce's theoretical thinking, however, was always connected with and supported by his experience of religious life. His mother had been his first teacher in philosophy and the Bible his first textbook. Although he could claim to be born nonconformist and to be without connection with "any visible religious body," it was religious problems that drove him to philosophy, and it was religious faith that was regarded by him as the foundation of human solidarity and social loyalty, as the binding element of a community.

While in Royce's *Religious Aspect of Philosophy* (1885) the influence of Hegel is prevalent, Royce later, in *The World and the Individual* (1900-01) came closer to Fichte and Schopenhauer, and shifted his emphasis from thought, which in the earlier work designates the processus of the Absolute, to will, calling himself "a voluntarist and empiricist who yet believes in the Absolute." To Royce, will, as the manifestation of the Absolute, seems fit to reconcile idealist metaphysics and human experience; to corroborate in man the cardinal virtues of courage, industry, loyalty, and solidarity; and above all to unite the religious conception of God with the philosophical idea of the Absolute. While the Absolute had been conceived at first as the

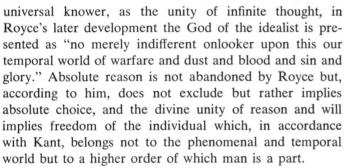

William James and Royce, 1903

BOWNE, BORDEN PARKER

universal knower, as the unity of infinite thought, in Royce's later development the God of the idealist is presented as "no merely indifferent onlooker upon this our temporal world of warfare and dust and blood and sin and glory." Absolute reason is not abandoned by Royce but, according to him, does not exclude but rather implies absolute choice, and the divine unity of reason and will implies freedom of the individual which, in accordance with Kant, belongs not to the phenomenal and temporal world but to a higher order of which man is a part.

In his last years, Royce studied the works of Charles Peirce and, in *The Problem of Christianity* (1913), exposed a triple logic of perception, conception, and interpretation. Voluntarism became an integral factor in Royce's theory of knowledge. Knowing is characterized as an act. An idea, to become cognitive, must be part of a judgment or itself a judgment. This change, however, confirms Royce's early conviction that all reality is reality because true judgments can be made about it. The decision as to which judgments are true and which are false is up to the infinite thought of the Absolute, Supreme Being.

For about thirty years, Royce and William James were intimate friends and staunch adversaries. James secured Royce's appointment as professor at Harvard. While criticizing one another, they inevitably also influenced one another, be it by provoking contrasting ideas or by agreeing on certain views. Royce sometimes expressed his sadness about being forced to attack the philosophy of James to whom he felt himself obliged for practically everything he had written. James, whose criticism of Royce's books sometimes could be devastating, once exclaimed, "Two hundred and fifty years from now, Harvard will be known as the place where Josiah Royce once taught."

BOWNE, BORDEN PARKER (1847-1910). For more than thirty years, Bowne was professor of philosophy at Boston University where, although the spiritual atmosphere of religious traditionalism was agreeable to him, he endeavored to and succeeded in liberalizing religious thought.

An acute critic of positivism and naturalism, he untiringly maintained the cause of theism, defending it from the viewpoints of epistemology, logic, psychology, metaphysics, and religious and social thought. He categorized his views as Kantianized Berkeleyanism, transcendental empiricism and, finally, Personalism—a term used by other philosophers, who differ from Bowne in all fundamental theses, to characterize their systems. Bowne's was chiefly influenced by Lotze.

Bowne's religious and philosophical problems conjoin in their attitude toward change and identity. Epistemologically and psychologically, Bowne regarded identity as the foundation of personality. He argued that without identity, recognition is impossible; without recognition, memory cannot be formed; that memory, the essence of the self, is the primary condition of mental life. He insisted that the mind, not the sense, gives evidence of reality; that reality is comprehended by more than the cognitive faculties; that life and aspiration are more deeply rooted in the person than logical thought; therefore, it becomes necessary to justify aesthetics, ethics, and metaphysics. Bowne stated that no fundamental antagonism exists between thought and feeling. The question of freedom intimately enters into the structure of reason. All knowledge is the result of considerable searching effort. Science is the consequence of human freedom, not of automatically functioning truth. Bowne applied his philosophy of change and identity to the experiences of daily social life, and tried to establish a balance between the claims of progress and conservatism.

Felix Adler

Paul Carus

ADLER, FELIX

ADLER, FELIX (1851-1933). Brought to the United States at the age of six by his father, a rabbi, Felix Adler was also educated for the rabbinical office. He received his doctorate from Heidelberg University and returned to preach at the Temple Emanu-El in New York City. It was here that he failed to refer to God in his sermons. Although he was not disloyal to Judaism, as a rationalist he could not accept the rituals in any literal sense.

He left the rabbinate and his friends established a professorship of Hebrew and Oriental literature for him at Cornell University.

It was his belief that the principle of the good life can be achieved independently of religious ritual and dogma that led him to found the American Ethical Union and the Society for Ethical Culture in New York. (From there it spread to many groups throughout America and the Continent.) He maintained that the idea of a personal God is unnecessary; that the social and ethical behavior of man, if it makes for harmonious relationships among men, constitutes the Godhead; that man's personality because of its unique and inviolable nature is the central force of the religion. He advocated more than mere religious tolerance: men should reverently respect the religious differences among themselves.

In his books *Creed and Deed* (1878) and *Moral Instruction of Children* (1892) he was able to fuse his heterogeneous influences: Judaism, Christianity, Kant, Emerson, and the cogent socialistic ideas of his lifetime. He is noted for his social efforts in such areas as kindergarten and manual training schools, and the abolition of child labor.

CARUS, PAUL

CARUS, PAUL (1852-1919). The memory of the eclectic Paul Carus is kept alive by the Carus Foundation, the Carus Lectures, and the American Philosophical Association. Carus preferred to consider himself a theologian rather than a philosopher. He referred to himself as "an atheist who loved God." The fact was that he was a pantheist who insisted that God, as a cosmic order, was a name comprising "all that which is the bread of our spiritual life." He held the concept of a personal God as untenable. Carus' monism was more frequently associated with a kind of pantheism, although it was occasionally identified with positivism. His pantheistic theology regarded every law of nature as a part of God's being. Although when he maintained that the laws of mechanics represented the action of spiritual existence, it was never quite clear whether he meant that mechanics were a part of God's being, or more simply, that the matter was identical with mind; thus he did not commit himself as to the character of divinity. He acknowledged Jesus Christ as a redeemer, but not as the only one, for he believed that Buddha and other religious founders were equally endowed with the same qualities.

Carus tried to steer a middle course between idealistic metaphysics and materialism. He disagreed with metaphysicians because they "reified" words and dealt with them as though they were realities. He objected to materialism because it ignored or overlooked the importance of form. Carus constantly emphasized form by conceiving of the divinity as a cosmic order. He also objected to any monism which sought the unity of the world not in the unity of truth but in the oneness of a logical assumption of ideas. He referred to such concepts as *henism,* not monism. He stated that truth was independent of time, human desire, and human action. Therefore, science was not a human invention, but a human revelation which needed to be apprehended; discovery meant apprehension; it was the result or manifestation of the cosmic order in which all truths were ultimately harmonious.

VEBLEN, THORSTEIN

VEBLEN, THORSTEIN (1857-1929). Before Veblen turned to the study of social and economic facts and theories, he had concentrated upon philosophy, especially the works of Kant, Comte and Spencer, and, in his later years, the problems of economics remained closely connected in Veblen's mind with fundamental problems of life, civilization and the general theory of science. Intending to integrate political economy into the general movement of science, Veblen discussed the evolution of the scientific point of view, the place of science within the framework of civilization, and the function of evolution within political economy. Although Veblen was strongly impressed by the doctrine of evolution, he was opposed to the simple application of the evolutionary principles to the study of social phenomena. He was also strongly opposed to positivism, and relied more upon German idealism and romanticism. He sometimes flirted with theorists of racialism like Gobineau and H. S. Chamberlain, and, if not influenced by Georges Sorel, he came in his own way very close to the latter's standpoint. Both Sorel and Veblen were inspired by Marx and criticized him by similar arguments. Both were enthusiasts of the idea of promoting industrial production by social and political changes. Also, both considered the capitalist unfit to achieve technical progress and they advocated recruitment of industrial leaders from the classes of salaried technicians and workers.

Veblen's violent attacks on the business class and its ideology have caused violent controversies in America. In Europe Veblen remained nearly unknown. Brought up in

a clannish community of immigrants from Norway, Veblen never became completely at ease with the American way of living. He had no talent for teaching, and his academic career was hampered by the troubles of his private life. But his writing, especially his first and principal book *Theory of the Leisure Class* (1899), had a fermenting effect on economic and social thinking in America.

DEWEY, JOHN

DEWEY, JOHN (1859-1952). At the celebration of his ninetieth anniversary, John Dewey declared that losing faith in our fellow men means losing faith in ourselves, "and that is the unforgivable sin." Dewey is generally recognized as America's leading philosopher, and the foremost apostle of the faith in the essential union of the democratic and philosophical spirit. Since his revolt against German philosophy, he repudiated the separation of the individual and the social, both of which, according to him, are concrete traits and capacities of human beings. He always regarded reason, not as something existing timelessly in the nature of things, but simply as a fortunate and complex development of human behavior. His criticism of the traditional notions of truth is embodied in his theory of *instrumentalism,* which he defines as "an attempt to constitute a precise logical theory of concepts, judgments and inferences in their various forms, by primarily considering how thought functions in the experimental determinations of future consequences." Dewey made inquiry, rather than truth or knowledge, the essence of logic.

He regarded philosophy as the criticism of those socially important beliefs which are part and parcel of the social and cultural life of human communities. This criticism involves an examination of the way in which ideas, taken as solutions of specific problems, function within a wider context. It is in this way that a theory of knowledge—logic, ethics, psychology, aesthetics, and metaphysics becomes necessary and explainable. These are not to be derived from the assumption of an abstract truth, that is, a higher reality or a reality different from that within which we live and act, nor from everlasting values. Dewey objects to transcendental philosophers, because they ignore the kind of empirical situations to which their themes pertain; even the most transcendental philosophers use empirical subject matter, if they philosophize at all. But they become nonempirical because they fail to supply directions for experimentation. The supply of such directions is the core of Dewey's philosophy. His standard of belief and conduct claims to lie within, rather than outside of, a situation of life, that can be shared. Idealists, in contradistinction to Dewey's search for a guide to the beliefs of a shareable situation, deny to common life the faculty of forming its own regulative methods; they claim to have private access to truth. In Dewey's democratic philosophy,

386

Old American classroom, showing authoritarian system of discipline against which Dewey rebelled

Progressive classroom in New York City, with pupils deriving their sense of discipline from constructive work

common life is the reality of a dignity equivalent to that of nature or the individual.

Dewey devoted his studies not only to the conditions but also to the consequences of knowledge. He never made philosophy subservient to the vested interests of any class or nation; nor was he afraid to hurt any sensibility. He insisted that philosophy, in contrast to all other human activities, must be allowed to remain outside and above the public domain in order to maintain sound relations with these other human activities and to whose progress it must contribute. Dewey was opposed to any isolation of cognitive experience and its subject matter from other modes of experience and their subject matter, because he attempted to integrate spiritual life into the precise framework of natural phenomena, and, for the sake of all-embracing experience, tried to do away with the distinction between the objective and the subjective, and the psychical and the physical. He denied that the characteristic object of knowledge has a privileged position of correspondence with an allegedly ultimate reality; he insisted that action is involved in knowledge and that knowledge is not subordinate to action or practice; that it is in experimental knowing that genuine intellectual integrity is found.

Dewey did not accept any alternative between knowledge or intelligence and action. To him it is "intelligent action" that matters. The failure of human intelligence in social areas has made Dewey strongly emphasize the social aspects of his philosophy. Throughout his long life he tried not only to apply his experimental methods to social philosophy, but he also actively participated in disputes and struggles of political, social, and cultural relevance. Political, social, cultural, and theoretical motives have enhanced Dewey's interest in education. He recognized the important role education plays in the survival of democracy, and the importance of democratic thought and action in the improvement of education. For more than forty years, Dewey maintained a leadership in American education, bringing increased human interest into school life and work, making for the increased encouragement of pupil initiative and responsibility. Dewey's instrumentalism was first expressed in his *Studies in Logical Theory* (1903) where he acknowledged his obligation to William James. His other principal works are: *Democracy and Education* (1916); *Essays in Experimental Logic* (1917); *Reconstruction in Philosophy* (1920); *Human Nature and Conduct* (1922); *The Quest for Certainty* (1929), and *Logic: The Theory of Inquiry* (1938).

WHITEHEAD, ALFRED NORTH

WHITEHEAD, ALFRED NORTH (1861-1947). Whitehead had become famous as a scientist, as one of the founders of modern mathematical logic, before he concentrated upon philosophy. He was sixty-three years old when he renounced his professorship of mathematics at the Imperial College of Science and Technology, London, in order to become professor of philosophy at Harvard. However, his mathematical investigations remained relevant to his metaphysics, and even Whitehead, the metaphysician who protested that "the final outlook of philosophical thought cannot be based upon the exact statements which form the basis of special sciences," retained his grand vision of the possibilities of abstract theory.

Whitehead never hesitated to confess his indebtedness to William James, Samuel Alexander and Henri Bergson for the development of his own philosophical thoughts, or that Minkowski's assimilation of space and time and Einstein's theory of relativity had stimulated his thought. But this indebtedness meant not so much an actual influence as rather the creation of a new situation which allowed Whitehead to proceed in his own way.

The decisive feature of this new situation was shaped by James' denial that the subject-object relation is fundamental to knowledge. By denying that in the occurrence of knowing one entity, regarded as the knower, as a mind or soul, standing in front of an object, be it externally existent or the self-consciousness of the knower himself, James also removed the habitual distinction of mind and matter. Whitehead, while constantly contending that the "bifurcation of nature," the sharp division between nature and mind, established by Descartes, had "poisoned all subsequent philosophy" and jeopardized the very meaning of life, restored the subject-object relation as a fundamental structural pattern of experience, "but not in the sense in which subject-object is identified with knower-known." To Whitehead, "the living organ or experience is the living body as a whole." Human experience has its origin in the physical activities of the whole organism which tends to readjustment when any part of it becomes unstable. Although such experience seems to be more particularly related to the brain, Whitehead held that "we cannot determine with what molecules the brain begins and the rest of the body ends." Human experience therefore is defined as "an act of self-origination, including the whole of nature, limited to the perspective of a focal region, located within the body, but not necessarily persisting in any fixed coordination within a definite part of the brain."

Upon this concept of human experience, Whitehead founded his new philosophy of the organism, his cosmology, his defense of speculative reason, his ideas on the process of nature, his rational approach to God. The aim of his speculative philosophy was "to frame a coherent, logical, necessary system of general ideas in terms of which every item of our experience can be interpreted." Whitehead thought that philosophy, speculative metaphysics included, was not, or should not be, a ferocious debate between irritable professors but "a survey of possibilities and their comparison with actualities," balancing the fact, the theory, the alternatives and the ideal. In this way the fundamental beliefs which determine human character will be clarified.

The first period of Whitehead's activities was devoted to mathematics and logic. It began with *Universal Algebra* published in 1898 after seven years of work, continued with *Mathematical Concepts of the Material World* (1905) and culminated in the monumental *Principia Mathematica* (1910-1913) written in collaboration with Bertrand Russell. Characteristic of Whitehead's second period, in which he was preoccupied with a philosophy of natural science without metaphysical exposition, are *An Enquiry Concerning the Principles of Natural Knowledge* (1919), *The Concept of Nature* (1920), *The Principle of Relativity* (1922) and *Science and the Modern World* (1925), which already mentions but not yet attempts a metaphysical synthesis of existence.

Most significant of Whitehead's metaphysical views are *Process and Reality* (1929), *Adventures of Ideas* (1933) and *Modes of Thought* (1938).

MEAD, GEORGE HERBERT (1863-1931). After Mead's death, one of his graduate students declared that for many years to come articles and even books would continue to be published of which the first author was George Mead. John Dewey, his intimate friend, has said that Mead had "a seminal mind of the first order," and Alfred Whitehead, after reading some of Mead's posthumously published books, publicly endorsed this view. Dewey also recognized that Mead, whose scholarship in the natural sciences was superior to his own, had influenced him by conversations which were continued over a period of years.

Mead published little during his lifetime, and wrote no systematic work, but he was a consistent thinker. He constantly expressed his antipathy for metaphysics and was equally opposed to idealism and materialism. His principal interests were devoted to the investigation of the consequence of biological theories to scientific psychology. He held that psychological phenomena, including those of thinking and knowing, must be described as actions or reactions of the organism that lives in an environment and regulates its relations to objective conditions of life by means of the nervous system of which the brain is a part. To Mead, the psychical is the state which occurs when previously formed relations of the organism to its environment break down and new ones are not yet built up. Acts are the unity of existence of the individual that is proclaimed as a concrete, inimitable, nonrationalizable unit, but modifiable through its relation to society. Mead tried to maintain a balance between the determination by the individual of the whole, be it society or the world, and the determination by the whole of the individual.

Münsterberg (Seated behind Table. Center) in his Psychological Laboratory

CALKINS, MARY WHITON

CALKINS, MARY WHITON (1863-1930). The creed of Calkins is expressed in four principal statements which are developed in her books: *The Persistent Problems of Philosophy* (1907) and *The Good Man and The Good* (1918). She proceeded from the conviction that the universe contained distinct mental realities; that although the mind had emerged from a lower level of existence, it no longer belonged to that level, but rather to a new order of existence which had special laws of behavior. These mental realities were ultimately personal; consciousness never occurred impersonally. She defined psychology as a "science of the self as conscious." She also asserted that the universe was throughout mental; that whatever was real was ultimately mental and therefore personal. She concluded that the universe was an all-inclusive Self; an absolute Person; a conscious being. She maintained that philosophy meant metaphysics, which she defined as "the attempt by reasoning to know what is ultimately real." To her, metaphysics did not imply a return to animism, and she stated that it was compatible with the concepts of scientific laws and that reasoning separated metaphysics from mysticism. She was considerably influenced by Royce; opposed logical atomism and instrumentalism. On several problems, she agreed with Samuel Alexander, but claimed a greater consistency.

MÜNSTERBERG, HUGO

MÜNSTERBERG, HUGO (1863-1916). The current of Münsterberg's life, which had seemed to take a slow course along German university lines, was suddenly turned to new tasks, experiences and ideas by a letter written to him by William James on February 21, 1892. James, who had met Münsterberg at an international congress three years before, had been impressed by his psychological methods and philosophical views, and now invited him to direct the Psychological Laboratory of Harvard University, claiming that in the whole world no better man could be found for that post than Münsterberg. The latter accepted and, apart from the years 1895 to 1897 and 1910 to 1911, taught at Harvard until his death.

Throughout his life in America, Münsterberg's scientific interests were intertwined with cultural and political interests. Fascinated by American life, he tried to interpret it to Germany, his native country, and to acquaint Americans with German cultural performances and scientific methods. His position became precarious after the outbreak of the First World War, when Münsterberg did not conceal his sympathy with Germany, without, however, approving all the measures taken by the German government.

Münsterberg's scientific creed was that psychology must fit into a system of causally connected elements. The function of psychology is to analyze life into elements parallel to the elements of matter that physics reconstructs; but he emphatically warned against confusing that existence, postulated by psychological analysis, with the immediate reality of life, such as becomes manifest in moral and practical activities, in the arts and religion. Causal psychology must be completed by purposive psychology, and the latter must be founded upon a theory of values.

Münsterberg also took great care in applying psychology to education, psychotherapy, the courtroom, vocational training and increase of industrial efficiency. He was the first psychologist to recognize the artistic importance and possibilities of the motion picture.

Paul Elmer More (1864-1937), American critic and philosopher, who taught at Harvard and Bryn Mawr and lectured at Princeton. Leading exponent of twentieth century American humanism, his essays aroused considerable critical furor in their time

WOODBRIDGE, FREDERICK JAMES EUGENE

WOODBRIDGE, FREDERICK JAMES EUGENE (1867-1940). Woodbridge, one of the most attractive and stimulating teachers in the history of American universities, called himself a naive realist. In his later years he was deeply impressed by Santayana's writings which he highly praised and acknowledged as illuminating and enhancing his own understanding of philosophical and cultural problems. But the basis of his philosophy, such as it is presented in his books *The Purpose of History* (1916) and *The Realm of Mind* (1926), was laid before he became acquainted with Santayana's thoughts.

The originality of Woodbridge's realism is veiled by his own characterization of his philosophy as "a synthesis of Aristotle and Spinoza, tempered by Locke's empiricism." Woodbridge avowed his indebtedness to Aristotle's naturalism and the conception of productivity, and to Spinoza's "rigid insistence on structure," while it was Locke who he said had taught him "fundamentally sound thinking." "Far less acute than Descartes, and far less subtle than Kant, he was far more solid than any of them."

But it is taken for granted that Woodbridge, by historically deriving his own thoughts from Aristotle, Spinoza and Locke, had wronged himself. The three philosophers were more influential to him as examples of philosophizing than as transmitters of ideas, and Spinoza and Locke particularly impressed him more as human personalities than as shapers of doctrines. Woodbridge's inquiry into the nature of structure and activity and their relations is the work of an independent thinker. To him, structure determines what is possible, and activity determines what exists. These concepts were elaborated by cautious and flexible analysis of reality as Woodbridge himself saw it.

Frederick J. E. Woodbridge
(*Painting by Ercole Cartotto*)

SANTAYANA, GEORGE

SANTAYANA, GEORGE (1863-1952). Santayana was the son of a Spanish father and an American mother. He hints at his own Spanish strain when he describes the southern mind as long-indoctrinated, disillusioned, distinct, sceptical, malicious, yet in its reflective phase detached and contemplative, able to despise all entanglements, to dominate will and to look truth in the eye without blinking. He thinks of the American mind as being more ingenuous than wise. American is the texture, Spanish is the structure of Santayana's mind. America impressed his spiritual outlook. But, successful as he was as an influential professor at Harvard, he never felt himself at ease there. The Spanish tradition corresponded more by far to his inclinations, and, although he did not care about authorities, he highly esteemed the soil of history, tradition or human institutions without which thought and imagination became trivial.

When Santayana resolved to spend the rest of his life in an Italian convent as guest, he did not give up his philosophical conviction, one of whose striking features was unrelenting materialism. He was "attached to Catholicism" but "entirely divorced from faith," and protested that his scepticism had rather confirmed than dispelled this attachment. He continued to hold that "most conventional ideals, the religious ones included, are not adequate to the actual nature and capacities of men who accept them." He did not acknowledge any Christian dogma but liked the Christian religion for aesthetic and historical reasons. Nevertheless he was far from holding romanticist predilections, and even farther from having any adoration of the tragic sense of living.

What was true for Santayana's attachment to Catholicism was also true for his relation to Platonism. Santayana thought in terms of two realms of being, that of existence and that of essences. Concerning existence, he professed materialism. His realm of essences was of Platonist origin. But Santayana declined to regard essences as truer realities than existent things, or to found the realm of essences upon divine activity or to oppose essence to accident and modification.

According to Santayana, essences neither necessitate nor explain thoughts, nor do they determine the ground of concrete existence. The seat and principle of genesis is matter, not essence, which, for its part, is explanatory of intuition, assures the form of apperception, elucidates existence, and helps the mind to grasp and to retain the character and identity of the changing existences. However, while the evolution of existing things changes their character at every moment, the essences, representing every moment of this change, remain in their logical identity. An essence is anything definite capable of appearing and being thought of: it is senseless to believe in it because belief involves the assumption of real existence. Intuition of essence is no knowledge at all because illusion and error are also intuitions. Knowledge is a compound of instinctive conviction and expectation, animal faith and

intuition of essence. It is essence by means of which the pursuit, attention and feelings which contribute to knowledge are transcribed in aesthetic, moral or verbal terms into consciousness. Matter is in flux; mind, conceived by Santayana as "simply sensibility in bodies," is existentially carried along the movement of that flux but is capable of arresting some datum, different from what the stimulated sensibility can articulate. This datum is essence in whose language alone mind can express its experiences.

Disillusioned, Santayana, although convinced of the truth of his work, did not except his philosophy from his general judgment of philosophical systems. To him they were all personal, temperamental, even premature. They were human heresies. The orthodoxy around which these heresies play, is no private or closed body of doctrine. It is "the current imagination and good sense of mankind," a body of beliefs and evaluations far too chaotic, subject to errors and too conventional to satisfy a reflective mind, but capable of correcting its errors. Hence the need for personal philosophical thought, hence the impossibility to attain the goal to shape a philosophy satisfying mankind. As for Santayana he acquiesced in this insight, and was fond of stating divergencies between his mind and that of his critics.

McDOUGALL, WILLIAM

McDOUGALL, WILLIAM (1871-1938). McDougall has called himself "arrogant," and the behaviorists, psychoanalysts, Gestalt psychologists, pragmatists and a host of men of other philosophical and psychological schools attacked by him are far from denying him that quality. Honored as McDougall was as a professor at Oxford and Harvard, he always felt himself living in an adverse intellectual atmosphere. Indeed, he had reason for becoming embittered, for he was aware that his theories were often misrepresented. His work has been discussed from the viewpoint of instinct theory. But, in fact, McDougall regarded the instinctive nature of man only as a foundation, and maintained that the theory of sentiments furnishes the key to his system according to which in the man of developed character very few actions proceed directly from his instinctive foundation.

In addition to extensive travels through India, Indonesia and China in order to "hear the East," McDougall prepared his approach to the problems of the human mind by neurological and psychological studies. However, after his *Physiological Psychology* (1905), he concentrated upon psychological introspection and retrospection. His *Introduction to Social Psychology* (1908) challenged all previous conceptions and provoked animated controversies. He held that neither instinct, regarded as a working hypothesis, nor the human individual, characterized as an abstraction, can provide the basic data for social psychology but rather molding influences of social environment. The basic fact of human behavior is *purposive striving.* Consequently, McDougall calls psychology *hormic,* from the Greek *horme*—vital impulse, urge to action, which is to him a property of the mind, while he regarded intellect not as a source of energy but as the integrated system of man's beliefs (later as the sum total of man's innate and acquired cognitive abilities). In *Body and Mind* (1911) McDougall stated that mind must be considered a potent cause of evolution. McDougall also wrote *The Group Mind* (1920), *The Frontiers of Psychology* (1936) and *The Riddle of Life* (1938).

Arthur Oncken Lovejoy

Morris Raphael Cohen

LOVEJOY, ARTHUR ONCKEN

LOVEJOY, ARTHUR ONCKEN (1873-   ). Shortly before the twentieth century began, two young, and then unknown, American philosophers made a horse-car trip during which one, named William P. Montague, asked the other whose name was Arthur O. Lovejoy, what he considered the chief end of man, and Lovejoy answered: self-consciousness, just what most philosophers regard as the starting point of their thinking. This viewpoint has remained characteristic of Lovejoy's philosophy. What other thinkers are apt to take for granted, he deals with as a problem.

Lovejoy calls his position "temporalized realism." To him, the most indubitable fact of all our experience is that experience itself is temporal. This cognition has been used by him as a touchstone to be applied to all theories about the nature of reality or of knowledge. He has used it for the rejection of all dominant forms of idealism and monism. He maintains that rationality, when conceived as complete and excluding all arbitrariness, becomes itself a kind of irrationality, excluding any limiting and selective principle. The world of concrete existence is a contingent world whose laws show some inexpugnable traits of arbitrariness. Otherwise it would be a world without power of choice, without character. Man is, by the most distinctive impulse of his nature, an interpretative animal who seeks to know the causes of things through trial and error in the course of time. The history of man's reflection, and the history of philosophy especially, is, to a large extent, a history of confusion of ideas, and Lovejoy has devoted much of his energy to analyze and unravel this confusion. An outstanding example of his method is in his book *The Great Chain of Being* (1936). Thus Lovejoy's interest in critical philosophy is closely interwoven with his interest in historical thought and research.

COHEN, MORRIS RAPHAEL

COHEN, MORRIS RAPHAEL (1880-1947). When Cohen was a boy in Minsk, Russia, he was called Kallyeleh, the Yiddish equivalent of moron. At the age of twelve, he emigrated to the United States. People from Cohen's native town were considerably astonished to hear, in later years, that the so-called moron was generally acknowledged as one of the strongest intellectual forces in American education and philosophy. Many of the greatest contemporary minds—Einstein, Woodbridge, Dewey, Russell, Oliver Wendell Holmes, Jr., and Cardozo—considered Cohen their equal. His disciples admired his wisdom and his teaching methods. His cardinal virtue was his integrity of mind and conscience. He was outstanding as a logician and mathematician, and was chiefly responsible for the renaissance of philosophy in American law.

Cohen's interest in the philosophy of law and religion dated back to his "moronic" boyhood, when he was educated in Biblical and Talmudic law and read Maimonides and Judah Halevi's *Kuzari*. As a young man, he was attracted to Marxian socialism, but his strong belief in democracy helped him to discover other ways of serving the common good and acting in accordance with his social conscience. Felix Adler influenced his approach to ethics; but Cohen was essentially a logician, devoted to mathematical logic and to the investigation of the relationships between science and philosophy. He characterized himself as a realistic rationalist who conceived of reason as "the use of both deductive and inductive inferences working upon the material of experience." He regarded reality as a category that belonged to science not religion.

BRIDGMAN, P. W.

BRIDGMAN, P. W. (1882-   ). A professor of mathematics and natural philosophy at Harvard University, an authority on thermodynamics, electricity, and various other physical sciences, Percy Bridgman is noted for his promulgation of the "operational" theory of meaning in his books *The Logic of Modern Physics* (1927) and *The Nature of Physical Theory* (1936). He asserts that the classical concepts of physics are inadequate. He defines concept as a set of operations comprised of mental and physical activity. Truth is identical with verifiability, and the criterion of scientific truth is the experimental method. Although Bridgman has been influenced by neither Dewey nor James, his operationalism parallels John Dewey's instrumentalism.

Bridgman enlarged his scope of observation and thought in *The Intelligent Individual and Society* (1938). His starting point is the irrationality of Man in contemporary society; Man's awareness of this makes him long for an intelligent, orderly life, even though such longing may not be directed at the perfectibility of human desires. If a perfect life is unattainable, a satisfactory life can be secured by apprehending the relations, consequences, implications of the drive, or by intelligently satisfying these drives. These drives are not subject to argument, but only to examination and modification through education. Rationality does not have all the qualities requisite for this task. Emotional adjustment can complete it.

Ideally, education should provide the technique for criticism and modification of the specific drives by the individual. Thus, Bridgman seeks to secure individual freedom in society. His human ideal is a synthesis of intellectual and emotional honesty.

P. W. Bridgman

The Einstein Tower at Potsdam, where Einstein pursued his observations in pre-Nazi days

ALAN W. RICHARDS

EINSTEIN, ALBERT

EINSTEIN, ALBERT (1879-1955). The overwhelming majority of scientists continually testify that Einstein has accomplished "one of the greatest generalizations of all time" and "has revolutionized our nineteenth century concepts not only of astronomy, but also of the nature of time, space, and of the fundamental ideas of science." Modern humanity reveres Einstein as one of its profoundest thinkers, as well as a man of the highest intellectual integrity, free of personal ambition, an intrepid fighter for human rights, social justice, and social responsibility. In the few decades that have passed between the time that Einstein made his theory of relativity known to the public and his seventieth birthday, more than five thousand books and pamphlets in every language have been published about him and his work. Although Einstein himself did nothing to popularize his ideas, his fame spread internationally after he predicted that the deflection of light in a gravitational field would occur in 1916 and 1919. He had and still has opponents, some of whom are prejudiced against him because he remained conscious of his Jewish origin. But humble people throughout the world are comforted by the knowledge that Einstein, whose thoughts pervade the universe, feels with all who suffer from oppression and persecution. Seldom has it happened that any man has become

so popular, even though his theory is largely beyond popular imagination and common-sense thought. While the achievements of Copernicus, Galileo, Newton, and Darwin have been, at least in broad outline, explicable to the public, it has been impossible up to the present time to translate Einstein's theory of relativity adequately into the nontechnical language of popular literature.

The most important consequence of Einstein's special theory of relativity for scientific and philosophical thought has been the change in the concepts of time and space. Einstein destroyed the assumption that there is a single all-embracing time in which all events in the universe have their place. He has shown that "it is impossible to determine absolute motion by any experiment whatever." As long as time and space are measured separately, there always remains a kind of subjectivity which affects not only human observers but all other things. Time and space, which for classical physics are absolute constituents of the world, are conceived by Einsteinian physics as dependent upon each other, forming a relationship which can be analyzed in many different ways into what is referred to as spatial distance or lapse of time. Time which previously had been regarded as a cosmic measure is presented by Einstein as "local time" connected with the motion of the earth. He conceives of time as so completely analogous to the three dimensions of space that physics can be trans-

396

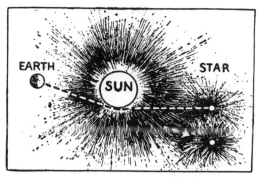

Einstein's theory says that light-rays will be bent, due to gravitation, in passing a large body like the sun. In the above diagram, the arrow points to the place from which it *seems* that the star's light is coming. Experiments seem to prove the theory correct.

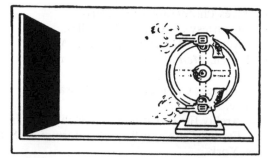

The two pistols which are attached to the rapidly rotating wheel are both fired at the same instant.

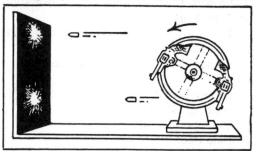

The light-flashes from the two pistols travel at the same speed and arrive at the target together. One bullet, however, will hit the target before the other.

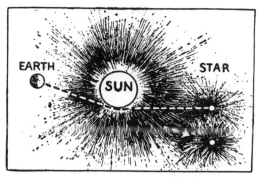

Einstein's Credo as a Jew

formed into a kind of four-dimensional geometry. On the other hand, the special theory of relativity confers an absolute meaning on a magnitude, namely the velocity of light, which had only a relative significance in classical physics.

After this special theory, Einstein formulated his general theory of relativity which offers new explanations of the size of the universe, of gravitation and inertia. Einstein's achievements are by no means limited to the special and general theories of relativity. He was awarded the Nobel Prize in 1922 for his studies in photo-chemical equivalents. Later, he took a leading part in the investigation of atomic energy. On many occasions, he has expressed his personal views on problems of daily life, contemporary history, war, peace, education, religion, science and the fate of the Jews.

Studying in Switzerland and Germany, Einstein quickly rose to international prominence. The mature years of his life were spent in his beloved America, which became a haven for him as it has for millions of other victims of aggression. His special Theory of Relativity as well as his Unified Field Theory were developed at the Institute for Advanced Study in Princeton.

Picture Credits*

2. Bildarchiv Foto Marburg.
6. B.—Library of Congress.
10. Yale University Press.
14. L.—Yale University Press.
18. R.—Jewish Theological Seminary.
19. R.—Jewish Theological Seminary.
20. L.—Jewish Theological Seminary.
34. U.R.—Gräflich Wallenrodtsche Bibliothek, Königsberg.
38. La Vieille Russie Gallery, New York City.
48. B.—Wide World Photo.
55. Archaeological Survey of India.
56. Self-Realization Fellowship, Los Angeles, Calif.
57 U.R. and L.R.—The Vedanta Society.
77. U.L., C.L., and L.L.—Charles Singer, *The Evolution of Anatomy,* copyright by Dover Publications, Inc., 1957.
80. B.—Culver Service.
88. U.R. and L.R.—Charles Singer, *op. cit.*
89. U.L., C.L., L.L., U.R., and L.R.—Charles Singer, *op. cit.*
124. T.—New York Public Library Picture Collection.
136. The Frick Collection.
137. U.L.—*Franciscan Herald Press,* Chicago, Ill.
L.L.—Badische Landesbibliothek, Karlsruhe.
141. L.R.—Yale University Library.
156. U.R.—*Medieval Contributions to Modern Civilization,* Hearnshaw.
160. L.R.—New York Public Library Picture Collection.
163. L.L.—Culver Service.
167. C.L.—University of Edinburgh Library.
168. U.R.—University of Edinburgh Library.
174. Archives Photographiques, Paris.
175. B.—Culver Service.
182. Culver Service.
183. Services Culturels de l'Ambassade de France, New York.
185. U.L.—Archiv für Kunst und Geschichte, Berlin.
186. Archives Photographiques, Paris.
187. L.L.—French Office of Information, New York.
L.R.—Archives Photographiques, Paris.
188. R.—Archives de la Gironde, Paris.
191. B.—Culver Service.
195. U.L.—Services Culturels de l'Ambassade de France, New York.
197. Culver Service.
198. R.—Culver Service.

199. Archives Photographiques, Paris.
202. R.—Courtesy of A. C. L. Bruselles.
205. L.—*Révue de Métaphysique et de Morale.*
207. E. T. Bell, *Men of Mathematics,* Simon & Schuster, Inc.
208. L.—Services Culturels de l'Ambassade de France, New York.
209. L.—Archiv für Kunst und Geschichte, Berlin.
214. L.—French Embassy Press & Information Service, New York.
R.—"Agip."
215. L.—French Embassy Press & Information Division, New York.
R.—Photo by Marton, French Embassy Press & Information Division, New York.
216. L.—French Embassy Press & Information Division.
226. L.—Culver Service.
247. University of Glasgow.
248. L.—University of Glasgow.
251. Keystone Photo.
253. British Office of Information.
267. R.—University of Southern California.
271. L.—British Office of Information.
277. New York Public Library Picture Collection.
290. L.—Propyläen-Verlag, Berlin.
296. L.—Kurpfälz. Museum, Heidelberg.
300. L.R.—Ullstein-Bilderdienst, Berlin.
301. U.L.—Ullstein-Bilderdienst, Berlin.
L.L.—Copress, Munich.
306. R.—Kurpfälz. Museum, Heidelberg.
317. T.—Bildarchiv, Kurpfälz., Heidelberg.
319. National Library, Vienna.
322. L.—Royal Library, Copenhagen.
323. R.—National Library, Vienna.
330. L.—Photo by Hildegard Jäckel.
335. Photo by Marvin Aronow.
337. B.—Archives of Austrian National Library.
340. U.R.—H. Hoffmann, Burke.

*KEY

T.—Top	U.L.—Upper Left
C.—Center	C.L.—Center Left
B.—Bottom	L.L.—Lower Left
L.—Left	U.R.—Upper Right
R.—Right	C.R.—Center Right
	L.R.—Lower Right

Where no key is given, all pictures on the page are from the same source.

350. R.—H. Hoffmann, Burke.
356. C.L.—*Story of America,* Collins, Doubleday and Co.
     L.R.—American Antiquarian Society.
357. T.—Yale University Library.
     B.—Essex Institute Collection.
358. L.—Massachusetts Historical Society.
359. New York Public Library Picture Collection.
361. Courtesy Franklin Institute.
363. R.—Courtesy Franklin Institute.
366. Yale University Art Gallery.
367. L.L.—New York Historical Society.
     U.L. and L.R.—Massachusetts Historical Society.
368. Historical Society of Pennsylvania.
370. New York Historical Society.
374. L.R.—Concord Antiquarian Society.

375. L.—Concord Free Public Library.
377. U.R.—New York Public Library Picture Collection.
380. R.—Harvard University Press.
382. R.—Brown Bros. Photo.
383. R.—Boston University.
386. Columbia University.
387. T.—Brown Bros. Photo.
     B.—*New York Times.*
388. Harvard University.
392. Brown Bros. Photo.
393. Duke University.
396. L.—Alan W. Richards, Princeton, N.J.
397. U.L. and C.L.—Drawings from *Einstein,* by C. R. Goedsche and W. E. Glaettli, American Book Company, 1954.

General Acknowledgments

Academy of San Fernando, Madrid, Spain
Albright Art Gallery, Buffalo, N.Y.
American Foundation for the Blind, Inc.
American Museum of Photography, Philadelphia, Pa.
American University of Beirut, Lebanon
Anthroposophical Society in America, New York
Archiv für Kunst und Geschichte, Berlin
The Art Collections of the University of Glasgow
Collection The Art Gallery of Toronto, Bequest of
    Sir Edmund Osler, 1924
Atlantis Verlag, Zürich
Aufbau, New York
Basic Books, Inc., New York
Bettmann Archive, New York
La Biblioteca Apostolica Vaticana, Vatican City, Rome
Bibliothèque Nationale, Paris
Bildarchiv Foto Marburg, Marburg, Germany
Birkhäuser Verlag, Basel
Crane Brinton, John B. Christopher and Robert Lee Wolff,
    A History of Civilization, copyright, 1955, by Prentice-
    Hall, Inc., Englewood Cliffs, N.J.
Bodleian Library, Oxford, England
Boston Public Library
Boston University College of Liberal Arts, Boston, Mass.
Trustees of The British Museum, London, England
Burke Publishing Company, Ltd., London, England
Caisse Nationale des Monuments Historiques, Paris
Christ's College, Cambridge, England
The Clarendon Press, Oxford, England
Alan C. Collins, New York
Comité de l'Encyclopédie Française, Paris
The Concord Antiquarian Society, Concord, Mass.
Concord Free Public Library, Concord, Mass.
Consulate General of the Federal Republic of Germany,
    New York
Consulate General of Switzerland, New York
Collection of A La Vieille Russie, 785 Fifth Avenue,
    New York
Copress, München
Frederic R. Coudert, Jr., Washington, D.C.
Culver Service, New York
George M. Cushing, Jr., Boston, Mass.
B. F. Dolbin, Jackson Heights, N.Y.
Drei Masken Verlag, A.G., Munich, Germany
Duke University, Durham, North Carolina
East and West Library, London, England
Editions d'Art Lucien Mazenod, Paris
Editions Du Pont Royal, Paris
Fotoarchiv der Staatlichen Museen, Berlin
Franciscan Herald Press, Chicago, Ill.

Fratelli Alinari, Istituto di Edizioni Artistiche, Firenze
Free Lance Photographers Guild, Inc., New York
Freie Universität Berlin
French Embassy Press & Information Division, New York
The Frick Collection, New York
Friedrich-Schiller-Universität, Jena
Fruitlands Museum, Harvard, Mass.
Government Printer, Jerusalem, Israel
Charles Gratry, Paris
Harper & Brothers, New York, N.Y.
Hebrew Publishing Co., New York
Hebrew University Bulletin, New York
The Historical Society of Pennsylvania
Historisches Bildarchiv, Lolo Handke, Bad Berneck I.F.,
    Germany
Iber-Amer, Publicaciones Hispanoamericanas, S.A.,
    Barcelona, Spain
Instituto de Filosofía, Rosario, Argentina
Instituto de Filosofía de la Facultad de Filosofía y Letras,
    Buenos Aires, Argentina
Istituto per la Collaborazione Culturale, Rome
Italian State Tourist Office, New York
Jews' College, London
Jubilee Magazine
Horace M. Kallen, New York
Keystone Press Agency, Inc., New York
Det Kgl. Bibliotek, Copenhagen, Denmark
Kunsthistorisches Museum, Vienna
Librairie Fernand Nathan & Cie, Paris
Library of the Boston Athenaeum, Boston, Mass.
Library of Congress, Washington, D.C.
The Library of the Jewish Theological Seminary of
    America
Life Magazine, Time & Life, New York
Longmans, Green & Co., Inc., New York and London
Arthur D. Lovejoy, Baltimore, Md.
Marathon Edition, c/o Tiroler Graphik, Innsbruck,
    Austria
Massachusetts Historical Society, Boston, Mass.
Irene Tufts Mead, Chicago, Illinois
Merton College, Oxford, England
The Metropolitan Museum of Art:
    Bequest of Mrs. H. O. Havemeyer, 1929;
    Hewitt Fund, 1913;
    Rogers Fund, 1917;
    Gift of Mr. and Mrs. Carl Stoeckel, 1897
Ministry of Public Education, Superintendency of Galleries
    and Objects of Art, Venice
Musée Condé, Chantilly
Musée Guimet, Paris

Musée National d'Athènes, Greece
Musei Comunali, Rome
Museo del Prado, Madrid
Museo Nazionale, Naples
Museum of Fine Arts, Boston, Mass.
Nasjonalgalleriet, Oslo
National Library, Naples, Italy
National Portrait Gallery, London
Det Nationalhistoriske Museum PAA Frederiksborg, Denmark
National History Magazine, The American Museum of Natural History, New York
The New School for Social Research, New York
The New York Historical Society, New York
The New York Public Library
The New York Times, New York
Nietzsche-Archiv Louis Held, Weimar
19 King's Parade, Cambridge, England
Öffentliche Bibliothek der Universität, Basel
The Open Court Publishing Company, La Salle, Ill.
Oxford University Press, London, England
Palais du Louvre, Paris
Palazzo Spade, Rome
Paroisse Notre-Dame, Reims, France
Philosophical Publishing Co., Quakertown, Pa.
Philosophische Fakultät, Der Universität, Freiburg, Germany
R. Piper & Company Verlag, München, Germany
Pix, Incorporated, New York
Princeton University Press, Princeton, N.J.
Propylaen-Verlag, Berlin
Psychologisches Institut der Universität, Würzburg
Ramsey & Muspratt, Cambridge, England
The Rand Corporation
Rijksmuseum voor de Geschiedenis der Natuurwetenschappen, Leiden
H. Roger-Viollet, Paris
Rowohlt Verlag, Hamburg, Germany
Royal College of Physicians, London, England
Royal Greek Embassy, Washington, D.C.
Science Museum, London, England
Self-Realization Fellowship, Los Angeles, Calif.
Services Techniques & Commerciaux de la Réunion des Musées Nationaux, Paris

Shankaracharya Reception Committee, Cambridge House, New York
Shengold Publishers, Inc., New York
Sociedad Filosofica Argentina, Buenos Aires
Société des Amis de la Bibliothèque Nationale et des Grandes Bibliothèques de France, Paris
Société Nouvelle de l'Encyclopédie Française, Librairie Larousse, Paris
The Society for Ethical Culture, New York
Soprintendenza alle Antichita della Campania, Naples, Italy
Soprintendenza alle Antichita dell'Etruria Meridionale, Rome, Italy
Soprintendenza alle Antichita delle Province di Napoli Avellino e Benevento, Naples, Italy
Soprintendenza alle Gallerie ed alle Opere d'arte Medioevali e Moderne per il Lazio, Rome, Italy
Sovfoto, New York
Staatliche Museen zu Berlin
Arno Stanke, Göttingen
Stedelijk Museum, Amsterdam
Süddeutscher Verlag, München, Germany
Solatia M. Taylor Co.
The Theosophical Press, Wheaton, Ill.
Theosophical Society, New York
Ullstein-Bilderdienst, Berlin-Tempelhof, Mariendorfer Damm
Universita di Napoli, Naples, Italy
Université de Paris, Paris
Université de Rennes, Neuilly
University of California, Berkeley, Calif.
The University of Edinburgh Library, Edinburgh, Scotland
University Press, Oxford, England
Michel A. Vallon, Danville, California
Verlag Ullstein, Ullstein Aktiengesellschaft, Berlin-Tempelhof
Victoria & Albert Museum, London
C. A. Watts & Co., Ltd., London, England
Wide World Photos, Inc., New York
Yale University Art Gallery, New Haven
Yeshiva University, New York
The Yoga-Vedanta Forest University, Sivanandanagar, Rishikesh, India
Zionist Archives, New York
Zionist Organization of America, New York

Index

Abailard, Peter, 123, 124
Aboab, Isaac, 28
Abraham, 2, 143
Abraham, Karl, 310
Abravanel, Isaac, 27
Abravanel, Judah, 27
Absalom, 5
Abulafia, Samuel, 24
Abu Yakub Yusuf, Sultan, 172
Achad, Haam, *see* Asher Ginzberg
Acosta, Uriel, 35
Adams, Henry, 381
Adams, John, 106, 189, 364-365
Adams, John Quincy, 106
Adler, Alfred, 310-311
Adler, Felix, 384, 395
Aeschylus, 69, 70, 71
Akiba, Rabbi, 13
Alain, *see* Émile Auguste Chartier
Albertus Magnus, i, 21, 125, 126, 172
Albo, Joseph, 25
Alcibiades, 80
Alcott, Amos Bronson, 372, 378
Alcott, Louisa May, 372
Alcuin, Flaccus Albinus, 120, 121
Alexander of Hales, 18, 21, 127
Alexander, the Great, i, iii, 72, 88
Alexander II, Tsar, 343, 347
Alexander, Samuel, 266, 267, 388, 390
Al-Farabi, 169
Alghazzali, Abu Hamid Mohammed ibn
    Ghazzali, 171
Ali, 167
Al-Kindi, 168
Allen, Ethan, 359, 360
Al-Mukammas, David ibn Merwan, 18
Ameinias, 93
Ammonius Saccas, 111, 118
Anaxagoras, 70, 92
Anaximander, 90, 91
Anaximenes, 91
Antisthenes, 78, 96, 97, 98
Anselm, Saint, 122, 247
Antoninus Pius, 110
Aquinas, Thomas, i, 18, 21, 126, 127,
    128, 129-132, 133, 172, 213, 219, 229,
    272, 286
Arcesilaus, 102
Archimedes, 74, 103
Ardigo, Roberto, 221·
Aristippus, 78, 97
Aristotle, i, ii, 21, 25, 65, 70, 72, 73, 86,
    87-89, 95, 96, 104, 128, 157, 168, 169,
    172, 173, 213, 272, 284, 303, 333, 364,
    391
Arnold, Matthew, 94, 139
Arrian, 110
Asher ben Jechiel, 24
Aspasia, 70
Augustine, Saint, 111, 118-120, 128, 133,
    134, 135, 161
Augustus, Emperor, 108
Aurelius, Marcus, 110, 111
Aurobindo, 58, 59
Autolycus, 102

Avenarius, Richard, 321, 354
Avenpace, 172
Averroës, 172, 173
Avicenna, 169-170
Axelrod, Pavel Borissovich, 347

Baader, Francis Xavier von, 290
Baal Shem-Tov, 15, 30
Bacon, Francis, 109, 179, 187, 229, 232-
    233, 234
Bacon, Nicholas, 232
Bacon, Roger, 229-231
Bahya ibn Pakuda, 19, 24, 129
Bain, Alexander, 381
Bakunin, Michael, 342, 347
Balzac, Honoré, 143, 214
Bancroft, George, 204
Barnard, Henry, 304
Baudelaire, Charles, 334
Baxter, Richard, 245
Beauvoir, Simone de, 216
Bebel, August, 351
Beecher, Henry Ward, 376
Belinski, Vissarion, 341, 342
Benda, Julien, 228
Beneke, Friedrich Eduard, 307
Bentham, Jeremy, 65, 180, 239, 247, 248,
    250-251, 252, 254
Berachyah, 24
Berdyaev, Nicholas, 343, 348
Bergson, Henri, 1, 183, 206, 209, 212,
    266, 272, 290, 328, 332, 388
Berkeley, George, 83, 179, 225, 237-238,
    266, 337
Bernard of Clairvaux, 124, 125
Bernstein, Eduard, 351
Besant, Annie, 331
Bèze, Théodore de, 164
Bias of Priene, 168
Bismarck, Prince Otto Eduard, 268, 292
Blake, William, 237
Blondel, Maurice, 209
Bloy, Léon, 212
Blum, Léon, 211
Boeckh, August, 351
Boehme, Jacob, 142, 290
Boethius, 112, 121
Boileau, Nicolas, 104
Bolingbroke, Viscount, 190, 245, 364
Bolzano, Bernard, 220
Bonaventura, Saint, 127-128
Bonhours, Pierre, 39
Boole, George, 255, 261, 324
Bosanquet, Bernard, 265, 292
Boutroux, Emile, 206, 209
Bowdoin, James, 358
Bowne, Borden Parker, 383
Bradley, Francis Herbert, 264, 265, 267,
    292
Brant, Sebastian, 273
Brentano, Franz, 320, 326, 329
Brentano, Lujo, 320
Bridgman, P. W., 395
Broglie, Louis de, 215
Brown, John, 371

Browne, Sir Thomas, 243
Bruno, Giordano, 25, 146, 157
Brunschwicg, Léon, 211
Buber, Martin, 44
Buber, Solomon, 44
Bucer, Martin, 164
Büchner, Ludwig, 316
Buddha, Gautama, 45-49, 61, 385
Bulan II, King, 20
Bullinger, Heinrich, 164
Bulwer-Lytton, Edward, 253
Bunyan, John, 29
Burckhardt, Jakob, 221, 315
Burke, Edmund, 104, 249, 361
Burns, Robert, 217
Buxtorff, Johannes, 36
Byron, Lord, 193, 266

Cabanis, Pierre, 183
Caesar, Julius, 106
Caird, Edward, 272, 292
Caird, John, 272
Calas, Jean, 190
Caligula, 69
Calkins, Mary Whiton, 292, 390
Calvin, John, 103, 161, 164, 165
Campanella, Tommaso, 158
Canisius, Peter, 138
Caracalla, Emperor, 117
Cardano, Geronimo, 154
Cardozo, Benjamin, 395
Carlyle, Thomas, 139, 196, 260, 347
Carneades, 102
Caro, Joseph, 13, 28
Carus, Paul, 384, 385
Cassirer, Ernst, 326
Cataline, 107
Catherine, Queen, 145
Catherine II, Empress, 198, 199
Cecilius, 104
Celsus, 116
Chamberlain, H. S., 385
Charlemagne, 120, 121
Charles II, King, 234
Charles the Bold, 121
Chartier, Émile Auguste, 214
Chaucer, Geoffrey, 112
Ch'eng I Ch'uan, 68
Ch-eng Ming-tao, 68
Chernyshevsky, Nicolai, 343
Chesterfield, Lord (Philip Dormer Stan-
    hope), 189
Christina, Queen, 36, 174, 175
Chrysippus, 100
Chuang Chou, 64, 66
Chü Lu, 63
Cicero, Marcus Tullius, 106-107
Claudel, Paul, 215
Cleanthes, 100
Clement of Alexandria, 116-117, 118
Cohen, Hermann, 43, 218, 225, 327, 336
Cohen, Morris Raphael, 394, 395
Coleridge, Samuel Taylor, 237, 252, 254,
    258, 373
Colet, John, 150